Virginia Vallejo

LOVING PABLO, HATING ESCOBAR

Virginia Vallejo was the most important Colombian radio anchorwoman and television presenter in the late 1970s and '80s. In 1982, she met Pablo Escobar, head of the Medellín Cartel. In 1983, they began a romantic relationship that ended in 1987, six years before his death.

In July 2006, she offered her testimony against a former justice minister on trial for conspiring with Escobar in the assassination of a presidential candidate. That same month, the DEA took her out of Colombia, on a special flight to save her life, so she could testify in other leading criminal cases.

Originally published in 2007 by Random House Mondadori, *Amando a Pablo, Odiando a Escobar* (*Loving Pablo, Hating Escobar*) became a number one international bestseller in Spanish. Due to brutal attacks and threats from the Colombian government, paramilitary, and media, she received political asylum from the United States in 2010. She continues to live in Miami, where she is writing two more books.

LOVING PABLO, HATING ESCOBAR

LOVING PABLO, HATING ESCOBAR

Virginia Vallejo

Translated from the Spanish
by Megan McDowell

ANCHOR CANADA

Originally published in Mexico as *Amando a Pablo, Odiando a Escobar* by
Random House Mondadori, S.A., de C.V., Mexico, D.F., in 2007.

Library and Archives Canada Cataloguing in Publication data is available
upon request.

ISBN 978-0-385-69013-3
eBook ISBN 978-0-385-69014-0

All photographs courtesy of the author's private collection.

Book design by Anna B. Knighton

Printed and bound in the USA

Published in Canada by Anchor Canada,
a division of Random House of Canada Limited
A Penguin Random House Company

www.penguinrandomhouse.ca

10 9 8 7 6 5 4 3 2 1

Penguin
Random House
ANCHOR CANADA

To my Dead,
to the heroes and the villains.
We are all one,
one single nation,
just one atom
recycled infinitely
always and forever.

Contents

CONTENTS

LOVING PABLO, HATING ESCOBAR

Introduction

IT IS SIX IN THE MORNING on July 18, 2006. Three bulletproof cars from the American Embassy pick me up from my mother's apartment in Bogotá to drive me to the airport, where a plane headed to some place in the United States is waiting for me with its engines running. A vehicle with security personnel armed with machine guns precedes us at top speed, and another one is behind us. The night before, the embassy's head of security had warned me that there were suspicious people at the other end of the park that the building overlooks, and he informed me that his mission was to protect me; I shouldn't get close to the windows for any reason or open the door to anyone. Another car with my most precious possessions left one hour earlier; it belongs to Antonio Galán Sarmiento, president of the Bogotá City Council and brother of Luis Carlos

Galán, the presidential candidate assassinated in August 1989 under orders from Pablo Escobar Gaviria, head of the Medellín Cartel.

Escobar, my ex-lover, was shot to death on December 2, 1993. To bring him down after a hunt that lasted nearly a year and a half, it was necessary to offer a reward of twenty-five million dollars and to employ a Colombian police commando unit specially trained for the purpose, plus some eight thousand men from the state security organizations; the rival drug cartels and the paramilitary groups; dozens of agents from the DEA, the FBI, the CIA, the Navy SEALs, and U.S. Army Delta Force; and U.S. planes with special radar as well as money from some of the richest men in Colombia.

Two days earlier, in Miami's *El Nuevo Herald*, I had accused the ex-senator, ex–minister of justice, and former presidential candidate Alberto Santofimio Botero of instigating the murder of Luis Carlos Galán and of having built golden bridges between the bosses of the drug cartels and the presidents in Colombia. The Florida newspaper dedicated a fourth of the front page, plus a complete inside page, of Sunday's paper to my story.

Álvaro Uribe Vélez, who has just been reelected president of Colombia with more than 70 percent of the vote, is preparing to take his oath on August 7. After my offer to the nation's attorney general to testify in the open case against Santofimio, which should have lasted for another two months, the judge has abruptly closed it. In protest, Colombia's ex-president and ambassador to Washington has resigned, Uribe has had to cancel the naming of another ex-president as the new ambassador to France, and a new minister of foreign affairs has been named to replace the former, who went to occupy the embassy in Washington.

The United States government knows perfectly well that if they deny me their protection, I could well be killed in the coming days, because I am the only witness in the case against Santofimio. They also know that with me, the keys to some of the most horrendous crimes in Colombia's recent history would also die, along with valuable information about the penetration of narco-trafficking into all the most powerful and untouchable levels of presidential, political, judicial, military, and media power.

Officials of the American Embassy are posted at the plane's stairs; they're there to carry up the suitcases and boxes I managed to pack in a few hours with help from a couple of friends. They look at me curiously, as though wondering why an exhausted-looking, middle-aged woman awakens so much interest in the media, and now also from their government. A DEA special agent six and a half feet tall, who identifies himself as David C. and sports a Hawaiian shirt, informs me that he has been tasked with escorting me to American territory. He also tells me that the bi-engine plane will take six hours to reach Guantánamo, and after an hour-long stop to fill up on fuel, two more to reach Miami.

I don't feel at ease until I see, safe in the back of the plane, two boxes containing evidence of the crimes committed in Colombia by the convicted felons Thomas and Dee Mower, owners of Neways International of Springville, Utah, a multinational company that I am facing in a lawsuit from 1998 worth thirty million dollars. Although in only eight days a U.S. judge has found the Mowers guilty of some of the crimes

I've spent eight years trying to prove before Colombian courts, all my offers to cooperate with Eileen O'Connor's office in the Justice Department in Washington—plus five IRS attachés in the American Embassy in Bogotá—have blown up. Reacting furiously when they learned about my calls to the DOJ, the IRS, and the FBI, the embassy's press office has sworn to block any attempt at communication with the government agencies of the United States.

The reason for their resistance has nothing to do with the Mowers and everything to do with Pablo Escobar: in the embassy's Human Rights office works a former collaborator of Francisco Santos, the vice president of the republic, whose family owns the publishing house Casa Editorial El Tiempo. The media conglomerate occupies 25 percent of Álvaro Uribe's ministerial cabinet, which allows the company access to a gigantic cut of the state publicity budget—the largest Colombian advertiser—on the eve of *El Tiempo*'s sale to one of the main editorial groups in the Spanish-speaking world. Another member of the family, Juan Manuel Santos, has just been named minister of defense and tasked with renovating the Colombian Air Force fleet. So much State generosity for a single media family serves a purpose far beyond securing the country's main newspaper's unconditional support of Uribe's government. It guarantees the newspaper's absolute silence on the imperfect past of the president of the republic. It's a past that the United States government already knows about. I do too, and very well.

ALMOST NINE HOURS AFTER TAKEOFF, we reach Miami. I am starting to worry about the abdominal pain that has been with me for almost a month. It seems to get worse with every hour that passes. I haven't seen a doctor in six years, because Thomas Mower has stripped me of my modest estate and the perpetual hereditary income generated by their South American operation, which I led.

The chain hotel is impersonal and large, as is my room. Minutes later, half a dozen officers of the DEA make their entrance. They look at me with inquisitive eyes while they examine the contents of my seven Gucci and Vuitton suitcases, loaded down with dresses by Valentino, Chanel, Armani, and Saint Laurent, and the small collection of artworks that have been in my possession for almost thirty years. They inform me that, in the coming days, I will meet with several of their superiors and Richard Gregorie, prosecutor in the case against General Manuel Antonio Noriega, so I can talk to them about Gilberto and Miguel Rodríguez Orejuela, the top bosses of the Cali Cartel. The criminal case against Pablo Escobar's archenemies will begin in a matter of weeks in a Florida court, led by the same prosecutor who won the Panamanian dictator's conviction. If they are found guilty, the U.S. government will be able to not only ask for life in prison or its equivalent, but also reclaim the fortune of the two drug kingpins. In my most polite tone of voice I ask the officials for an aspirin and a toothbrush, but they reply that I'll have to buy them. When I explain that all my worldly capital consists of two quarters, they find me a tiny toothbrush, the kind given away on planes.

"Looks like it's been a while since you've stayed in an American hotel. . . ."

"It's true. In my suites at the Pierre in New York and the Hotel Bel-Air bungalows in Beverly Hills, there were always aspirin and toothbrushes. And dozens of roses and champagne!"

I tell them, sighing with nostalgia. "Now, thanks to a couple of convicts in Utah, I am so poor a simple aspirin is a luxury item."

"Well, in this country, the hotels don't have painkillers anymore: since it is a drug, it must be prescribed by a doctor, and as you surely know, that costs a fortune here. If you have a headache, try to ride out the pain and sleep. You'll see, it'll be gone tomorrow. Don't forget, we just saved your life. For security reasons, you can't leave the room or communicate with anyone, especially the press; and that includes the journalists from the *Miami Herald*. The United States government still can't promise you anything, and starting now, everything will depend on you."

I express my gratitude and tell them they don't have a thing to worry about, since I wouldn't have anywhere to go. I remind them that I was the one who offered to testify in various cases of exceptional importance, both in Colombia and in the United States.

David—the DEA agent—and the others withdraw to go over the next day's agenda.

"You've just arrived, and already you're asking the American government for things?" reproaches Nguyen, the police chief who stayed in the room.

"Yes, because I have terrible abdominal pain. And because I know that I can be of double use to your government: those two boxes contain evidence of the Colombian-Mexican part of a fraud against the Internal Revenue Service that I estimate in the hundreds of millions of dollars. In Russia, the class-action suit brought by Russian victims of Neways International was withdrawn after all the witnesses died and twenty-three million dollars were paid out. Imagine the size of the fraud in

8

three dozen countries, against their distributors and against the IRS!"

"Overseas evasion isn't our territory. We are antidrug officers."

"If I had information on the location of ten kilos of coke, you all would find me an aspirin, right?"

"You don't seem to understand that we aren't the IRS or the FBI of the state of Utah, but the Florida DEA. And don't confuse the Drug Enforcement Administration with a drugstore, Virginia!"

"What I understand, Nguyen, is that *USA v. Rodríguez Orejuela* is two hundred times bigger than the current *USA v. Mower!*"

The DEA officers return and inform me that all the TV channels are talking about my flight from Colombia. I reply that in the past four days I have declined almost two hundred interviews from all over the world and that, really, I'm not interested in whatever they're saying. I beg them to turn off the TV, because I haven't slept in eleven days or eaten in two; I am exhausted, and I just want to try to rest a few hours so I can offer all possible cooperation tomorrow.

When I'm finally alone with all my luggage and that sharp pain as my only company, I mentally prepare myself for something much more serious than possible appendicitis. Over and over I wonder if the United States government has really saved my life or if these DEA officers plan, instead, to squeeze me like an orange before returning me to Colombia. They could argue that the information I had on the Rodríguez Orejuela family turned out to be previous to 1997 and that the state of Utah is another country. I know perfectly well that back in Colombian territory, everyone who has skeletons in their closet will use me as a lesson for any informant or witness who might be tempted to follow my example: members of the security organizations will be waiting for me at the airport with some "arrest warrant" issued by the minister of defense or the state security organizations. They'll load me into an SUV with tinted windows, and when they're all finished with me, the media belonging to the presidential families involved with the drug cartels or in the service of the president re-elect will blame my torture and death either on the Rodríguez Orejuelas—"the Pepes," persecuted by Pablo Escobar—or on the capo's wife.

I have never felt more alone, sicker, or poorer, perfectly aware that if I am returned to Colombia, I will not be the first or the last to die after offering cooperation to the American Embassy in Bogotá. But my departure from the country in the DEA's plane seems to be news all over the world, which means that I'm much more visible than a César Villegas, alias "el Bandi," or a Pedro Juan Moreno, the two people who best know the president's past. That's why I decide that I won't let any government or any criminal turn me into another Carlos Aguilar, alias "El Mugre," who died after testifying against Santofimio; or Patricia Cardona, who even under maximum protection from the Colombian prosecutor was murdered after her husband— the accountant to the Rodríguez Orejuela family—left for the United States in another DEA plane.

I know perfectly well that, unlike some of those people, may they all rest in peace, I have never committed a crime. And it is because of thousands of deaths like theirs that I have the obligation to survive. And I say to myself: "I don't know how I'm going to do it, but I won't let anyone kill me, nor will I let myself die."

PART ONE

Days of Innocence and Reverie

True love suffers, and is silent.

—OSCAR WILDE

✧ *The Kingdom of White Gold*

IT WAS MID-1982, and Colombia was plagued by various rebel groups. They were all Marxist or Maoist, and rabid admirers of the Cuban model. They lived off subsidies from the Soviet Union, from the kidnapping of people they considered rich, and from stealing landowners' livestock. The most important of these groups was the FARC (Fuerzas Armadas Revolucionarias de Colombia, or the Revolutionary Armed Forces of Colombia), born of the violence of the fifties, an era of unlimited cruelty so savage that it is impossible to describe without feeling ashamed to belong to the species of man. Other groups had fewer members: the ELN (National Liberation Army) and the EPL (Popular Liberation Army), which later would lay down arms to become a political party. In 1984, the Quintín Lame Armed Movement would be born, inspired by the brave man of the same name who fought for the cause of protecting indigenous peoples.

And there was the M-19: the movement characterized by spectacular, cinematic attacks, whose members were an eclectic mix of university students and professionals, intellectuals and artists, children of bourgeois and military parents, and those hard-liner combatants who in the argot of the armed groups were known as *troperos*. Unlike the other armed groups—which operated in the jungles and countryside that cover almost half the Colombian territory—"the M" was eminently urban and counted several women among its leadership who were just as prominent and publicity-loving as their male counterparts.

In the years after Operation Condor in South America, the rules of combat in Colombia were written in black and white: when any member of one of these groups fell into the hands of the military or state security services, they were jailed and often tortured to death without trial or mediation. Likewise, when a wealthy person fell into guerrillas' hands, they were not freed unless the family handed over the ransom, often after years of negotiations; he who didn't pay died, and his remains were rarely found. With few exceptions, this situation holds as true today as it did then. Any professional Colombian can name more than a dozen people among their friends, relatives, and employees who were kidnapped—some returned safe and sound, others who never came back. These last, in turn, can be subdivided into those whose families did not have the means to satisfy the kidnappers' demands, those whose ransom was paid but were still never returned, and those whose existence was deemed not to merit the surrender of the wealth accumulated over several generations, or just over one lifetime of honest work.

. . .

I HAVE FALLEN ASLEEP with my head resting on Aníbal's shoulder, and I'm woken by that double jump that light aircraft give when they touch ground. He caresses my cheek, and when I try to stand up, he tugs gently at my arm, as if to say I should stay sitting down. He points out the window, and I can't believe my eyes: on both sides of the landing strip, two dozen young men, some with dark glasses and others with their brows furrowed in the afternoon sun, have the small plane surrounded and are pointing their machine guns at us; their expressions say they are used to shooting first and asking questions later. More of them seem to be half-hidden in the brush, and two are even playing with their mini-Uzis the way any of us would play with car keys; I can only imagine what would happen if one of those guns hit the ground, spraying six hundred bullets a minute. The boys, all very young, are wearing comfortable, modern clothes: colorful polo shirts, imported jeans and sneakers. None of them is wearing a uniform or camouflage.

As the small plane careens down the runway, I calculate how much we would be worth to a rebel group. My fiancé is the nephew of the previous president, Julio César Turbay, whose government (1978–1982) was characterized by a violent military repression of insurgent groups, especially the M-19, throwing a large number of their upper leadership in jail. But Belisario Betancur, the new president, has promised to free and give amnesty to all fighters willing to participate in his peace process. I look at Aníbal's children, and my heart sinks: Juan Pablo, eleven years old, and Adriana, nine, are now the stepchildren of the second-richest man in Colombia, Carlos

Ardila Lülle, owner of all the soda companies in the country. As for the friends who are with us, Olguita Suárez—who in a few weeks will marry the friendly Spanish singer-songwriter Rafael Urraza, the organizer of today's outing and whom we call "the Singer"—is the daughter of a millionaire cattle rancher from the Atlantic coast, and her sister is engaged to Felipe Echavarría Rocha, member of one of the most important industrial dynasties of Colombia; Nano and Ethel are decorators and *marchands d'art*, Ángela is a top model, and I am one of the most famous TV anchors in the country. I know perfectly well that if we fell into guerrilla hands, all the people on board the plane would be identified as oligarchs and, in consequence, "*secuestrables*" or "kidnappable," an adjective as Colombian as the prefix and noun "narco," which we'll get to later.

Aníbal has gone silent, and he looks unusually pale. Without bothering to wait for their answers, I fire off two dozen questions in a row:

"How did you know that this was the plane they sent for us? Don't you realize they might be kidnapping us? How many months are they going to keep us when they find out who the mother of your children is? And these aren't poor *guerrilleros*; look at their guns and tennis shoes! But why didn't you tell me to bring my tennis shoes? These kidnappers are going to make me walk through the whole jungle in Italian sandals, and without my straw hat! Why didn't you let me pack my jungle-wear in peace? And why do you accept invitations from people you don't know? The bodyguards of people *I* know don't aim machine guns at their guests! We fell into a trap! All because you go through life snorting coke and you don't know where reality is. If we get out of this, I am not marrying you, because you're going to have a heart attack, and I do not intend to be a widow!"

Aníbal Turbay is big, handsome, and free; he is loving to the point of exhaustion and generous with his words, his time, and his money, despite the fact that he's not a multimillionaire, as all my ex-boyfriends are. He is equally adored by his eclectic collection of friends—people like the treasure hunter Manolito de Arnaude—and by hundreds of women whose lives are divided into "before Aníbal" and "after Aníbal." His only defect is an irremediable addiction to nasal powder; I hate it, but he adores it more than his children, me, money, everything. Before the poor man can respond to my scolding, the plane door opens, and in wafts the warm, humid air of the tropics of what in my seasonless country we call Tierra Caliente—the Hot Land. Two armed men enter, and on seeing our stupefied faces, they exclaim:

"Oh, God! You aren't going to believe this: we were expecting some cages with a panther and several tigers, and it looks like they were sent in a different plane! A thousand apologies! How embarrassing, with the ladies and the children! When the *patrón* finds out, he's going to kill us!"

They explain that the property has a very large zoo, and evidently there has been a coordination problem with the guests' flight and the one bringing in the beasts. And while the armed men fall all over themselves apologizing, the pilots emerge from the plane with an indifferent expression that says, *We don't owe explanations to strangers; our job is to follow a flight plan, not review the cargo.*

Three jeeps are waiting to drive us to the hacienda's house. I put on my sunglasses and safari hat and descend from the plane, unaware that I am taking my first steps in the place that will change my life forever. We get into the vehicles, and when Aníbal puts his arm around my shoulders, I feel calm, ready to enjoy every remaining minute of our stay.

"What a beautiful place! And it looks huge. I think this trip is going to be worth it . . . ," I tell him in a quiet voice, pointing to two herons taking flight from a distant shore.

Absorbed, in complete silence, we take in that magnificent scene of earth, water, and sky that seems to stretch out beyond the horizon. I feel a burst of happiness, the kind you don't see coming, the kind that invades you suddenly and enfolds everything and then departs without a good-bye. From a cabin in the distance, in the unmistakable voice of Roberto Torres, come the notes of "Caballo Viejo" (Old Horse) by Simón Díaz, that hymn to the Venezuelan plains that older men have adopted as their own throughout the continent, singing it to chestnut mares when they want to throw off their reins and hope the mares will do the same. *Cuando el amor llega así, de esta manera, uno no se da ni cuenta . . .* (When loves arrives this way, you don't even realize it . . .), warns Torres as he narrates the old stud's feats. "When love arrives like this, you just can't help it . . . ," the plainsman justifies himself, ultimately demanding that the whole human species follow his example, "because after this life, you get no more chances," in a tone full of popular wisdom and rhythm, the accomplices of warm air heavy with promise.

I am too happy and caught up in that view to start inquiring about our host's name or his life story.

"The man who owns all this must be just like that: one of those old, crafty politicians, with plenty of money and mares, who think they're the king of the town," I tell myself as I lean my head against Aníbal's shoulder again. Aníbal, that hedonist huge man whose love of adventure died with him only a few weeks before I gathered the strength to start telling this story, woven from moments frozen in the nooks and crannies of my memory, peopled with myths and monsters who should never be brought back to life.

THOUGH THE HOUSE IS ENORMOUS, it lacks all the refinements of Colombia's traditional large haciendas: there is no chapel, stable, or tennis court; there are no horses, English riding boots, or purebred dogs; no antique silver or artworks from recent centuries; no oil paintings of virgins and saints or gold-painted wooden friezes over doorways; no colonial columns or varnished figures of ancestral Nativity scenes; no studded chests or Persian rugs of every size; no hand-painted French porcelain or tablecloths embroidered by nuns; no roses or orchids cultivated by the proud lady of the house.

Nor do I see the humble servants once typically found on my country's rich estates, people who are almost always inherited along with the property—long-suffering folk, resigned and immensely sweet, who for generations have chosen security over freedom. Those peasants in *ruanas*—short ponchos of brown wool—with missing teeth but always smiling, who respond without hesitating to any request, doffing their old hats with a deep bow of the head: "Right away, sir!" "Eleuterio González at your service, here to serve!" and who never found out that the concept of tipping existed in the rest of the world. They are almost extinct today, because the *guerrilleros* taught them that when the Revolution triumphs, someday in the not-so-distant future, they could also have land and live-stock, weapons and booze and women like the bosses', pretty and free of varicose veins.

The hacienda's bedrooms are off a very long hallway and are decorated in a Spartan fashion: two beds, a nightstand with a locally made ceramic ashtray, a cheap lamp, and photos of the property. Thank God, our room's private bath has cold and hot water, not just cold, like almost all the farms of the Hot Land. The interminable terrace is dotted with dozens of tables with umbrellas and hundreds of white plastic chairs. The size of the social area—equal to any country club—leaves not the slight-est doubt that the house was built to host on a large scale and receive hundreds of visitors; from the guest rooms, we deduce that, on weekends, they must be counted by the dozen.

"Imagine what the parties are like!" someone in the group comments. "They probably bring the Vallenato King in from Valledupar, with two dozen accordions!"

"Noooo, more like Sonora Matancera and Los Melódicos, together!" someone else says, with a sarcastic tone that lets just a bit of envy show through.

The property manager informs us that the hacienda's owner has been held up by a last-minute problem and won't arrive until the next day. It's clear that the workers have received instructions to take care of our slightest need so our stay is comfortable and pleasant, but from the very first moment, they let us know that the tour of the place excludes the second floor, where the owner and his wife and son have their private rooms. The workers are all men, and they seem to feel a great admiration for their boss. Their high quality of life, superior to that of servants of other rich families, is clear from their con-fidence and utter lack of humility; these peasants seem to be family men, and the work clothes they're wearing are new and well made. They are more discreet than the young men on the landing strip; unlike that group, they aren't carrying weapons of any sort. We move into the dining room for dinner. The main table, made of wood, is enormous.

"This could feed a whole battalion!"

The napkins are white paper, and the food is served by two efficient and silent women—the only ones we've seen since we arrived—on dishes from the region. Just as we had anticipated, the menu consists of a delicious *bandeja paisa*, a typical dish of the Antioquia region and the most basic of Colombian cuisine: beans, rice, ground meat, and fried egg, accompanied by a slice of avocado. Not a single thing on the property reflects a particularly refined or luxurious ambiance. Everything on this estate—more than seven thousand acres between Doradal and Puerto Triunfo in the burning Colombian Magdalena Medio region—seems to have been planned with the practical and impersonal taste of an enormous Hot Land hotel, and not in the style of a large country house.

Nothing, then, on that warm, calm tropical night—my first at Hacienda Nápoles—could have prepared me for the world of colossal proportions I would discover the next day, or for the size of that kingdom that was so different from any I'd seen before. And no one could have warned me about the colossal ambitions of the man who had built it all, from only stardust and the spirit that makes myths that forever change the history of nations and the fates of their people.

AT BREAKFAST we are told that our host will arrive at noon, and will have the pleasure of personally showing us his zoo.

Meanwhile, we're going to take a look at the hacienda from dune buggies, those vehicles designed for young people with no responsibilities, to ride over the sand at high speeds. They consist of a very low, almost ground-level frame that can resist anything, two seats, a steering wheel, a gearshift, a fuel tank, and a motor that makes an infernal racket. Wherever those vehicles go, they leave behind a little cloud of smoke and dust and a wake of envy, because someone who drives a dune buggy is radiant and tan, in shorts and sunglasses, with a pretty and slightly scared girl beside him, her long hair flowing in the wind, or with a half-drunk friend who won't change himself for anyone. The dune buggy is the only vehicle that can be driven on the beach by highly intoxicated people without anything bad happening to them, without turning over, with the ability to suddenly stop, and, above all, without the police locking up the crazy guy at the wheel.

The first morning of that weekend unfolds in utter normality, but then strange things begin to happen, as if a guardian angel were trying to warn me that present pleasures and innocent adventures are almost always the masks that cover the face of future sorrows.

Aníbal is certainly one of the craziest human beings to ever walk the planet, a superlative that greatly entertains my adventurous spirit, and all my friends predict that our engagement will end, not at the altar, but at the foot of a cliff. Though he drives his Mercedes on narrow and winding two-lane mountain roads at more than one hundred miles per hour, with a glass of whiskey in one hand and a half-eaten snack in the other, the truth is that he has never had an accident. And I ride happily in the dune buggy with his little girl on my lap, the wind in my face and my hair flying, enjoying the pure delight, the indescribable joy you feel when you ride for miles and miles over flat, virgin terrain at top speed with nothing to stop or limit you. At any other Colombian hacienda, those vast expanses would be dedicated to raising zebu cattle, and they would be peppered with barred and locked gates to safeguard thousands of cows gazing languidly and dozens of bulls on eternal alert.

For nearly three hours we travel over miles and miles of grasslands in every shade of green, interrupted only by the occasional lake or slow-moving river, a mustard-colored hill, soft as velvet, a slight undulation in the distance, similar to those prairies where, years later, I watch Meryl Streep and Robert Redford in *Out of Africa*, only without the baobab trees. The whole place is populated only by trees and plants, birds and small animals native to the American tropics, impossible to describe in detail because every new scene starts before the previous one has finished parading before our eyes—vistas that first went past by the dozens now seem to pass by the hundreds.

At vertiginous speed we head toward a long hollow of thick and junglelike vegetation, about half a mile wide, to cool off for a few minutes from the burning noontime sun under the giant feathered fans of a guadua bamboo forest. Seconds later, flocks of multicolored birds take flight with a shrill squawking, the buggy jumps over a depression hidden by dead leaves, and a stick about seven feet long and almost two inches thick enters like a bullet through the front part of the vehicle, crosses the narrow space between Adriana's knee and mine at about sixty miles per hour, and stops exactly one millimeter from my cheek and two inches from my eye. No damage done—to me or Adriana, at least—because dune buggies stop on a dime. And because, it seems, God has a very singular destiny reserved for me.

In spite of the distance we've covered, and thanks to that invention called the walkie-talkie, which I had always considered snobbish and superfluous, in a matter of twenty minutes, several jeeps come to rescue us and to collect the "cadaver" of the first totaled dune buggy in the whole history of humanity. Half an hour later we are in the hacienda's small hospital receiving tetanus shots and Mercurochrome swabs on the scrapes on our knees and my cheek, while everyone breathes a sigh of relief because Adriana and I are alive and have all four eyes intact. Aníbal, wearing the expression of a chastised child, grumbles about the expense of having that blasted machine repaired or possibly replaced, for which he'll need, first of all, to find out how much it costs to ship one from the United States.

We are informed that the hacienda owner's helicopter arrived a while ago, though none of us remembers hearing it. Somewhat uneasy, my fiancé and I prepare ourselves to offer apologies for the damage we caused and to ask about how to repair it. Minutes later, our host makes his entrance into the small salon where we've gathered with the rest of the guests. His face lights up when he sees how astonished we are at his youth. I think he senses how relieved my buggy-assassin boyfriend and I are that he's the same age as most of the members of our group, because a mischievous look flits over his face, and he seems to fight against one of his guffaws that, I later learn, are the precursors to peals of laughter.

Some years before, during a visit to Hong Kong, I was looking at the Rolls-Royce Silver Ghost that was parked in front of my hotel twenty-four hours a day with its chauffeur in hat, uniform, and black boots. Its owner, the venerable and elegant "Captain" Chang, answered: "Don't worry, dear madam, we have seven more just for our guests, and that one is yours!"

In the same tone of voice, our smiling young host exclaims with a dismissive wave of his hand: "Don't worry about that buggy, we have dozens of them!" eliminating all our worries straightaway—and with them, any shadow of doubt about his resources, hospitality, or total willingness to share the infinite entertainment of his paradise with us. Then he sets about greeting us one by one in a voice that first calms, then disarms, and finally seduces us—women, men, and children alike. His smile makes each of us feel like the accomplice chosen for some carefully planned joke that only he is in on.

"Delighted to meet you in person, finally! How are those scrapes? We promise to more than make up for the time the kids lost; they won't be bored for a minute! Nice to meet you, I'm Pablo Escobar."

Though he is a fairly short man—under five foot six—I feel absolutely certain he has never cared a whit. His body is solid and of the type that in a few years will tend to gain weight. His double chin, premature and prominent, over a thick and abnormally short neck, detracts youth from his expression but adds a certain authority, the air of a respectable older gentleman, to the carefully measured words that emerge from his straight, firm mouth. He speaks with a serene voice—neither high nor deep, polite and truly pleasant—utterly sure that his wishes are commands and that his dominance of the subjects that concern him is complete. He sports a mustache under a nose that in profile is almost Greek and, along with his voice, is the only striking characteristic of a man who, in another setting, would be described as perfectly ordinary, more ugly than beautiful, and who could be confused with millions of others in the streets of any Latin American country. His hair is dark and curly, with an untamed triple wave across his forehead that he brushes away from time to time with a quick movement; his skin is fairly light—he's not tan like us, who are golden year-round, though we live in Tierra Fría—the Cold Land. His eyes are very close-set and are particularly elusive; when he feels he's not being watched, they seem to withdraw into unfathomable caves under his sparse eyebrows to scrutinize those outside. I notice that he looks almost constantly toward Ángela, who observes him with polite disdain from her stature of five foot seven, her twenty-three years, and her superb beauty.

We take the jeeps and head to the part of the Hacienda Nápoles where the zoo is. Escobar drives one of the vehicles, accompanied by two Brazilian girls in thongs, pretty cariocas of small stature and perfect hips who never talk and who caress each other, though with growing discretion because of the children and the elegant beauties who are now taking all of the host's attention. Aníbal notices their utter indifference to what is happening around them, which for an authority in his field is an indisputable symptom of repeated and deep inhalation of Samarian Platinum. Remarkably, on this sumptuous property Samarian Gold is merely cheap pot. We notice that both girls, tender like little angels about to fall asleep, sport one-carat diamonds on their right index fingers.

Three elephants appear in the distance, perhaps the main attraction of any respectable circus or zoo. Though I've never been able to distinguish between Asian and African species, Escobar tells us they are Asian. He also informs us that all the larger species and the ones in danger of extinction have two a man we'd met just a few hours ago, and who five minutes ago had been chatting breezily with him.

Approaching the water's edge, Escobar and I touch bottom and stumble onto the shore. He holds me firmly by the arm and I ask him why, among so many people, he was the only one who realized I was about to die.

"I saw the desperation in your eyes. Your friends and my men only saw your hands waving."

I look at him and tell him that it wasn't just that—he was the only one to see my anguish and the only one who cared about my life. He seems surprised, and more so when I add, with the first smile I'm capable of after the fright, "So now you'll be responsible for me as long as you're alive, Pablo. . . ."

He puts an arm around my shoulders, which can't stop shaking. Then, with a cheerful expression, he exclaims, "As long as I'm alive? What makes you think I'm going to die first?"

"Well, it's just a saying . . . but let's make it as long as I'm alive, so we can both take it easy, and you can pay for my funeral!"

He laughs and says he's sure that will be a century from now, because judging from the events of today, I have more lives than a cat. When we reach the shore where the group is, I let myself be wrapped in the towel that Aníbal's loving arms hold out to me; it's warm, and because it's large, it hides what he doesn't want me to see in his eyes.

The grilled beef is as good as the best *parrillada* in an Argentine estancia, and the view from the cabin above the river is simply a dream. In complete silence, and a bit withdrawn from the rest of the group, I contemplate the opposite side of the river with the eyes of Eve granted a second chance in paradise. In the years to come, I would relive that afternoon in my mind time and time again, with me gazing toward the calmest part of that Río Claro, mirroring the magnificent wall of tropical foliage behind it and now covered with a million sparkling emeralds, the sunlight bathing every leaf of every tree, God shining in the wings of every butterfly. Several months later, I would beg Pablo to take me back to that place of reverie, but he would answer that such a thing was no longer possible because it had been taken over by guerrillas. Then, on a random day almost a quarter of a century later, I would finally come to understand that we must never return to the places of splendid beauty where we were once incredibly happy for a few hours, because all that is left of them is the nostalgia for the colors and, above all, the longing for the laughter.

EVERYTHING IN HACIENDA NÁPOLES seems colossal. We find ourselves now on the Rolligon, a gigantic tractor with the strength of three elephants, wheels almost seven feet in diameter and a basket that fits fifteen people.

"Bet you can't get that one, Pablo!" we shout, pointing to a medium-sized tree.

"Bet we can knock that one down, too!" shouts Escobar, delighted, steamrolling the poor tree without compassion, arguing that anything that can't stand up under his attack doesn't deserve to live and should return to the earth and become food.

On the way back to the house, we pass a car riddled with bullet holes; it looks to be a Ford from the late twenties.

"It's Bonnie and Clyde's!" he informs us proudly.

I ask if he means the real couple's or the one from the movie, and he replies that it's the original—he doesn't buy fakes.

ance by exclaiming in front of everyone, "This is the only woman in the world who wakes up looking like a rose. . . . It's like seeing a miracle of creation every morning."

"Just look at them!" says the Singer to Escobar. "Two sex symbols, together . . ."

Pablo looks at us, smiling. Then he stares straight at me. I lower my eyes.

Back in our room that night, Aníbal comments in a low voice, "Really, a guy who can smuggle three giraffes here all the way from Kenya is capable of getting tons of anything into the United States!"

"Such as what, love?"

"Coke. Pablo is the King of Coke, and there is so much demand that he's on his way to becoming the richest man in the world!" he exclaims, raising his eyebrows in admiration. I tell him I would have sworn Pablo financed that lifestyle of his with politics.

"No, no, my darling, it's the other way around: he finances the politics with this!"

And half closing his eyes, rapturous with pleasure after his fortieth line of the day, he shows me a fifty-gram rock of cocaine that Pablo gave him.

I am exhausted, and I fall deeply asleep. When I wake up the next day, Aníbal is still there, but the rock isn't. His eyes are bloodshot, and he's looking at me with enormous tenderness. I only know I love him.

‹ℛ Presidential Aspirations

A FEW WEEKS LATER, Aníbal gets a call from Escobar, inviting us to visit the hacienda and zoo of Jorge Luis Ochoa, near Colombia's Caribbean coast. Ochoa is Escobar's best friend and his partner in the social project Medellín sin Tugurios (Medellín Without Slums). Pablo sends a plane for us, and when we land we see that he is already waiting for us, and only the crew of his own plane is with him. It's clear that, not being the owner of the house, he is there to join us as one more guest in the group, which again includes our friend Ángela. We weren't able to bring Aníbal's children this time because their mother was truly horrified when she heard about the adventures we'd had in Nápoles; she strictly forbade him from bringing the kids on "weekends with those extravagant nouveau riche people."

There is very little traffic on the highway that leads from the airport to Ochoa's hacienda. After a few minutes of driving under a merciless sun, with Escobar at the wheel of a convertible jeep, we reach the checkpoint where the toll is the equivalent of three U.S. dollars. Our driver slows down, greets the collector with his widest grin, and keeps right on going, relaxed and slow, leaving the poor boy stupefied. First he stands openmouthed with the ticket in his hand, and then he runs after us, waving his arms uselessly to get us to stop. Surprised, we ask Pablo why he *voló el peaje*, as Colombians say, or "blew the toll."

"Because if there are no police in the booth, I don't pay. I only respect authority when it's armed!" he cries triumphantly, in the tone of a schoolteacher giving a lesson to his little students.

The Ochoas are renowned breeders and exporters of champion horses; thousands of them can be found in La Loma, their hacienda near Medellín that's run by their father, Fabio. This ranch, La Veracruz, is dedicated to breeding fighting bulls. Although the size of their property and its zoo can't compare with Nápoles, the house is beautifully decorated, and everywhere I see those little electric Ferraris and Mercedeses, red and yellow, that so many children dream of. The oldest of the three Ochoa brothers is Jorge Luis—his friends call him El Gordo—an affable man the same age as Pablo. He's married to a tall, pretty woman, María Lía Posada, cousin of the soon-to-be minister of communications, Noemí Sanín Posada. While Jorge doesn't display the same magnetic quality as Escobar when he sets out to have fun, it's clear the two men share a great affection and deep respect, born of loyalty that has been repeatedly put to the test over the years.

After a day spent eating and touring the grounds, we said good-bye, and I told Jorge that I wish I could see his famous champion horses. With his wide smile, he promises to plan something special very soon, and that I won't be disappointed.

We go back to Medellín in another of Escobar's planes. Though his efforts to win over Angelita have again been fruitless, the two of them seem to have become good friends. Medellín is the City of Eternal Spring, and for the *paisas*, its proud inhabitants, it is the capital of the Antioquia department—the name given to states in Colombia—as well as the country's industrial capital and the capital of the world. We stay at the Intercontinental, located in the beautiful El Poblado neighborhood and near Pablo and his cousin Gustavo's mansion-office, a property that belongs to the manager of the Medellín Metro, a great friend of theirs. That part of the city is characterized by an infinite number of streets that curve between hills covered in exuberant, semitropical vegetation. For visitors like us, used to Bogotá's flat streets, which are numbered like New York's, they are a true maze. The *paisas*, though, drive at top speed as they go up and down through the residential neighborhoods, lined with trees and gardens, and through the noisy city center.

"Since today is Sunday and everyone goes to bed early, at midnight I'm going to take you on a thrill ride in James Bond's car," announces Pablo.

When he presents us with the jewel of his collection, we're terribly disappointed. Still, though it's no Aston Martin and it boasts only a supreme dose of automobile anonymity, the dashboard is covered in buttons. He sees our faces lit up by curiosity, and in his pride of ownership he begins to reel off the characteristics of a car that could only have been designed with the police in mind:

"This button lets out a cloud of smoke that throws off anyone chasing you; this other one releases tear gas that leaves them coughing and desperate for water; that one pours oil so they slide in a zigzag and go off a cliff; this one drops hundreds of tacks and nails to puncture their tires; this is a flamethrower that you activate after this one that sprays gasoline; that one sets off the explosives, and on either side are the machine guns, though today we've removed them in case the car falls into the hands of some vengeful panther. Oh! And if all that fails to work, this last button emits a frequency that destroys the eardrum. We're going to give a demonstration of the practical utility of my treasure; unfortunately, though, only the ladies fit in Bond's car. Ángela will be my copilot. The men . . . and Virginia . . . will go in the cars behind."

And he pulls away very slowly, while we get in the other car and take off at top speed. After several minutes, we see him coming up behind us like a bat out of hell; we don't know if he's flown right over us, but somehow, seconds later he's in front of us. Again and again we try to pass him, but just as we're about to do it, he careens off and vanishes around the curves of El Poblado's deserted streets, only to reappear when we're least expecting it. I implore God to let no other vehicle cross his path, because it would surely tumble off the road or be flattened on the asphalt like a stamp. The game draws out for almost an hour, and while we pause to catch our breath, Escobar comes out from the shadows, tires squealing, and leaves us floating in a sea of smoke that forces us to stop. It takes us several minutes to find our way, and when we finally do, he passes us in a flash and we're wrapped in clouds of gas that seem to multiply and grow more inflamed as the seconds pass. We feel like the sulfuric acid is burning our throats and going up our noses to cloud our vision and invade every fold of our brains. We cough, and with every mouthful of poisoned air we breathe, the burning is multiplied by ten. We hear the bodyguards groaning behind us, and in the distance we can hear the occupants of James Bond's car laughing as they flee the place at 125 miles per hour.

Somehow, at the side of the road, we find a spigot. Escobar's boys get out of the car at a run, cursing and bumping into one another while they fight for a sip of liquid. When I see them crying, I stand to one side, and to set an example, I get in the back of the line. Then, with my hands on my hips and in the little voice I have left, I yell at them with all the contempt I can muster, "Act like men, dammit! From what I can see, the only brave one around here is me: a woman! Aren't you ashamed? Have a little dignity; you're like little girls!"

Once Pablo and his accomplices reach us, they burst out laughing. Over and over he swears to us that his copilot is to blame, because he only authorized her to throw out the curtain of smoke. And that evil witch, who can't stop laughing, admits, "I pushed the tear gas button by mistake!"

Then, in a militaristic tone, he orders his men: "Have some dignity! You really do look like little girls. And let the lady through!"

Coughing and swallowing my tears, I say I'll let the "señoritas" go ahead, and I'll drink water when we get to the hotel, two minutes away. Then I add that his bucket of bolts is nothing but a stinking skunk, and I leave.

ON ANOTHER OF OUR TRIPS to Medellín in the second half of 1982, Aníbal introduces me to a drug trafficker named Joaquín Builes who is quite different from Pablo and his partners.

"Joaco" looks exactly like Pancho Villa, and his family are relatives of Monsignor Builes. He is very rich and friendly, and he also boasts that he is very evil—"but *really* evil, not like Pablito"—and that he and his cousin Miguel Ángel have ordered hundreds and hundreds of people murdered, so many they could be the entire population of an Antioquian town. Neither Aníbal nor I believe a word, but Builes cackles and swears it's true.

"The truth is that Joaco is harmless," I'll hear Pablo say later. "But he's so, so stingy! He'd rather waste an entire afternoon trying to sell you a Persian rug for $1,000 than invest that same time and effort in dispatching five hundred kilos of coke, which would earn enough to set up ten warehouses full of rugs!"

In that entertaining gathering with Joaco, Aníbal, and the Singer, I find out that as a teenager, Pablo started his successful political career as a cemetery gravestone thief. He would file off the names of the deceased, and then he and his partners sold them as new. And not just once, but several times. I find the story hilarious, because I imagine all those tightfisted old *paisas* turning over in their graves when they find out their heirs paid a fortune for a headstone that wasn't even secondhand but third- or fourth-. I also hear them talk admiringly about Escobar's inarguable and very laudable talent for "deboning" stolen cars of any make in just a few hours and selling them off in pieces as "discount parts." I conclude that it was the rookie congressman's encyclopedic knowledge of automobile mechanics that allowed him to order that "exclusive, unique, and absolutely handmade" product that is James Bond's car.

Someone mentions that our new friend was also a kind of *gatillero*, or trigger man, during the Marlboro Wars. When I ask what that means, no one wants to clue me in and every-one rushes to change the subject. I imagine it must be some-thing like stealing thousands of packs of contraband Marlboro cigarettes that, certainly, weigh less than a gravestone. And I conclude that Pablito's life has much in common with the Virginia Slims slogan: "You've come a long way, baby!"

SOME DAYS LATER, we receive an invitation from Jorge Ochoa to travel to Cartagena. Awaiting us there is one of the most unforgettable nights I've ever experienced. We stay in the presidential suite of the Cartagena Hilton, and after dining at the city's finest restaurant, we prepare for the outing Jorge and his family planned after the promise he'd made me: a trip through the city streets—the old and new parts—in carriages drawn by horses they've had brought in from La Loma.

The scene seems straight out of *One Thousand and One Nights*, planned by an Arabian sheikh for his only daughter's wedding or produced by a Hollywood art director with the pomp of some celebration on a nineteenth-century Mexican hacienda.

The horse-drawn carriages are a far cry from the ones in Cartagena or New York or even a Spanish grandee's at the Fair of Seville. Like those, they have two lights silhouetting an impeccably uniformed driver, but each of the four coaches is pulled by six champion Percheron horses, white as snow, har-nessed, chests puffed like the horses pulling Cinderella's car-riage, pleased as can be at their own size and splendid beauty. Stepping with the intense, sensual exactitude of twenty-four flamenco dancers, they parade through those historic streets as though synchronized. Pablo informs us that each team is worth a million dollars, but for me, my sublime enjoyment is worth all the gold in the world. The vision leaves a wake of astonishment behind: people emerge onto the old city's white balconies; tourists are enchanted; poor Cartagena coachmen watch openmouthed as the display of magnificent ostentation passes by.

I don't know if the whole performance is an act of generosity on Jorge's part or if Pablo planned it as a subtle attempt to seduce Angelita with something so romantic and unique. Or maybe it's the Ochoa family expressing their gratitude to Escobar, who had bravely orchestrated the successful return of Jorge's sister after she was kidnapped a year earlier. All I know is that none of the great Colombian magnates I've met will ever be able to coordinate their daughters' weddings with such irrefutable style.

On another long weekend we travel to Santa Marta, located on the Caribbean Sea in the cradle of the legendary Samarian Gold. There we meet the Dávilas, the kings of marijuana. Unlike the coke kings, who with few exceptions—like the Ochoas—are of poor or lower-middle-class extraction, the Dávilas belong to the old landowning aristocracy of the Atlantic coast. And in contrast to the *coqueros*, who for the most part aren't very attractive—or, as Aníbal would say, "a bit thickset"—almost all of these men are tall and handsome, though ordinary. Some of the Dávila women have married such notable people as President López Pumarejo, or President Turbay's son, or Julio Mario Santo Domingo, the richest man in Colombia.

Aníbal tells me that the Santa Marta airport closes at six in the evening, but the Dávilas are so powerful that it reopens at night just for them. That's how they can quietly dispatch planes loaded with what is famed as the world's best marijuana. I ask him how they do it, and he replies that they grease everyone's palms: the control tower, the police, and here and there a navy officer. Since at this point I already know many of his most "newly rich" friends, I comment, "I thought all these narcos had their own runways at their haciendas. . . ."

"Noooo, my love. That's only the big ones! Weed doesn't pay enough, and there's a lot of competition coming from Hawaii. Don't get the idea that's in everyone's reach, because you need a million permits for a private landing strip. You know how much paperwork is involved in putting the plates on a car in this country, right? Multiply that by a hundred, and you can register a plane; now multiply that by another hundred, and you get the license for a private landing strip."

I ask how Pablo manages, then, to have his own landing strip and a fleet of planes, ship tons of coke, bring giraffes and elephants from Africa, and smuggle in Rolligons and six-foot-tall boats.

"It's because his business has no competition. And he's the richest of all because Pablito, my love, is a jumbo: he has a key contact at the Civil Aviation Agency, a young guy who's the son of one of the first narcos . . . an Uribe, cousin of the Ochoas . . . Álvaro Uribe, I think. Why do you suppose all these people end up financing the campaigns of the two presidential candidates? Don't be naive!"

"That's some position the kid's got for himself! All these guys must be lining up."

"That's life, my love: the bad name goes away, but the money stays at home!"

. . .

THOSE ARE THE DAYS of wine and roses, honey and laughter, and enchanting friendships. But nothing lasts forever, and one fine day that captivating song stops playing just as suddenly as it had started.

Aníbal's addiction is growing with every rock Pablo gives him, and as it grows, the most absurd and embarrassing scenes of jealousy come to replace declarations of love and expressions of tenderness. Whereas before those scenes had been reserved for strangers, now they are directed at our mutual friends and even my fans. After every argument comes a two-day separation, and Aníbal seeks consolation from an ex-girlfriend, a couple of mud wrestlers, or three flamenco dancers. On the third day, he'll call and beg me to take him back. Hours of pleading, dozens of roses, and an artful tear overcome my resistance . . . and the cycle starts all over again.

One night, while we are chatting with the group in an elegant bar, my boyfriend takes out a gun and aims it at two fans who only wanted my autograph. When our friends manage to disarm him nearly an hour later, I beg them to take me home. And this time, when Aníbal calls to try to explain away what happened, I tell him, "If you quit coke today, I will take care of you and make you happy for the rest of your life. If not, I am leaving you this instant."

"But, my love . . . you have to understand that I can't live without 'Snow White,' and I'm never going to leave her!"

"Then I no longer love you. It's over."

And like that, in the blink of an eye, in the first week of January 1983, we say good-bye forever.

. . .

IN 1983, there are still no private television channels in Colombia. Each new government leases off airtime to private production companies called *programadoras*, and TV Impacto—the company I started with the well-known hard-line journalist Margot Ricci—has received several spaces in the AA and B time slots. But Colombia is going through a recession, and the large companies are only advertising in AAA or prime time, 7:00 to 9:30 p.m. We are only a year into the project, and our profits aren't enough to cover the costs of the National Institute of Radio and Television; practically all the small producers like us are broke.

MARGOT ASKS ME for a meeting so we can decide what to do, but when I arrive at the office on Monday, the first thing she says is "Did Aníbal really shoot you on Friday?"

I reply that if he had, I'd be in the cemetery or the hospital, and not the office.

"But that's what all of Bogotá is saying!" she exclaims, in a tone that says other people's words take precedence over what's right before her eyes.

I reply that I can't change reality just to please all of Bogotá. But I also say that, while it is false that Aníbal fired the gun, I'd left him for good and I haven't stopped crying in three days.

"You finally left him? What a relief; I'm so glad! Now, get ready to cry for real, because we're $100,000 in debt. At the rate we're going, in a few weeks I'll have to sell my apartment, my car, and my son! Of course, before I sell my son, I'll sell you to the bedouin with five camels, because I don't know how we're going to get out of this!"

Eight months earlier, Margot and I had traveled to Israel on an invitation from the government, and then we visited Egypt to see the pyramids. While we were in the Cairo bazaar haggling over a turquoise necklace, a scrawny, toothless bedouin some seventy years old, carrying a shepherd's crook and smelling of goat, had leered at me lasciviously. He circled us nervously and tried to catch the attention of the stand's owner. After exchanging some words with the old man, the merchant gave Margot a brilliant smile and addressed her in English: "The rich gentleman wishes to give the necklace to the young lady as a gift. And that's not all: he wishes to marry her and negotiate the dowry now. He is willing to offer five camels for her!"

Offended by the figure, but quite entertained by the unbelievable proposal, I told Margot to ask for at least thirty camels for me, and while she was at it to tell that mummy from the Fourth Dynasty that the young lady was not a virgin: she'd been married, and not just once, but twice.

Exclaiming that only a sheikh had thirty camels, the old man, alarmed, asked Margot if I had buried my two husbands.

After smiling with compassion at the man seeking my hand in marriage, Margot warned me to get ready to run and turned to the merchant with a triumphant expression: "Tell the rich gentleman that she didn't bury them: this young thirty-two-year-old lady already kicked two husbands to the curb, both twenty years younger than him, twenty times better-looking, and twenty times richer!"

And we ran off to disappear in the market while the old

man chased us, howling in Arabic and waving his crook furiously in the air. We didn't stop laughing until we reached the hotel and were happily looking out from our room at the legendary Nile River, jade-colored and shining under the stars.

Margot's mention of the bedouin brings to mind a dromedary collector who is not yet septuagenarian, nor is he cantankerous, fetid, or toothless. And I say to Margot, "I know someone with more than five camels who once saved my life, and who could maybe save this company, too."

"Sheikh or circus owner?" she asks ironically.

"Sheikh, with thirty camels. But first I have to consult with someone."

I call the Singer and explain that Margot and I are about to lose our television production company, and I tell him I need Pablo's phone number so I can ask him to advertise with us, or to buy our *programadora* outright.

"Well . . . the only business of Pablo's that I know of is the 'Coca-Cola' one! But this is precisely the kind of problem he loves to solve with a flick of his wrist. . . . Stay right where you are, and he'll call you."

Minutes later, my phone rings. After a short conversation, I go to my partner's office, and with a radiant smile I tell her, "Margarita, the congressman Escobar Gaviria is on the line, and he wants to know if he can send his jet for us tomorrow at three in the afternoon."

ON RETURNING FROM MEDELLÍN, I find an invitation to dine with Olguita and the Singer. She is sweet and refined, and he is the friendliest and most candid Andalusian in the world. When I get to their house—they hardly wait for me to sit down—

Urraza asks me how it went. I reply that, thanks to the advertisement for Osito Bicycles that Pablo offered us, we'll be able to pay all the company's debts, and that the next week I'm going to film a program with Pablo at the municipal dump.

"Well . . . for that kind of money, I'd *eat* garbage! And you're going to put him on TV? ¡*Hostia!*"

I tell him that every journalist interviews half a dozen unimportant congresspeople every week, and that Pablo is a member of the House; an alternate, yes, but a congressman nonetheless. And I add, "He's in the process of giving away twenty-five hundred houses to the 'residents' of the dump, and others to people who live in slums. If that isn't news in Colombia, I'll eat my hat!"

He wants to know if Pablo made the interview a prerequisite, and I tell him no: I was the one who required it as a condition to accept the advertising; he asked only for a five-minute segment. I explain that I feel so grateful for his generosity, and have so much admiration for what Medellín sin Tugurios is doing, that I'm going to dedicate the whole hour of my Monday program to it, from 6:00 to 7:00 p.m.; the show will air in three weeks.

"You've certainly got balls! . . . And I'm starting to think Pablo is interested in you."

I reply that all I'm interested in is saving my company and advancing my career, which is the only thing I have.

"Well, if Pablo falls in love with you and you fall in love with him—as I think could happen—you won't have to worry about your career again, or your future, or that damned production company! And you're going to be thanking me for it for the rest of your life, believe me."

Laughing, I tell him that's not going to happen: my heart

is still very bruised, and Pablo has always been fascinated by Ángela.

"But don't you realize that was all just child's play? And that she's the kind of girl who will always be in love with some polo player? Pablo knows Angelita isn't for him; he's not an idiot. He has very big political aspirations and he needs a real, elegant woman at his side, one who knows how to speak in public, not a model or a girl from his own class, like the last girlfriend. . . . Did you know he left her with two million dollars? What wouldn't he, a man who wants to be president and who's on his way to becoming one of the richest men in the world, give to a princess like you!"

I say that men who are so rich have always liked very young girls, and I'm already thirty-three years old.

"Oh, stop that bullshit, you look twenty-five, *hostia*! And multimillionaires have always liked sensational women— role models—not little girls who have nothing to talk about and don't know how to make love. You're a sex symbol, and you've got twenty years of beauty ahead of you. What more do you want? Do you know any man who cares how old Sophia Loren is, silly girl? You're this country's professional beauty with a pedigree, something Pablo has never had! *Hostia*, and here I thought you were an intelligent woman. . . ."

To add a final flourish to his rant, he exclaims in horror, "And if you plan to show up at that dump wearing Gucci and Valentino, I'm warning you, you won't be able to get rid of the stench for a week! You can't even imagine what it's like there. . . ."

ભ *Ask Me for Anything!*

IT IS LIKE THE STENCH of ten thousand bodies on a battlefield
three days after a historic defeat. Miles before we get there,
we can already smell it. The Medellín dump is not a mountain
covered with garbage: it is a mountain made of millions and
millions of metric tons of decomposing trash. It is the stench
of organic matter accumulated over centuries, in every state
of putrefaction. It is the smell of gas emanations erupting all
around us. It is the reek of all that remains of the animal and
vegetable world after it mixes with chemical waste. It is the
smell of every form of absolute poverty, the stench of injustice,
corruption, arrogance, and utter indifference. It impregnates
every molecule of oxygen around us, entering our pores and
shaking our bodies to their core. It is the sweetish aroma of
death, a perfume made for Judgment Day.

We start up along the same ash-gray road used by the trucks
to deposit their cargo at the peak. Pablo drives, as always. I

can feel him observing me every minute, scrutinizing my reactions: those of my body, of my heart, of my mind. I know what he's thinking, and he knows what I'm feeling: a fleeting glance catches us by surprise; a certain smile confirms it. I know that with him by my side I'll be able to stand everything that awaits us; but, as we approach our destination, I begin to wonder if the cameraman and my assistant, Martita Bruges, will be able to work the full four or five hours in that nauseating environment, on that unventilated stage, in that stifling heat enclosed by the metal walls of a cloudy day that was more oppressive and suffocating than any I remember.

The smell was only the preface to a spectacle that would make the toughest of men recoil in disgust. The Dante's inferno that spreads before us seems to measure several square miles, and the mountaintop is terror itself: above us, against a dirty gray sky that no one would think to associate with heaven, swarm thousands of buzzards and vultures with razor-like beaks under cruel little eyes and revolting feathers that haven't been black for a long time. Haughtily—as if they were eagles—the members of this underworld's reigning dynasty take a few seconds to evaluate the state of our health, then go back to feasting on horse carcasses with wet viscera glinting in the sun. Below, hundreds of newly arrived dogs greet us by baring teeth sharpened by chronic hunger; beside them, other, more veteran canines—less skinny and more indifferent—wag their tails or scratch their patchy, flea-infested fur. The whole mountain seems to tremble with undulating and frenetic movement: it is the thousands of rats, big as cats, and millions of mice of all sizes. A swarm of flies hovers above us, and storm clouds of gnats and mosquitoes celebrate the arrival of fresh blood. For the lower species of the animal world, this place seems to be a paradise of nutrients.

Some ashy figures, different from the rest, start to appear. First, out peek curious little ones with swollen bellies, full of worms; then, some males with sullen expressions; and, finally, some females so gaunt that only the pregnant ones seem alive. And almost all the younger women are expecting. The drab creatures seem to emerge from all around us, first by the dozen and then by the hundred; they circle us to block our way or prevent us from fleeing, and in a matter of minutes they have us surrounded. Suddenly, that close, oscillating tide explodes in a clamor of joy, and a thousand white sparks illuminate their faces.

"It's him, it's don Pablo! Don Pablo is here! And he's brought the lady from TV! Are you going to put us on TV, don Pablo?"

Now they look radiant with happiness and excitement. Everyone comes to greet him, to hug him, to touch him, as though wanting to keep a piece of him for themselves. At first glance, only those miraculous smiles separate these dirty and emaciated people from the rest of the animal kingdom; but in the following hours those beings will teach me one of the most splendid lessons that life has seen fit to give me.

"WOULD YOU LIKE TO SEE my Christmas tree, miss?" asks a little girl, tugging at my silk blouse.

I imagine she's going to show me a branch from some fallen tree, but it turns out to be a little frosted Christmas tree, nearly new and made in the USA.

Pablo explains that Christmas arrives here almost two weeks late, that all of these people's possessions come from the garbage, and that rich people's boxes and castoffs are treasures and construction materials for the poorest.

"I want to show you my Nativity scene, too!" says another little girl. "It's finally finished!"

Baby Jesus is a one-eyed, one-legged giant, the Virgin Mary is medium-sized, and Saint Joseph is small. The plastic donkey and ox obviously belong to commercial models. I try to hold back my laughter on seeing this pleasant incarnation of a modern family, and I continue my tour.

"Can I invite you to see my house, Miss Virginia?" one affable woman asks with the same self-assuredness of any middle-class Colombian woman.

I imagine a shack of cardboard and tin like the Bogotá shanties, but I'm wrong: the little house is made of bricks held together with cement, and the roof is made of plastic tiles. Inside, it has a kitchen and two bedrooms, with furniture that's worn but clean. Her twelve-year-old son is doing his homework at the table.

"I got lucky—someone threw out their whole living room set!" she tells me. "And look at my dishes: they have different patterns, but six of us can eat on them. The silverware and glasses don't match like yours do, ma'am, but mine were free!"

I smile and ask if they also get their food from the garbage.

She replies, "Ugh, no, no. We would die! And in any case, the dogs get to the food first. We go down to the market and buy food with the money we earn recycling."

A youth with the look of a gang leader, sporting American jeans and modern tennis shoes in perfect condition, proudly shows me his 18K-gold chain; I know that in any jewelry store it would cost $700, and I ask how he managed to find something so valuable, and so small, amid millions of metric tons of garbage.

"I found it with these clothes in a plastic bag. I didn't steal it, miss, I swear to God! Some angry woman threw out her man along with all of his stuff, right down to the kitchen sink. . . . These *paisa* women are fierce, my God!"

"What's the strangest thing you've ever found?" I ask the group of children following us.

They look at one another and then answer almost in unison:

"A dead baby! The rats were eating it when we got there. Then there was the body of a little girl who had been raped; but it was much farther away, up by the spring." They point toward the place. "But those are things bad people from the outside do. The people here are good, right, don Pablo?"

"Right you are: the best in the world!" he says, with absolute conviction and without an ounce of paternalism.

TWENTY-FOUR YEARS LATER, I have forgotten almost everything that Pablo Escobar said to me in that interview, his first for national media, about the twenty-five hundred families who lived in that inferno. A videotape of his enthusiastic words and my face bathed in sweat must still exist somewhere. Only my heart and my senses still hold the memories of those hours that forever changed my scale of material values, my concept of what human beings need in order to experience a little happiness. Counteracting that omnipresent stench, there was Pablo's guiding hand on my forearm, transmitting his strength to me. A few of those survivors were clean, most were fairly dirty, and they all seemed proud of their ingenuity and grateful for their luck. They told stories about where their humble possessions had come from or how they'd discovered some small treasure. The women's faces lit up as they described the houses they could soon call home; the men were eager to recover the respect of a society that had treated them like scum, and young boys were hopeful at the prospect of leaving that place behind and growing up into honest men. They all shared collective dreams of faith in a leader who would inspire them and a politician who wouldn't betray them.

HAPPINESS HAS SPREAD through the place, and something like a festive air floats around us now. My initial impression of horror has given way to other emotions and to a new understanding. The elementary sense of dignity of these human beings, their courage, their nobility, their capacity to dream, all intact in an environment that would plunge any one of us into the deepest chasms of desperation and defeat, have turned my compassion into admiration. At some point along that dusty path, one that perhaps I'll find again in some other time or space, an infinite tenderness for all those people suddenly knocks on the doors of my consciousness and floods every fiber of my spirit. And I no longer care about the stench or the shock of that dump, or how Pablo gets his tons of money, but the thousand forms of magic that he makes with it. And like a spell, his presence beside me erases the memory of every man I had loved before then. He is my present and my past and my future, and my only everything. Now only he exists.

"What did you think?" he asks me as we walk toward the cars.

"I am deeply moved. It was an enriching experience, like nothing else. From afar they seem to live like animals; from up close, they seem like angels . . . and all by yourself you're going to return them to their human condition, right? Thank you for inviting me to meet them. And thank you for what you're doing for them."

He is silent for a long time. Then he puts his arm around my shoulders and says, "No one says things like that to me. . . . You're so different! What do you say you have dinner with me tonight? And since I think I know what you're going to say . . . I took the liberty of making sure the beauty salon is open until whatever time you want, so you can get that skunk smell out of your hair."

I tell him that he stinks like a *zorrillo*, too, and laughing happily, he exclaims that he could never be anything that ended in the diminutive "*illo.*" Because he is nothing more and nothing less than . . . Zorro!

OUR ENTRANCE into the restaurant leaves a wake of stunned looks and a crescendo of whispers. We're led to the table farthest from the door, where we'll have a view of everyone who enters. I mention that I have never gone out with an interviewee, much less with a politician, and he says that there's a first time for everything. Then, staring at me and smiling, he adds, "You know? Lately, anytime I'm sad or worried . . . I start to think about you. I think of you yelling at all those tough men in the middle of that cloud of tear gas: 'Aren't you ashamed? Have a little dignity; you're like little girls!' as if you were Napoleon at Waterloo. It's the funniest thing I've seen in my entire life! I laugh to myself for a good while, and then . . ."

While he pauses to pique my curiosity, I mentally prepare my answer.

"I think about you soaked in freezing water and turned into a panther, with that tunic stuck to your body. I laugh for a while again . . . and I say to myself that you are, really, a very . . . very . . . brave woman."

Before I can reply that no one has ever recognized that virtue in me, he goes on: "And you have a capacity for gratitude that's very rare, because beautiful women aren't in the habit of being grateful for anything."

I tell him that I have an excessive capacity for gratitude because, since I'm not beautiful, no one has ever given me anything or recognized any talent in me. He asks me what I am, then, and I reply that I'm a collection of rare defects that for the moment aren't noticeable, but will be with the passage of time. He asks me to tell him why I started the programming company with Margot.

I explain that, in 1981, it seemed to be my only option for professional independence. I had quit my job as the anchor of the 7:00 p.m. newscast *24 Horas*, because when director Mauricio Gómez had tried to make me refer to the M-19 as a "criminal band," I changed the terms to "*guerrilleros*," "insurgents," "rebels," or "subversive group." Mauricio reprimanded me almost daily, threatening to fire me and reminding me that I earned the equivalent of $5,000 a month. I replied that he might be the grandson of Colombia's most archconservative president and the son of Álvaro Gómez, who was possibly the next, but right now, he was a journalist. One fine day, I blew up and left the best-paid job in TV, and although I know I made a tremendous mistake, I would die before admitting it to anyone.

Pablo says he's grateful I could confide in him and asks whether the "insurgents," "rebels," or "subversives" know about what happened. I tell him they have no idea; I don't even know them. And in any case, I didn't quit out of political sympathies, but rather on principle of journalistic rigor and linguistic integrity.

"Well, they don't have your principles: they kidnapped Jorge Ochoa's sister, among others. I *do* know them, very well . . . and now they know me, too."

I tell him I'd read something about the rescue and ask him to tell me how he managed it.

"I got eight hundred men and placed them at every one of the eight hundred public phones in Medellín. Then we followed everyone who made a call at six p.m., the appointed time for the kidnappers to call and discuss how the twelve-million-dollar ransom would be paid. Through tracking, we ruled out the innocent people one by one until we found the *guerrilleros*. We located the leader of the band and kidnapped his entire family. We rescued Martha Nieves, and the 'rebels,' 'insurgents,' or 'subversives' found out they can't mess with us."

Astonished, I ask how one manages to find eight hundred trustworthy people.

"It's a simple matter of logistics. It wasn't easy, but it was the only way. In the next few days, if you let me take you to see my other civic and social projects, you'll see just where all those people came from. But tonight I just want to talk about you: What happened with Aníbal? You two seemed so happy together."

I tell him that the rocks of coke that he gave to Aníbal as a gift led me to decide that a woman like me could not live with an addict. And I add that, on principle, I don't talk about a man that I've loved with another. He notes that that is an unusual trait, then asks if it's true that I was married to an Argentine director who was twenty years older than me. I admit that, unfortunately, I'm still married to him.

"Even though we've split our property, he absolutely refuses to sign the divorce papers, so I can't get married again and he cannot marry the new woman in his life."

He looks at me in silence, as though memorizing my words. Then he transforms, and in a tone that leaves no room for the slightest argument, he tells me what I have to do.

"Tomorrow, your lawyer is going to call David Stivel and tell him he has until Wednesday to sign the divorce papers, or there will be consequences. You and I will talk after the notaries close, and you can tell me what happens."

With my eyes shining in the amber light of the candles, I ask if Zorro would be able to kill the ogre keeping the princess locked in the tower. Taking my hand in his, he replies very seriously, "Only if the ogre is brave. Because I don't waste lead on cowards. But you're worth dying for . . . aren't you, my love?"

With those words, and the question in his eyes and the touch of his skin, I finally know that he and I are leaving our friendship behind, because we are destined to become lovers.

WHEN HE CALLS on Wednesday night, my news is not good.

"So he didn't sign, then. . . . He's a stubborn *che*, isn't he? He sure wants to complicate our lives. This is a serious problem!

But before we figure out what to do about it, I need to ask you something: Once you're finally a free woman, will you have dinner with me again, at my friend Pelusa Ocampo's restaurant?"

I reply that it's fairly improbable that in the year 2000 I'll still be free, and he persists, "No, no, no! I'm talking about Friday, day after tomorrow, before some other ogre beats me to it."

With a resigned sigh, I note that this is the kind of problem that cannot be solved in forty-eight hours.

"Day after tomorrow you will be a free woman, and you'll be here with me. Good night, love."

ON FRIDAY, when I come home for lunch after spending hours in the studio editing the program we'd filmed at the dump, my housekeeper informs me that my lawyer, Hernán Jaramillo, has called three times because he needs to speak with me urgently. When I call him, he exclaims, "Stivel called this morning, desperate to tell me he had to sign the divorce papers before noon, or he was dead! The poor guy came to the notary pale as wax and shaking like a leaf; he looked like he was about to have a heart attack. He almost couldn't sign his name! Then, without a word, he ran away like a bat out of hell. I can't believe you've been married for three years to such a chicken! But anyway . . . you're a free woman now. Congratulations, and let me know about the next one. Just make sure he's rich and good-looking this time."

At two thirty in the afternoon, my housekeeper announces that six men are here bearing flowers; the arrangement won't fit in the elevator and they're asking for permission to carry it up the stairs, which seems suspicious to her. I tell her it's possible the man who sent them isn't just suspicious but "a criminal." I ask her to put our minds at ease and run down to reception to find out who they're from. She comes back and hands me the card:

For my freed Panther Queen,
from El Zorro. P.

WHEN THE MEN LEAVE, I'm confronted by a thousand *cattleya trianae*, Colombia's national flower, and orchids in every shade of purple, lavender, lilac, and pink, with white phalaenopsis here and there like foam in a vivid violet sea. My housekeeper's only comment, with arms crossed and brow furrowed: "I didn't like those characters one bit . . . and your friends would say that this is the most ostentatious thing they've seen in their lives!"

In fact, I know that if I showed them something so splendid, they would die of envy. I tell her that this arrangement could only have been done by the famous *silleteros* of Medellín, the artists of the Flower Festival.

At three in the afternoon, the phone rings; without bothering to ask who's calling, I ask where he'd pulled a revolver on David. At the other end of the line, I sense surprise and then happiness. He bursts out laughing and tells me he has no idea what I'm talking about. Then he asks what time I want him to pick me up at the hotel to go to dinner. Glancing at the clock, I remind him that the Medellín airport closes at 6:00 p.m. and the last flight on Friday must have about twenty people on the wait list.

"Oh hell . . . I hadn't realized. . . . And here I was hoping to celebrate your freedom! What a shame! Well, we'll have dinner another day, maybe in the year 2000."

And he hangs up. Five minutes later, the phone rings again. This time I pray to God it isn't one of my friends when, without waiting for him to identify himself, I say that his thousand orchids are overflowing out the windows, and they're the most beautiful thing I have seen in my life. I ask him how long it took to pick them.

"They're just like you, my love. And I've had people gathering them since . . . the day I saw you with Band-Aids on your face and knees, remember? Anyway, I just wanted to tell you that Pegasus has been waiting for you since last night. You can fly him today, tomorrow, day after tomorrow, in a week or a month, because he's not going to move from there until you're on him. I'm only going to hope . . . and wait for you."

Now, this is really a carriage for a modern Cinderella: a brand-new Learjet, white and shining, with three handsome and smiling pilots instead of six white shire horses. It's 5:15 p.m., and we have just enough time to get to Medellín before the airport closes. I could have made him wait a week or a month, but I also love him, and I can't wait a single day. While I slide through the clouds, I wonder if Pablo will make me suffer the way a couple of other men I'd loved ages before had, cruel men who were perhaps richer than him. Then I remember the words of Françoise Sagan: "I'd rather cry in a Mercedes than on a bus," and I tell myself happily:

"Well, I'd rather cry in a Learjet than in a Mercedes!"

There are no unicorn-drawn carriages or moonlit dinners beneath the Eiffel Tower, no emeralds or rubies, no fireworks displays. Only him close to me, confessing that the first time he felt me holding on to his whole body in the Río Claro, he knew he hadn't saved my life just so I could belong to another man, but so that I would be his. Now he is begging me, pleading, imploring, repeating over and over:

"Ask me for anything, everything you want! Just tell me what you desire most," as if he were God, and I'm telling him that he's only a man, and not even he could stop time to freeze or draw out for a second longer that flood of golden moments that the gods' splendid generosity has decided to pour over us.

That secret night at Hacienda Nápoles is the last of my innocence and the first of my reverie. When he falls asleep, I go out onto the balcony and look up at the bright stars shimmering in all that unfathomable cobalt expanse. Flooded with happiness, I smile as I remember the conversation between Pilar and Maria in *For Whom the Bell Tolls*, and I think about the earth trembling beneath the bodies of earthly lovers. Then I turn to go back to the arms that await me, my universe of flesh and blood, the only thing I have and the only thing that exists.

❧ *Death to Kidnappers!*

I **RETURN TO BOGOTÁ** to tape my TV programs, and the next weekend I'm back in Medellín. This pattern will repeat for fifteen months, the happiest of my life and, according to Pablo, the fullest of his. What neither of us realizes is that this brief time will contain the last perfect, easy days of either of our existences.

"You have my eleven planes and my two helicopters at your disposal. And you can ask me for anything you want. Anything, my love. What do you need first?"

I reply that I'll just need one of his planes to bring my assistant and cameraman back to Medellín. I want to take some more shots to fill out the report, and I'd like to ask him a few more questions in a different setting: a political meeting, perhaps.

Again and again he insists that he wants to give me a fabulous gift, saying I am the only woman who hasn't asked him for anything in the first week. He tells me to choose the most beautiful penthouse in Bogotá and whatever Mercedes I want.

"And how would I explain that to the Treasury Department? Or my friends, my colleagues, my family? I would look like a kept woman, my love. Plus, I don't drive, because if I did they'd lock me up for life. Thank you, Pablo, but I have my little Mitsubishi and my chauffeur, and I don't need anything else. I'm definitely not a car lover, and in this country a luxury car is just an invitation to kidnappers."

He insists so much that I decide to give him two options: either a Pegasus like his—I *am* turning into a plane lover, it seems—or a million kisses. He bursts out laughing and chooses the latter, but instead of counting one by one, he counts hundred by hundred, then thousand by thousand, and, finally, a hundred thousand by a hundred thousand. When he finishes in a couple of minutes, I accuse him of being a kiss thief, and I ask him what I can give him in return. After thinking about it a few seconds, he says I could teach him how to give interviews, because over the course of his life he'll have to give more than a few; he praises mine and asks what my secret is. I tell him there are three: the first is to have something important, interesting, or original to say, and also something witty, because everyone likes to laugh. As for the second and the third, since I like to take things slow, I categorically refuse to share them in the first week.

He takes the bait, and with a smile that's something between mischievous and guilty he swears that if I teach him my professional secrets, he'll confide some of his own to me.

Fast as lightning I reply that the second secret is not to answer every question the journalist asks, but instead to say what you want to say. But I insist that to play ball well you need years of practice; that is, years of fame. Someone like him should not grant interviews except to media editors or directors—since they know where curiosity ends and insult begins—or to journalists who are friends.

"Purebred bulls are for expert bullfighters, not *banderilleros*. Since you're still what a Hollywood insider would call a 'civilian,' I recommend for now that you don't give interviews except to a matador who knows some of your professional secrets and who loves you with all his heart in spite of them. Now, you're going to tell me when you stopped stealing headstones and stripping stolen cars, and started exporting 'snuff.' Because that's what really marked a turn in your philanthropic activity. . . . Isn't that right, my love?"

Offended, he looks at me and lowers his eyes. I know I've caught him off guard and crossed a line, and I wonder if I've touched his Achilles' heel too soon. But I also know that Pablo has never been in love with a woman his age or of my class. And I know that if we're going to love each other on completely equal terms, I'll have to teach him from the start where the fun and games of two overgrown kids ends, and where the relationship between an adult man and woman begins. The first thing I tell him is that a senator has to submit to scrutiny from the press—and that in his case, it will be unrelenting.

"Okay, what do you want to know? Let's play ball," he says, raising his head defiantly.

I explain that when the program we filmed airs, the whole country is going to wonder not only how he made his fortune but also what the real purpose of all that generosity is. And with a simple phone call to Medellín, any journalist will be able to learn a couple of open secrets in a matter of minutes. I warn him that the owners of media companies are going to shoot to kill when they see him strutting around with his millions, showing off his charity projects. The media elite have been feeding off the people for years, and Pablo's generosity will be a threat to the avarice of nearly all the established powers in Colombia.

"Fortunately, you have a formidable mental quickness, Pablo. And I'll tell you from the start none of the big Colombian tycoons could admit the whole truth about where their own fortunes came from. That's why the superrich don't give interviews, not here or anywhere else. What sets you apart from them is the size of your social projects, and that's what you'll have to mention when everyone starts going after you."

Animated now, he starts to tell me his story: When he was still a boy, he directed a massive fund-raising drive to build a school in the La Paz neighborhood in Envigado, near Medellín, because he didn't have anywhere to study. The result was a school building for eight hundred students. When he was little he rented bicycles, as a boy he sold used cars, and at a very young age he started out in land speculation in Magdalena Medio. At one point he stops and asks if I think he's lying; I reply that, though I'm sure it's all true, it could hardly be the origin of such a colossal fortune. I ask him to tell me what his parents did. He says that his father was a worker on the hacienda of Joaquín Vallejo, a well-known industrial leader, and his mother was a rural schoolteacher.

I recommend, then, that he start by saying something like: "From my father, an honest Antiochian peasant, I learned the ethic of hard work, and from my mother, a teacher, the importance of solidarity with the weakest among us." But I remind him that no one likes to have their intelligence insulted; he has to prepare for the day when some veteran reporter will ask him, in front of a camera and the entire country:

"How many marble headstones do you need for a new bicycle? Or is it the other way around: How many secondhand bicycles can be bought with a good gravestone, a real beauty, Honorable Father of the Nation?"

He replies that he would say, without a second's hesitation: "Why don't you go and find out how much both of them cost? You can do the numbers yourself. Then get your own group of kids who aren't afraid of gravediggers or the dead, send them into the cemetery at night, and have them carry those damned stones that weigh a ton!"

And I exclaim that with stone-faced arguments like that, any journalist would have no choice but to recognize his unique talent, his innate leadership, his heroic bravery and unusual strength.

Pablo asks me whether, if we had met each other when he was poor and anonymous, I would have fallen in love with him. Laughing, I tell him definitely not: we never would have met! No one in their right mind would have thought to introduce me to a married man because while he was sanding names off tombstones, I was going out with Gabriel Echavarría, the most beautiful man in Colombia and son of one of the ten richest. When he was stripping cars, I was already dating Julio Mario Santo Domingo, a bachelor, heir to the largest fortune in the country, and the most handsome man of his generation.

He points out that if those are my parameters, I must really love him. And I admit that it's precisely because of the points of comparison that I love him so much. With a caress and a grateful smile, he tells me I am the most brutally honest and generous woman he's met, and that's why I make him so happy.

Over and over we practice the answers, serious or hilarious, that he would give in order to publicly account for his donations, his planes, and especially his giraffes. We conclude that he's going to need the parameters of logic, used by the Greeks twenty-five hundred years ago. Because to justify his fortune he'll have to forget about "land speculation in Magdalena Medio" and start thinking in terms of "real estate investments in Florida," even if no one believes it, and even if it could bring everyone from the DIAN in Colombia to the IRS and the Pentagon in the United States down on him.

"Fame, good or bad, is forever, my love. Why don't you keep a low profile, at least for now, and wield power from the shadows, like *capi di tutti capi* all over the world? Why do you need to be well known, when it's far better to be a quadruple-millionaire? And in Colombia, fame only brings you mountains of envy. Just look at me."

"At you? But all the women in this country would love to be in your shoes!"

I tell him we'll talk about that another day, not now. To change the subject, I tell him I find it very hard to believe that the rescue of Martha Nieves Ochoa was done only through exhaustive tracking. He seems surprised at my frankness, and he replies that it's also a matter for another day.

I ask him to explain to me what MAS is. Lowering his eyes, and in a voice full of determination, he tells me that "Muerte a Secuestradores!" (Death to Kidnappers!) was founded at the end of 1981 by the big drug traffickers, and that it already has many supporters among the rich landowners and some state organizations: the DAS (Administrative Department of Security), the B-2 unit of the army (military intelligence), the GOES (Grupo Operativo Antiextorsión y Secuestro, or Operative Group Against Extortion and Kidnapping), and the F2 unit of the police. MAS wants to keep rich people's money from going to Miami, and their partners' and associates' money from having to stay out of the country. To that end, they were determined to end a plague that exists only in Colombia.

"We all want to invest our money in the country, but with that sword of Damocles hanging over us it's impossible! That's why we're not going to let a single kidnapper go free: every time we catch one, we'll hand him over to the army to deal with. No drug trafficker wants to go through what I did with my father's kidnapping, or what happened with the Ochoas' sister, or the torture my friend Carlos Lehder del Quindío had to endure in the flesh. Everyone is joining together around MAS and Lehder and making large contributions: we already have an army of almost twenty-five hundred men."

I suggest that starting now, and given that his associates are also farmers, businessmen, exporters, or industrialists, he should try to always refer to them as his "professional colleagues." I express my horror about what happened to his father and ask if Pablo also managed to free him in record time.

"Yes, yes. We got him back safe and sound, thank God. Some other time I'll tell you how."

I'm learning to leave for another day any question about what seems to be rescue methods of exceptional force and effectiveness. But I express my skepticism about the MAS's ability to achieve the same results in every one of the three thousand kidnappings that happen each year in Colombia. I tell him that to end all the abductions he would first have to get rid of several guerrilla groups that total more than thirty thousand men. In a third of a century of trying, the army hasn't been able to eradicate them. Rather, their numbers seem to grow with every day that passes. I tell him that the rich establishment is going to be happy with MAS—because they won't have to provide a single peso, or a bullet, or a life—while he will have to bear the costs, the enemies, and the deaths.

He shrugs and replies he doesn't care. The only thing he's interested in is being the leader of his profession and having his colleagues' support in backing a government that would end the extradition treaty with the United States.

"In my line of work, everyone's rich. And now, I want you to rest so you'll be very beautiful tonight. I invited two of my partners—my cousin Gustavo Gaviria and my brother-in-law Mario Henao—and a small group of friends. I'm going to go check on the work they're finishing up with on the soccer field we're donating next Friday. You'll meet my whole family there. Gustavo is like a brother to me. He's very intelligent, and he's the one who practically runs the business. That way I have time to dedicate myself to the things that really interest me: my causes, my social work, and . . . your lessons, my love."

"What's your next goal . . . after the Senate?"

"I've told you enough for today. If I'm going to give you all of those million kisses I owe you, we're going to need about a thousand and one nights. See you later, Virginia."

A while later I hear a helicopter's propeller as it moves off over the vast expanse of his little republic, and I wonder how this man with the heart of a lion is going to manage to balance all those contradictory interests and achieve such out-sized goals in just one lifetime.

Well, at his age he has all the time in the world ahead of him. . . .

I sigh, observing a flock of birds that also disappears over a limitless horizon.

I know that I am attending the birth of a series of events that is going to split the history of my country in two, that the man I love is going to be the protagonist of many of them, and that almost no one seems to be aware of it. I don't know if this man that God or Fate has placed in my path—so utterly sure of himself, so ambitious, so passionate about every one of his causes and about everything—one day will make me cry oceans the same way he makes me laugh now. But he certainly has all of the elements to become a formidable leader. Luckily for me, he isn't beautiful or educated, and he's not a man of the world: Pablo is, simply and completely, fascinating. And I think to myself, *He has the most masculine personality I have ever known. He's a diamond in the rough, and I think he's never had a woman like me. I am going to try to polish him and teach him everything I've learned. And I'm going to make him need me like water in the desert.*

MY FIRST ENCOUNTER with Pablo's partners and family members takes place that night on the terrace of Hacienda Nápoles.

Gustavo Gaviria Rivero is inscrutable, silent, secretive, distant. Every bit as sure of himself as his cousin Pablo Escobar is, this race-car champion rarely smiles. Though he's the same age as us, he is, without a doubt, more mature than Pablo. From the first moment my eyes meet those of that small, thin man with straight hair and a fine mustache, everything about him warns me that he doesn't touch the subject of his business with "civilians." He seems to be a great observer, and I know he's there to evaluate me. My intuition quickly tells me that not only is he uninterested in Pablo's aspiration to fame, but he's also beginning to worry about his partner's exorbitant spending on social projects. Unlike his cousin, who is a liberal, Gustavo is affiliated with the Conservative Party. Both of them consume alcohol in minimal quantities, and I notice that they are not interested in music or dancing, either. They are alert: all business, politics, power, and control.

They are capos recently arrived in the world of the very rich and the even more ambitious, and they have just acquired a new connection: an exquisite diva who by profession is an insider of the most select ranks of political and economic power and who is related to the Holguines, Mosqueras, Sanz de Santamarías, Valenzuelas, Zuletas, Arangos, Caros, Pastranas, Marroquines. And so, as if hypnotized, for the next six hours, none of the three men will glance at another table, another woman, a man, or anything else, not even for an instant.

Mario Henao, brother of Pablo's wife, Victoria, has an exhaustive knowledge of and furious adoration for the opera. I realize that he wants to impress me and maybe even instruct me on the subject that would least interest Pablo or Gustavo. And since I know he's the last ally someone in my position could aspire to, without the slightest consideration for Caruso or Toscanini or La Divina—or for the Capones' and Gambinos' legendary passion for those three gods—I steer the conversation directly to Pablo's and Gustavo's competencies.

It takes me hours to get that ice king Gustavo to lower his guard, but my effort bears fruit. I spend nearly two and a half hours interviewing him, and almost as long listening to an enthusiastic lesson about the discipline and precision needed to control a car going 150 miles per hour—the life-or-death, split-second decisions that must be made in order to leave the competition behind and come in first. In the end, both of us know we have won, if not the affection, at least the respect of a key ally. And I have learned where Pablo and his partner get that fierce determination to always be number one, rolling right over anyone who stands in their way, which seems to extend to each and every aspect of their lives. Around us, two dozen tables are occupied by people with last names like Moncada or Galeano, whose first names and faces it would be impossible for me to remember today. Toward midnight, two boys armed with automatic long-range rifles and soaked in sweat run up to where the four of us are talking and yank us back to reality.

"Mr. X's wife is here looking for him," they tell Pablo, "and he's here with his girlfriend. Imagine the problem, boss! The woman's mad as a hornet. She's here with two friends, and they're demanding we let them in. What should we do?"

"Tell her to learn to act like a lady. Tell her no self-respecting woman goes looking for a man—whether husband, boyfriend, or lover—anywhere, especially at night. Tell her to be smart and go home and wait there with the frying pan and the rolling pin so she can beat him up when he gets there. But she cannot come inside."

The boys return after a while and inform Pablo that the women are determined to get in; they say he knows them.

"I *do* know that kind of wild animal, and very well . . . ," he says with a sigh, as if he had suddenly remembered an episode that made him deeply sad. Then, without hesitation or holding back because of my presence, he orders them:

"Fire two shots in the air very close to the car. If they keep coming, aim directly at them. And if they still don't stop, shoot to kill without hesitation. Is that clear?"

We hear four gunshots. I imagine them reappearing with at least three bodies, and then I wonder who the fourth one might be. Some twenty minutes later, the boys come in panting and sweaty, their hair disheveled. They have scratches all over their faces, hands, and forearms.

"What a fight, boss! They didn't get scared even with the gunshots: they punched and kicked us, and you can't imagine those nails like tigresses' claws! We had to march them out at gunpoint, with help from two other guys. Poor guy, with what's waiting for him when he gets home, completely drunk."

"Yes, yes, you're right. Get a room ready for him so he can spend the night here," orders Pablo, flaunting his masculine solidarity with his long-suffering peers. "Otherwise, tomorrow we'll have to bury him!"

"These *paisas* women are fierce, aren't they? Ave María!" say the three little angels with me, sighing in resignation.

I'm like Alice in Wonderland as I learn more and more about Pablo's world. I find out that many of these tough and rich men are literally kicked around by their wives . . . and I think I can guess why. I wonder about that other "wild animal" he knew so well, and something tells me that it is not his wife.

With a group of Pablo and Gustavo's friends, we decide to go out one Sunday and play with the Rolligon. Looking around while we knock over trees with the giant caterpillar-tractor, I long for the laughter of my own friends from seven months ago. I feel nostalgia for my "beautiful people," the ones I've always lived among and with whom I feel at ease anywhere in the world, no matter the language. But the truth is I don't have time to miss them much because, as we hit a tree trunk, a black and buzzing swarm about three feet wide comes charging at us like a train. I don't know why—maybe because of that singular destiny God has reserved for me—in a fraction of a second I free-fall out of the Rolligon, hide in the tall grass, and stay so still that I don't dare to breathe until a quarter of an hour later.

What seems like a million wasps go flying after those dozen and a half people who derive their living from the traffic of cocaine. Miraculously, not a single one stings me. When Pablo's men find me an hour later, thanks to my lavender dress, they tell me that some of the guests even had to be hospitalized.

IN THE FOLLOWING YEARS I would spend a thousand hours by his side and maybe another thousand in his arms, but for reasons that I would only come to understand many months later, from that afternoon on Pablo and I would never return to Nápoles to enjoy time with friends in the place where I had thrice been on the verge of dying, and had almost died of happiness as well. Only once—and to live the most perfect day of his existence and mine—would we return to that paradise where he had saved me from that whirlpool because he wanted all my life for himself. He had decided to steal me from the arms of another man and take over the unexplored spaces of my imagination, the already forgotten times of my memory, and every single inch of skin that in those days housed my existence.

Eleven years later, all those men who were the age of Christ on the cross would be dead. And this "chronicler of the Indies" survived them all, it's true; but if someone were to paint today the picture of Alice in Wonderland in that hall of mirrors and mirages, he would see, repeated to the infinite, only the shattered reflections of Munch's *The Scream*, my hands clasped to my ears to blot out the blasting of bombs and the moans of the dying, the buzzing of chainsaws and cries of the tortured, the explosions of airplanes and the weeping of mothers, my mouth open in a cry of impotence that only a quarter of a century later has finally managed to escape from my throat, my eyes wide open in horror and fright under the red skies of a country ablaze.

That huge hacienda still exists—it's also true—but from the place of reverie where, for a fleeting moment, we shared the most delicious expressions of freedom and beauty, the most loving moments of joy and generosity, and all those of passion and tenderness, the magic vanished almost as quickly as it had arrived. All that is left of that enchanted Eden is the longing of the earthly senses for the colors and the caresses, the laughter and the stars. Hacienda Nápoles would soon become the stage for the legendary conspiracies that would forever change the destiny of my country and its relationship to the rest of the world. But—as in those first scenes of *Chronicle of a Death Foretold* or *The House of the Spirits*—today that paradise of the damned is populated only by ghosts.

All those young men have now been dead for quite some time. But, when it comes to their loves and their hatreds, their pleasures and their pains, their causes and their utopias, their struggles and their battles, allies and rivals, loyalties and betrayals, triumphs and defeats, when it comes to the lives and the deaths that comprise the rest of this story, all this chronicler can tell you is that she wouldn't dream of trading this story for a briefer time or a less plentiful space.

PART TWO

Days of Splendor and Fear

Oh courage, could you not as well
Select a second place to dwell
Not only in that golden tree
But in the frightened heart of me?

—The old poet NONNO reciting Tennessee Williams's
"How Calmly Does the Orange Branch" in *The Night of the Iguana*

℘ *The Caress of a Revolver*

PABLO ESCOBAR had belonged to that small group of privileged children who knew from the tenderest age exactly what they wanted to be when they grew up. He also knew what he *didn't* want to be: little Pablo never dreamed of being a pilot or a fireman or a policeman.

"I just wanted to be rich, richer than the Echevarrías of Medellín and richer than any of the rich people in Colombia, whatever it cost, using all my resources and every one of the tools life placed at my disposal. I swore to myself that if I didn't have a million dollars by the time I was thirty I would kill myself. With a bullet to the brain," he confesses to me one day while we're boarding his Learjet, parked in its private hangar in the Medellín airport along with the rest of his fleet. "Someday soon I'm going to buy a jumbo and fit it out as a flying office, with several bedrooms, bathrooms with showers, a living area, bar, kitchen, and dining room. Sort of a flying yacht. That way, you and I can travel all over the world without anyone knowing or bothering us."

Once we're on the plane, I ask him how we'll manage to fly around incognito in an aerial palace. He replies that when we get back I'll find out, because, from now on, every time we see each other he's going to have a surprise for me that I'll never forget. He tells me he's noticed something very interesting: as he tells me his secrets, my own seem to parade across my face, especially my eyes. He adds that when I burst out in joy at discovering something new, my happiness and excitement make him feel as if he'd just won a car race and I was the champagne.

"Has anyone ever told you you're the most effervescent thing in the world, Virginia?"

"All the time!" I exclaim happily, because I know that when it comes to lack of modesty, we've both met our match. "And from now on, I'm going to have to close my eyes when I want to protect my deepest secrets. You're only going to be able to extract them veeeeerrrry slowly . . . with a bottle opener, made especially for Perrier-Jouët rosé!"

He replies that that won't be necessary because, for the next surprise, he plans to blindfold me, and he might also have to handcuff me. With a wide smile I tell him I've never been blindfolded or handcuffed, and I ask him if he is, by chance, the kind of sadist you see in the movies.

"I'm a depraved sadist a thousand times worse than the ones in horror movies, or hadn't you heard, my love?" he whispers into my ear. Then he takes my face in both his hands and sits looking at it, as if it were a deep well where he sought to quench his most hidden longings. I caress him and tell him we're the perfect couple because I'm a masochist. He kisses me and tells me he's always known that.

When the day of the surprise arrives, Pablo picks me up at the hotel around ten at night. As always, a car with four of his men follows at a prudent distance.

"I can't believe that a woman like you doesn't know how to drive a car, Virginia," he says, taking off at top speed.

I reply that any half-literate guy can drive a five-gear bus and that I, who am nearly blind, don't need my IQ of 146 to drive a car but to cram ten thousand years of civilization into my head. Not to mention to memorize half-hour news programs in five minutes, because I can't see the teleprompter. He asks me what I would guess his IQ is, and I say it must be around 126, if that.

"No, ma'am: my minimum confirmed is 156. So don't be so cocky!"

I tell him he's going to have to prove it to me, and I ask him to slow down, because at 110 miles per hour, we're going to be two prematurely dead prodigies.

"We already know that neither of us is afraid of death. Or are you, miss know-it-all? Now you're going to see what you get for being so arrogant. Today I'm in a very bad mood, and I'm sick of these bodyguards following us everywhere. They don't leave us alone for a minute, and I'm bored with it. I think there's only one way to escape them. You see on the other side of the highway, there to my left? You have your seat belt on, right? Well, hold on, because in thirty seconds we're going to be down there heading in the opposite direction. If it doesn't work, see you in the next life, Einstein! One . . . two . . . threeeeee!"

The car swerves and rolls over the grass-covered median. After rolling once and spinning three times, it stops ten feet below. I hit my head hard, twice, but I don't make a sound.

Pablo recovers in seconds, puts the car in reverse, and with tires squealing starts driving on the opposite lane of the highway, careening like a madman toward his apartment. We're there in a few minutes, driving at top speed into the garage; the door clicks shut behind us and the car slams to a stop millimeters from the wall.

"Pheeew!" he says, exhaling air. "We've lost them now, but I think I'm going to have to fire those guys tomorrow. Can you imagine what would've happened if someone like me had tried to kidnap me?"

I smile to myself and keep quiet. I'm in pain, and I'm not going to give him the satisfaction of saying what he wants to hear, which is that another person with his sangfroid hasn't been born yet. We go up to the penthouse, which is deserted, and I notice a camera across from the bedroom door. I sit down in a low-backed chair, and he stands in front of me with his arms crossed. With a threatening tone and an ice-cold expression in his eyes, he says to me:

"So now you see who has the higher IQ here. Not to mention who's got the balls, right? And if you complain or make one false move while I'm preparing the surprise, I'm going to rip that dress in two, film what comes next, and sell the video to the media. Understood, Marilyn? And since I'm a man of my word, we're going to start by . . . blindfolding you. I think we'll also need a roll of duct tape." He puts a black blindfold over my eyes, tying it firmly with a double knot, all the while humming "Feelin' Groovy" by Simon and Garfunkel. "And some handcuffs . . . where did I put those?"

"Not that, Pablo! We agreed you would only blindfold me. I just nearly broke my neck, and it doesn't make sense to handcuff a groggy featherweight. As for gagging me, you should at least wait until the circulation between my head and my body starts up again!"

"Agreed. I'll only handcuff you if you try to jump up, because I never underestimate a panther with delusions of genius."

"And I wouldn't jump, because I would never underestimate a criminal with the delusions of a schizophrenic."

After a long pause that seems to last an eternity, he says suddenly, "We're going to see how true it is that the blind have extra-sharp hearing. . . ."

I hear his shoes treading on the carpet and a combination safe being opened. Then, the unmistakable sound of six bullets entering the chamber of a revolver, one after the other, and the snap of the gun when the safety is removed. After that, everything is silent. Seconds later he is behind me, speaking into my ear in a whispery voice while his left hand holds me by the hair and the other slides the barrel of the gun in circles on my neck, around and around:

"You know, people in my line of work are referred to as 'the magicians.' That's because we work miracles. As the king of those magicians, only I know the secret formula to reattach this body that drives me crazy to that little head I adore. Abracadabra . . . imagine we're gluing it with a diamond necklace . . . around this swan's neck . . . so thin . . . so fragile I could break it in two with my bare hands. Abracadabra . . . once around . . . twice . . . three times. How do they feel?"

I tell him the diamonds are cold, and they hurt, and they're very small for my taste. And that it's not the promise he made me, and since it's improvisation, it doesn't count.

"Everything counts between the two of us, my love. You've

never felt a gun on your skin before. This silken skin ... so golden, so perfectly cared for ... without a scratch ... without a scar, isn't that right?"

"Careful with the blindfold, it could fall off and ruin the surprise of the century, Pablo! I think you should know that I practice shooting with the police in Bogotá—with a Smith and Wesson—and that, according to my trainer, I have better aim than some officers with twenty-twenty vision."

He tells me I'm just full of surprises, but that it's one thing to have a gun in my hand and another for it to be held by a murderer and pointed at my temple. He adds that he's been in that position, too, and he asks if it's not absolutely terrifying.

"Quite the opposite: it's absolutely exquisite! Ooohhh ... what could be more divine ... more sublime," I say, throwing my head back and sighing in pleasure while he unbuttons my shirt dress and the gun starts to descend along my throat toward my heart. "And, in any case, you're only a sadist ... not a murderer."

"That's what you think, my dear. I am a serial killer. ... Now tell me why you like it so much. You surprise me. ... Go on!"

Slowly, I tell him that a gun is always ... a temptation. Eve's sweet apple. An intimate friend who offers us the option of ending it all and flying up to heaven when there's no other way out ... or to hell, in the case of ... confessed murderers.

"What else? Keep talking until I give you permission to stop," he says in a hoarse voice, lowering the upper part of my dress to kiss me on the nape of my neck and my shoulders. I obey and continue:

"It's silent ... like the perfect accomplice. It's more dangerous than all your worst enemies put together. When it explodes, it sounds ... let me think ... like ... like ... the bars of San Quentin prison! Yes, yes, the bars slamming in a gringo prison sound like bullets, morning, noon, and night. Now, that must be absolutely terrifying, right, my love?"

"So that's how it is, you perverse little creature. Now tell me what it's like . . . physically. And if you stand up, I'll gag you with tape over your mouth and nose so you won't be able to breathe, and I won't be responsible for what this mere sadist would do to you!" he orders as he starts to caress me with his left hand, and the revolver descends slowly in a straight line down my breast and my diaphragm, across my waist and toward my abdomen.

"It's big . . . and I think it's very masculine. It's rigid . . . and hard . . . and it has a duct in the center. But it's cold, because it's metal . . . and it's not made of what you are, is it? And now that you've heard what you wanted to hear, I swear to you, Pablo, if you go one millimeter lower I'll get up from this chair, go back to Bogotá, and you'll never see me again!"

"Okay, okay, okay," he says, with a guilty little laugh of resignation. "The things that occur to a guy when he's got an utterly defenseless sex symbol in his hands. Okay, wet blanket, let's move on . . . but I warn you that you'll have to wait for me to finish my job with the duct tape, because I'm almost as much of a perfectionist as you are."

"And you have to understand that for someone like me, these games are really very elementary. I've been waiting days for my surprise, and you'd better hope it's up to my expectations!"

In an authoritative voice he tells me that here, the only one who decides what is and isn't elementary is him.

"I know what you're going to show me: your gun collection, because you're going to give me one! Like the ones the Bond girls have, of course! Can I take off the blindfold now so I can choose the prettiest and deadliest one?"

"You take the blindfold off when I say! Have you not realized yet that the only one who gives orders here is the murderer who owns the gun, the sadist who owns the camera, the macho who has the brute strength, and the rich man who owns the territory, and not a poor little woman who weighs a hundred and twenty pounds and has an obviously inferior IQ? You only have to wait a few minutes. I'm just going to cover . . . where these last four are from . . . and there we are! It's for your own good: imagine if in the future someone was torturing you horribly, for days and days, to get information on what you're about to see. Or what if you turn out to be a Mata Hari, and someday . . . you betray me?"

"They're stolen diamonds, right, my love? Thousands and thousands of carats, that's it!"

"Don't be such an optimist. I would never show you those, because you'd steal the biggest ones and swallow them, and then I'd have to cut you open with these scissors to fish them out of your belly!"

I can't stop laughing at the image of me choking down diamonds. Then I think of another theory.

"I've got it. How did I not think of this sooner? You're going to show me the kilos of coke 'made in Colombia' and packed for exportation to the United States! Do you seal them with duct tape? Finally, I'm going to get to see them. Is it true that each one looks like two pounds of butter and has the brand La Reina?"

"But what a lack of imagination! You're a real disappointment. Any one of my partners can see that, or my men, my pilots, my customers, even the DEA. I told you that what I'm going to show you, no one has seen—or will ever see. No one but you. Okay . . . we're ready. Now I can sit at the feet of my queen to watch the reaction on her face. I promise you're never going to forget this night. One . . . two . . . three: I order you to take off the blindfold!"

There are blue ones, green ones, wine-colored, brown, black ones. And, before I can leap forward to try to examine them up close, a steel handcuff closes with a *click!* around my right ankle, and my foot is attached to the chair. The only reason I don't fall face-first on the floor with the chair on top of me is because Pablo jumps up and catches me in the air. He squeezes me in his arms and kisses me again and again, laughing non-stop as he exclaims, "I knew you were dangerous, you tricky panther! You're going to pay for that! If you want to see them, you have to first tell me that you love me as you've never loved anyone before! Ha, ha, ha! Ha, ha, ha! Say you adore me. Go on, say it now! If you don't, I won't let you look, not up close or from far away!"

"I'm not going to say what you want to hear, I'm going to say what I want, understand? And that is that you are . . . you are . . . you're a genius, Pablo! The greatest prodigy of the underworld, ever!" And in a nearly inaudible voice, as if someone could be listening to us, I shoot off a barrage of questions, which I know he loves:

"Are they all yours? How many are there? How much do they cost? How do you get them? Let me see the photos and your names! Give me the key to the cuffs, Pablo, they're hurting my ankle! Let this poor blind girl look at them from up close; don't be such a sadist, I'm begging you! I want to take the duct tape off the names of all the countries so I can see!"

"No, no, no! I bet you, my prodigy of the up-and-up world,

never would have thought someone from my world could be so, so popular that fourteen nations have granted him citizenship!"

"Wooow! Now I know what all that money—along with an exceptional criminal IQ—is good for. It looks like half the UN is fighting for the honor.... But I don't see the United States anywhere, which in your profession must be priority number one, right?"

"Well, my love ... Rome wasn't built in a day! And seven percent of all the countries in the world isn't such a bad start ... and at my tender age. For now you can only see the photos. My nationalities and names you'll find out as we use them. Not even I know them yet."

"You see? I'm the only person you can trust who can help you with the correct pronunciation in five languages! At the tender age of seventeen, I was already a phonetics teacher at the Instituto Colombo Americano. Aren't I just a treasure of a girlfriend? How are we going to go to a foreign country if you can't pronounce your own name, Pablo? We have to start practicing now, so you don't arouse suspicion down the road. You have to understand it's for your own good, dearest love of my life."

"No and no, period. For now there's only one more phase to the surprise, and then comes the champagne reward. The pink rosé that comes in the most beautiful bottle of all, isn't that right?"

Without taking off the cuffs, he makes me sit back down in the chair, and he kneels down in front of me, facing the double line of passports spread out on the floor six feet away. He has covered the names of the countries with duct tape, and also his own names and birth dates on the inside pages. Then, like a child with new toys on Christmas morning, he starts to show me each of the fourteen photographs. Hypnotized, I watch the parade of unimaginable, inconceivable, unthinkable versions of the face of the man I love.

"In this one I have my head shaved. Here I am with glasses and a goatee, like a Marxist intellectual. I have an Afro in this one. Awful, isn't it? Here I am as an Arab; my friend the Saudi prince got it for me. I dyed my hair blond for this one; and for this other one, where I'm a redhead, I had to go to a beauty salon, where the women looked at me like I was a *marica*, a fag. In this one I'm wearing a wig. Here I don't have a mustache, and here I've got a thick beard. How about this one, bald on top and with little glasses, like Professor Calculus in *Tintin*? It's great, right? I look horrible in almost all of them, but not even my own mother would recognize me! Which one's your favorite?"

"All of them, Pablo, all of them! You look hilarious! I've never seen a more sensational collection. You're the most lawless person I've met in my life, the biggest bandit who's walked the face of the earth," I say in praise, laughing nonstop while he returns his passports to their places. "How could anyone get bored with you? You really know how to have fun!"

He closes the safe, leaves the revolver on the desk, and comes toward me. He caresses my face with great tenderness, and without a word, he removes the cuffs. He kisses my ankle—which now boasts a thick red line—over and over. Then he places me on the bed and gently massages the part of my head that hit the roof of the car.

"You may not believe it, but what I love most in the world isn't this head or this body that are so . . . multidimensional," he tells me, now with his usual voice. "And bruised!" he adds, laughing. "It's all that gold of yours pressed up against me, like this, the way we are now."

Surprised, I tell him that if there's anyone in that room who doesn't have an ounce of gold, it's precisely me. And he murmurs in my ear that I have the biggest heart of gold in the world, because, he says, I start out as his challenge, and in spite of all the terrible tests he puts me through, I never complain and, in the end, I am his prize.

"Since my heart is inside yours, I know everything about you. And now that we've both won, we can lose our heads together, right? Abracadabra, my darling Marie Antoinette . . ."

When he falls asleep, I check the revolver. It's loaded with six bullets. I go out onto the terrace and I see that below there are four cars with bodyguards parked on each corner of the street. I know they would give their lives for him. I would, too, without thinking twice. I am now soothed, and I fall asleep happy. When I wake up, he's already gone.

❧ *Two Future Presidents and* Twenty Love Poems

AFTER AMASSING A COLOSSAL FORTUNE, Pablo's goal is to use his money to become the most popular political leader of all time. And, how could it be anything else but madness, delusions of grandeur, an overwhelming cult of personality? His aspiration is an unheard-of extravagance; to give away ten thousand houses to homeless families and to end hunger in a city of one million people—a useless expenditure in Colombia, possibly a country with the stingiest tycoons in all of Latin America.

People who possess fabulous riches live in constant doubt as to whether they are loved only for their money. Thus they are almost as insecure and untrusting in matters of the heart as women who are famous for their beauty, who are always wondering if men really need them as wives or girlfriends, or just want to show them off as possessions or hunting trophies. But when it comes to Pablo, he is utterly convinced he is loved not for his wealth but for himself—by his followers, his army, his women, his friends, his family, and, obviously, by me. While he is correct, I can't help but wonder if his extreme sensitivity, combined with what seems to be a pathologically obsessive personality, will be able to handle the pitfalls of the fame that's approaching. In particular, the antagonism it will bring him in a country where people proverbially "don't die of cancer, but of envy."

I see Pablo for the second time in public at the grand opening of one of his basketball courts. His political movement, Civismo en Marcha (Civic-mindedness in Motion), extols healthy recreation and he has a passion for sports, so Pablo plans to donate a court to all the poorest neighborhoods in Medellín and Envigado, and to install lighting on all the city's soccer fields. When we met, he had already donated several dozen.

That evening, he introduces me to more of his family, lower-middle-class people without an ounce of evil in their very serious faces. I also meet his twenty-three-year-old wife, Victoria Henao, mother of Juan Pablo, his six-year-old son. The Nanny, "La Tata" as everyone calls her, isn't pretty, but her face has a certain dignity. Only her earrings—two solitary diamonds of unheard-of size—could give her away as the wife of one of the country's richest men. She wears her hair very short, she's dark and small, and her evident timidity contrasts with his poise. Unlike Pablo and me, who feel like fish in water when we're in a crowd, she doesn't seem to enjoy the event very much. Something tells me she is starting to view her husband's growing popularity with some unease. She greets me coldly and with the same mistrust I read in the eyes of almost all of Pablo's family. She looks at him with absolute adoration, and he stares at her enraptured. I watch them both with a smile, because

I have never felt jealous of anyone. Fortunately, my passion for Pablo is not exclusive or possessive; I love him with heart and soul, body and brain, madly but not irrationally, because I love myself above him. And my insight leads me to question if, after seven years of marriage, those mooning lovers' gazes might not really answer to the need to publicly clear up any doubts about their relationship.

As I study his family with the triple perspective afforded by the lover's intimacy, the journalist's objectivity, and the spectator's distance, I seem to see an enormous shadow hanging over the idyllic scene and the crowd of people pushing toward Pablo to thank him for the thousands of supplies he distributes weekly among the poor. The kind of sadness that accompanies a premonition—inexplicable and heavy with doubt—enfolds me suddenly, and I wonder if those triumphant scenes of multicolored balloons and raucous music could be mere illusions, fireworks, houses of cards. When the shadow moves away, I can clearly see what no one else seems to have noticed: that over Pablo's whole extended family—dressed in their new clothes and jewelry sprung from a formidable newly born fortune—fear looms. Fear of something that has been gestating for a long time, and that could explode at any moment like a volcano of biblical proportions.

These disturbing feelings pass through me and disappear while Pablo is basking in the warmth of the crowd, the admiration and applause. Things that for me are everyday reality, tokens of my job as a TV host and at countless events, accustomed since age twenty-two to the cries of *bravo!* in a theater or a jeering stadium. But for Pablo they are oxygen, the only reason for his existence, the first steps on the path to fame. It's clear that his ardent political discourse touches something deep in the common people's hearts. As I listen to him, I think of the words of Shakespeare that Mark Antony says at Julius Caesar's burial: "The evil that men do lives after them; the good is oft interred with their bones." I wonder what the fate of this man will be, this strange combination of benefactor and bandit, so young and naive, with whom I've also fallen in love. Will he know how to play his cards right? Will he learn someday to speak in public with a less marked accent and a more mannered tone? Will my diamond in the rough polish his elementary speeches to transmit a powerful message that can reach beyond the provinces? Will he manage to find some more controlled form of passion in order to get what he wants, and an even more intelligent one to keep it? After several minutes pass, the joy that has come over all those poor families spreads to me, and I share in their hopes and illusions. I thank God for sending the only large-scale benefactor that Colombia has produced for as long as I can remember, and full of enthusiasm, I join in the people's celebration.

The program filmed in the dump causes a national sensation. All my colleagues want to interview Pablo Escobar and find out where he gets his money: a thirty-three-year-old alternate congressman who seems to have inexhaustible resources and a generosity never seen before, as well as an unnerving flair for political leadership that comes from his unusual blend of money and heart. Many want to know, as well, the nature of his relationship with a high-society TV star who has always jealously guarded her private life. I roundly deny any romance with a married man, and I advise Pablo not to grant any interviews until after the test I plan to give him before a camera in his TV studio. He agrees, but grudgingly.

"Next week I'm going to invite you to the First Forum

Against the Extradition Treaty, here in Medellín," he tells me. "And at the next one, in Barranquilla, you'll meet the most important men in my trade, who are also now the richest men in the country. Almost all of them are with us in MAS, and they're determined to defeat that monstrosity, whatever it takes. By force, if necessary."

I tell him that that bellicose language is going to win him many enemies in the initial stage of his rising political career. I advise him to study Sun Tzu's *The Art of War* so he can learn strategy and patience. I teach him some of the wise philosopher's maxims, such as "Don't attack uphill." He says that when it comes to strategy, he adapts his to the needs of the moment. And anyway, books bore him terribly, and he has me, who has read voraciously since I was little, so he doesn't have to study. He knows this is the last thing a desirable woman in love wants to hear, so he adds in a merry tone, "I bet you can't guess the alias I've instructed my men to use for you when you land at the airport? None other than . . . 'Belisario Betancur,' the president, so you can enter the underworld at the highest level! You can't complain, my dear V.V.!"

And he laughs with that mischievousness that disarms me, that in one fell swoop erases all my worries and melts me in his arms as if I were a caramel ice cream with vanilla and chocolate chips, left outside on a summer afternoon.

The people who travel in his plane with me are an ever more varied group. One person is coming back from speaking to Kim Il Sung in North Korea. Another passenger, returning from the most recent summit of Non-Aligned Nations, knows Petra Kelly, founder of the German Green Party, whom Pablo has decided to invite to see his zoo and his social projects. Another guest is a personal friend of Yasser Arafat's. Once we are in Pablo and Gustavo's offices, the color blue replaces red, very dark glasses are everywhere, and the green is not exactly the one of European environmentalists: that group is from the police F2; the Paraguayan man is close to Stroessner's son or son-in-law; those men over there are Mexican three-star generals; the ones with the suitcases are Israeli arms dealers; and those in the back have come from Liberia. Pablo's life in those first months of 1983 seems like the Permanent Assembly of the United Nations. And I learn gradually that the man I love, on top of a talent for disguising himself and buying nationalities, has a chameleonlike ability to adapt his political ideology to the consuming audience. His discourse is extremely leftist to appeal to his poorest listeners, political parties, and the media; it becomes the most bone-chilling and repressive right to defend his family, his business, his property and interests when he's in front of multimillionaire associates or uniformed allies. And he flaunts both extremes in front of the challenging woman he loves, showing off his talents as a puppeteer of history, in perfect control of the multicolored strings of that formidable web he's weaving. He has chosen her as the observer of his evolutionary processes, and as a possible accomplice so that she can see how every form of masculine power converges in him. And, as he makes her into the sole witness of his ability to subjugate all other men, she's discovering as well his ability to seduce other women.

The first Forum Against Extradition is held in Medellín. Pablo invites me to sit at the main table beside the priest Elías Lopera, who is sitting to his right. There, for the first time, I hear his fiery nationalist speech against that legal concept. Over time, the fight against extradition will become his obsession, his cause and his fate, the plight of an entire nation. It will affect millions of our countrymen and claim thousands of victims, and it will be a cross for him and for me to bear. In Colombia, justice almost always takes twenty years or more in coming—if it comes at all, because along the way it's often sold to the highest bidder. The system is designed to protect the criminal and wear down the victim, which means that someone with Pablo's financial resources is destined to enjoy the most egregious impunity throughout his life. But a black cloud has now appeared, not only on his horizon but on that of everyone in his trade: the possibility that any accused Colombian can be requested for extradition by the U.S. government. In other words, they could be tried in a country with an efficient judicial system, high-security prisons, multiple life sentences, and the death penalty.

In that first forum, Pablo speaks before his peers using much more belligerent language than I have heard from him. He doesn't hold back in his fierce attacks on the rising political leader Luis Carlos Galán. Pablo berates the presidential candidate for having expelled him from his movement, Renovación Liberal (Liberal Renewal), whose main cause is the fight against corruption. In 1982, after Galán found out where Pablo's money really came from, he had notified Escobar of his expulsion—though without mentioning him by name—in front of thousands of people gathered in Berrío Park in Medellín. As long as he lives, Pablo will never forgive him for that.

I had met Luis Carlos Galán twelve years before in the house of one of the nicest women I ever remember meeting: the beautiful and elegant Lily Urdinola, from Cali. I was twenty-one years old, and I had just divorced Fernando Borrero Caicedo, an architect who looked exactly like Omar Sharif and was twenty-five years older than me. Lily had just separated from the owner of a sugar mill in the Cauca del Valle, and now she had three suitors. One night she invited them all to dinner, and she asked her brother Antonio and me to help her choose among them. There was the Swiss millionaire who owned a bakery chain, the rich Jewish owner of a clothing chain, and the shy young man with an aquiline nose and enormous blue eyes whose only capital seemed to be a brilliant political future. Although that night neither of us voted for Luis Carlos Galán, a few months later, at twenty-six years old, the quiet young man with light eyes became the youngest minister in Colombia's history. I never told Pablo about this "defeat," but for the rest of my life I would regret not having given my vote to Luis Carlos that night, because if Lily had let him court her, between the two of us I'm sure we could have fixed that blessed problem between him and Pablo, and thousands of deaths and millions of horrors could have been avoided.

The photograph of Pablo and me at the first Forum Against the Extradition Treaty becomes the first of many to document the beginning of the most well-known part of our relationship. A few months later, the magazine *Semana* will use it to illustrate an article on "the *paisa* Robin Hood," and with that generous description, Pablo will begin to build his legend, first in Colombia and then in the rest of the world. After that, in all our encounters, Pablo will greet me with a kiss and a hug followed by two spins, and then he'll always ask me:

"What are they saying in Bogotá about Reagan and me?"

And I'll tell him in detail what everyone thinks of him, because what they say about President Reagan is only interesting to Nancy's astrologist and the Republican congresspeople in Washington.

For the second Forum Against the Extradition Treaty we travel to Barranquilla. We stay in the presidential suite of a recently opened grand hotel, instead of El Prado, one of my favorites. Pablo likes only the most modern things, while I like only the most elegant, and we will always argue over what he considers "antiquated" and what I see as "magical." The event takes place at Iván Lafaurie's splendid residence. The house was beautifully decorated by my friend Silvia Gómez, who has also done all my apartments since I was twenty-one.

This time, the media has not been invited. Pablo tells me that the poorest of the participants has ten million dollars, while the fortunes of his partners—the three Ochoa brothers and Gonzalo Rodríguez Gacha, "the Mexican"—plus his own and Gustavo Gaviria's, total several billion dollars and far exceed those of Colombia's traditional tycoons. While he is telling me that almost all the attendees are members of MAS, I'm reading disconcertion in the expressions on many faces when they see a well-known TV journalist is present.

"Today you will witness a historic declaration of war. Where do you want to sit? In the first row down below, looking at me and the bosses of my movement, who you met in Medellín? Or at the main table, looking out at the four hundred men who are going to bathe this country in blood if that extradition treaty is approved?"

As I'm starting to get used to his Napoleonic speaking style, I choose to sit at the far right of the main table. It's not that I want to get to know those four hundred faces of the new millionaires who could eventually replace—and even guillotine—my powerful friends and ex-lovers in the traditional oligarchy (a thought that produces mixed emotions in me, from deepest fear to the most exquisite delight). Rather, I want to try to read on those hardened and leery faces what people really think of the man I love. While I don't like what I see, what I hear makes my blood run cold. I don't know it, but this starry night, in this mansion surrounded by gardens beside the Caribbean Sea, is the baptism by fire of the Colombian narco-paramilitarism. And I am attending it as the only woman, the only witness, and the only possible historical chronicler.

When the speeches are over and the forum ends, I descend from the stage and walk toward the pool. Pablo stays, chatting with the hosts and his partners, who all congratulate him effusively. A crowd of curious people surrounds me, and several of the attendees ask me what I'm doing here. One man, who looks like a traditional landowner and livestock breeder from the Coast—with one of those last names like Lecompte, Lemaitre, or Pavajeau—emboldened by rum or whiskey, says in a loud voice for all to hear:

"Now, I'm too old for one of these kids to come in and tell me who to vote for! I'm a *godo* [member of the Conservative Party], the old-fashioned and lifelong sort, and I'm voting for Álvaro Gómez, period! That's a serious guy, not like that rascal Santofimio! Where does this Johnny-come-lately Escobar get off, thinking he can barge in and give me orders? Does he think he has more money and more cattle than me, or what?"

"Now that I know you can get a TV star with the coke money, I'm going to get rid of Magola, my wife, and marry the actress Amparito Grisales!" brags another one behind me.

"Does this poor girl know that the guy was a 'trigger man' who's got more than two hundred deaths under his belt?" taunts a third one in a low voice to a small group gathered around him. They celebrate his words with nervous laughter before beating a fast retreat.

"Doña Virginia—" an older man who seems to be listening to the others with displeasure addresses me. "My son was kidnapped by the FARC over three years ago, and they still have him. May God bless Escobar and Lehder and all these men who are so brave and determined. People like them are what this country needs, because our army is too poor to fight alone against the guerrillas who've gotten rich off kidnapping. Now that we're joining forces, I know that I can dream of seeing my son again before I die. And that he will be able to hug his wife again and finally meet my grandson!"

Pablo introduces me to Gonzalo Rodríguez Gacha, "the Mexican," who is accompanied by some of the Boyacá emerald dealers. He receives warm congratulations from almost all the participants, and we stay chatting for a while with his friends and associates. When we return to the hotel, I don't say anything about what I heard. I only comment that some of the people—like the right-wingers they clearly are—seem to feel a deep distrust for someone as liberal as Santofimio, Pablo's candidate.

"Wait till someone kidnaps their sons, and the first one of our colleagues is extradited, and you'll see how they run to vote for whoever we tell them to!"

After he was expelled from Luis Carlos Galán's movement, Pablo Escobar had joined that of Senator Alberto Santofimio, the liberal leader from the Tolima Department. Santofimio is very close to ex-president Alfonso López Michelsen, whose son's mother-in-law is his cousin. Gloria Valencia de Castaño, "the First Lady of Colombian TV," is the unrecognized daughter of an uncle of Santofimio's, and her only daughter, Pilar Castaño, is married to Felipe López Caballero, the editor of the magazine *Semana*.

In every Colombian presidential and senate election, the flow of *santofimista* votes constitutes a substantial part of the total obtained by the Liberal Party, which exceeds the Conservative Party in number of votes and presidents elected. Santofimio is charismatic and has a reputation for being an excellent public speaker, as well as the most able, ambitious, and astute politician in the country. He is around forty years old and is figured to be a presidential hopeful. A short and chubby man, he has a satisfied face and is almost always smiling. We have never been friends, but I like him and I've always called him Alberto. (In 1983, everyone calls me Virginia socially, and I call other well-known personalities by their first names; I only use the term "Doctor" with those I want to keep at a distance, and "Mr. President" with heads of state. In 2006, after twenty years of ostracism, people will call me "señora" and I'll call them "Doctor" and "Doctora," while former presidents, when they see me coming, will take off at a run.)

A few months before Escobar and I met, he and Santofimio, along with other Colombian congresspeople, had attended the inauguration of the socialist Felipe González as prime minister of Spain. González's trusted adviser, Enrique Sarasola, is married to a Colombian woman. I had interviewed González for TV in 1981, and I'd met Sarasola in Madrid during my first honeymoon. With a terribly serious expression, Pablo has described for me the scene in which the other politicians in the retinue asked him for cocaine in a Madrid nightclub, and how offended he was. And thus I confirmed what I already knew: the King of Coke seems to detest, almost as much as I do, the export product on which he is building a tax-free empire. The only person Pablo has given coke rocks to without even being asked is his girlfriend's previous boyfriend, and he didn't exactly do it for humanitarian or philanthropic reasons.

Since in 1983 the liberal senators Galán and Santofimio are the two surest options for a generational changing of the guard in the 1986–1990 presidential term, Pablo and Alberto have become fierce allies against the presidential campaign of Luis Carlos Galán. Escobar has admitted to me that for the midterm elections in 1984, he is investing millions into Santofimio's political movement. I try to convince him that it's time for him to call the recipient of his donations by his first name, as Julio Mario Santo Domingo does with Alfonso López, but Pablo will always call his candidate "Doctor." In the following years, "El Santo" will be the constant link between Escobar's operation and the political class, the bureaucracy, the Liberal Party, and, above all, President López. El Santo even connects him to parts of the Armed Forces. In fact, his cousin is the son of a well-known army general and is married to the daughter of Gilberto Rodríguez Orejuela, one of the heads of the Cali Cartel.

TODAY I AM RADIANT WITH HAPPINESS. Pablo is coming to the congressional sessions in Bogotá, and he's finally going to come to my apartment. And he says he's bringing another surprise! Every petal on every rose is perfect, and so is everything else: my bossa nova music on the stereo, the rosé champagne in the refrigerator, my favorite perfume, the dress from Paris, and the copy of *Twenty Love Poems* by Pablo Neruda on the coffee table. Clara, my best friend at the time, has come from Cali. She sells antiques, and she wants to offer Pablo a Christ from the seventeenth century for Father Elías Lopera. For the moment, only she, Margot, Martita, and Pablo's partners know about our relationship.

The doorbell rings. I dash down the steps that separate the study and the three bedrooms from the social part of my apartment, which is more than two thousand square feet. When I reach the living room, I find myself face-to-face not only with the candidate and his patron but also with more than half a dozen bodyguards. They insolently look me over from head to toe and then take the elevator down to wait for their boss in the garages or the lobby. The elevator comes up again with another dozen men and goes back down with half a dozen. The scene is repeated three times, and three times Pablo reads the displeasure on my face. Everything in my reproachful expression warns him that this will be the first and last time in his life that I allow him to enter the place where I'm waiting for him—especially my own house!—accompanied by bodyguards or strangers.

Over the years I will see Pablo some 220 times, around 80 of them surrounded by an army of friends, followers, employees, or bodyguards. But starting after that day, he will arrive at either of our apartments or my hotel suite completely alone, and when we meet in his country houses, he will order his men to vanish before they see me. He has understood in seconds that when a married man visits the woman he loves—and who, by the way, is a diva—he cannot act like a general but must behave like any other man in love. Also, that the first honor one lover owes another is an almost blind trust. For the rest of our days together, I will always thank him—with gestures, never words—for his tacit acceptance of the conditions I imposed that night with only those three looks.

Clara and I greet Gustavo Gaviria, Jorge Ochoa and his brothers, the Mexican, Pelusa Ocampo, owner of the restaurant where we eat sometimes, Guillo Ángel and his brother Juan Gonzalo, and Evaristo Porras, among others. Porras's jaw is trembling and at first I have the impression that he's afraid, but Pablo explains that he has consumed cocaine in industrial quantities. I'd never seen Aníbal Turbay's teeth chatter like that, and I conclude that Evaristo must have snorted at least a fourth of a kilo. Pablo takes him to another room to reprimand him in private, then takes a videocassette from him and sends him away. He pushes Evaristo gently toward the door as if he were scolding a child and orders him to go back to the hotel to wait for them. Then he tells me we have to watch the video together, because he wants to ask me for a favor he says is urgent. I leave Clara in charge of the guests, and we go up to the study.

Every time we see each other, Pablo and I spend six, eight, or more hours together, and in all that time he has confided some basics of his business. Tonight he explains that Leticia, capital of the Colombian Amazon, has become key for him in the shipment of cocaine paste from Peru and Bolivia into Colombia, and that Porras is his organization's man in the southeast of the country. He also tells me that to justify his fortune to the tax man, Evaristo has bought the jackpot-winning lottery ticket three times and has won a reputation as the world's luckiest man!

We turn on the TV, and on the screen appears the figure of a young man talking with Porras about what seems to be business of an agricultural nature. The images were filmed at night and are blurry, and the conversation isn't clear, either. Pablo tells me that it's Rodrigo Lara Bonilla, Luis Carlos

Galán's right-hand man, and, as such, his archenemy. He explains that what Evaristo is taking from a package is a check for a million pesos—some $20,000 then—for a bribe, and he confesses that the setup has been carefully coordinated between him, Porras, and the cameraman. When we finish watching the tape, Pablo asks me to denounce Lara Bonilla on my TV program, ¡Al Ataque! And I refuse. Roundly and categorically.

"I would also have to denounce Alberto, who's downstairs, for receiving much larger amounts from you. Plus Jairo Ortega, your principal in Congress, and who knows how many more people! What happens if tomorrow you give me the money for Clara's Christ, and someone films me so they can say it was a cocaine deal, just because you gave it to me? My whole life I've been a victim of slander, and so I never use my microphone to hurt anyone. How do I know Lara isn't doing some legal business with Porras, other than that planned setup? You have to understand that it's one thing for me to show that infernal dump and your impressive social projects on my program, and quite another for me to be an accomplice in setups to attack your enemies, whether they're guilty or innocent. I want to be your guardian angel, my love. Ask someone else to do you this favor—someone who wants to be your viper."

He looks at me, stupefied, and lowers his eyes in silence. Since I see that he doesn't want to fight me, I go on: I tell him that I understand him like no one else, because I am also the sort who never forgives or forgets, but that if we all decided one day to finish off those who have done us harm, the world would be deserted in seconds. I try to make him see that with his luck in business, in family, in politics, and in love, he should consider himself the most fortunate man on earth, and I beg him to forget about that thorn he carries around festering in his heart, because it will end up infecting his soul with gangrene.

He stands up as if spring-loaded. He takes me in his arms and rocks me a long time. There is nothing, nothing in the world that could make me happier—ever since the day Pablo saved my life, those arms bestow all the security and protection a woman could ever want. He kisses my forehead, breathes in my perfume, runs his hands over my back again and again, and tells me he doesn't want to lose me, because he needs me at his side for many things. Then, looking me in the eyes and smiling, he tells me, "You're completely right. I'm sorry! Let's go back to the living room." And my soul returns to my body. It seems to me that he and I are growing side by side, like two little bamboo trees.

Many years later I will wonder if behind Pablo's long, downcast silences there really lay that thirst for revenge he always talked about, or just a terrifying and unspeakable presentiment. Could he have been seeing, perhaps, visions from a future that was bearing down on us like an out-of-control train, and that we were helpless to avoid?

When we go downstairs, everyone is happy, and Clara and Santofimio are reciting the most famous verses of Neruda's *Twenty Love Poems* in unison.

Pablo and I interrupt them and ask them to let us choose our own.

"Dedicate this one to me," I say, laughing. "I only want your wings, your twenty-four wings, those of the eleven airplanes and the two on the jumbo jet!"

"So that's what you want, you rascal, to escape from me? Don't even dream about it! I want all of you, and this is your real Neruda verse, autographed and everything!"

After signing his name, he says that now he wants to give me a poem of his own that is exclusively for me. He thinks for a few seconds and writes:

Virginia:
Don't think that if I don't call you,
I don't miss you a lot.
Don't think that if I don't see you,
I don't feel your absence.
Pablo Escobar G.

I think that so much repetition of "don't" is a bit strange, but I keep my comments to myself. I praise his mental agility and thank him for the gift with my most radiant smile. Santofimio also dedicates the book to me: "To Virginia: the discreet voice, the majestic figure, the [two illegible words] of our Pablo. AS."

Around eight at night, the *capi di tutti capi* say good-bye because they have to attend a social engagement of a "very, very high level." Clara is happy because she sold the Christ to Pablo for $10,000, and she writes a dedication in the book of Neruda poems that she can't wait to see him become president of the republic. When she leaves and his associates have gone downstairs, Pablo tells me that his whole group is now headed to the apartment of ex-president Alfonso López Michelsen and his wife, Cecilia Caballero de López, but he asks me not to tell anyone.

"Good for you, my love! Why worry about those *galanistas*

when you have access to the most powerful, most intelligent, richest, and, especially, the most pragmatic president? Don't even think about Galán or Lara. Just keep going with Civic-mindedness in Motion and Medellín Without Slums. As the Bible says: 'You will know them by their works.'"

He asks me if I'm going to go out campaigning with him, and with a kiss, I tell him he can count on me there. Always.

"We start this week. I want you to know that I can't call you every day to tell you all the crazy things that occur to me, because my phones are tapped. But I think about you all the time. Don't ever forget, Virginia, that 'You are like nobody else since I love you.'"

○ﾗ *The Lover of El Libertador*

IT'S APRIL 28, 1983, and I receive a call from Pablo in my office. He announces that he's going to give me some historically important news, but he asks me not to report on it or share it with anyone in the media; only with Margot, if I want to. In an excited tone that's unusual in him, Escobar informs me that the plane of Jaime Bateman Cayón, head of the guerrilla movement M-19, has exploded over the Darién Gap while it was flying between Medellín and Panama City. I ask him how he knows, and he tells me that he's in the loop about everything that goes on at the Medellín airport. But, he adds, Bateman's death is the only part of the news that will be on all the international programs in a few hours. The part no one knows is that the rebel leader was carrying a suitcase with $600,000 in cash, and it hasn't appeared anywhere. I'm disconcerted and I tell him so. How can anyone know, a few hours after a plane accident over one of the densest jungles on the planet, whether a suitcase turned up among the plane's wreckage or alongside some incinerated bodies? From the other end of the line, Escobar laughs slyly and says that he knows perfectly well what he's talking about, for the simple reason that one of his planes already found the wreckage of Bateman's!

"Pablo, finding destroyed airplanes in the middle of the jungle takes weeks, if not months. Those pilots of yours are some real marvels, to be sure!"

"That's right, my love. And since you are another marvel, I'll leave you with that information so you can connect the dots! Say hi to Margot and Martita, and I'll see you on Saturday."

THE COLOMBIAN GOVERNMENT would take nine months to recover the bodies. On Bateman's death it was learned that the M-19's account in a Panamanian bank was under the name of the founder's mother, Ernestina Cayón de Bateman, an important fighter in the cause of human rights. She and the group's leaders would later get tangled up in a bitter conflict over a million dollars her son had deposited in Panama. Years later, an Ecuadorean banker designated as a go-between would end up with nearly all the money.

Pablo and I would never speak again about the mysterious suitcase. But I'd learned a valuable lesson from the only gravestone thief and auto mechanic with an aerial fleet I've ever met: helicopters and small planes belonging to controversial people who have many enemies rarely crash because of technical failures of divine origin; they almost always crash because of human intervention. Thus, the importance of tracking. About that $600,000—a figure from twenty-five years ago— today I can only cite that famous gringo saying: "If it walks like a duck, swims like a duck, and talks like a duck . . . it's a duck!"

COUNTLESS SENATORS AND REPRESENTATIVES have been joining Santofimio's movement, including many of my acquaintances from Bogotá, like María Elena de Crovo, one of ex-president López's best friends; Ernesto Lucena Quevedo; Consuelo Salgar de Montejo, my father's first cousin; and Jorge Durán Silva, "the People's Mayor" and my fifth-floor neighbor. We spend many weekends out campaigning, and in every region we visit, liberal leaders and *lopistas* are added to our group of *santofimistas*.

One day, I hear loud laughter behind me, and I ask Lucena what's so funny. Reluctantly, he tells me that Durán Silva has been mocking me in public, saying that Escobar sends his plane for me every time he wants to take me to bed. Unfazed and without turning around, I say at the top of my lungs so that everyone can hear:

"These guys today don't know anything about women! I am the one who requests the biggest of the eleven airplanes every time I want to sleep with their owner!"

A tomb-like silence follows. After a brief pause, I add, "How naive, poor guys!" and I withdraw.

What my neighbor is ignoring is that all men in love listen to the woman who sleeps with them more than to anyone else. And Escobar is no exception. Pablo and I are well aware that because of the nature of the business feeding Santofimio's campaign and my fame, we are exposed to all kinds of mockery and criticism, so we protect ourselves fiercely. Since he has an empire to manage and can't be present for all the rallies and political meetings, we almost always see each other afterward or the following day, when I give him a detailed report on everything that's happened. When I tell him about the People's Mayor, he reacts like a lion.

"And why else would I send a jet that uses thousands of dollars in fuel for the woman I adore, who lives in another city? Am I going to take catechism lessons from a beauty like you? Are you Saint Maria Goretti, or what? That bum's been asking me for money for weeks. . . . Now he won't get a cent from me as long as he lives! And if he comes within a thousand feet of me, I'll send a dozen men to kick his ass and I'll order them to castrate him! For being a *marica*! And stupid!"

As the campaign advances, I start to realize the impressive influence Santofimio exercises over Pablo. On the night of *Twenty Love Poems*, I'd heard them say several times that Luis Carlos Galán was the only thing standing between them and power. By now it's absolutely clear to me that not only is Santofimio determined to be the next president, but Pablo plans to be his successor on Bolívar's throne. They don't make the slightest effort to hide their intentions to end *galanismo*, whatever the price.

More than any policy content, his furious speeches involve virulent attacks against Galán "for having divided the Liberal Party, which had always come to elections united, and for having cost the presidency of Doctor Alfonso López Michelsen, the most qualified man in the country and one of the most illustrious on the continent!" They characterize Galán as a "traitor to the nation for defending an extradition treaty that will hand over the sons of Colombian mothers to an imperialist power, to none other than the very gringos who took Panama from us, because another traitor sold it to Teddy

Roosevelt for a handful of coins!" And Santofimio's followers shout things like:

"Down with Yankee imperialism, and long live the glorious Liberal Party! Santofimio for president in '86, Escobar in '90! Pablito is a patriot who won't give in to the gringos or the oligarchy, because he has more money than all those parasites put together! Hear our cries, Pablo Escobar Gaviria, who came from the entrails of this long-suffering people, and who the Lord and the Virgin protect! And you, too, Virginia, so the next time you bring all the TV actors, who are of the people, too! And long live Colombia, *carajo!*"

I give speeches, too. I almost always speak before the candidate, and I launch guns blazing into a tirade against the oligarchy.

"I know it from the inside! I know firsthand how four families are bleeding this country dry, families who only care about acquiring the embassies and the state's publicity budget for themselves! There's a reason so many guerrillas exist, but thank God, Santofimio and Pablito are democrats, and they're going to take power through the ballot boxes and win Simón Bolívar El Libertador's throne, and to make true his dream of a united, strong, and dignified Latin America! And long live the mothers of Colombia, long live the motherland that will weep tears of blood the day the first of her sons is extradited!"

"You sound like Evita Perón," Lucena tells me. "Congratulations!" The others congratulate me as well, and since I know everything I'm saying is true, I go along with it. One night, as we're sitting by the fire at my apartment, I tell Pablo what they'd said. He smiles proudly and is silent for a moment. Then, he asks me to name the South American personage I love most. Without a second's hesitation, I say El Libertador.

More seriously, he tells me, "Now, that's better. Because you and I don't truly like Perón, do we? And I'm already married, my love. But since you're so brave, you have a different fate in my life: you will be my Manuelita. And I'll whisper it in your ear now, nice and slow, so you won't ever forget this: You ... Virginia ... will ... be ... my ... Manuelita."

Next thing I know, that son of a schoolteacher will start recounting the details of the September conspiracy, when Manuela Sáenz, Simón Bolívar's Ecuadorean lover, saved his life. I admit that I hadn't thought about that brave and beautiful woman since I was in high school. I know that Pablo is no Libertador, and that no one in her right mind could do anything but laugh at the image he has of himself, his outsized dreams and ambitions. But, absurd as it seems now in light of the horrors that came later, I have always been grateful for that homage, the deep love implicit in his idealization of the two of us as a couple. As long as I live, I will carry in my heart the sound of Pablo Escobar's voice uttering those six words and remember the enormity of a minuscule moment of tenderness.

IN COLOMBIA, everyone who is anyone in a given part of the country is a first, second, fourth, or eighth cousin of everyone else. That's why I'm not surprised when one night, after one of his sports field openings, Pablo introduces me to the former mayor of Medellín, whose mother is a cousin of the Ochoas' father. Pablo calls him "Doptor Varito," and I like him immediately. He seems to be one of a very few of Pablo's friends with a decent face and, as far as I can remember, the only one with the look of a scholar. He was director of the Civil Aviation Agency from 1980 to 1982, and now, at thirty-one years old, everyone is predicting a brilliant political career ahead of him; more than one person has ventured to say that he could even make it to the Senate one day. His name is Álvaro Uribe Vélez, and Pablo idolizes him.

"My business and that of my associates is transportation, for $5,000 per kilo, insured," Pablo explains to me later. "And it's built on a single foundation: landing strips, planes, and helicopters. That blessed kid, with help from subdirector César Villegas, got us dozens of licenses for the first and hundreds for the second. Without landing strips and planes of our own, we would still be bringing cocaine paste in tires from Bolivia and swimming to Miami to get merchandise to the gringos. It's thanks to him that I'm informed about everything that happens in Civil Aviation in Bogotá and at the Medellín airport, because his successor was trained to collaborate with us. That's why Santo and I demanded from both electoral candidates a favorable appointment of the head of aviation. Álvaro's father, Alberto, is one of ours, and if one day something keeps Santofimio and me from the presidency, that boy would be my candidate. He may look like a church boy, but he's a fierce fighter."

In June of that year, Alvarito's father dies in an attempted kidnapping by the FARC, and his brother Santiago is wounded. The Uribe family's helicopter is damaged, and Pablo lends him one to bring the body from their hacienda to Medellín. For several days, Pablo is deeply sad. One night, when his spirits are low, he admits, "It's true that drug-trafficking is a gold mine, and that's why they say there's no such thing as an ex-*marica* or an ex-narco. But it's a business for tough guys, my love, because it's a parade of bodies and bodies and more bodies. Those who call the money you earn from coke 'easy' don't know anything about our world. They don't know it from inside the way you're starting to. If something were to happen to me, I want you to tell my story. But first I have to know if you're up to the task of really conveying what I think and feel."

Pablo always suffered from a strange condition: he knew who his enemies would be before they struck the first blow, and what each person who crossed his path could do for him.

Starting that night, our happy and passionate meetings at the hotel are almost always followed by work meetings.

"This week I want you to describe what you saw and felt at the dump."

The next Saturday, I give him six handwritten pages. He reads them carefully and exclaims, "But . . . it makes you want to go running with a handkerchief over your mouth to keep from throwing up! You feel things with your gut, don't you?"

"That's the idea, Pablo. And I write viscerally; 'gut' is your word."

A week later his assignment for me is to describe what I feel when he . . . makes love to me. On our next encounter I give him five and a half pages, and I sit watching him, not looking away for a second, while he devours them.

"But . . . this is the most salacious thing I've read in my entire life! If I didn't hate *maricas* so much, I'd say it makes me want to be a woman. They're going to put you in the Vatican's index. Honestly . . . this'll give me multiple erections!"

"That's the idea, Pablo. And . . . you didn't have to tell me that."

The third week my assignment is to describe what I would feel if I was told he had died. Eight days later, I give him a seven-page manuscript, and this time, while he reads it, I look silently out the window toward the hills in the distance.

"But . . . what's this nightmare? This is heartbreaking! You think you love me this much, Virginia? If my mother read this, she would cry for the rest of her life. . . ."

"That's the idea, Pablo."

He asks me if I really feel everything I write. I reply that it's barely a fraction of what has been in my heart since the day I met him.

"Well then, you and I are going to talk about many things. But, oh, don't start criticizing or judging me! You have to know that I'm no Saint Francis of Assisi, got it?"

By now I hardly ever ask him questions, and I let him choose what he wants to talk to me about. Now that he trusts me, I've been learning to recognize his boundaries, to try not to ask any questions whose answer might be "I'll tell you another time," and not to issue value judgments. I discover that, like nearly everyone on death row in the United States, Pablo has a perfectly rational explanation and moral justification for all of his illegal actions: according to him, refined human beings with imagination need to try all kinds of pleasure, and he is simply the provider of one of them. He explains that if religions and moralists didn't punish those pleasures, the way they did with alcohol during Prohibition—which only brought dead policemen and economic recession—his business wouldn't be illegal, he would pay tons of taxes, and Colombians and gringos would get along splendidly.

"You, a pleasure-seeker and freethinker, understand perfectly well that governments should live and let live, right? And that if they did, there wouldn't be so much corruption, or so many widows and orphans, or so many people in prison. All those lives lost are a waste for society and very expensive for the state. You'll see, someday drugs will be legal. But, well . . .

until that day comes, I'm going to show you that everyone has a price."

And then he opens a briefcase and takes out two checks. They're made out to Ernesto Samper Pizano, the head of Alfonso López Michelsen's presidential campaign.

"This is the price of the country's most powerful, intelligent, experienced president. And the most independent, because López doesn't sell out to the gringos!"

"It's about . . . $600,000. That's all? That's the price of the richest president in Colombia? If I were him, I'd have asked you for . . . at least three million, Pablo!"

"Well, let's say it's . . . the initial installment, my love. Because toppling that extradition treaty is going to take a while. Do you want to have these copies?"

"No way! I could never show them to anyone, because I support anyone who's on your side. And anyone who's at all well informed knows, too, that Alfonso López has anointed Ernesto Samper as a future president of Colombia . . . when he's older and more mature, of course, because he's a year younger than us."

I recommend to Pablo that he listen to the speeches of Jorge Eliécer Gaitán, not only to train his voice but also for their content. The only popular leader of titanic proportions that Colombia has produced in its entire history was assassinated in Bogotá on April 9, 1948, when he was about to reach the presidency. He was murdered by Juan Roa Sierra, a man who served obscure interests and who was then horribly lynched by enraged mobs. For days they dragged his mutilated cadaver through the streets, and they set fire to the city center and the presidents' houses, making no distinction between parties. My great-uncle Alejandro Vallejo Varela, writer and close friend of Gaitán's, was at his side when Roa shot him, and in the clinic where he perished minutes later. The following weeks, which would go down in history as El Bogotazo, became an orgy of blood, fire, and drunken snipers. Stores were sacked, people were murdered indiscriminately, and thousands of cadavers piled up in the cemetery because no one dared to bury them. During those days of terror, the only Colombian statesman, Alberto Lleras Camargo, took refuge in the house of his best friends, Eduardo Jaramillo Vallejo and Amparo Vallejo de Jaramillo, my father's elegant sister. After Gaitán's death came that era of limitless cruelty in the fifties known as La Violencia. When I was a teenager, I saw the photographs of what men do in wartime with the bodies of women and their fetuses. I vomited for days and swore that I would never bring children into the world just so they could live in that country of brutes, monsters, and savages.

I talked about this history one night with Gloria Gaitán Jaramillo, the hero's daughter, over dinner. We were joined by her daughters, María and Catalina, two adorable and very Parisian girls who had inherited inquisitive minds from their brilliant mother, their mythic grandfather, and an aristocratic grandmother who was related to mine. Some days earlier, on learning that Virginia Vallejo was looking for a CD or cassette of her father's speeches, Gloria had come out of her office in the Jorge Eliécer Gaitán Center in Bogotá to ask me, with her charming smile, why I was interested. From my (recent) ex-husband—a socialist Peronist and a great friend of the Jewish millionaire banker of the Argentine Montoneros— I had learned that if there is anything that makes a revolutionary heart beat faster, it's a tycoon who sympathizes with their cause. I told Gloria that the *paisa* Robin Hood—son of a teacher, just like Gaitán—had asked me for her father's speeches. He wants to see if, after studying them thoroughly and with my help, he can learn to wield his voice in such a way as to awaken something of what the hero inspired in the masses. After an hour of enthusiastic conversation on participatory democracy, and a tour of the center's facilities and the Exploratory Wing under construction, Gloria had invited me to have dinner with her daughters the following Friday.

Gaitán's daughter is a refined woman and a great cook. While we are enjoying the exquisite food she's prepared, I tell her that Pablo Escobar financed part of Alfonso López's presidential campaign, and that his conservative partners, Gustavo Gaviria and Gonzalo Rodríguez, did the same for President Betancur. Gloria knows almost all the world's socialist heads of state and the resistance leaders in many countries. Among other things, she tells me she was once the lover of Salvador Allende, the assassinated Chilean president; that she had been López Michelsen's ambassador to (the Romanian dictator) Nicolae Ceaușescu's government; and that she is a great personal friend of Fidel Castro's. I don't know whether it's because she believes in reincarnation and the concept of circular time, but Gloria feels a particular curiosity about people born in 1949, the year after her father's assassination. So when Pablo and I invite her to Medellín, she accepts with pleasure. For several hours, as though hypnotized, we listen to her as she analyzes Colombia's history in light of her father's omnipresent absence; she speaks of the irreparable loss his death entailed and the void that no other Colombian leader could fill, because all who have come after him lack his integrity, courage, and greatness, not to mention his magnetism. She also talks about his ability to communicate his faith in the people, moving audiences, regardless of class, gender, or age. She recalls the sheer power of that vibrant voice, trained to sell his ideology with the perfect dosage of reason and passion, the formidable strength of his gestures, and the power that radiated from that imposing and unforgettable masculine presence.

While we're flying back to Bogotá in Pablo's jet, I ask Gloria what she thinks of him. She responds with a few polite phrases recognizing his ambition and his existential curiosity, his enormous social projects and generous philanthropy, his passion and generosity toward me. Then, she tells me with enormous affection and frankness:

"Look, Virgie: Pablo has one great defect, and it's that he doesn't look people in the eye. And people who look down at the ground when they're talking to you are either hiding something because they're false, or they aren't being sincere. But in any case, you two look so good together! Like Bonnie and Clyde!"

Gloria is the most intelligent and astute woman I have ever met. We will be excellent friends for the next six years, and she will be one of only three people I introduce Pablo to, along with Margot and Clara, two exceptionally shrewd women. Gloria possesses an impressive lucidity—a Virgo and a Bull in the Chinese horoscope, coincidentally, my signs as well. From her I would gradually learn slowly that true intelligence comes not only from a capacity for deep analysis and rigorous classification, or from exceptional mental quickness like Pablo Escobar's, but above all, from strategy. And, although Gloria will often hear me say that trading my innocence for discernment was the worst deal I'd ever made, over time I would take back my words: not only was it the best deal, it was also my only choice.

When Escobar asks me about Gaitán's daughter's impression of him, first I tell him what I know he wants to hear and then what I know that I have to communicate to him: I insist on the subject of strategy and the imperative need to divide Antioquian voters into zones by town, neighborhood, block, and house. Finally—for the first time, and for reasons I can't explain—I talk to him about the bullet-ridden, naked body of Bonnie Parker on the floor of the morgue, displayed beside Clyde's for the press cameras.

Before another burning fireplace, Pablo will hug me and smile with infinite tenderness, contemplating me with a serious face and saddened eyes. After a few seconds, he'll give me a kiss on the forehead and pat my shoulder, something he knows will soothe me. Then, sighing in silence, he'll look away into the fire. Among the many things that he and I will always know and never put into words is that, for all those with the genes of power running through their blood, I am nothing but a bourgeois diva, and he a multimillionaire criminal.

I think I am one of the few people who rarely thinks about Pablo's money. Very soon, though, I would learn the true dimensions of the fortune possessed by that man I love as I've never loved another, and whom I believe I understand as no one else in the world could.

◌ In the Devil's Arms

PABLO AND I are up very early—something unusual for both of us—because he wants me to meet his son, Juan Pablo, who stayed the night at the Tequendama Hotel in his bodyguards' care. When we come down from my bedroom and pass through the study on the way to the elevator, he stops to look out at my neighbors' gardens in daylight. My apartment occupies the entire sixth floor, and it has a lovely view. He asks me who owns the enormous house that takes up the whole block across the street from me. I tell him it belongs to Sonia Gutt and Carlos Haime, head of the Moris Gutt Group and the richest Jewish family in Colombia.

"Well, from this window—after some tracking—I could kidnap them in about . . . six months!"

"No, you couldn't, Pablo. They live in Paris and in the South of France, where they raise horses that run with Aga Khan's, and they almost never come to Colombia."

Then he asks who owns the lawns at the back that are so well cared for. I tell him that it's the residence of the American ambassador.

"Well, from here I could . . . hit him with a bazooka and blow him to bits!"

Astonished, I tell him that of all the people who have looked through that window, he is the only one who thought of it as the watchtower of some medieval fortress.

"Ohhh, my love, it's just that there is nothing, nothing in the world I like more than being naughty! If you plan things carefully, they will always, always work out."

With an incredulous smile, I pull him away from the window. In the elevator I tell him he has to promise me he's going to start thinking like a future president of the republic and stop thinking like the president of an organized crime syndicate. With another smile, full of mischief, he promises me he'll try.

Juan Pablo Escobar wears little glasses and is adorable. I tell him that at his age I didn't see well, either, and that when I got glasses I became the best student in my class. I look at Pablo and add that it was then that my IQ started to really climb. I tell him his father is number one, too, in car and boat races and in everything else, and that he's going to be a very important man. I ask him if he would like to have a very long electric train, with an engine that whistles and a lot of cars. He replies that he would love it, and I tell him that when I was seven, I was dying to have one, but no one gives trains to little girls and that's why it's better to be a boy. We say goodbye, and when I watch the young man I love walk down the hotel hallway holding that happy child's hand, it reminds me of Charlie Chaplin and the Kid in one of my all-time favorite film scenes.

A few days later I get a call from the director of Caracol Radio, Yamid Amat, who wants a phone number for the *paisa* Robin Hood so he can interview him. I pass the message on to Pablo.

"Don't tell him I get up at eleven! Tell him that, from six to nine a.m.—the time of his news show—I . . . have French classes. And that from nine to eleven . . . I go to the gym."

I advise him to make Amat wait about two weeks. Also, to prepare an original and evasive answer for any attempt to find out the nature of our relationship. Pablo gives the interview, and when the journalist asks him what woman he would like to make love to, he replies: Margaret Thatcher! As soon as the program is over, he calls me to find out what I think and, of course, to hear my reaction to his public declaration of love for the most powerful woman on the planet. I analyze the report and then congratulate him effusively.

"You're learning to play on my field, love, and you're doing it very well! The student is exceeding the master, and you can be sure that Thatcher quote will go down in history."

We both know that any of the "richest men in Colombia"—and any men less brave than him—would have answered with an anxious "Sir, I am offended!" or perhaps some nonsense like "I only make love to my esteemed and respectable wife, the mother of my five children!" After reiterating that "Thatcher is for the public and you, only you are for me," Pablo says good-bye until Saturday. I am beaming: he didn't say Sophia Loren, or Bo Derek, or Miss Universe. But best of all, he didn't say "my adored wife."

Escobar makes news again when he attends sessions of Congress for the first time and the police at the Capitol won't let him in. But it's not because of his criminal mind, or his criminal beige linen jacket—it's because he's not wearing a tie.

"But, Agent, don't you see it's the famous *paisa* Robin Hood?" protests someone in the entourage.

"*Paisa* Robin Hood or coastal Robin Hood, only ladies enter without ties!"

Parliamentarians of all stripes run to offer Pablo theirs, and he takes the tie from one of his companions. The next day, the story is all over the news.

My Pablito superstar! I think with a smile.

SOME WEEKS LATER, I'm in New York. First I go to FAO Schwarz and spend $2,000 on a toy train for Juan Pablo, just like the one I always wanted. Then I walk down Fifth Avenue, trying to think of a really useful gift for the boy's father. He already has someone to buy him ties, and he also owns toy airplanes, toy boats, toy tractors, a toy James Bond car, and toy giraffes in bulk. When I pass a window display with unusual electric devices, I stop. I go inside, and after studying the products on offer, I observe the Arabs who manage the place: no doubt about it, they have the look of businessmen. I ask the one who seems to be the manager if he knows of a place to buy equipment to tap phones. In another country, of course—not in America, God forbid! He smiles and asks me how many lines we'd be talking about. I take him to one side and tell him it's the whole Secret Service building in a tropical country, because the man I love is the leader of the Resistance and aspires to be the next president; he has many enemies and needs to protect himself from them and from the opposition.

He tells me that an angel like me couldn't appreciate what he has to offer. I tell him that maybe *I* couldn't, but our movement certainly could. He asks if the movement could pay fifty thousand dollars. I say sure. Two hundred thousand? I say yes. Six hundred thousand dollars? I say of course, but for that kind of money we would be talking about a variety of high-tech products. He calls to the other man, who seems to be his father and the owner of the store. Biting his nails, he says a few phrases in Arabic that end with what sounds like the word "Watergate." They both give me radiant smiles, and I in return smile appreciatively. They look around and then invite me into the back of the store, where they inform me that they have access to all kinds of equipment thrown out by the FBI and even the Pentagon. First, with carefully measured phrases, and then with manifest enthusiasm, they tell me that they are in the position to offer us things like a briefcase that can decipher a million codes in a dozen languages, glasses and telescopes to see at night, and some suckers that you put on the wall to listen to the conversations in the room next door—in a hotel, for example. But the pièce de résistance is a device to intercept a thousand phone lines simultaneously—it would have been the dream of Richard Nixon's reelection campaign and costs a million dollars—and another that guarantees your phone can't be bugged. But first, they want to know if the Resistance has cash. Since I know perfectly well that the movement's only problem is excess liquidity in American territory, I flash a movie-star smile and tell them that's a matter for our leader's secretary; I was only passing through to buy a lighted makeup mirror. I say he'll be in touch in a couple of days, and I dash off to the hotel to call Pablo.

"Well, aren't you a treasure of a girlfriend! What heaven

did you come down from? I adore you!" he exclaims in a state of terrible excitation. "My associate, Mr. Molina, will leave for New York on the next flight."

I'm learning how to play on his field, but that's as far as I go: not being a soccer player myself, I prefer to leave the goals to the professionals.

Pablo's gratitude is, and will always be, the greatest gift he gives me; his passion is the second. Back in Medellín, he showers me with praise and caresses, then tells me he's decided to confess the real reason he's in politics: it's the parliamentary immunity, plain and simple. A senator or representative cannot be detained by the police, or by the Treasury Department, the Armed Forces, or state intelligence agencies. But he doesn't tell me this because I'm a treasure of a girlfriend, or his guardian angel, his interview trainer, or his future biographer. Rather, it's because *El Espectador*, a newspaper that staunchly supports Galán, has been doing its own tracking, looking into Pablo's past; and beneath all those stolen gravestones, they've found two dead men clamoring for justice: agents from DAS (Departamento Administrativo de Seguridad, or the Administrative Department of Security), who had caught Escobar and his cousin Gustavo in 1976 on the Colombian-Ecuadoran border with one of their first shipments of pure cocaine and had sent them to jail.

Pablo already knows my capacity for compassion toward every kind of human suffering. And as he tells me the details of that tragedy that marked his life, I realize he is scrutinizing every one of my reactions.

"When they were putting me on that plane in Medellín to go serve my time in Pasto, I turned around in handcuffs to say good-bye to my wife, who was fifteen and pregnant with

Juan Pablo, and my mother, both in tears. I swore that I would never again let them put me on a plane to send me to jail, and much less on a DEA plane! That's why I went into politics: to put out an arrest warrant for a congressperson, they have to lift parliamentary immunity first. And in this country, that takes somewhere between six and twelve months."

He tells me that thanks to the money and threats they'd dispensed left and right, he and Gustavo had gotten out of jail only three months later. But in 1977 the same agents had captured them again and forced them to beg for their lives, on their knees with their hands up. The only way to get out of it alive was to offer them a massive bribe. After handing over the money, and in spite of Gustavo's opposition, Escobar killed the DAS detectives with his own hands.

"I gave them '*chumbimba corrida*' till I got tired! Otherwise, they would have extorted us for the rest of our lives. And I swore to a judge who sentenced me that she would always ride the bus: every time she buys a car, I set it on fire! There's no such thing as a small enemy, my love. That's why I never underestimate them, and I get rid of them before they grow strong."

It's the first time I've heard him say "*chumbimba corrida.*" Others say "pump full of lead"; people like me say "bullets in bulk." Since I know what it means, I ask him in his own language:

"And did you also give *chumbimba corrida* to your father's kidnappers? And to how many of Martha Nieves Ochoa's?" Without waiting for an answer or hiding my sarcasm, I go on: "In the end, are there two dead, or twenty, or two hundred, my love?"

Everything in him transforms. His face hardens and he

grabs my head with both hands. He shakes it, trying to communicate an impotence and pain of the kind a man can never admit to a woman, much less a man like him to a woman like me. He gazes at my face with a look of anguish, as if it were a liquid dream trickling through his fingers to disappear forever. Then, with something between a roar and a moan that seems to come from the throat of a wounded lion, he cries, "But don't you realize they discovered that I am a murderer? And that they're not going to leave me in peace? And I will never be able to be president? And before I answer you, you're going to answer this: When they prove all this, are you going to leave me, Virginia?"

I confess that for an angel caught by surprise, it can be terrifying to find herself in a murderer's bloodied hands, a demon's warm lips on hers. But the dance of life and death is the most voluptuous and erotic of all, and in the lifesaving arms of a demon who'd snatched her from death's embrace, the poor angel finds herself wrapped in an exquisite sensation, one of such perverse and sublime ambivalence that, in the end, she surrenders. And for having been dragged in ecstasy to heaven, she is returned to earth, punished. And that angel, now condemned to the sinful human form, ends up murmuring into the ear of that pardoned demon that she will never leave him, that he will always be inside her, like right now, and in her heart and her mind and her existence until the day death does come for her. And that murderer, comforted, his face still pressed against my tear-dampened neck, surrenders completely and ends confessing, "I adore you as you can't even dream. . . . Yes, I gave it to my father's kidnappers, too, and with twice as much pleasure! And now the whole world knows that no one, no one, will extort me or harm my family.

And that anyone who has the slightest ability to hurt me is going to have to choose between *plata o plomo*, money or lead. What they wouldn't give, all the rich men of this country, to be able to kill the kidnapper of a father or a son with their own hands! Right, my love?"

"Yes, yes . . . what wouldn't they give! And how many of Martha Nieves's kidnappers did you give *chumbi* to?" I ask, calmer now.

"We'll talk about that another day; it's much more complicated. That was the M-19. . . . Enough for today, my love."

For a long time we embrace in complete silence. Each of us believes we know what the other is thinking. Once again he looks radiantly happy. My tears vanish as though by magic and turn into laughter as he begins to sing and dance for me.

IN THAT DEFENSE of impunity put to a salsa rhythm, Rubén Blades says that "*la vida te da sorpresas y sorpresas te da la vida*" (Life gives you surprises, and surprises give you life). And since our life has been turning into a roller coaster, in June 1983 a circuit court judge in Medellín requests that because of his possible ties to the deaths of the two DAS agents Vasco Urquijo and Hernández Patiño, the Honorable Chamber of Representatives lifts the parliamentary immunity from the congressman Pablo Emilio Escobar.

✤ A Lord and a Drug Lord

I HAD MET my first version of "the richest man in Colombia" in 1972 at the presidential palace; I was twenty-two, and he was forty-eight and divorced. Days earlier, my first lover had told me he was the second-richest man in Colombia, but a few weeks later, when I saw that smiling reincarnation of Tyrone Power, whom the president's diminutive secretary introduced as Julio Mario Santo Domingo—and when he saw me in hot pants under a coat that reached my ankles—sparks flew, and the rest was history. For the next twelve years of my life, my boyfriend or secret lover would always be whoever occupied the throne of Colombia's richest man.

Ultimately, exceptionally rich or powerful men are every bit as solitary as women who are famous for their glamour or sex appeal. The latter want to find the illusion of protection or security in the arms of a great magnate, and the former dream of holding the illusion of all that beauty against their bodies for a brief moment, before it flees and becomes part of their past. The richest man in the country—who in Colombia is always the stingiest—has two advantages as a boyfriend or lover, and they have nothing to do with money. The first is that a great tycoon is terrified of his wife and of the press, and as such is the only man who doesn't flaunt a sex symbol like a hunting trophy or say indiscreet things in front of his friends. The second is that, like a peacock, he will parade his encyclopedic knowledge of the exercise and manipulation of power for the woman he is seducing or falling in love with, as long as she shares his codes of social class. Otherwise, they would have no one to laugh about together, and complicit laughter is the greatest of all aphrodisiacs.

By January 1982, all my exes know I left that poor, ugly Argentine I'd married in 1978, who'd taken off with a chorus girl. Today, the ex who calls me, happy as can be, is Julio Mario Santo Domingo.

"Since you are the only Colombian woman one can present everywhere in the world, I want you to meet my great friend David Metcalfe. He's not that rich, or an Adonis; but next to that guy you were married to, he's a multimillionaire who looks like Gary Cooper. He's a legendary lover on two continents, and I've been thinking that he's just what you need now that you ditched that husband. This is the man who's good for you, doll, before you go falling in love with another poor asshole!"

Santo Domingo, the Colombian beer mogul, explains that Metcalfe is the grandson of Lord Curzon of Kedleston, viceroy of India and the second man of the British Empire during Queen Victoria's reign. I learn that the Mountbattens—the last viceroys of India—had been in the wedding party of Curzon's daughter Lady Alexandra and "Fruity" Metcalfe.

That Fruity and "Baba" Metcalfe, in turn, were in the Duke of Windsor's wedding party after he abdicated the British throne to marry the twice-divorced American Wallis Simpson. That Edward VIII (whose family called David) was godfather of his best friend's son. And that David Metcalfe, upon his father's death, had inherited the ring and cuff links bearing the Duke of Windsor's family crest from when he was Prince of Wales. He adds that David Metcalfe is friends with all the richest people in the world, hunts with British royals and with the king of Spain, and is one of the most popular men of international high society.

"He's going to pick you up on Friday for a dinner at my apartment, and you'll adore him, you'll see! Bye, my pretty, precious, dreamy doll."

As David is coming into the living room, my mother is on her way out, and I introduce them. The next day, she will say to me, "That six-foot-tall man, in black tie and patent leather shoes, must be the most elegant in the world. He looks like one of those cousins of Queen Elizabeth!"

He is a nearly bald and perfectly tanned Englishman, with narrow shoulders and enormous hands and feet, an angular and quite wrinkled face, opera glasses perched on an aquiline nose, gray eyes that are wise and generous but somewhat cold. He has eight hundred years of pedigree and fifty-five of life. He looks at me with an enchanting smile and says that "Mario" has told him I am every man's dream. I tell him that's right and also that, according to our friend, he is every woman's. And then I change the subject, because the truth is that Metcalfe, as they say in Colombia, doesn't inspire the slightest salacious thought in me. I share Brigitte Bardot's maxim: "The only thing necessary for a man to be a perfect lover is physical attraction." And any animal lover knows that at the hour of truth, the Prince of Wales's ring on the finger, the six-person staff in Belgravia, and the Van Gogh in the dining room are not enough.

Among the strict rules that the elegant and haughty Lord Curzon considers inarguable are that "a gentleman does not wear brown in the city," and "a gentleman does not eat soup at lunch." Eighteen months have passed since I'd met his grandson, and it's the middle of 1983. The "richest man in Colombia" is not an English lord or a local gentleman. He doesn't get up at 6 a.m. to call his ambitious "slaves," but summons his sinister "boys" at eleven. He has bean soup at his daily brunch, and he doesn't even wear a brown suit to congressional sessions, but rather a beige jacket. He doesn't know what the hell chalk stripe or Prince of Wales fabrics are, and he lives in sneakers and blue jeans. He is thirty-three years old, not fifty-nine, and he doesn't have a clear idea of who Santo Domingo is, because since he owns a small republic, he is only interested in the presidents he finances and the dictators who cooperate with him in everything. In a country where none of the stingy tycoons have their own planes yet, he puts an aerial fleet at my disposal. He shipped sixty tons of coke last year—but this year plans to double production—and his organization controls 80 percent of the world market. He is five feet five inches tall and has no time for tanning. While he's not as ugly as Tirofijo ("Sureshot"), the leader of the FARC, his conviction that he bears a certain resemblance to Elvis Presley is stretching things a bit. He has never cared about Queen Victoria, only the beauty queens of Caquetá, Putumayo, or Amazonas. He makes love like a peasant boy but believes himself a stud, and he only has one thing in common with the four richest men in Colombia: me. And I idolize him. Because he adores me, because he's the most exciting and fun person to ever have walked the face of the earth, and because he isn't stingy, but lavish.

"Pablo, I'm afraid to enter the United States with this much money," I'd said to him before my first shopping trip to New York.

"The American government doesn't care how much money you bring in, only how much you take out, my love! Once, I arrived in Washington with a million dollars in a briefcase, and they gave me a police escort so no one would assault me on the way to the bank! Me, can you believe it? But woe on you if they catch you taking out more than $2,000 cash, even if the law says $10,000. Always declare all the money when you go in. You spend it or deposit it in your bank account $2,000 at a time, but never, ever, ever even think about bringing it back. If the Feds catch you with cash, they give you a thousand years in jail, because money laundering is a much bigger crime than even drug trafficking. I'm a moral authority on these matters. Don't tell me I didn't warn you."

Now when I travel, I always put $10,000 rolls of bills in a Kleenex box in each of my three Gucci suitcases, and another in my Louis Vuitton carry-on, and I declare it all. When the customs agents ask me if I robbed a bank, I invariably reply, "The dollars are bought on the black market, because that's how it's done all over Latin America, where the peso is the currency. The Kleenex are because I never stop crying. And I take many trips a year because I'm a TV journalist; just look at all these magazine covers."

And the officer invariably replies, "Go ahead, beautiful, and give me a call the next time you're sad!"

And I go out like a queen to the limousine that's always there waiting for me, and when I reach the hotel—after passing some Rothschild, Guinness, or Agnelli in the lobby, or the retinue of a Saudi prince, a French first lady, or an African dictator—I throw the Kleenex in the trash and climb happily into a bubble bath to polish my shopping list for the next day. I've already labored over it for three hours in my first-class seat on the plane, while I drank rosé champagne and ate caviar blinis, because now my lover's Pegasus is almost always busy carrying thousands of kilos of coke to Norman's Cay in the Bahamas. That place belongs to his friend Carlitos Lehder and is an obligatory stop for the other queen—the white one you inhale—on the way to the Florida Keys.

Any civilized and brutally honest woman will admit that one of the greatest delights in existence is to go shopping on Fifth Avenue with a lavish budget. That's especially true if she's already had four moguls at her feet who are worth twelve billion combined, and none of them had even sent her flowers.

And on each return to Colombia, there is my Pablo, "crowned" again, with Pegasus and the rest of his fleet, his political ambitions—the result of aspirations of a different kind by millions of grateful and happy gringo fans—and his adoration, his passion, and all of his crazy and terrible need for me. And the Valentino or Chanel falls to the floor, and Cinderella's crocodile shoes fly through the air, and any suite or shack is the same earthly paradise for death's embrace or the demonic dance, because, when your lover acts like an emperor and pays for a series of shopping sprees, his past is as irrelevant as Marilyn Monroe's or Brigitte Bardot's in some lucky man's bed.

But the problem with many exceptionally rich men is the lengths to which they are willing to go to cover up yesterday's crimes or indiscretions. Horrified at the revelations about Pablo Escobar's past, Margot Ricci has destroyed every copy of the program we filmed at the dump and informed me that she doesn't ever want to hear from Pablo or me again. We sell the TV production company, now debt-free, to her boyfriend, Jaime, a good-natured man who dies soon thereafter. She marries Juan Gossaín, director of RCN, the radio network that belongs as well to the soft-drink tycoon, Carlos Ardila, who is married to Aníbal Turbay's ex-wife.

The *paisa* Robin Hood has by now learned to deal with the media. He competes with me for magazine covers, and he's enjoying his newfound fame to the utmost. When Adriana, daughter of the banking and construction mogul Luis Carlos Sarmiento, is kidnapped, I urge Pablo to put his thousand-man army at his disposal. Not just out of principle, but because he needs to start sowing seeds of gratitude among decent people, including the most powerful members of the establishment. Very moved, Luis Carlos tells me that the negotiations to free his daughter are already well under way, but that he will always be grateful for congressman Escobar's gesture.

Pablo's life takes a complete turn the day President Betancur names a new minister of justice: Rodrigo Lara, he of the agricultural business deal with Evaristo Porras, the triple jackpot winner. Immediately, Lara accuses Escobar of drug trafficking and of having ties to MAS, and Escobar's followers, who feel betrayed by Betancur, display Evaristo's million-peso check in Congress. And the key minister of Luis Carlos Galán's New Liberalism starts bearing down on Pablo like a freight train: the Chamber of Representatives lifts his parliamentary immunity, a Medellín judge issues an arrest warrant over the deaths of the two DAS agents, the American government revokes his tourist visa, and the Colombian government confiscates the animals in his zoo as contraband. When they are auctioned, though, Escobar buys them back through intermediaries; after all, except for the Ochoas and the Mexican, no one in the country has enough room for thousands of exotic animals to graze, or a veterinarian to take care of them, and especially not enough rivers and straw for the elephants and two dozen hippopotamuses who are nearly as territorial as their owner.

Pablo begs me not to be alarmed by his avalanche of problems, and he tries to convince me that his life has always been this turbulent. He is either a great actor or the most self-confident man I have ever met. One thing I have no doubt about: he is a formidable strategist and has nearly inexhaustible resources with which to mount devastating counterattacks, because money is pouring in. I never ask him how he launders it; but sometimes, when I'm worried, he gives me some clues as to the size of his income. He has more than two hundred luxury apartments in Florida, bundles of hundred-dollar bills are sent right to Hacienda Nápoles camouflaged in household appliances, and the cash that's entering the country is enough to finance the presidential campaigns of all the political parties until the year 2000.

The arrest warrant drives Pablo into partial hiding. Our need for each other's skin has been growing in intensity right along with the manhunt and the bugging of our phones. Since neither of us confides in anyone, we both need our interlocutor/lover's voice more and more. But every one of our encounters now demands careful logistical planning, and we can no longer see each other every weekend, much less at the Intercontinental Hotel.

As the months pass and our trust grows, I have also started to hear him and Santofimio use much more bellicose language. It's not unusual for the latter to say things in front of me like:

"Wars are not won halfway, Pablo. There are only winners and losers, not half winners and half losers. You're going to have to chop off a lot of heads to get things done; or in any case, the most visible ones."

And Escobar unfailingly replies, "Right, Doctor. If they keep fucking with us, we're going to have to start giving a lot of *chumbimba*, so they learn some respect."

In the course of a tour through the Department of Tolima, Santofimio's native soil and political stronghold, he starts to embrace me in front of his local leaders in a way that makes me terribly uncomfortable. But when his "caciques" leave, the candidate transforms and is all business: he tells me I have to help him convince my lover to increase his campaign contributions, because the money he's giving now isn't enough for anything, and Santofimio is the only senatorial and presidential option that guarantees Pablo not only that the extradition treaty will end, but also that his past will be completely buried.

When I return to Medellín, I'm mad as a hornet, and before Pablo can even kiss me, I start reeling off the events of recent weeks in a crescendo of complaints, finger-pointing, accusations, and questions without answers:

"I held a cocktail fund-raiser for his campaign and invited the leaders from all the poor neighborhoods of Bogotá. Only because you asked me to, I crammed a hundred and fifty nosy people into my apartment. Santofimio got there after 11 p.m., stayed fifteen minutes, and then rushed off. He didn't even call the next day to thank me. He's a classless, ungrateful, two-faced pig! This poor country matters shit to him! He's going to finish off your idealism, and you'll end up just like him. Here, in your territory and in front of your people, he would never have dared embrace me in public like he did in Tolima! Haven't you yet realized the price I'm already paying for putting my clean image in the service of your interests, so that an Iago like him—if you even know who Iago is—will try to use me in such a sleazy way in front of that gang of provincial criminals who think an unscrupulous crook like him is God?"

An invisible wall seems to descend from the ceiling and comes between the two of us. Pablo stands still as a rock, paralyzed. Then, he looks at me in shock and sits down. With his elbows on his knees, head in his hands, and eyes fixed on the floor, he starts talking to me in an icy voice, carefully measuring his words:

"It pains me to the core, Virginia, but I have to tell you that that man you call an ungrateful pig is my link to the whole political class of this country, from Alfonso López on down, not to mention his connection to sectors of the Armed Forces and security organizations that aren't with us in MAS. I'm never going to be able to dispense with him, and it's precisely his lack of scruples that makes him so invaluable to someone like me. And, in fact, I *don't* know who Iago is, but if you say he and Santofimio are similar, it must be true."

All my respect for him shatters like a mirror hit by a bullet. In terrible pain, my face washed in tears, I ask him: "Is that sewer rat perhaps trying to tell me that it's high time I start considering other options ... because you've already found them, my love? That's what this whole show of grabbing me in public is about, right?"

Pablo stands up and looks toward the window. Then, with

a sigh, he tells me, "You and I are adults, Virginia. We're free, and we can both consider all the options we want."

For the first time in my existence, and without caring that I could lose the man I've loved most in my life, I throw a jealous fit. Unable to control myself, I punch the air with every phrase I shout:

"You've turned into a scoundrel, Pablo Escobar! And I want you to know that the day I trade you in for someone else, it won't be some poor swine like your beggar candidate! You don't even know how spoiled I am when it comes to men. I can have the richest or the handsomest, and I don't have to pay like you do! I treat kings like pawns and pawns like kings, and when I trade you in for a pig, it'll be a pig who's richer than you. And one who wants to be president. No, one who wants to be a dictator, yes, sir! And you, who have never underestimated me, you know that's exactly what I'm going to do. I'll swap you for a dictator, but not a half-assed one like Rojas Pinilla. Not like that, no, one like . . . like . . . like Trujillo! Or Perón! Like one of those two, I swear to God, Pablo!"

When he hears this, he bursts out laughing. He turns around and, still laughing, comes toward me. He grabs both my arms to keep me from punching him in the chest and he wraps them like a noose around my neck. Then he holds me firmly around the waist and presses against my body while he tells me: "The problem with that future husband of yours is that he's going to need me to bankroll him. And when he sends you to pick up the cash, we'll go at it nonstop, won't we? Your other problem is that the only two pigs as rich as I am are Jorge Ochoa and the Mexican . . . and neither of them is your type, are they? You see that I'm the only option for a woman like you? And you're my only option, because where else am I going to find another box of surprises that makes me laugh so much . . . with that heart of yours? Or another Manuelita . . . with that Einstein IQ? Or another Evita . . . with that body of Marilyn, hmm? Are you going to abandon me at the hands of powerful enemies who have started a ruthless hunt for me . . . that's going to end with my early death and my poor humanity under some terrible gravestone that someone had to buy for me? Swear you're not going to trade me in yet for some Idi Amin Dada who would extradite me . . . or barbecue me! Swear to me, my adored torment, on what you love most. And what you love most . . . is me, right?"

"And when do you propose I trade you in, then?"

"How about in . . . a hundred years. No, more like seventy, so you don't think I'm exaggerating!"

"I'm not giving you more than ten!" I reply, drying my tears. "Anyway, you're sounding like Augustine of Hippo, who before becoming Doctor of the Church, prayed: 'God grant me chastity, but not yet!' And I warn you, now I'm really going to sack the stores on Fifth Avenue. This time I'll clean them out!"

He looks at me with something like profound gratitude. Exhaling in relief, he says with a smile, "Pheeeew! Go sack them whenever you want, my adored panther, as long as you promise we'll never, ever talk about these things again." Then he laughs and asks: "And how old was that saint when he went impotent, miss know-it-all?"

Facing the prospect of a closet full of Chanel or Valentino, what average woman is going to worry about Santofimio's duplicity? I dry the last of my tears, reply that he was forty, and inform Pablo that I'm never going out on the campaign trail again. He says that the only absence he cares about is that of my face on his pillow—and all the rest of me in his bed—and he starts to caress me. As he lists each of those possible absences, I have only my present and Pablo's presence.

Pablo seems to have forgotten that I never forgive and that when it comes to the opposite sex, any one of my options is more interesting than all of his put together. So, I finally let my arm be twisted, and I accept the invitation I have declined over and over during the previous eighteen months: a first-class ticket to New York, an enormous suite at the Pierre Hotel, and the passionate, elegant arms of David Patrick Metcalfe. And the next day, when I go out to spend $30,000 at Saks Fifth Avenue, I leave the bags in the limo and go into Saint Patrick's Cathedral. I light one candle for the patron saint of Ireland and another for the Virgin of Guadalupe, patron saint of the generals of the Mexican Revolution who were ancestors of mine. For the rest of my life I will carry in my heart a nostalgia for something that was lost forever on that night of dictators and pigs, and from that day on, I will never care about Pablo's one-night stand with a model or a weekend with a beauty queen, much less about a couple of lesbians in some Jacuzzi in Envigado.

One day, in the central library of my friends Hans and Lilly Ungar, I meet with the man who'd been my first TV director, now the former minister of foreign affairs, Carlos Lemos Simmonds. He advises me to go back to radio, and he recommends the Grupo Radial Colombiano, now the fourth-largest network in the country. It has a stellar team, and it belongs to the Rodríguez Orejuela family of Cali, who owns banks, drugstore chains, cosmetics laboratories, Chrysler of Colombia, and dozens of other companies.

"They keep a low profile. Gilberto Rodríguez is very

intelligent and is on his way to becoming the richest man in the country. Also, he's a gentleman."

A few weeks later I receive a job offer from Grupo Radial. It's a pleasant surprise, and since I've heard such good things from Carlos Lemos, I delightedly accept. My first assignment is to cover the Cali Fair and Sugar Cane Beauty Pageant the last week of December and the first of January. Pablo is spending the holidays at Hacienda Nápoles with his family, and he has sent me a Christmas present: a beautiful gold watch with a double strand of Cartier diamonds. He bought it from Joaco Builes's girlfriend, Beatriz, who is quite a businesswoman and sells jewelry to all the drug traffickers of Medellín. She cautions me:

"Virgie: don't even think, never ever, of taking it to Cartier in New York for repairs! I admit it, the watches Joaco and I sell are stolen, and they could seize it or throw you in jail. Don't say I didn't warn you! In any case, Pablo is convinced that watches as gifts are very lucky."

One night I am dining in Cali with Francisco Castro, the young and handsome president of the Banco de Occidente, the most profitable of all the banks owned by Luis Carlos Sarmiento. Two men enter the restaurant and a hush falls; everyone turns to look, and a dozen waiters rush to attend them. In a low voice full of contempt, "Paquico" Castro tells me, "Those are the Rodríguez Orejuela brothers, the kings of coke in the Valley. A couple of foul, awful mobsters. They may both have a billion dollars and a hundred companies, but they're the kind of customer Luis Carlos would immediately have kicked out of his banks!"

I'm surprised, and not because the news reaches me through someone with a reputation for being a child prodigy in financial matters. I thought that, by now, I knew the names of everyone who's anyone in Pablo's line of work; so, it is very strange that I've never heard of them. The next day, the radio station director informs me that Gilberto Rodríguez and his wife want to meet me. They've invited me up to the presidential suite of the Intercontinental Hotel, their base of operations during the fair, where they will personally give me my first-row tickets to the bullfights. (In a bull ring, the first row is really the third, behind the *barrera* and the *contrabarrera*. The *barrera* row looks directly onto the alley where the bullfighters congregate, along with their teams, cattle breeders, and the male journalists. Never the female ones, because supposedly they bring bad luck, and because sometimes the bulls jump the fence into the alley and charge at everything in their way.)

Rodríguez Orejuela looks very different from the bosses in Medellín; all that is obvious in them is subtle in him. He looks like an ordinary businessman, and he would go completely unnoticed anywhere but Cali. He is very courteous and polite, as all rich men are with pretty women, and he has a certain crafty, cunning element that he camouflages perfectly with another that, to the eyes of a less perceptive observer, could seem like shyness or even a discreet hint of elegance. I would say he is a little over forty years old; he isn't tall, his face and hands are round, and he lacks Pablo's masculine presence. The truth is that both Pablo Escobar and Julio Mario Santo Domingo have what on the Colombian coast they call *mandarria* (potency), a word whose unique sonority says it all. When one of them enters a place, everything in their movements and attitude seems to cry out: "Here comes the king of the world, the richest man in Colombia! Stand back! Don't anyone dare get in my way, because I am danger on two legs and today I woke up in a bad mood!"

Rodríguez's wife is around thirty-seven; her face is fairly ordinary and has scars from juvenile acne. She is taller than either of us, and under her tunic printed in green tones she clearly has a good figure, like nearly all women in the Cauca del Valle. She has eagle eyes, and everything seems to indicate that her husband doesn't move a muscle without her permission.

I have always believed that behind every exceptionally rich man there is either a great accomplice or a great slave.

This is no "Nanny," like Escobar's wife. She's more like a "Beast," and she seems like the general's general!

On my return to Bogotá, I'm surprised by a call from Gilberto, who invites me to the bullfights with him and the sports commentators of Grupo Radial. I reply, "Thanks very much. But you should know that I only sit in the first row—that is, with the poor people—when I'm at a fair working like a slave, exploited by the radio network of some presidential family, or some banker with hundreds of drugstores. Meaning, since I am blind, the only place I can see from and where I can be seen, is the *barrera*. See you on Sunday!"

After the bullfight, the group takes me home. A few days later, Myriam de Rodríguez calls to ask me why I went to the bullfight with her husband. Extremely displeased, I reply that she should be asking the owner of Grupo Radial Colombiano himself why he sent the sports commentators and the international editor to cover the bull season. And before hanging up, I make a suggestion: "Next time, you could ask him to bring you, too—with your microphone, of course—so you can see why, as the Agustín Lara song goes, 'when Silverio faces the bull, nobody changes a shady *barrera* for a throne!'"

Afterward I wonder why I didn't taunt that beast some more. Why didn't I tell her that her husband couldn't interest me for anything, absolutely anything in the world? That I am madly in love with his rival, who is much richer than him, well married, adores me, and can't wait to return from his estate and melt in my arms? That he's going to be either a president with a past or a dictator with no record, and that he is, whether she likes it or not, the only, true, inarguable universal King of Cocaine? Why didn't I ask her what percentage of the market her Gilberto had—if last year Pablo already had 80 percent, and this year he's doubling production—so I could take pleasure in her replying: "Well, my husband has another eighty percent!"

Once my rage has passed, I start to remember those four tycoons of the establishment I had loved in the past: their privileged intellects, those hearts of stone, their incapacity for any form of compassion, their legendary capacity for revenge. Then, and with a smile that comes from some hidden corner of my heart, I also remember their gifts for snake charming, their laughter, their weaknesses, their hatreds, their secrets, their lessons . . . all that capacity for work, that passion, ambition, and vision . . . their power to seduce, their presidents . . .

How would they react if they knew Pablo Escobar aspired to the presidency? If he were to retire from the business, which one of them could be an ally? Which his rival and which his enemy? Which one could become a mortal danger for Pablo? I think none of them, because by now everyone knows that Escobar has more money, more cunning, and more balls . . .

and is twenty or twenty-five years younger than any of them. In any case, as Machiavelli says, "Keep your friends close and your enemies closer."

And I'm left thinking that it isn't women's bodies that pass through men's hands, but rather men's heads that pass through women's hands.

❧ *The Seventh-Richest Man in the World*

OUR FIRST HUG of 1984 is followed by two spins and a piece of news that falls on me like gallons of freezing cold water. Pablo plans to retire from politics, and he wants to know what I think, so he can weigh it against the opinions of his family, his partners, and, obviously, his candidate, "Doctor Santofimio."

I reply that you don't have to be Einstein to know what all of them think, and I beg him for once in his life to say to hell with all of them and think only of himself. I implore him not to fold to Minister Lara, or *galanismo*, or the government, or public opinion, or the gringos. I ask him to remind his family where the diamonds and Mercedeses come from, and all the Boteros and Picassos. I advise him, instead of attacking the extradition treaty head on and throwing away millions on politics, to start social projects in Bogotá of the same scope as Medellín sin Tugurios, so that his popularity can protect him and make him untouchable, and also to start thinking about retiring from the business or leaving it in the hands of his partners, who are loyal and solid as rocks.

"Do you think that yours will be the only dynasty in this country that bears the weight of two deaths? The only difference is that, at thirty-four years old, you already have a billion or two dollars! And vote-buying in this country is the norm, so you're not inventing anything new, just paying them with houses and sports fields instead of sandwiches! I will never understand why Belisario Betancur named as minister of justice the sworn enemy of the people who had financed most of the presidential campaigns! Alfonso López would never have done something so stupid. You don't need Santofimio, and stop calling him 'Doctor'! People like you and me say 'Doctor' to someone like Álvaro Gómez, not Alberto Santofimio!"

Pablo never loses his calm. Pablo never complains. And Pablo never interrupts me when I'm on fire. By now, he has learned that I only stop talking and calm down completely when he takes me in his arms, and that's why he behaves with me like one of those animal trainers who whisper into horses' ears until they relax. It's been that way since the day I told him that if in hell they glued me to his body with Krazy Glue for all eternity, I would never get bored for a second, and I'd feel like I was in heaven. He told me that was the most perfect declaration of love of all time.

That night, he tells me that he and his candidate have agreed to separate officially, although they'll go on cooperating below board. Santofimio's gifts of persuasion with other congresspeople are more indispensable now than ever to Pablo's trade in their efforts to bring down the extradition treaty. He explains that there is another big reason why he has decided, for the moment, to leave politics in the hands of professionals:

the route through Norman's Cay with Carlos Lehder is having serious problems, and sooner or later it's going to fall. His partner is turning into a megalomaniacal drug addict and is causing all kinds of problems for Lynden Pindling's government in the Bahamas.

"I've already made contact with the Sandinistas. They're desperate for money, and they're offering me whatever I want if I'll use Nicaragua as a stopover point and distribution base for merchandise on the way to Miami. In a few weeks you and I will go to Managua together, and we'll try out one of my passports. I want you to meet the junta and tell me what you think of them. Everything you've said is true, but you have to understand that my business comes before politics, and I have to milk it until it's impossible to get anything else from it. Then, I can think about retiring, and when the storm is over, I will return to Congress. You'll see, in six months things will start getting better. You know that I see problems coming months in advance, and when they arrive, I have the solution carefully planned and ready to go into action. Everything, except death, can be fixed with money. And I've got money pouring in, my love."

I ask him how the founders of MAS manage to get along with a communist government so close to the rebel groups of Colombia. He replies that when we are there I will understand everything. In the end I keep quiet. Two weeks later Pablo announces he's withdrawing from politics. I think that, as long as it's provisional and not definitive, it's the right decision, because it will take him out of the path of the publicity storm.

In the following weeks we are immensely happy. Our relationship is known about only by his partners, three friends of mine, and a handful of his staff: Fáber—his secretary and a

very kind man, always in charge of picking me up and drop-
ping me off at the airport—and three of his men whom he
trusts completely, Otto, Juan, and Aguilar, who is known as
"El Mugre" (the Dirt). Pablo and I roundly deny any romance
out of consideration for his wife and also for my career, which
is in ascendance: *El Show de las Estrellas* (*Show of the Stars*), my
program on Saturdays at 8:00 p.m., is shown in several countries and has a fifty-three-point rating. In 1984, there are only
three television channels in Colombia, and no one watches the
official one. My other program, *Magazín del Lunes* (*Monday
Magazine*), steals viewers away from the news show hosted
by Andrés Pastrana on the other channel, supposedly because
I cross my legs in a very sensual way. And, for that same reason, Di Lido Stockings, property of the Kaplan family from
Caracas and Miami, has hired me to go to Venice to film a
second commercial for them. The first one captured 71 percent
of the national market; so, this time, I am requesting from the
owners of Di Lido a fee equal to the country's one hundred
best-paid models combined, plus first-class plane tickets and
a suite in the Cipriani Hotel or the Gritti Palace. I've happily told Pablo that, after Venice, the Kaplans will have to pay
me like a movie star in a country without a movie industry!
And he smiles because he knows that in 1981 I had received
an offer from a Hollywood producer. I stayed in a bungalow
at the Hotel Bel-Air, Princess Grace's favorite hotel, and he
invited me to join Michael Landon, Priscilla Presley, and Jür-
gen Prochnow in his upcoming film. I turned it all down after
Margot's withering questions: "Do you want to be a serious
journalist or a movie star? Are you going to leave me with this
company now that we're finally getting out of poverty?"

One morning around eleven, Pablo arrives at my apartment

unannounced. He says he's come to say good-bye: he's leaving for Panama and Nicaragua, and he can't take me with him. The people who act as his liaisons with the Sandinista junta have forbidden him from bringing a TV journalist with him. He tells me he'll be gone only a week, and he promises that when he's back we'll take a trip together, maybe to Cuba to meet Fidel Castro. I don't believe a word of it, especially when he proposes that while he's gone I take a shopping trip so I won't be sad about the change in plans. I'm furious, but I don't complain: New York is definitely more chic than Managua, and the Pierre is another earthly paradise. Not just because it's a block and a half away from Bergdorf Goodman, but also because vengeance is sweet.

The scene in the enormous suite a week later is surreal: on one phone line, in his room, David is laughing on the phone with "Sonny," the Duke of Marlborough. On the other, in my room, I am laughing on the phone with Pablito, the King of Coke, who is asking me to buy all the copies of *Forbes* magazine before they run out, because they've just listed him as the seventh-richest man in the world! And when both of us hang up, there, in the little living room between us, is Julio Mario, the King of Beer, laughing his head off because, he says, Metcalfe is going to get some cement shoes! (Among the capos of the illustrious Genovese, Bonanno, Gambino, Lucchese, and Maranzano families, there was a tradition of coating their enemies in liquid concrete and waiting patiently while it solidified, before throwing them to the bottom of the sea; it could be called the New York way of making people disappear, or the contemporary version of "a millstone around the neck.")

Julio Mario asks me how rich, really, all those "peasant friends" of mine are. I reply that they are now among the richest in the world, and he says that I must have lost my mind from all that shopping. And since the bearers of all those titles are so happy today, I leave Metcalfe and Santo Domingo laughing at the demimonde and go down to buy cigarettes. I also buy all the copies of *Forbes* I can find. I head back to the suite, and without a word I hand them each a copy open to the page with the list of that year's richest people. The Ochoas are in sixth place, and Pablo Escobar is seventh.

"So my competition has three *billion*," says David. "Well, that kind of money should be enough not just to buy giraffes, pay El Mugre, and finance your shopping trips, but also to live with a little style, like Stavros Niarchos!"

"You should have his baby, doll face!" says Julio Mario in a companionable tone. "You're not getting any younger, are you?"

David reacts in horror: "Virginia is not that kind of girl!"

I look at Julio Mario, and I tell him in Spanish so that David can't understand: "If I didn't have children with you, who are beautiful, why would I have them with that 'peasant'? And don't forget that I'll always be twenty-six years younger than you."

I say that both of them are just jealous because the new moguls work on a global scale and aren't just domestic. And also because my friends are the same age as me, not to mention they're very intelligent peasants.

"My God, darling," cries David with an elegant wave of his hand and sounding like Lord Curzon discovering that Pablo eats soup at brunch. "Intelligence is Henry Kissinger!"

"One thing's for sure: now I really do think you're the bravest man alive," says Julio Mario, roaring with laughter. "Oh, what a fright, David. Your days are numbered before Junior Corleone puts you in a concrete suit!"

Now that my two favorite men are looking at me with new eyes, I feel that this is the happiest day of my life. I tell myself that God has a plan, and that's why I am here today, laughing with them, my two dozen shopping bags in my room, instead of looking at the face of "La Piña" Noriega or Danielito Ortega.

A few days later I'm back in Pablo's arms, and we're both celebrating, though for different reasons. And even if the King of Coke is, along with the grandson of the Viceroy of India, the bravest of men, at the hour of truth he is as human as any King of Beer.

"Oh, what a fright, my love! There I was, alone with all those ugly guys in their military uniforms . . . thinking how they could just toss me into the sea because I had told them that no one in the world has fifty million dollars in cash. Can you believe it? That's how much those sons of bitches wanted, 'in advance'! Just that little chump change, how about that? Do communists think money grows on trees, or what? We were in a yard surrounded by a little white wall about three feet high, and I just kept looking at it, trying to figure out if I could jump it and make it to my plane before they could kidnap me or sell me off to the gringos. And the whole time I was thinking: Why didn't I bring my beloved beauty with me? I miss her so much! Because oh, what ugly women they have there! . . . Well, the important thing is that we're together now. Plus, they lowered the price to a fraction of what they were asking, and now I have that route in case the gringos start putting pressure on Noriega. He's been ours since he helped us mediate when

Martha Nieves Ochoa was abducted, but he could turn on us, because he always works for the highest bidder. And how did things go for you in New York?"

"And are the Sandinistas the ones who are going to introduce you to Fidel Castro?" I ask, before I answer his question.

"Yes, but down the road, supposedly once they make sure we understand each other."

"And why do you want to meet Fidel Castro?"

"Because his island is closer to the Florida Keys than anything else. And now that we know we can pay the price set by communist dictators . . ."

"Yes, but he's intelligent and rich, not ignorant and poor like those Sandinistas. Don't count on him for anything, Pablo. Fidel doesn't just have the gringos close: they're right on top of him in the Keys, not to mention inside, in Guantánamo!"

I change the subject and tell him that while I was dining with a girlfriend at Le Cirque, I ran into Santo Domingo and an English lord who is an acquaintance of mine. They had heard something about us and were dying of curiosity about the *Forbes* list; they asked me about him, and I sensed they were just a bit jealous of his billions. And Julio Mario had the nerve to suggest I have an heir! Pablo asks me what I said, and I tell him, "That he knew perfectly well that in my family several generations of very pretty women had always taken the precaution of getting married before they had children. And that you were already very well married."

Pablo sits thinking for a while, processing this information. I don't realize the nerve I've touched until he starts talking:

"That was very, very good, my love. And now, I'm going to tell you a story I've never told a woman before. You see, before I met you, the woman I loved most in life was named Wendy.... Yes, like in *Peter Pan*, don't laugh. And Wendy Chavarriaga was not a lioness, no, no, no: she was a pack of hounds! Every time she thought I was with another woman, she crashed her car into mine, cut down the door with a chain saw; she came after me with a hammer, kicked me, threatened to kill me, flay and dismember me; she threw every four-letter word in Spanish, Colombian, and Chibcha at me ... and I took it all, everything, because I adored her, I idolized her. Quite simply, I craved Wendy! And she used to go to New York with a dozen girlfriends, not alone like you, and I paid for everything they wanted. But in spite of my warnings, one day she got pregnant. And she went to find my wife at the beauty salon and yelled triumphantly: 'Now, this is a child conceived out of love, not out of duty like yours!'

"The next day I sent four boys for her. They dragged her to a veterinarian and had an abortion performed on her without anesthesia. I never saw her again, and I haven't missed her for a second. Thank God that you are a princess. And next to Wendy, even if you do throw your tantrums sometimes, you're my oasis, Virginia."

I'm stunned. I'm frozen. I'm terrified. A shiver runs down my spine as I tell him, "Yes, thank God my name isn't Wendy or Chavarriaga."

Something of my adoration for him starts to die that night after I hear that horrible story, a painful punch to the gut of any woman with a heart. And I think how God has a plan, and I'm glad I know how far I can go with that man who is so brave in general, and so monstrous in his exceptions. Silently, I wonder if someday that cruel streak will also turn against me; but I tell myself it won't happen, because I'm the exact opposite of that poor girl, and there's a reason why he calls me his "sweet panther."

PABLO IS NOT ABOUT TO CHANGE after appearing in seventh place on the *Forbes* list. He gives a radio interview and says that neither he nor the Ochoas really have that much money, and that they don't even know how much that would be in pesos! He says that those are the fortunes of Santo Domingo and Ardila, and that *Forbes* got them confused. And that if he did have three billion dollars, he would give $2.9 billion to the poor and keep only a hundred million so his family could live peacefully for a century!

Of course, Pablo isn't really interested in pesos, because he knows more about dollars than any Swiss banker. And not only do we always talk in dollars: we do it in dozens of millions, in hundreds of millions, in billions. First, because that's the currency he does business in, and because, in 1984, it is still one of the most stable currencies in the world. And second, because we're both absolutely convinced that estimates in pesos are not reliable in either the medium or long term. The constant devaluations of the Colombian currency, which come to 35 percent annually, make any calculation with strings of zeros to the right grow distorted with the passage of time: a million pesos—a tidy sum in 1974—will be insignificant in 1994, while in those twenty years a million dollars depreciates around only 50 percent.

A week later, Pablo announces that he's brought me a present: it's hidden somewhere on his body, and I have to look for it very, very slowly. He opens his arms in a cross and his hands are empty, so I think it must be something very small and very valuable, like an "oil drop" emerald or a "pigeon blood" ruby. He stays very still and silent while I start at his scalp, and as my fingers move down over every centimeter of his body, I start to undress him. First I take off his shirt, then his belt, his pants . . . and nothing! When I reach his feet, and after stripping him of his shoes, I find hidden in his sock a nine-millimeter Beretta with a marble grip, engraved with his four initials and fully loaded.

"What have we here? Now it's my turn, Mr. Alternate Congressman, and I'm going to get revenge for the night of the revolver. Hands up!"

In a fraction of a second he's on top of me. He twists my arm, disarms me, and puts the barrel in my mouth. I think he must have found out about David, and he's going to kill me.

"This time it's not a game, Virginia. I brought you this because you're going to need it. The license is in my name and it's a loan, got it? If you have to use it, I want you to know I have the best carpet-cleaning service in the country: I don't leave a drop of blood behind. And now you're going to know the truth, my love: I'm not going to be a congressman anymore, or president, or any of that. Very soon you're going to be a warrior's woman, and I came to explain just what the security organizations will do to you the day they show up here asking for me. I'm going to teach you, too, how to shoot yourself so you die right away and you don't end up disfigured or paraplegic. You may have very good aim at the shooting range, but if you don't overcome the fear of killing, an expert can disarm you in seconds. And the first thing all those butchers will do is tear off your clothes . . . and you are the most beautiful thing in the world, right, my darling? So you're going to take off that dress that cost $2,000 or $3,000 before I rip it, and then you're going to come into the bathroom and stand in front of all those full-length mirrors. And I said now! What are you waiting for?"

I obey, because I'm not going to let him ruin a Saint Laurent. Also because I feel extremely relieved and enormously curious, and because the truth is, I have always adored those inflamed looks that precede his caresses. Pablo unloads the gun and stands behind me. He tells me that if you pull a gun with the intention to kill, you have to do it with a completely cool head, knowing you're in control. Then he starts to instruct me on how to place my feet and legs, torso and arms, shoulders and head, when I'm facing several men but protected by a firearm. He shows me what the expression in my eyes should be, my mouth, my whole face, and what my body language should say. He explains what I should feel, how I should think, what they will try to do. With a strange glint in his eyes, he indicates which one I should kill first if there are two, if there are three, or if there are four and they're unarmed or at a prudent distance. Because if there are five or more, and they are armed or coming closer, I should shoot myself before I fall into their hands. He shows me what to do in that case: where to place my fingers and where, exactly, to put the barrel. Again and again he pulls the trigger, again and again he twists my arm until I can't stand the pain anymore and I learn not to let myself be disarmed. While I observe in those mirrors the images of our two naked bodies fighting for control of the gun, I can't help thinking of two Athenian discus throwers or two Spartan wrestlers. Since he is a hundred times stronger than I am, he overpowers me again and again, exploiting that choreography mercilessly to send me on a roller coaster of emotions. He forces me to feel terror, then to lose my fear, to take control, to imagine the pain ... to die of love. Suddenly, he tosses the Beretta to the floor and grabs me by the hair with his left hand, while the final part of that lesson starts to flow out of his lips and into my ears, from his other hand and into my skin: endless, detailed descriptions of the most aberrant forms of torture, the most terrifying, unimaginable, chilling styles that torment can fit itself out in. I try to silence him, to cover my ears with my hands so I can't hear, but he restrains both my arms and covers my mouth while he goes on, not stopping for a second. Finally he finishes reciting all of that punishment dreamed up by a Benedictine inquisitor, all that suffering designed by the depraved mind of some South American military man during Operation Condor. Then, that devil who robs me of life and returns it to me, this man who spoils me and loves me like no one else can, whispers in my ear with a sibilant voice that it's all only a fraction of what awaits me if I don't learn to defend myself from his enemies. He tells me I must hate them with the same ferocity he does, be ready to kill them without hesitation when they're in front of me, and not to doubt for a second that I'll be able to pull the trigger the day they dare come to me to find out about him.

After two minutes of heavenly silence, I ask him why he knows so much about those things. Still exhausted, he replies, "Because in my life I've had to squeeze a lot of people ... a lot of kidnappers. That's why, my love."

After another two minutes of idyllic repose, I ask him how many people. After a pause, he sighs and he replies with the utmost calm that ... it's about two hundred. After another two minutes I ask him how many of those two hundred "died on him."

After another pause and another sigh, he replies "a lot, a

lot." This time I don't give him a rest before I ask him what happened to all the others who were left alive. And this time Escobar doesn't answer. I get up from the place where our pitched battles always end, gather up the bullets, and load the Beretta. I carry it to my safe, take out the copy of the key to the private elevator that opens directly into my apartment, and return with the gun in one hand and my gold key ring in the other. I hand him the key.

"I've never given this to anyone, Pablo. If someday you don't have anywhere else to go, you can always hide here. No one in their right mind would think of looking for you at my house; maybe they'll come here for me, but not for you. Here, in this little heart locket, is the combination to my safe; you'll always find your gun there when I'm out of the city, because from now on it will always be with me and I'll only leave it behind when I take a commercial flight. Now tell me what name you want me to leave with the concierge so they let you into the garage and you can come up when I'm not here."

A tender caress in a long silence, the same deep sadness as always in his eyes, and three words impossible to forget are his response to the infinite gratitude that I deposit in the hands of that formidable, unique, and terrible man. He gives me a gun; I hand him a gold heart. And after we say good-bye, I'm left with not two but two hundred souls vying for my compassion and my sanity. Some inner demon whispers to my conscience that if lovers always replied truthfully to each other's questions, the entire world would freeze in seconds.

AS THE PROVERB GOES, "If you want to kill the bird, cut down the tree where it nests." March 1984 sees the downfall of "Tranquilandia," the largest cocaine-processing laboratory in the world. The citadel in the Yarí jungle was detected by a U.S. satellite, and the American government passed the information on to Minister Lara and the Colombian police. The group of fourteen labs that stretch the length and width of twelve hundred acres produces 3,500 kilos of cocaine a week. It has its own landing strips to ship the drugs immediately out of the country as well as its own roads and comfortable facilities for nearly three hundred workers. The police throw fourteen tons of coke into the Yarí River, and they seize seven planes, a helicopter, vehicles, weapons, and almost twelve thousand drums of chemical supplies for processing cocaine paste into pure cocaine.

I see Pablo a few days before I leave for Venice. He is smiling and calm. He tells me that the laboratories at Tranquilandia and Villa Coca belonged to Jorge and Gonzalo, not to him, and that only a fraction of the figures the police reported had actually been seized. He explains that they all learned a valuable lesson: from now on, the jungle "kitchens" will be mobile, and in the guerrilla-controlled zones they'll pay tolls to the rebel groups. In any case, the merchandise that "fell" is only 10 percent of their total. Compared with the 90 percent that is "crowned," it's irrelevant. He earns $5,000 from every kilo he transports and insures for his clients, and for every kilo of his own he realizes double net profits, because he doesn't have to pay transportation. That's after subtracting all the expenses, like pilots, gasoline, and payments to authorities who cooperate in each country. The last are known in the profession as "the route." The shipments are several tons each, and the crew can earn up to a million dollars per trip; that way, if they're caught by the law and bribery doesn't work, the pilots can hire the best lawyers and pay fines without having to call Colombia. I gradually learn that except in the United States and Canada, bribes always work. The key people along the route are the dictator or ruler, the commander of the air force or police, or the head of customs in whichever tropical country the plane stops to refuel. All of them—chemists, "cooks," guards, pilots, accountants—earn extravagant salaries to make sure they won't steal, turn in their superiors, or hand over the routes. Pablo almost always uses the word "merchandise," not cocaine, and he tells me these things to reassure me, so I'll stop worrying so much about Minister Lara Bonilla's implacable pursuit.

This time, I am going to Italy, so my shopping budget is $100,000. I ask for leave from Grupo Radial, pre-record TV programs for three weeks, and happily depart for Venice, the city founded by the richest merchants in history and the most splendid place ever built on the face of the earth and the waters of the sea.

At the beginning of April 1984, everything in my world is nearly perfect: my young lover is perhaps the most lavish merchant of his own time, and thanks to him I also feel like the happiest, most pampered and beautiful woman on earth. I stop first in Rome to buy dresses for the commercial we'll film in Venice. Today, I've emerged from Sergio Russo's beauty salon wondering why I can never look like this in Colombia. I suppose it's because this style has just cost me hundreds of dollars, and that's a mere fraction of the price of my Odicini dress and my crocodile shoes and handbag.

After Pablo, nothing makes me happier than people staring at me as I walk past the luxury stores lining the city's main street; I have a handsome, elegant, smiling, and proud man on either side of me, both sporting impeccable navy-blue blazers and rings with coats of arms on their fingers. On this perfect day I'm walking down Via Condotti with Alfonso Giraldo Tobón and Count Franco Antamoro de Céspedes. Alfonso is a legendary playboy, and the most adorable and refined man Colombia has ever produced. His father made an enormous fortune after inventing the dandruff product Caspidosán, and Alfonso frittered it away dancing with Soraya, the dreamlike Persian empress, and drinking with princes like Johannes von Thurn und Taxis, the richest in the Holy Roman Empire, "Princie" Baroda of India, and Raimondo Orsini d'Aragona, of the Pontifical Throne. After taking intensive classes from the greatest expert in women, Porfirio Rubirosa—first Trujillo's son-in-law and later married to the two richest women in the world—Alfonso now lives in his favorite city in a wing of a palazzo owned by Orsini. Franco, for his part, is partner in a private bank in Geneva and the grandson of Carlos Manuel de Céspedes, the hero who rang the bells of freedom in Cuba and the first of the great hacienda owners to set all his slaves free. My two old friends make me laugh nonstop, have tender nicknames for me, and are incredibly generous with their words.

Franco exclaims, "At thirty-four you are disgustingly young, Cartagenetta. Forty is the best age for beautiful women. What is someone like you doing living in Colombia? Such a luminous creature urgently needs a rich, handsome husband who's great in bed and has a title!"

"Tomorrow," says Alfonso, "you're going to have dinner with a polo player who is the most beautiful man in Rome, and on Sunday he'll take you to the Polo Club, where all the handsomest men in Italy are. Now, that's eye candy, lover! I already told my friends that the most beautiful woman in Colombia was coming to Rome, and they're all dying to meet you."

I smile happily, because now I finally have a title, too! And I laugh to myself, because I adore the seventh-richest man in the world with all my soul, I have an alternate lover at the level of Porfirio Rubirosa, and I've managed not to lose my head yet over the most beautiful polo player in Colombia. And since Alfonso has perfect taste in all that has been or will ever be, I beg him to take me to Battistoni to buy shirts and to Gucci to buy the most divine layers and leather jackets for "an untamable stud who only wears jeans and tennis shoes to supervise, whip in hand, hundreds of ponies, and about a thousand grooms on his estate." When Aldo Gucci comes into his store, Alfonso introduces us and accuses me with a broad grin of having bought twenty-five thousand dollars' worth of crocodile bags. Though it's really only five thousand, the delighted owner disappears and comes back minutes later with two scarves as gifts, one with little polo horses and another one with flowers that I still have today.

I travel to Venice with half a dozen suitcases loaded down with treasures, and I settle into my suite at the Gritti Palace. I happily tour the city, buy Murano crystal and a bronze for "The Nanny" as Pablo requested, and I prepare to film the commercial. Everything has been planned down to the last detail, but working in the Grand Canal turns out to be simply impossible. I am wearing a spectacular white Léonard dress with flowers, a large straw hat, my turquoise and diamond necklace and earrings, and I have my legs crossed at that perfect angle. Boatloads of tourists catch sight of the cameras, and six or seven of them surround us. The guides point to me and shout "*Un' attrice, vieni! Un' attrice!*" and dozens of Japanese sightseers approach to take my picture and ask for my autograph. At first I find it all very funny; but after a hundred attempts that stretch out over nearly three days, we decide to move to a *caneletto* with a little bridge, from where a *ragazzo* in medieval dress throws me a rose, which I receive smiling and blowing a kiss. Finding the *bello ragazzo biondo* has been another drama, because in Venice everyone lives on tourism, and a blond model charges thousands of dollars. In the end it all works out, and my Venetian commercial will become one of the most memorable in the history of Colombian advertising. For the rest of my life, and because of that unforgettable trip and my high fees, my colleagues will say contemptuously that I was "just a model." The evil tongues of my country will even say that "to cut travel and hotel costs, Alas Publicidad had to reconstruct much of Venice on the Magdalena River!"

Pablo calls me twice a week to tell me that all is well and things are calmer now. Back home, I am counting the hours until I see him, when we'll melt into each other's arms and say how much we missed each other. I'll give him his gifts and rave about life's generosity, and about how marvelous people are to me when I leave Colombia, because in other countries it's not a crime to always look radiant with happiness. And I know he'll smile at me with tenderness and look at me proudly, because he understands me like no one else, and he knows more than anyone the harm envy can do.

After almost a month away, and with so many reasons to celebrate and be happy, who could have imagined the dimensions of the rage and hatred of the owners of a twelve-hundred-acre citadel after it was lost? And at the seizure of a trifling fourteen or sixteen tons of coke at $40,000 or $50,000 a kilo in the streets of the United States, plus the planes, the supplies, and the rest? How could I have guessed that Tranquilandia also belonged to Pablo, and that the losses amounted to nearly a billion dollars at the time, around $2.5 billion today?

And the shot that is fired the day after I return to Bogotá rings out in every corner of Colombia, on all the news programs and in all the newspapers of the planet. It explodes in my head, my happiness dissolves into atoms, and all my hopes are shattered. It explodes in my ears, and my world crumbles in seconds, my dreams crushed. And I know nothing will ever be the same again. That as long as I live, I will never know another day of complete happiness. That the man I have most loved in my life has stopped living and has condemned us to merely survive. That from now on, the freest being on earth will be a mere fugitive from justice, and the man I love will be an eternal outlaw until the day they capture him or the night they kill him.

Why didn't I realize the day of the Beretta that he planned to kill the minister of justice? Why did I go to Italy instead of staying at his side and giving him a million arguments against making a mistake like that? Why is he only surrounded by idiots who don't see the consequences of their actions and assassins for hire who obey him in everything as if he were a god? And why do you punish me so, Lord, when I never hurt a soul? And why is life so cruel, and everything so fleeting? Why does nothing last? And why did you put him in my path to be my cross to bear, when he already had a family and women, partners and politicians, followers and an army, while I had no one and nothing?

At Rodrigo Lara Bonilla's funeral, President Belisario Betancur announces the extradition treaty with the United States will be signed and will go into effect ipso facto. Over and over I see the young, widowed Nancy Lara on TV, her face bathed in tears like mine. Two hours later Pablo calls me. He asks me not to talk, not to interrupt him, and to memorize every one of his words:

"You know they're going to put that death on me, and I have to leave the country. I'm going to be very far away, and I won't be able to write or call, because from now on you'll be the most watched woman in Colombia. Keep that ivory I gave you with you at all times, and practice everything I taught you. Don't trust anyone, especially girlfriends and journalists. Anyone asks about me, you're going to tell them, without exception, that you haven't seen me in almost a year and that I'm in Australia. Leave the presents from Italy at the house of a friend, and I'll send for the suitcases later. If I can't come back to Colombia, I'll send for you as soon as things calm down. And you'll see that with time, everything does calm down. Remember that I love you with all my soul and I'm going to miss you every day. See you soon, Virginia."

"VAYA CON DIOS, *mi vida. Vaya con Dios, mi amor,*" sings Connie Francis in that heartbreaking good-bye that, I don't know why, has moved every fiber of my heart since I was a little girl. But . . . how could I tell a murderer to go with God, knowing that my idealist, my leader of the people, is dead, and this heartless avenger has been born?

All I know is that I'm only an impotent woman. That starting now he will be ever more a stranger, less and less mine . . . that he will be ever more absent, ever more distant . . . that his self-defense will make him ever more merciless, and his thirst for revenge will turn him more ruthless every day . . . and that from now on, every one of his dead will also be mine, and bearing them all is perhaps my only fate.

✂ Cocaine Blues

IN THE WEEKS AFTER Rodrigo Lara Bonilla's assassination, there are hundreds of arrests and raids; confiscated planes, helicopters, yachts, and luxury cars. For the first time ever in Colombia, driving a Mercedes through the city or a Ferrari on the highway is enough to make the police stop you on suspicion, yank you out of the car, barking insults, and unceremoniously cart you away. The proverbial "palm greasing" doesn't work anymore, because the army is everywhere. The Colombians who pay taxes proudly say that *finally!* the country is changing and all the corruption is coming to an end, we couldn't take any more, we were being *Mexicanized*, and Colombia's image is in the trash. The big bosses flee in a stampede to someplace that, it's rumored, could be Panama, because that's where they have their money stashed so the gringos can't confiscate it. Everyone assumes that the United States is going to invade us to build a naval base on the Pacific coast, because

the Panama Canal is drying up and they have to start thinking about its replacement, and about clearing the Darién to
build the Pan-American Highway from Alaska to Patagonia.
Supposedly they're also going to build a military base on the
Atlantic coast just like Guantánamo, because the guerrillas
are building up such strength that all our neighbors—how
embarrassing!—are already complaining that their countries
are being *Colombianized*. The nation is inflamed, the mood is
heated, and everyone understands that decent people are in
favor of both bases, because 60 percent of those against them
are narco-traffickers or communists.

For several weeks my life becomes an authentic hell: every
half hour some unidentified person calls to scream in my ear
everything they could never say to Pablo, things very much
like those he had recited into my ear on that night of the
Beretta and the mirrors. Over time I get used to the insults
and threats, and to the days passing with no news of him; I
also stop crying, I grow stronger, and I think things are better this way, because that murderer was no good for me and
maybe it's best for him to stay in Australia raising sheep and
to leave Colombians—the best and most hardworking people
in the world—in peace. And since life is very short, and in the
end we only have our experiences—"what we've lived, what we
ate and how we danced." As a test to see if Pablo has stopped
hurting me, I go with David Metcalfe to Rio de Janeiro and
Salvador de Bahía to eat *moqueca baiana* and hear Gal Costa,
Caetano Veloso, Maria Bethânia, Gilberto Gil, and all the
other marvels of that subcontinent, a place that must have
been created in heaven by some merciful god and intended for
the most hedonistic people on earth. We tour Brazil's city of
artists and thinkers, which has recently been painted in every

color because of the success of *Dona Flor e Seus Dois Maridos*, the film with Sonia Braga, whom I have just interviewed on one of my TV programs. David looks great in his resort wear—his Savile Row blazers and his pink, coral, and canary pants from Palm Beach—and in the *cidade maravillosa cheia de encantos mil* (the wonderful city of a thousand delights) I debut all the pareo wraps and bikinis I had bought in Italy, and I feel like the Girl from Ipanema as I gaze out at the lagoon, shining under the starry sky of the carioca night. I don't dance samba, because a member of White's Club who stands six foot six inches tall and is twenty-two years older than me may drink caipirinhas, but he roundly refuses to dance to samba, salsa, reggae, vallenato, and all that "Spanish music" of Latin Americans from my generation. For a few short days I feel like I'm in paradise, and I think that finally, after crying a river for Pablo and another for myself, one for the people Pablo has killed and another for our country, life is smiling on me again.

After a few months, everything seems to return to normal. It's said that the Organization of American States supported Colombia and opposed the gringo invasion because one Guantánamo base was enough, and two wouldn't be good for the hemisphere's stability. Also because who wants to deal with all those whining European environmentalists if the gringos destroy the Darién rain forest, with imperialist arguments disguised as pro–free trade? The entire country, without exception—rebels, students, workers, middle and upper class, and domestic workers—celebrates that the Yankees were left all dressed up with nowhere to go, and the big businessmen start to return to the country and retake the helms of their banks, drugstore chains, and soccer teams.

And who better to know the truth about everything that's happening with Pablo and his world than Gilberto Rodríguez Orejuela, his colleague emeritus and lord and master of dozens of journalists? Thank God the Rodríguezes are not enemies of the establishment but rather friends of all the political and bureaucratic elite. They don't have blood on their hands or torture people—well, it's rumored that many years ago they participated in the kidnapping of some Swiss people in Cali, but that was so long ago it's no longer true. Gilberto doesn't keep his money buried in cans underground, like Pablo and the Mexican, but rather in his own banks. He doesn't murder ministers but is a personal friend of Belisario Betancur. They call him "the Chess Player" because he has the brain of one and not the mind of a serial killer. He doesn't wear beige linen in Bogotá but instead navy blue. He doesn't wear tennis shoes; he wears Bottega Veneta, because he's John Gotti. And, lately, all my coworkers comment in low voices that after the billion-dollar blow to the owners of Tranquilandia, Gilberto Rodríguez has become the richest man in Colombia.

Rodríguez is spending more and more time in Bogotá, and every time he's in town he invites me up to his office at Grupo Radial so I can tell him everything that's going on. He claims he's just a simple man from the province and not well informed about the latest news of the capital. Of course, Gilberto knows everything, because his three best friends are Rodolfo González García, Eduardo Mestre Sarmiento, and Hernán Beltz Peralta, the crème de la crème of the Colombian political class. All the representatives from the Valle del Cauca and many from other departments call him frequently. He gives ten or fifteen minutes of his time to each one, and I hear their names while I watch him from the sofa across from his desk. What Gilberto really wants to show me is that he is elegant, popular, and powerful, and that he buys ministers and senators by the dozen; that now my lover is just a fugitive from justice, and he has become the power behind the throne in Colombia. To everyone who calls asking for money—and that's the only thing they call for—he responds in the affirmative. He tells me that to his friends, he sends 100 percent of what he had promised; but to those he doesn't like, he transfers 10 percent, and once he knows their price, he promises that the rest will come another day. To President Alfonso López Michelsen—whom Gilberto Rodríguez idolizes for possessing what he calls "the most formidable, complete, and perverse intelligence in the country"—he gives first-class tickets to Europe. And President López and his wife, Cecilia Caballero, are always traveling to London and Paris, and to Bucharest for procaine injections from the famous gerontologist Anita Aslan, whose patients have a reputation for staying in a perfect state of health, conservation, alertness, and lucidity until the dawn of their second century.

Gilberto is a dyed-in-the-wool liberal. As a child, he and his family had fled from the conservative-led violence in his native Tolima, the rice and coffee region, to settle in the Valle del Cauca, the sugar region. Unlike Escobar and the Ochoas in Antioquia, he owns the entire police force in the valley as well as the security organizations and the army. Gilberto and I talk about everything, but we never mention Pablo by name, not even if the subject is Picasso's *Guernica* or Neruda's "New Love Song for Stalingrad." Escobar and Rodríguez are polar opposites in almost everything. When Pablo sees me, he only has one thing in mind: get my dress off; the eight hours of conversation will come much later. When Gilberto looks at me, the only thing on his mind is Escobar's girlfriend. And when I look at Gilberto, I only have one thing in mind: Pablo's rival. If Pablo is the drama, Gilberto is the comedy, a snake charmer and a box of surprises, one of his Italian shoes in the underworld and the other firmly planted in the establishment. And, for some time now, we have both spoken the same language. We not only enjoy laughing together, but we are also the best-informed people in the country. Ultimately, each of us sympathizes with the other's cause, and the compassion we feel goes both ways.

"But how could a man have such a beauty, such a queen, such a goddess, as a girlfriend? A woman like you is for marrying! You tend her needs every day and never look at another woman again for the rest of your life. And to think I'm already married . . . and to such a beast! It's like living with Kid Pambelé and Pelé, punching all day, kicking all night. Not even in your dreams could you imagine, my queen, what it's like to have to spend every day putting up with a beast who leads you down such a bitter path, while society and the other bankers beat you with the lash of contempt, like you were a pariah. Thank God you understand me. The rich cry, too, don't you believe otherwise. You, to be sure, are a refuge of peace!"

The other fundamental difference between Pablo and Gilberto is that the man I still love, and whom I miss so much, has never underestimated me. Pablo doesn't insult my intelligence, and he doesn't flatter me except when he sees me undone, suffering for him over things I would never dare talk to him about. Also, Pablo would never accept defeat, not from anyone, even the woman he loves. Pablo doesn't talk badly about his accomplices, only about the *galanistas*, his sworn enemies. Pablo always sends 100 percent of what he promises the next day, and he never asks for a receipt. Pablo doesn't talk about small things and never lowers his guard with anyone, especially with me, because for the two of us, nothing is good enough: everything should be better, a thousand times bigger, the utmost, the maximum. Everything in our world—our relationship, our language, our conversations—is macro. We are equally elemental and earthly, dreamy and ambitious, terrible and insatiable, and the only problems we have are two different codes of ethics that are forever clashing. I tell him that I'm forever frightened by the cruelty of evolution, which made the son of God come down to earth to teach us compassion. After a byzantine discussion I have convinced him that his concept of the present should be a hundred years, because for a protagonist of history like him, to live always within the conventional definition of something that doesn't exist, without analyzing causes or foreseeing consequences, is very dangerous. Pablo and I never cease to surprise each other, to shake, contradict, confront, and scandalize each other, to push one another to the limit and feel, briefly, like an all-powerful, human god for whom nothing is impossible. Because there is nothing, nothing in the world that makes an ego thrill more than finding another one of equal size, as long as that ego is of the opposite gender, and the body that encases it ends up under the body of the other.

One night, Gilberto Rodríguez invites me to the celebration of a historic triumph of América de Cali, the soccer team his brother Miguel owns. Miguel is a friendly and chivalrous man, serious and without an ounce of the charming irony that characterizes his older brother. My instinct tells me that he also lacks Gilberto's intellectual curiosity, which is extensive and more of the artistic and existential type than political or historical, like Pablo's. I interview Miguel Rodríguez, chat with him for a few minutes to see how he reacts to my presence—because I'm sure that Gilberto the Big Mouth has already mentioned me to him—and we pose for the photographs. I meet Gilberto's children from his first marriage, who are all very cordial to me, and I take my leave. He insists on walking me to my car, and I insist it isn't necessary, because I know that when he sees my Mitsubishi, the Rodríguez family is going to score the only goal they've been missing.

"But, how lovely your car is, my queen!" he exclaims triumphantly, as if he were standing before a Rolls-Royce Silver Ghost.

"Don't talk nonsense, it's not Cinderella's chariot. It's the little car of a journalist exploited by the Grupo Radial Colombiano. Plus, I think it's time to admit that . . . my heart's not in cars. It's in planes. A fleet of them, in fact."

"Uuuuyyy! And whose hangars are those planes kept in, my dear?"

"Those of a man who's in Australia and will be back soon."

"But . . . don't you know he's been back for a while now? And that his whole fleet is in just one hangar: the police hangar? And when are you coming to Cali, my love? Let's see if, finally, you and I can go out to dinner one night."

I reply that Bogotá has had restaurants since the colonial era, but that on Saturday I'll be in Cali buying antiques from my friend Clara, and I say good-bye.

I don't stop crying until seven at night on Saturday, because Clara already knows, through Beatriz—Joaco's girlfriend and Pablo's sister's neighbor—that Pablo returned to Colombia and went straight to the Jacuzzi with a beauty queen or the pair of models seasoned with marijuana. I thank God that

Gilberto doesn't seem to like lesbians or the Dávilas' Samarian Gold, that he isn't a fugitive from justice, and that he is, definitively, the absolute crowned king of the Valle del Cauca. And, since I treat kings like pawns and pawns like kings, and he and I have already spent some two hundred hours talking and laughing about everything human and divine, about politics and finance, music and literature, philosophy and religion, with the first sip of whiskey I ask him about the real world—in his condition as importer of supplies and chemicals summa cum laude, and not as banker emeritus or any such nonsense:

"What is the formula for cocaine, Gilberto?"

He accepts the blow and immediately gives me a big smile.

"Well . . . you've sure turned into a *mafiosa*, my love! Can it be that in all this time, they didn't give you some intensive classes? What did you talk about with that Australian, then? Did you count sheep, or what?"

"No, we talked about the theory of relativity, which I explained to him step by step until I made him see stars, and he finally understood! And never, ever, ask me about that psychopath again because, on principle, I never talk about one man I've loved with another. So let's have it, your recipe . . . and I promise not to sell it to anyone for less than a hundred million dollars."

"Yes . . . he has never accepted that in this business, like everything in life, sometimes you win and sometimes you lose. Someone steals two hundred kilos here, three hundred there . . . and you resign yourself, because what else can you do? He, on the other hand . . . every time someone steals five kilos, he leaves five people dead! At that rate, he's going to kill off all of humanity!"

And then he gives me an intensive chemistry course: this much cocaine paste, this much sulfuric acid, this much potassium permanganate, this much ether, this much acetone, et cetera, et cetera. When he finishes, he says, "Well, my love, since we speak the same language . . . I'm going to propose a perfectly legal business that will make you a multimillionaire. How well do you get along with Gonzalo, the Mexican?"

I reply that all the bosses respect me, that I was the only TV star present at the forums against extradition, that sooner or later that position is going to cost me my career, and that was the reason why I accepted the job at Grupo Radial Colombiano.

"It's the only parachute I'm going to have the day they take away all my other programs. . . . It's my tragedy to always see these things coming."

"No, no, Virginia! Don't even think about that. A queen like you wasn't born to worry about such silly things. Look: since I'm spending more and more time in Bogotá and Gonzalo lives there, I'd like you to help me convince him that what's best for him, after the blow they've just been dealt in the Yarí, is to work with us, because we are the country's biggest chemical importers. Now, he's truly smart. In Los Angeles, there are a million Mexicans desperate for work of any kind, and they're the best and most honorable people in the world! The people who move the Mexican's merchandise don't steal one gram of it. On the other hand, your friend from Miami has to work with all those *Marielitos*—the murderers, rapists, and thieves that Fidel Castro sent to the gringos in 1980—and they only understand the hard way. That's why the man's gone so crazy! I'm not so ambitious, and I don't want to win every battle: I'll settle for the Wall Street market and the rich kids at Studio 54.

That'll give me enough to live in peace for the rest of my life. The things one does for one's children, *mijita* . . ."

I know how Pablo Escobar, Gustavo Gaviria, Jorge Ochoa, and Gonzalo Rodríguez think and act: as a single concrete block, and more so now that the whole world is after them. I'm not in the business of selling chemical supplies, but I *do* have a passion for the collection, processing, classification, and storage of every kind of information, useful or useless. I don't miss an opportunity, and I ask Gonzalo for a meeting.

The Mexican receives me at the country training site of the Millonarios Club, his soccer team. He comes out and asks me to wait for him, because he has some generals in his office and he doesn't want them to see me. I take a walk through the gardens, which are beautiful and dotted with duck ponds. The time passes quickly as I study the behavior of the dominant male with his rivals and the female ducks. I wait patiently until everyone has gone and Gonzalo is free to talk to me. Pablo's associates have always treated me very well, and I'm delighted at his smile when I tell him I like them all much better than Pablo himself. Gonzalo tells me that he can't speak freely anymore, even in his offices, because anyone could hide a microphone in there. He is a terrible man who began his career as an emerald dealer in the lowest underworld, and next to him, Pablo looks like the Duchess of Alba. He is two years older than us, very dark, thin, and about five feet seven inches tall. He is silent, calculating, and very crafty. He has seventeen haciendas in the eastern plains on Colombia's border with Venezuela, and although they are worth much less, some of them are larger than Nápoles. Like every Colombian landowner, he is ferociously anti-communist, with a virulent hatred for the guerrillas who live off kidnapping and livestock theft. That's why the army is always welcomed to his properties with a *ternera a la llanera* (roasted veal) and boots for the soldiers, who have holes in theirs because of the army's tight budget. When I give him Gilberto's message, the Mexican reflects for a long while, and then he says, "I don't know what's going on between you and Pablo, Virginia . . . I can't stick my nose into it because he's my friend, but that man has been crazy for you since he met you. Personally, I think he doesn't dare show his face to you after what happened. But you have to understand that the blow they hit us with was monumental, the kind no one forgives . . . and things couldn't have been left at that, because one has to demand respect."

And then he starts to tell me everything that's been happening in Panama, and he explains why, with the help of ex-president Alfonso López, things are going to start righting themselves very soon. He adds that almost all of their planes are already safely in several Central American countries, because that's what having the Civil Aviation director in your pocket is for. I tell him about the daily threats I have been receiving since Minister Lara's death, and about the terror I'm living in, and he offers to put men at my disposal to trace the calls and eliminate the people who are turning my life into hell. I respond that I have enough on my conscience with the deaths Pablo is responsible for. And also that, unfortunately for me, I'm the sort who would rather be a victim than a victimizer, and maybe that's why I perfectly understand people who, in a country like ours, take justice into their own hands. He tells me that I'll always be able to count on him, especially when Pablo isn't around, because for the rest of his life he will be grateful for the TV program I made about Medellín sin Tugurios and for my presence at the forums against extradition. I say that his friend has never thanked me for anything, and he replies categorically and in a voice that grows more heated with each phrase:

"He doesn't say anything to you because he's very proud, and after he won your heart, he thinks he's king of the world! But he's talked to me often about your courage and loyalty. That man really needs you, Virginia, because you're the only educated and adult woman he's had in his whole life, and the only one who puts him in his place. Or do you think there's going to be another woman of your caste who bets it all on a criminal like him, without asking anything in return? But, changing the subject . . . how can you be so naive? Don't you know that Gilberto Rodríguez is the sneakiest enemy Pablo Escobar has? How can that scoundrel send a princess like you to run *mafiosos'* errands? If he wants to be my partner, let him get his hands bloody in MAS, killing kidnappers and communists, and quit acting like some great lord. He's nothing but an "Indian-made good" like the rest of us, a drugstore messenger with a bike! Unlike him, I know where my territory is and who my partners are. Tell him I have supplies to last till the year 3000, and that this is no business for an angel like you—it's for a son of a bitch like him, only with balls like Pablo Escobar's. I want you to know that I don't plan to say a word to my friend about this meeting. But remind that so-called Chess Player that there is nothing, nothing, more dangerous a man can do in this life than to test the anger of Pablo Escobar!"

Gonzalo knows perfectly well that neither he nor I will say any of that to Gilberto. I thank him for his time and his trust and say good-bye. I have just learned one of the most valuable lessons of recent years: and it's that the incredibly powerful guild of drug traffickers is much more deeply divided than anyone would believe, and that, wherever Pablo is, the toughest of them will always close ranks around him.

I never understood how Escobar managed to awaken that fierce loyalty and admiration in other strong men. I only saw Gonzalo three or four times in my life, and when they killed him in 1989, I knew that Pablo had only months left to live. They say the Mexican was just another psychopath, that he murdered an entire left-wing political party, and that he was one of the biggest monsters Colombia has produced in its entire history. All that, and much more, is painfully true. But, in honor of the truth, I must also say that that incredibly ugly and heartless man, who, in the eighties, with the help of the army and security organizations, sent hundreds of souls from the Patriotic Union Party and their presidential candidates off to heaven, had a quality that I rarely encountered in Colombia: the character of a real man. Gonzalo Rodríguez Gacha knew how to be a friend. And Gacha, as they called him, as if he were a bastard, was as solid as they come.

When I return to my apartment, I call Luis Carlos Sarmiento Angulo. I inform him that the president of his Banco de Occidente, in Cali, roundly opposes opening accounts there for the Rodríguez Orejuela family. They are now the richest in the Valle del Cauca, with a couple billion dollars and dozens of legitimate companies, including the Workers Bank, the First Interamericas of Panama, and several hundred drugstores.

"Whaaaat?" yells the richest man of the Colombian establishment.

I see Gilberto again in Cali, because he is convinced that my phone is bugged and I'm being closely watched. I tell him I have good news and bad news. The bad news is that Gonzalo thanked him for the offer but said he had supplies to last until 3000.

"Which means he told you to tell me to go to hell . . . and he told you he was the *paisa*'s partner and not mine, right? And I'm sure he told you I was a *marica* because I wasn't a member of MAS. How long did you talk?"

I tell him it was about a quarter of an hour, because he was very busy. Gilberto exclaims, "Don't lie to me, my queen. When it comes to a treasure trove of information like you, a guy talks for three hours, with pleasure. No one talks to you for fifteen minutes! What else did he say?"

"Well, he said that he understands perfectly that you and Miguel are too liberal to kill communists . . . and that he respects ideological differences . . . and that you, who are a brilliant man, know what that means, because he feels bad sending the message with a princess like me. But the good news is that Luis Carlos Sarmiento doesn't see why your drugstores can't be customers at his banks! I told him that you liked to pay your taxes down to the last cent—you and I know that's not out of patriotism, don't we?—and he loved that, because he's the largest taxpayer in the country. My humble theory is that the more magnates pay taxes for real, the more they'll relieve the tax burden on everyone. The problem is that except for you two, who are now the richest men in Colombia, everyone hears that and howls, 'Get back, Satan!' Sarmiento said to tell you he'll see you whenever you want."

"Well, you really are a marvel! You must be a dream of a girlfriend. No, no, not a girlfriend: you were born for much more important things, my love."

"Yes, I was born to be a guardian archangel. To do favors

without asking anything in return, not go into the supply business, Gilberto. Someone like me understands perfectly well that no one can have two billion dollars in just one bank. And now that you're on the right path, don't even think about getting into MAS with my *paisa* friends. Ever."

Since the occasion calls for celebration, we go dancing at Miguel's nightclub. That night Gilberto drinks a lot, and I realize that alcohol transforms him into someone else—he loses his self-control completely. Back at the Intercontinental Hotel, he insists on walking me to my room. I feel terribly uncomfortable as we cross the lobby, because everyone in Cali knows him and everyone in the country knows me. When we reach my door, he insists over and over that he open it himself. He pushes me inside, and the rest is history: because of a *banderilla* thrust into Pablo Escobar's hide, the Trojan War has just started.

A few days later Gilberto comes to Bogotá. He apologizes for what happened, saying he doesn't remember anything, and I tell him I don't, either, thank God. It's entirely untrue, because I have a savant's memory for even the most unremarkable things. He tells me that as proof of how important I am to him, he wants to take me with him to Panama to a meeting with ex-president Alfonso López. He asks me if I know him.

"Of course. At twenty-two years old, Julio Mario Santo Domingo was already seating me at the main table of the presidential campaign, along with President López and President Turbay. And since Pablo Escobar also sat me at the main table at the two forums against extradition, where you were conspicuous in your absence, I think I am the perfect person to cover the news."

In Panama I meet the directors of Gilberto's companies

and his partners. It seems that he has summoned them all to some cardinal conclave, but none of them is named Alfonso López Michelsen. The board is made up of a dozen middle-class men, and the partners seem to be experts in accounting and finance. I can't help thinking how the people around Pablo are always talking politics, while those around Gilberto only talk business. The last thing that could occur to me is that he's invited them there so he can show me off. All I know is that when I return to Bogotá four days later, I hear the first version of the story that will pursue me for the next twenty years of my life, and that will eventually cost me my career. In my absence, Jorge Barón Televisión, the production company of *El Show de las Estrellas*, has received a dozen phone calls from someone whose voice can only be mine, saying I can't attend the scheduled tapings because my face has been horribly slashed with a razor on orders from Pablo Escobar's wife, supposedly because she wanted to take away an enormous black SUV that her husband had given me! When I enter the studio looking perfectly tanned and radiant in my long dress, I hear the assistants and technicians commenting in low voices that I've just come back from having plastic surgery over the weekend in Rio de Janeiro, and the famous surgeon Ivo Pitanguy worked miracles to save my face. With Pablo's millions, they say, nothing is impossible. The entire country enjoys the endless versions of the story and the various models and colors of the car I was stripped of (others talk about a fabulous jewelry collection). Society ladies and almost all of my colleagues in the press gripe to each other about how Ivo and I are such good friends, since he operated on my nose in 1982, because he left me looking "younger and better than ever."

Many days go by before I realize that a certain female chess player has figured out how she can kill two birds with a single stone: while I haven't been hit, kicked, or disfigured except in the fantasies of a woman sick with evil—not to mention those of the journalists at *El Tiempo* and *El Espacio*, a hundred mic-wielding colleagues with whom I've never even gone for coffee, and a million women convinced that youth and beauty are purchased in plastic surgeons' clinics—I've now been made into the protagonist of the most sordid scandals. Plus, Pablo Escobar's innocent wife has been turned into a dangerous and vengeful criminal, and he is painted as an idiot who lets his girlfriend be violently stripped of his gifts and a coward who didn't lift one finger to stop it or to punish the guilty parties.

One night, I return home after a product launch for a publicity agency. After examining me under magnifying glasses for five hours, everyone has concluded that with my long white Mary McFadden gown and my hair pulled into an updo, I look ever so much better than I did two weeks ago. When I enter my apartment, I am surprised to see light coming from the living room. I look in, and there he is. Paging through my photo albums and, one presumes, relieved to see me so intact and unscathed. Happy as can be, as if he hadn't murdered Minister Lara. Smiling, as if I hadn't spent months listening to threats of torture and rape, and fifteen days setting straight stories of beatings and mutilations. Delighted, as if a century hadn't passed since the last time we saw each other. Radiant, as if among eight million Colombians he were my only suitor. Expectant, as if I were his Penelope pining for her Odysseus's return, obliged to rush to him and melt in his arms like passion fruit ice cream with bits of cherry. Just because he's in the newspaper every day and on the covers of magazines flaunting that movie villain's face, the face of a murderer, a psychopath, of an extraditable criminal and fugitive from Bogotá's Modelo prison!

I immediately realize that he doesn't know about the fleeting affair with Gilberto, because there isn't an ounce of reproach in his gaze, only the most absolute adoration. He also immediately realizes that I'm not the same as before. And he succumbs to the temptation of asinine flattery that he'd never used with me before: how I'm the most beautiful thing he's seen in his whole life, how he never imagined that in a long gown and with my hair pulled up I could look like a goddess descended from Olympus, et cetera, et cetera. I pour myself an enormous drink and reply that looking like that and speaking even better have been how I've made a living my whole life. He tells me he's been looking at my magazine covers and wondering why among the five dozen of them none show me as I look in real life. I tell him that, since Colombian magazines don't have the budgets to pay Hernán Díaz—a genius of photography with perfect taste—*Semana* magazine has started the trend of putting serial killers on the cover and turning them into modern myths.

His face is darkening as I go on.

"How did it go in Panama with the magazine owner's father? Is it true that your trade is going to turn over planes and routes and invest fortunes in the country, if Belisario Betancur withdraws the extradition treaty? And how does Alfonso López suggest they'll control the inflation that's going to hit us after an infusion of capital that is more than the entire external debt?"

"Who told you all that? And who is calling you every fifteen minutes at this hour, Virginia?"

I tell him we'll wait for the next call so that, if we're lucky, he can listen to a complete torture session. In his most persuasive voice he tells me not to worry, because the threats can only come from a bunch of harmless *galanistas*. When I don't say a word, he quickly changes his subject and tone.

"What did you do with the things you brought me from Rome? Beatriz says you didn't leave anything with her and that Clara is her witness."

I am stunned, destroyed.

"That's all I need right now, Pablo! Those gifts were worth over $10,000. I think by now you know of my generosity and integrity, but if you want to question them, you're free to do so. But what is this horror? And to think that before I went to Rome I gave both those witches $1,000 to go shopping at Saks! They thought you were gone for good . . . or that you and I would never talk again . . . and since they're both dealers, they stole your suitcase to sell it all, including the bronze, God knows for how much!"

He asks me not to say a word to anyone, because for both of our safety, no one can know that he is back and that we saw each other. He adds that it's time I accept that someone like me cannot have girlfriends, and that people like Clara and Beatriz are capable of doing anything for $10,000. Suddenly, he opens a suitcase and tosses a dozen and a half audiocassettes onto the floor. He informs me that they are my phone conversations and that they were recorded by the police's F2 unit, who work for him. He says they can't be listened to because they're scrambled. When he sees I don't believe him, that I'm neither surprised nor alarmed, and that I'm too emotionally exhausted to get any more furious, he begins asking in a threatening voice:

"Who is the husband of that *mafiosa* who's calling the media to say that my wife cut you? Because we both know perfectly well that this is not the work of Bogotá snobs but of some criminal's wife!"

"I think they're just *galanistas*, Pablo . . . and don't underestimate yourself so much, because my lover, on principle, is, has been, and will always be the richest man in Colombia, not 'some *mafioso*'! You can ask the F2 for the original tapes to find out what his name is. I'm pleased to know you arrived safely. I've spent the past five hours listening to the most refined insults disguised as adulation, and I'm very tired. Good night."

He tells me I'll never see him again in my life. Without answering, I go up to my room, and I hear the elevator going down. To take my mind off the night's events, I put in a cassette with my favorite songs and throw all the bath salts I can find into the tub. I close my eyes, thinking it was lucky that he saw me for the last time in a long gown and not in pajamas, and with my hair in an updo instead of curlers. I ask myself why the hell I need a *mafioso* serial killer like him, and I answer that I don't, I don't, not for anything except help killing myself, of course! But . . . then why am I crying like this while I listen to Sarah Vaughan's "Smoke Gets in Your Eyes" and Shirley Bassey's "Something"? And I tell myself it's only because I'm doomed to never trust anyone, condemned to the most utter solitude, to a life surrounded by vipers. . . . Yes, because that's what all those fat journalists are, and those society women on endless diets, and those spurned men, and that pair of thieves I'd thought were my best friends.

An object falls heavily into the tub. It makes a *splash!* and I open my eyes, terrified. And there, floating in a cloud of bubbles and foam, is the *Virgie Linda I*, the most beautiful toy boat in the world, its sails with striped colors and her name written in white letters.

"It's your first yacht, and if you don't tell me that *mafioso*'s name, I'll take it away right now! No . . . better to drown you in that tub. Yes . . . too bad there's a wall and I can't stand in front of your feet, grab them, and lift them up together . . . slowly . . . nice and slow . . . and you couldn't do anything about it. No, that would get your elegant hairdo all wet, and we want you to look divine in your posthumous photo in *El Espacio*, next to all those other cadavers oozing blood, under a headline that reads . . . mmm . . . 'Good-bye, Goddess'! Do you like that? Better than 'Murdered Mafiosa,' right? What shall we do so you'll tell me who that son of a bitch is, so I can cut him into little pieces? And so I can have his woman's face sliced up, so she'll learn not to mess with my woman's? And with my wife!"

"Bravo, Pablo! That's the way to talk! We'll look for that *galanista mafiosa* all over Colombia, and we'll leave her in pieces like a puzzle, yes sir. And the guy's girlfriend, too!" I exclaim, waving my fists up high and unable to contain an attack of laughter while I try to reach for my little sailboat.

Furious, he snatches it away with one hand and with the other grabs the tape player. He kneels next to the tub and says it isn't a joke, that he only came back to electrocute me, even if he has to spend the rest of his life regretting it. This man I have before me, arms out like he's been crucified, the terror of having lost me to another on every inch of his expression, seems to me the funniest and most pathetic thing I've ever seen. I also think I see in his eyes something of the same desperation that only he, among so many dozens of people, saw in mine that day of the whirlpool. Suddenly, much as I say that the past and the future are the only things that exist, I realize that he is the only thing that fills my existence with the present, the only thing that overflows it and contains it, the only thing that justifies every one of my past sufferings and all those that may await me. I reach toward him, and tugging on his shirt so I can put my arms around his neck, I tell him, "Hey, Pablo, why don't we electrocute ourselves together . . . and you and I can go to heaven, once and for all . . . eternity?"

He sways and for a moment I think he's going to slip into the tub, radio, toy ship, and all. Swiftly, he drops them to the floor and lifts me out of the water, swears that he will only be accepted into hell, wraps me in a towel, and starts rubbing me furiously. And as if all that had nothing to do with me, I start singing to him my translated version of "Fever," the song that's playing now. I admire the tiny details of the toy of my dreams and tell him that the *Virgie Linda II* is going to have to be worthy of a real *mafiosa* and measure at least a hundred feet. . . . Then, trying to recover every instant of the present we had lost, all his demon fantasies and all the nightmares of my poor archangel start up again, to the rhythm of "Cocaine Blues" and those macho songs Johnny Cash sang for convicted murderers. I don't have the slightest intention of translating those for him, because how could a person, in a moment like that, sing to Pablo Escobar in his own language:

I shot a man in Reno just to watch him die?

ℭℛ *Not* That *Pig Who's Richer Than Me!*

"BETTER A TOMB IN COLOMBIA than a jail cell in the United States!" roar the press releases put out by a newly formed insurgent group: Los Extraditables. Although the media outlets claim that its members' names are unknown, the identity of its founders, the profession they share, their proven capacity for revenge, and the amount of capital they have are known in the last town of the most remote corner of Colombia, down to the last village idiot. The detonator of the declaration of war is the new minister of justice, the *galanista* Enrique Parejo: a few days after taking over as Rodrigo Lara's replacement, Parejo has signed the extradition of Carlos Lehder, and of Hernán Botero, banker and the principal stockholder of the Atlético Nacional soccer team, requested by the U.S. government for laundering more than fifty million dollars. Lehder flees the country, but Botero is extradited. All the soccer games are canceled in mourning, and his photo, with feet and hands in chains while FBI agents drag him away, becomes the symbol of the nationalist cause of Los Extraditables.

Gilberto Rodríguez and Jorge Ochoa moved to Spain with their families. Gilberto has told me that the two of them plan to retire from the business to invest a large portion of their capital in Europe. He also says that he's going to miss me and that he'd like to see me again very soon. He knows I am possibly the only woman and journalist with whom he can safely talk about his activity, his colleagues, and the problems of his line of work with the absolute certainty that I would never commit an indiscretion. The truth is, now that I know the vulnerabilities of his profession, the last thing I would do is cause divisions or contribute to those that already exist. I am perfectly aware that at such a pivotal moment for all of them, any disloyal act could even cost me my life. And so, my relationship with that entire world is based on a self-imposed code of omertà, in the finest Cosa Nostra tradition. I watch Gilberto go with something of the *saudade* you feel for someone you're fond of but not in love with, having never been lovers. Although I tell him that I will also miss our long chats, the truth is I haven't forgiven him for handling that fleeting affair with a dose of indiscretion unpardonable in someone of his talents.

In the following months, Pablo and I return to the joy of our early times together, but now that each of our encounters demands careful logistical planning, we take advantage of every minute we can spend together to be deeply, intensely, and completely happy. The planes I travel in are rented, and only the two men who pick me up at the airport, armed with R-15 rifles, know that I am going to see him. Since I live less than 330 feet from the gardens of the American ambassador's residence in Bogotá, Pablo is terribly worried that the DEA could be watching me, or that I could fall into the hands of intelligence organizations. That's why, to put him at ease, I never ask his pilots or his men where they're taking me, or where he's hiding. Our encounters take place at night, in little houses that always seem to be under construction or have very rudimentary facilities. We reach them after traveling several hours, over terrible roads that are muddy and full of potholes. As we approach our destination, I start to see sentry booths to either side, and the boys tell me that we're going to one of Pablo's many houses scattered over the Antioquian country-side. On the way back we always reach the highway in five minutes, and I conclude that everything is designed to make access impossible and facilitate Pablo's flight if he finds himself surrounded. Only later do I learn that many of those incipient constructions were located within Hacienda Nápoles itself; as it was the only place on earth where he felt completely safe, he had begun to prepare the hideouts that would be his refuge during the long series of wars that—as he already knew and I was starting to sense—would consume what remained of his life.

Although we don't say it, we both know that any one of these encounters could be the last. Each has the flavor of a final good-bye, and when I watch him go, I sink into a deep sadness, thinking about what would become of me if they killed him. I still hold out hope that he'll retire from the busi-ness and reach some kind of agreement with the government or the Americans. I miss Fáber, the secretary who used to pick me up at the airport and was almost always the one to bring me money on the eve of my trips. But Pablo explains that his faithful employee is a good man, and that now he has to surround himself with young men who are unafraid to kill, because they've done it many times. The two who pick me up from the airport and bring me back are always different. We are all armed, me with my Beretta, Pablo with an M-5 machine gun or a German pistol, and the boys with mini-Uzi machine guns or R-15 or AK-47 rifles, the same ones the guerrillas use.

I always wait for him in the house, with the pistol in one pocket and the license for it in the other, completely silent. When I hear the jeeps coming, I turn off the light and look out one of the windows to be sure it isn't the Dijín—secret police—or DAS or the army. Pablo has taught me that if it is any of them, I must shoot myself before they can interrogate me. What he doesn't know is that I've also been mentally preparing myself to shoot him if he's arrested in front of me, because I know that in less than twenty-four hours he'd be in a cell he would never come out of again, and I'd rather take his life with my own hands than see him extradited.

I only breathe easy when I see him arrive with a small army of men who immediately vanish. Then everything is silent again, and only the crickets' song and the whisper of the breeze through the leaves can be heard. It seems to me that except for the two men who escort me there and back, none of those fifteen or twenty men in his convoy knows he is coming to see me. But from my window I begin to recognize some of the people who later on will become his most recognized mercenary assassins, baptized in Colombia as *sicarios*, or hit men, and by media and journalists on Pablo's payroll as the "Military Wing of the Medellín Cartel." In reality, his right-hand men are just a small gang of murderers from the Medellín ghettos, armed with rifles or machine guns and able to subcontract others just like them: hundreds of thousands of discontented youth who grew up with a visceral hatred of society and idolize Escobar as a symbol of anti-imperialist struggle; they are willing to do anything to fulfill his orders in the secret hope they'll catch some of the legendary financial success of "El Patrón," their boss. Some of his hit men have terrible faces, and others, like Pinina, are smiling and angelic. Pablo doesn't have deputies or confidants because, though he loves his men, he doesn't fully trust anyone. He is aware that a mercenary, no matter how well paid he is, will always sell his armed hand, his information, his heart and soul to the highest bidder, especially in such a profitable business. With some sadness, he admits to me one day that if he dies, he's sure they will all switch to the ranks of whoever kills him. On more than one occasion I've heard him say:

"I don't talk about my 'kitchens' with the accountants, or about accounting with the 'cooks.' I don't talk politics with the pilots, or with Santofimio about my routes. I never ever talk about my girlfriend with my family or my men, and I would never talk to you, either, about my family problems or the missions of my boys."

The "Financial Wing of the Medellín Cartel"—which sounds like a complex web of banks and corporations in the Bahamas, Grand Cayman Islands, and Luxembourg—is simply Pablo's brother "Osito" Escobar; Mr. Molina; Carlos Aguilar, alias "El Mugre"; a few bill counters; and another half-dozen men tasked with packing the rolls of bills into appliances in Miami. Laundering one hundred million dollars is much more complicated than stuffing it in two hundred freezers, refrigerators, and TVs and shipping them from the United States to Colombia. There, the proverbial friendliness of customs agents makes things easy, and it cuts down on one of the worst vices of the Colombian state: *tramitología*, or endless bureaucratic paperwork. Needless to say, bureaucracy is for dummies—that is, for honest people because who would ever make the rich stand in line and fill out forms, or open their suitcases and boxes at customs, as if they were common smugglers?

Among a dozen big bosses, only Gilberto Rodríguez Orejuela pays taxes down to the last cent on his legitimate companies and has a need for traditional banks, because he dreams that one day society will recognize his children as coming from businessmen and not drug traffickers. In Pablo's and Gonzalo's cases, their only use for their registered companies is to justify the acquisition of real estate, planes, and vehicles to the tax man. When it comes to serious money, and the purchase of weapons, giraffes, and luxury toys, they both laugh in the faces of domestic bankers, not to mention Swiss ones. They have haciendas of five to twenty-five thousand acres complete with landing strips, and in their minds big cans were invented so they could store their money under their own ground. They'll withdraw it in an emergency without asking some little bank manager's permission, and they'll spend it on protection, girding themselves against war and having their large-scale fun, all without explanations to the treasury.

Those are the days when the poor director general of police in Bogotá earns some $5,000 a month, and the poor police of some villages in semi-jungle territories earn between $20,000 and $50,000—and they don't have to worry about pensions for disability, retirement, or death or about working their way up the institutional ladder. All those zones that the central government had forgotten about ages ago start to develop at vertiginous speed, sprouting discos full of multicolored lights and good-time girls, where you can find the police commander conversing democratically with the region's trafficker, or the army captain chatting with the paramilitary commander, or the town's mayor with the guerrilla front's leader. And the next day, the Bogotá newspapers will be full of stories of these unlikely pairs killing each other, supposedly for political or military, ideological or patriotic, legal or judicial reasons, while, in fact, it had been spurred by alcohol and exacerbated by the whims of a common target in a skirt. Or else it's over a betrayal of a deal, the kind of financial arrangement that cannot be registered with a notary. Everyone in the southeast of the country drinks Royal Salute whiskey, the villages fill up with narco-Toyotas, and the people in the jungle have an even better time than in the discos owned by Pelusa Ocampo in Medellín and Miguel Rodríguez Orejuela in Cali. And they are, without a doubt, happier than in Bogotá, where it rains all the time and people live with crazy traffic jams, the lines at state offices, the *raponeros* who steal watches, handbags, and earrings, and thousands of buses that spit out black smoke during the day and white smoke at night. Another problem with the capital is that since Bogotá is not the jungle, drug trafficking is still taboo there and the narcos aren't socially acceptable. Not because they're illegal—who cares about *that*?—but because narcos come from lower classes and are short, dark, ugly, ostentatious, and covered with gold chains, or bracelets, or diamond rings on their pinkies. What *is* accepted and in fact very well looked upon in Bogotá—as in any self-respecting metropolis—is the consumption of pure cocaine rocks among the upper classes. They've also started to indulge in *basuco* (cocaine paste) and crack, because drugs fall into the same category as prostitution and abortion: it's in very poor taste to produce or offer them, but it's perfectly acceptable to consume them.

The King of Cocaine and founder and soul of Los Extraditables has a secret girlfriend, one who goes to target practice with the officers of the El Castillo police station and who, ever more elegant, frequents the presidential palace and cocktail parties at embassies and attends her cousins' weddings at the Jockey Club of Bogotá and the Club Colombia in Cali. One morning at three, when a sink collapses in her apartment and the surge of water shooting everywhere threatens to flood it, four fire trucks arrive in less than three minutes, making a frightening racket. The sirens at the American ambassador's residence sound, and her neighbors assume she's been assaulted again. The firemen save her from drowning, and wearing a Burberry raincoat over her negligee, she signs autographs for her heroes until 4:30 a.m.

Another night, someone very important picks her up in a little car to go to dinner, and when she asks her friend about all those rolls of red and black cloth in the back seat, her friend replies, "It's just that since you have such good taste, I wanted you to give me your opinion about the new flag for JEGA, the toughest urban guerrilla group of all time!"

Every well-informed person knows that some of the most interesting, attractive, and important women in the media are girlfriends of the M-19 commanders, but none of us talk about those things because we've been educated in the torture methods of the Holy Inquisition, and we prefer to keep a respectful distance. In 1984, there are some very pretty women in the Colombian media, some upper-class and a few very brave ones. On the other hand, the male journalists, actors, or commentators are incredibly boring, conceited, archconservative, fairly ugly, and from the middle or lower-middle classes, and neither those women nor I would ever consider going out with any of them. What they do have—like my colleagues on the board of directors of the Colombian Association of Announcers—are the most lovely and full professional voices I have heard in any Spanish-speaking country. None of my female colleagues ask me about Pablo Escobar, nor do I ask them about the *commandantes* Antonio Navarro or Carlos Pizarro, and I presume that after Martha Nieves Ochoa's kidnapping, Los Extraditables and M-19 must hate each other to death. But I always figure they tell their boyfriends everything, just as I tell everything to mine. Pablo laughs at the story of the firefighters for a long while, but then turns very serious and asks me in alarm, "And where was the Beretta while you were signing autographs for two dozen men in that negligee from Montenapoleone?"

I tell him it was in the pocket of the raincoat I put on top of it. He tells me not to insult his intelligence, because he knows perfectly well that when I'm in Bogotá I keep it stored in the safe. I promise that from now on I'll sleep with it under my pillow, and he only relaxes after I swear it over and over while I cover him with kisses. Although we've been nicknamed "Coca-Cola"—supposedly because Pablo supplies the product (coke) and I the anatomical part (*cola* means "tail" in Spanish)—the truth is that almost no one knows about this clandestine phase of our relationship. I tell anyone who tries to find out about Pablo that I haven't seen him in ages. I never ask him what he says when he's asked about me, because I don't want to risk hearing words from his mouth that could hurt me. Pablo thinks women suffer much more than men; I tell him that's true, but only during wartime, because in everyday life it's easier to be a woman than a man: we always know what we have to do—take care of the children, take care of the men, take care of the old folks, take care of the animals, take care of the crops or the garden, and take care of our house. With an expression full of compassion for his gender, I add that "being a man is much more difficult, just such a challenge every day." I do it to get rid of some of that blessed gender superiority of his, because Pablo only admires other men—the women he truly respects can be counted on the fingers of one hand. Though he'll never admit it to me, I know he divides the feminine sex into three categories: family, whom he loves although they bore him; the pretty ones, who entertain him and whom he always pays for one night of love before he says good-bye; and all the rest, who are "ugly" or "chickens," and to whom he is largely indifferent. When it comes to me, however . . . I come from another class and I am not impressed with him: he isn't tall or beautiful or elegant or wise. I am a real woman who makes him laugh, and I'm not nearly as disfigured as people say I am. I walk around armed and protect him with my life. I am his "panther." I talk to him about the things men talk about, and I know how to speak their language. Because of all of that, and because Pablo only admires and respects brave people, I think he has me in some kind of emotional limbo alongside Maggie Thatcher: not at all feminine but certainly 180 degrees from his masculine universe.

After his family, the most sacred thing to him are his partners. Although he would never say it, I get the feeling that the men in his family, except for his cousin Gustavo and his brother "Osito," bore him with their conventionality. Much more exciting are his friends Gonzalo, Jorge, and crazy Lehder, just as audacious, rich, hedonistic, gutsy, and unscrupulous as he is. I know that the departure of Jorge Ochoa, whom Pablo loves like a brother, has hit him terribly hard, because he may never return to Colombia. With the exception of Lehder, none of them have been requested for extradition because the United States still doesn't have concrete evidence that they are drug traffickers. All this is about to change.

After a few weeks of idyllic happiness, Pablo tells me he has to return to Nicaragua. I try to dissuade him with every argument I can think of, because I'm convinced the Sandinistas bring him bad luck. I tell him it's one thing that they are communists and he is a trafficker, and quite another that as sworn enemies of Uncle Sam they are linking the ideology of the former with the latter's billions. I insist that the gringos don't care about Marxist dictatorships as long as they don't directly challenge them or have any money. But take one that's a neighbor of both the United States and Fidel Castro, and enrich it with drug trafficking money, and with time it will become a dangerous threat. I also insist that he can't risk his life, his business, and his mental health for Hernán Botero and Carlos Lehder. He replies, offended, that the cause of each and every one of the Colombian extraditables, large and small, rich and poor, is, has been, and will be his as long as he lives. He promises he'll be back soon and we'll see each other again, or that we'll meet in the near future somewhere in Central America so we can spend some time together. Before he says good-bye, he warns me again to be very careful with my phones, with my friends, and with his gun. This time when I watch him go I'm not just sad, I'm terribly worried about his simultaneous dalliances with the extreme left and the extreme right. I wonder which of the Colombian rebel groups acted as mediator with the Sandinistas. Every time I try to bring the subject up, he replies that I'll know when the time is right.

Not only does the beginning of an answer arrive in the most unexpected way, but it also makes me realize immediately that what is at stake is much more complex than it appeared at first glance.

The photos are seen by the entire world: Escobar and Rodríguez Gacha loading seven and a half tons of coke onto a plane on a landing strip owned by the "Nica" government. One of the pilots of the organization—now baptized the "Medellín Cartel" by the Americans—had fallen into the DEA's hands. His name is Federico Vaughan. The DEA promised to help reduce his sentence to the minimum if he returned to Nicaragua as if nothing had happened, with cameras hidden in the plane's fuselage. The U.S. government would have photographic evidence that Pablo Escobar and his associates really are drug traffickers, and they could present official requests to the Colombian government for their extradition. But for the Americans, there is something else much more important than chucking Escobar, Ochoa, Lehder, and Rodríguez Gacha into a cell and throwing away the key: the evidence that the Sandinista junta is involved in narcotics trafficking, something that could morally justify military interventions in an area of the world that is quickly becoming a hotbed of threats to them—a belt of dictatorial, communist, military, or corrupt governments that could spread and prompt massive migration to the United States. In Mexico's case, the eternally dominant Institutional Revolutionary Party (PRI) is overtly sympathetic to Fidel Castro and some of the most leftist governments in the world. That nation with the strongest cultural identity in all Latin America—"so far from God and so close to the United States"—is also becoming an obligatory drug trafficking route that enriches not only the big Aztec bosses but also a police force and military famed to be among the most corrupt on earth.

With the photos of Pablo and Gonzalo in Nicaragua, the first chapter of the Iran-Contra affair has just been written, along with the beginning of the end of General Manuel Antonio Noriega's era in Panama. When I see them in all the world's newspapers, I thank God that Pablo didn't take me with him to Nicaragua on his first trip, or after Minister Lara's murder, and especially not now. He is starting to use ever more anti-American language against Reagan's government, and I harbor a deep-seated fear that in time the man I love will become one of the most wanted men in the world, because while it's true his best quality is his unique ability to anticipate everything that's bearing down on him and to prepare a crushing counterattack, his worst defect is an utter lack of humility in recognizing and correcting his mistakes, and an even greater inability to measure the consequences of his actions.

One day, Gloria Gaitán announces she's going to bring the journalist Valerio Riva, who's visiting from Rome, to see me. They arrive at my house with cameramen in tow, set up some lights, and almost without my permission, the Italian starts to interview me for his country's TV. Then, he tells me that the producers Mario and Vittorio Cecchi Gori—the most powerful in Italy, along with Dino De Laurentiis—are interested in making a movie about Pablo Escobar's life. I say I'll give them an answer as soon as Pablo is back from Australia, and after I meet with Riva and the producers in Rome, where I plan to travel soon. Yes, to Rome and to Madrid, because while the days of separation have been turning into another two months without hearing from Pablo, I've decided that this time I've had enough, and I'm not going to wait for him to get tired of "those ugly guys in uniform" or the beauty queen of the moment. And I've accepted an invitation to go to Europe from Gilberto Rodríguez, who does miss me a lot and can't talk to me over the phone. Whom does he have in Madrid to talk to about "La Piña" Noriega and Daniel Ortega, about Joseph Conrad and Stefan Zweig, about the M-19 and the FARC, about Peter the Great and Toscanini, the Mexican and the PRI, about his favorite works of art—Sophia Loren and all the Renoirs—about the convict banker Jaime Michelsen and Alfonso López Michelsen, about Kid Pambelé and Pelé, about Belisario Betancur and the Beast, and the correct way to eat asparagus? And who else can I talk to about Carlos Lehder, the informant pilot Barry Seal, the CIA, and another ton of subjects I've been suppressing, without my interlocutor running for the hills?

A few days before I leave, I pass by Raad Automobiles, owned by my friend Teddy Raad, whose wedding Aníbal Turbay and I had been in. Like the painter Fernando Botero, the decorator Santiago Medina, and the helicopter salesman and art dealer Byron López, the Raads have gotten very rich providing the emerging classes with luxury goods—in his case, Mercedeses, BMWs, Porsches, Audis, Maseratis, and Ferraris. I stop in to admire a few cars on sale for a quarter million and up, and I ask Teddy how often he sells one.

"I sell a Mercedes a day, Virgie, though it's another thing for them to pay me! But who's going to tell these guys they can't get a car on credit, when every time they 'crown' a delivery, they come the next day to buy half a dozen? Look, here comes one of our best clients, Hugo Valencia, from Cali."

Hugo is the archetype and embodiment of the *mafioso*, the

kind held in contempt by all the upper classes and honest people of Colombia: he's around twenty-five years old and has an insolent gaze, his skin is very dark, and he's utterly sure of himself. He's about five foot three, and he sports seven gold chains around his neck, four on his wrists, and enormous diamonds on both pinkie fingers. He looks happy as can be, he's ostentatious and very friendly, and I like him right from the first moment. And even better the second, when he says, "Aren't you classy, Virginia! And you're going to Rome? Well, it just so happens . . . I desperately need someone with perfect taste, someone who can convince the owner of Brioni to send a tailor to Cali with a million samples to take my measurements, because I want to order about two hundred suits and three hundred shirts. Would you be offended if I gave you an advance of $10,000 for putting you out like that? And, incidentally: Where do you get those jewels you wear on the covers of all those magazines? Because I want to buy them by the ton for all my girlfriends, who are divine! Though not like you, of course . . ."

With pleasure, I agree to do him the favor, and I promise to bring him back several pairs of Gucci shoes as gifts. And since today I want to see everyone happy, I forget about the theft of Pablo's suitcase, and I send Hugo to Clara and Beatriz so they can help him cover his girlfriends with diamonds and rubies, and in the process earn a small fortune for themselves. We are all enchanted with him and his enormous ego, and we baptize him "the Kid." Another person who is fascinated with Hugo and his liquid millions is that young president of the Banco de Occidente, the one who considered the Valle del Cauca's royal family of drug trafficking to be "a bunch of filthy *mafiosos.*" When the brilliant banker makes friends with the Kid, he decides that in the eyes of his Panamanian branch, Hugo Valencia is indeed a successful businessman, not "a disgusting narco" with competing banks in Colombia and Panama, like Gilberto Rodríguez.

Before going to Madrid, I stop in Rome for the meeting with Valerio Riva and the Cecchi Gori producers. The latter don't show up, but the aspiring scriptwriter for the film about *Il Robin Hood Colombiano* invites me to a Sunday lunch in the country house of Marina Lante della Rovere, who tells me she is a very good friend of the ex-president Turbay, Aníbal's uncle, and now the Colombian ambassador to the Holy See.

The next day, a horrified Alfonso Giraldo shows me one of the major newspapers with commentary on my TV interview: Valerio Riva has described me as the "lover of Latin American tycoons." While we go shopping along Via Condotti, Via Borgognona, and Via Frattina, my dear friend, a conversant and fervent Catholic, begs me to confess all my sins to him.

"Darling, tell me who they are right now. Because if the four boyfriends I know about are tycoons, I am the cardinal of Brunei! Don't tell me that the boy with the hundreds of ponies and the thousand grooms turned out to be the man with the pack of giraffes, the herd of elephants, and the private army. I think you're on the road to perdition, and we urgently need to go to lunch with a prince, like my friend Giuseppe, the legendary Luchino Visconti. They filmed *Il Gattopardo* in his Palermo palazzo, and Queen Isabel stays there when she visits *la Sicilia*."

Laughing, I explain that I have the Midas touch when it comes to the products I recommend, the magazines that put me on their covers, and the men I love, and so my ex-boyfriends have become the five richest men in Colombia. It isn't any fault of mine, but rather of their own ambition. And to reassure him, I tell him that I already left that barbarian with the ponies and the zoo, and that the owner of two banks is waiting for me in Madrid with his partner, another multimillionaire who breeds Thoroughbred horses and whose family is, according to *Forbes* and *Fortune*, the sixth richest in the world.

"Can't ask for anything more chic than that, Poncho!"

He asks if the Brioni suits are for the banker, because elegant men have always worn Savile Row.

"No, no, no. Leave those British tailors to Sunny Marlborough, Westminster, and Julio Mario! This is just a favor I promised to do for a 'baby' in Cali, who's very newly rich and has his hands full with fifteen-year-old girlfriends. He's the exact opposite of that untamed stud who couldn't care less about luxury clothes, gold watches, and all those things he thought were for '*maricas*.'"

I tell the manager of Brioni about the Kid's generosity—and that of his hundreds of colleagues. I also regale him with tales of Cali women's legendary beauty, the weakness the models have for Italians who work in the world of high fashion, the elegant sugar tycoons in the Cauca Valley, the salsa clubs in Cali, and the climate in neighboring Pance. His eyes bulge: he says he's seen a vision of the Virgin Mary, gives me a ton of gifts, and reserves his first-class ticket on Alitalia for the following Sunday.

I have lunch with Alfonso and Prince San Vincenzo on the terrace of the Hassler; here, at midday, a golden gauze floats above the old eternal rose that is Rome. Near the entrance to the restaurant, all the Fendi sisters are happily celebrating one of their birthdays. Asking a Sicilian prince about the Cosa

Nostra is like asking a German about Hitler or a Colombian about Pablo Escobar, and I decide to talk to Alfonso and Giuseppe about Luchino Visconti and the filming of *The Leopard*. As we're saying good-bye, the enchanting prince invites me to tour the Emilia-Romagna region over the weekend. I tell him that, unfortunately, I have to be in Madrid on Friday, because the following week I must go back to work.

And on Friday, I'm dining with Gilberto and Jorge Ochoa at Zalacaín, considered at this time to be the best restaurant in Madrid. They are both happy to see me so radiant, to listen to my stories and to learn that I declined a prince's invitation so I could see them. And I am happy to hear they have retired from the business and are thinking of investing their endless capital in chic things, like construction in Marbella or breeding fighting bulls, and not in hippopotamuses and armies of a thousand hit men armed with R-15 rifles. The name of Gilberto's rival and Jorge's partner is not mentioned for anything, as if he simply didn't exist. But, for some reason I couldn't care to explain, his presence floats above those tablecloths and over that whole sybaritic room, creating a disturbance as if we had been put into a particle accelerator that produces nuclear fission.

Over the weekend we go to lunch on suckling pig next to the Alcázar of Segovia. Gilberto points to a tiny window hundreds of feet up in the tower of the castle wall and tells me that centuries ago, a Moorish slave girl had dropped a little prince from there; a few seconds later, she threw herself after the baby. I'm left sad all afternoon, thinking about the terrors that crossed that poor creature's heart before she hurled herself into the void. On Sunday, several of Gilberto's executives take me to Toledo to see *The Burial of the Count of Orgaz* by

El Greco, one of my favorite artworks in this country of the world's greatest painters. I feel sad again, and again I don't really know why. That night Gilberto and I dine alone, and he asks me about my career. I tell him that in Colombia, fame and beauty only engender monstrous doses of envy, which are nearly always expressed through the media, and in phone threats made by other people sick with malice. He tells me that he's missed me a lot, and he's been feeling a deep need for the woman he can talk to about everything, and in "Colombian." He takes my hand and says that he'd like to have me close by, not in Madrid but in Paris, because he adores the City of Light more than any other, and he never thought that someone like him, of such humble origins, would be able to see it.

"I can't offer you passion by the ton, but since we get along so well, over time you and I could fall in love and maybe have something more serious. You could start your own business, and we'd spend the weekends together. What do you think?"

The truth is that the proposal takes me by surprise, but it's also true that he and I understand each other very well. And not only is the center of Paris a thousand times more beautiful than all of Bogotá's most elegant neighborhoods put together, but, in so many ways, the City of Light is light-years away from the City of Eternal Spring: Medellín. Slowly I start to reply; that is, to list my conditions for becoming the Parisian lover of one of Latin America's richest men—without sacrificing my freedom—and the reasons for each of them: I wouldn't live in a little apartment with a little car, because for that, I could marry any boring Colombian minister with a penthouse, Mercedes, and bodyguards, or any middle-class Frenchman. He would have to spoil me, like exceptionally wealthy men all over the world do with the emblematic women who make them feel proud in public and even prouder in private, because my refinement could fill his life with happiness without much effort, and my elegant friends could be incredibly useful to him in opening many doors. If we did come to fall in love, I would make him feel like a king every day we spent together, and he wouldn't be bored with his life for a minute. But if one day he decided to leave me, I would take only my jewels, and if I decided to leave him to marry another man, I would only take my haute couture wardrobe—requirement sine qua non in Paris for the wife of a man who wants to be taken seriously.

With a smile full of gratitude—because a man with over a billion dollars couldn't ask for more ample or generous conditions—he replies that as soon as he's finished getting settled in Spain and he makes all his investment decisions, we should meet again in person. The most complicated thing for him and Jorge Ochoa is the transfer of their capital, and he can't call me because of the problems with my phone. When we say good-bye, eager to meet again very soon, he recommends that I immediately withdraw my savings from the First Interamericas in Panama, because the Americans are pressuring General Noriega and at any moment they're going to close the bank and freeze all the assets in it.

I follow his advice before this does in fact happen, and two weeks later I travel to Zurich, to consult the Oracle of Delphi about Gilberto's offer; it's surprised me a great deal, and I want to hear the opinion of someone who knows all the rules of the game of international high society. When I see David Metcalfe arrive in our Baur au Lac suite loaded down with Wellington boots, rifles, and ammunition, I ask him how "a terrorist from the White's club" like him can manage to travel the world disguised as a pheasant murderer. He laughs delightedly at the characterization, and he tells me he's going hunting with the king of Spain, who is an absolute dear and not nearly as stuck-up as all those English royals. When I explain my reasons for accepting his invitation this time, he exclaims in horror, "But have you gone mad? You're going to become a don's kept woman? Do you think that all of Paris isn't going to know the very next day how that guy made his fortune? What you have to do, darling, is go right now to Miami or New York and find work at one of those Spanish TV channels!"

I ask him how he would feel if a woman with whom he spoke the same language, who keeps him laughing nonstop, and who has a billion dollars gave him such an offer: to set him up in Paris in a *hôtel particulier* decorated like the Duchess of Windsor's house, with a budget to cover art acquisitions from Sotheby's and Christie's, a chauffeured Bentley, the most demanding chef and the most beautiful flowers, the best tables in luxury restaurants, the perfect tickets to all the concerts and the opera, dream vacations to the most exotic locales . . .

"Weeeeellll . . . I'm human, too! Who wouldn't kill for all that?" he answers, with the little laugh of someone who knows he's been cornered.

"You see? You're like Princess Margaret admiring Elizabeth Taylor's diamond on her own finger: 'It doesn't look so vulgar now, does it, Your Royal Highness?'"

While we are dining in the restaurant that's across from the little Baur au Lac bridge, I tell him that Gilberto owns several labs, and I've always dreamed of a cosmetics business in South America. I add that with my determination and credibility in matters of beauty, I could almost certainly build something successful. With a serious and somewhat sad expression, he comments that I obviously know what someone with a billion dollars is good for, but that some don like Gilberto would never know what to do with a woman like me.

The next morning at breakfast he hands me the *Zeitung*, because he only reads his *Times* of London, *The Wall Street Journal*, and *The Economist*.

"I think those are your friends. You don't even know how lucky you are, darling!"

And there they are—in all the Swiss newspapers, and the American and British ones: photos of Jorge Ochoa and Gilberto Rodríguez. They've been arrested with their wives in Madrid, and they might be extradited to the United States.

I say good-bye to David, take a plane to Madrid, and go straight to the Carabanchel Prison. At the entrance they ask me about the nature of my relationship with the two inmates, and I say I'm a Colombian journalist. They don't let me in, and back at the hotel, Gilberto's executives tell me I need to return immediately to Colombia, before the Spanish authorities can detain me and ask me all sorts of uncomfortable questions.

Half a dozen police and agents follow my every step in the airport, and I only relax once I am on the plane. The truth is that rosé champagne is a palliative for almost any tragedy, and crying in first class is better than crying in economy. And any wailing woman would be consoled by the man who sits down next to me: a carbon copy of Agent 007 in the first James Bond movies. A few minutes later he offers me a handkerchief and shyly asks, "Why are you crying like that, lovely?"

For the next eight hours, that stupendous *madrileña* version of Sean Connery at forty will give me an intensive course on the March and Fierro economic groups, which he works with and are the largest in Spain, and I become a burgeoning authority in capital flows, stocks, and junk bonds, not to mention real estate in Madrid, Marbella, and Puerto Banús, Construcciones y Contratas, the Koplowitz sisters, the king, Cayetana of Alba, Heini and Tita Thyssen, Felipe González, Isabel Preysler, Enrique Sarasola, bullfighters, the Alhambra, the *cante jondo*, the ETA, and the most recent prices of Picassos.

I reach my apartment and listen to the messages on my answering machines. A hundred death threats on one, and on the other, a number only three people know, someone who hangs up dozens of times. To avoid having to think of the horrible way my trip had ended I decide to go to sleep, but I leave both phones connected in case there is news about Gilberto.

"Where have you been?" comes the voice that I haven't heard in almost eleven weeks and whose owner speaks as if he owned me.

"Let me think . . . ," I reply, half-asleep. "On Friday, I was in Rome at the Hassler, having dinner with a Sicilian prince, not a colleague of yours. On Saturday, I was at the Baur au Lac in Zurich consulting with an English lord—not a drug lord—about my possible relocation to Europe. On Monday, I was at the Villa Magna in Madrid, analyzing and considering that possibility. On Tuesday, I was crying at the doors of Carabanchel, because I would no longer be able to settle in Paris as God intended. Since they didn't let me in, on Wednesday I was on an Iberia plane, rehydrating with Perrier-Jouët after crying gallons of tears. And, yesterday, to keep from killing myself after so much tragedy, I was dancing the night away with a man who looked just like James Bond. I am exhausted, and I'm going back to sleep. Good-bye."

He has six or seven telephones, and he never talks more than three minutes on one. When he says "change" and hangs up, I know he's going to call back in a few minutes.

"But what a fairy-tale life you have, princess! Are you trying to tell me that now you can have the noblest or best-looking man because you've just lost the two richest?"

"Only one, because you and I lost each other a while ago— ever since you went to live in Sandinista-land with some little beauty queen. And what I'm trying to tell you is that I have a very busy social life, that I'm terribly sad, and I just want to sleep."

He calls again around three in the afternoon.

"I've made the arrangements to send for you. If you don't come nicely, they'll drag you out in your negligee. Remember, I have your keys."

"And remember that I have your 'ivory.' I'll give them *chumbi* and say it was in self-defense. Good-bye."

Fifteen minutes later, now employing his usual persuasive tone, he tells me that some very important friends of his want to meet me. In our secret code—made of the names of animals in his zoo and of numbers—he insinuates that he's going to introduce me to Tirofijo, leader of the FARC, and other rebel commanders. I reply that everyone, poor and rich, left and right, high and low, dreams of meeting the stars of the screen, and I hang up. But on the fifth call, he leads me to believe that he and his partners are working full steam with the Spanish government so that his best friend and "that lover of mine" are not sent "up" (to the United States), but "down" (to Colombia), and that he wants to tell me the details in person because he can't talk about it over the phone. And I decide that vengeance is sweet:

"He's not my lover . . . but he was going to be. And I'll come."

I hear silence on the other end of the line and I know I've hit the bull's-eye. He warns me: "It's pouring down rain. Bring your rubber boots and a ruana, okay? This isn't Paris, my love, it's the jungle."

I propose that we leave the meeting until the next day, because I still have jet lag and I don't want to get wet.

"No, no, no. I've already seen you bathed in a river, jugs of water, in the ocean, in the swamp . . . in the bathtub, in the shower, in tears . . . a little clean water now isn't going to hurt you, princess. See you tonight."

I decide that to meet Tirofijo one doesn't wear a ruana, but a Hermès parka. And a foulard on one's head and a Louis Vuitton bag, just to see how he reacts. And Wellingtons, not guerrilla boots, so he can see that I'm no communist.

I've never been in a guerrilla encampment, but this one seems to be deserted. The only sound is a radio playing, but very far away.

I guess these guerrilleros go to bed early so they can get up at dawn to steal livestock, nab the kidnappable people while they're still half-asleep, and get Pablo's coke out of their territory before the sun comes up and the police arrive, I conclude. *Old folks get up early, of course, and Tirofijo must be around sixty-five by now. . . .*

The two strangers leave me at the entrance to a little house that is under construction and then vanish. The first thing I do is circle the building with my hand in the pocket of my parka, to be sure that, in fact, no one is there. The little white door is very rudimentary, the kind that locks with a padlock. I go inside and see that the room is about 150 square feet and is made of bricks, cement, and plastic tiles. It's night and the place is cold and dark, but I can see a mattress on the floor in one corner, with a pillow that looks new and a brown wool blanket. I study the place, and I think I can see his radio, his flashlight, a shirt, his small machine gun hanging across from me, and an unlit kerosene lamp. When I lean over the little table to try to light it with my gold lighter, a man leaps from the shadows behind me and grips my neck with his right arm. I think he's going to break it, while he clasps my waist with his left arm and presses me against him.

"Look how I sleep, practically out in the open! See how people who are fighting for a cause live, while princesses travel around Europe with the enemy! Look close, Virginia," he says, letting go of me and lighting the lamp. "Because this, not the Ritz Hotel in Paris, is the last thing you're going to see in your life!"

"You chose to live like this, Pablo, like Che Guevara in the Bolivian jungle, only he didn't have three billion dollars. No one is forcing you, and you and I have been over for a while! Now tell me what you want from me and why you're not wearing a shirt in this cold, because I didn't come to spend the night with you or to sleep on that flea-infested mattress."

"Right, you didn't come to sleep with me. You'll soon find out why you're here, my dear, because the woman of the *Capo di Tutti Capi* doesn't cheat on him with his enemy in front of his friends."

"And no one cheats on the *Diva di Tutti Divi* with models in front of her audience. And stop calling me yours, because I am not 'The Nanny'!"

"Well, my diva, if you don't take off every one of those thousands of dollars you're wearing, I'll call my men in to cut them off with razors."

"Do it, Pablo, it's the only thing you haven't done yet! And if you kill me, you're doing me a big favor, because the truth is I've never much liked life, and I won't miss it. And if you mutilate me, no other woman will ever come near you. Go on, call all two hundred of them in here! What are you waiting for?"

He yanks off my parka, rips my blouse, throws me onto that enormous white mattress with blue stripes, tossing me around like a rag doll. He tries to cut off my breathing and starts to rape me while he moans and howls like a beast:

"You told me one day you'd trade me for another pig as rich as me . . . but did you have to choose that one? Precisely that one? Do you want to know what he said about you to my friends? Tomorrow that pathetic jailbird is going to know you've come back to me, one day after you were supposedly crying for him! And in jail, that's going to hit hard! The Mexican told me everything a few days ago . . . because I went through the F2 tapes and I asked him why you called him. He didn't want to tell me anything, but he had to. I couldn't believe that swine of a *maricón* had sent you to my partner . . . you . . . my girlfriend. To get my princess dirty with that kind of business . . . my enchanted princess . . . and that witch he has for a wife was the *mafiosa* who called the stations . . . right, my love? How did I not realize? Who else but her? While I was ready to suffer and die for all of them, that coward climber was trying to steal my girlfriend, my best friend, my partner, my territory, and even my president! Take you to Paris . . . how about that. If Jorge wasn't with him in jail, I'd pay those Spaniards to turn him over to the gringos! You have no idea how I hate you, Virginia, how I've dreamed of killing you all these days. I adored you, and you ruined everything! Why didn't I just let you drown? Look, this is what it feels like when you're drowning: feel it now! I hope you like it, my love, because now you're going to die in my arms. Look at me, I want to see that goddess face breathing its last sigh while I hold you. Die, today you are going to hell with me on top of you and inside you!"

Again and again he presses the pillow over my face. Again and again he holds my nose shut and covers my mouth with his hands. Again and again he squeezes my neck. That night, I experience suffocation in all its forms. I make a superhuman effort not to die, and another one a million times greater not to let out a single sound. For an instant I see the light at the end of the tunnel, but at the last moment he returns me to life and lets me gulp in air while I hear his voice, ever more distant, demanding that I scream, plead for my life, beg. When I don't answer his questions, or say a single word, or look at him, he goes crazy. Suddenly, I'm not struggling or suffering anymore because I don't know if I am alive or dead, and I also stop wondering what that thick layer of viscous, slippery liquid that joins us and separates us is made of—if it's sweat, or damp, or tears—and when I'm about to lose consciousness and he has finished punishing me, insulting me, torturing me, humiliating me, hating me, loving me, and taking revenge for another man or whatever all that horror was for, I hear his voice coming from somewhere neither near nor far, telling me:

"You look horrible! Thank God I'll never see you again. From now on, it's only little girls and whores for me. I'm going to get things ready for your trip home. I'll be back in an hour, and you better be ready! If not, I'll have them drop you in the jungle just as you are."

When life begins to return to my body, I look at myself in the mirror, to be sure I still exist, and to see if my face has changed like it did the afternoon I lost my virginity. Yes, I look terrible, but I know it's not the fault of my skin or my face, but because I've been sobbing and his beard was rubbing against me. By the time he comes back I'm almost completely recovered, and I even think I see a spark of recognition in a fleeting glance from him. In the intervening time I've decided that, since today I am leaving his life for good, the last word will be mine. And I've mentally prepared a good-bye that no man could forget, especially one whose goal is to be the most macho man in the world, twenty-four hours, every single day.

He walks slowly into the room and sits down on the mattress. He puts his elbows on his knees and takes his head in his hands, a gesture that tells me everything. I understand him, too. But I remember almost everything I hear and all that I feel, so I would never be able to forget even if I wanted to, and I know I will never forgive him. I am sitting in a director's chair and I look at him from above, with my left boot crossed over my right thigh. Now he leans against the wall and stares into space. And I do, too, thinking how odd it is that the gazes of a man and a woman who once loved each other madly and respected each other deeply always form a perfect forty-five-degree angle when they are about to say good-bye; they are never face-to-face. Since vengeance is a dish best served cold, I decide to use my sweetest voice to ask about a newborn baby.

"How is your Manuelita, Pablo?"

"She's the most beautiful thing in the world. But you have no right to talk to me about her."

"And why did you give your daughter the name that in other times you wanted to give me?"

"Because she's named Manuela, not Manuelita."

With something of my self-esteem recovered, and now

without fear of losing him—because today he is the one who is losing me—I remind him of the reason for my visit.

"Is it true you're working with Enrique Sarasola to have them sent to Colombia?"

"Yes, but that's not a subject for the press. These are private matters for the families in my trade."

After the two polite questions, I initiate the attack I had planned.

"You know what, Pablo? I was taught that an honest woman only has one fur coat . . . and the only one I've had in my life I bought with my own money, five years ago now."

"My wife has an entire cold-storage room with dozens of fur coats, and she's much more honest than you. If you're trying to get me to give you a new one now, you must be out of your mind!" he exclaims, raising his head in surprise and looking at me with absolute contempt.

Since that was exactly the reply I had anticipated, I continue.

"A girl should be taught that an honest man doesn't have more than one plane. That's why I will never again fall in love with a man who owns a fleet, Pablo. They are terribly cruel."

"Well, there aren't many of us, my dear. Or maybe . . . how many?"

"Three. Or did you think you were the first? And experience has taught me that the only, absolutely the only thing that terrifies a mogul is the possibility of being traded for his rival. Because he tortures himself over and over . . . imagining the woman he loved and who loved him in bed with the other . . . mocking his deficiency, laughing at his . . . shortcomings . . ."

"But do you still not know that that's precisely why I like innocent girls so much, Virginia?" he says with a triumphant look. "Didn't I ever tell you that I like them because they can't make comparisons, not with tycoons or anyone else?"

With a deep sigh of resignation, I pick up my travel bag and stand up. Then—like Manolete about to kill a Miura bull with the most calculated precision, and a tone of voice I have been practicing mentally over and over—I tell Pablo Escobar what I know no other woman has told him or will tell him as long as he lives.

"Well, you see . . . there aren't many women, either, who can make the comparisons I can, my dear. And what I have always wanted to tell you—what I'm absolutely sure of—is that the real reason why you like very young girls isn't because they can't compare you to other magnates, but because they can't compare you to . . . sex symbols. Good-bye, Pablito."

I don't even bother to wait for his reaction, and I leave that horrible place feeling jubilation and the most inexplicable sense of freedom, which briefly replaces all the rage inside me. After walking nearly two hundred yards in the rain that's begun to fall, I finally see Aguilar and Pinina, who are waiting for me with the same smiling faces as always. Behind me I hear the characteristic whistle from El Patrón, and I can picture his gesture as he orders them to communicate his instructions to the six men tasked with the complicated process of returning me home. This time he doesn't put his arm around my shoulder and walk with me, or send me off with a kiss on the forehead. I don't take my hand from the Beretta in my pocket until I reach my house; only as I am putting it away do I realize that it was the only thing he didn't strip me of.

Some days later, *Los Trabajos del Hombre* (*The Jobs of Man*), one of the most-watched prime-time programs of Colombian television, dedicates a complete hour to me to talk about my life as a TV journalist. I ask the jewelry seller to lend me the most eye-catching piece she has, and at some point in the interview, I come out against extradition. Just as soon as the broadcast ends, my phone rings. It's Gonzalo, the Mexican, calling to express his deepest gratitude in the name of Los Extraditables. He tells me I am the bravest woman he's ever met, and the next day Gustavo Gaviria calls to praise my character in similar terms. I tell them it's the least I could do in basic solidarity with Jorge and Gilberto. The director tells me it was the most-watched program all year; but there's not one single word from Pablo, or from the Ochoa or Rodríguez Orejuela families.

JORGE BARÓN informs me he has decided not to renew my contract for *El Show de las Estrellas* for a third year, as we had agreed. He doesn't give me any explanation except that the public watches his show to see the singers, not me. The program has fifty-four rating points on average, the highest in the history of the medium—there is still no cable TV in Colombia. It is shown in several countries, and though they only pay me $1,000 a month, I spend thousands of dollars on my wardrobe; as a result I make much more in product launches for advertising agencies. I warn Barón that he can forget about the international market. A few weeks later, all the foreign channels cancel their contracts, but he makes up for the losses by associating with soccer impresarios from his native Tolima in businesses that move millions of dollars. Later, those same businesses will be investigated by Colombia's attorney general's office, and when they call me to testify in the case against Jorge Barón for illicit gain, I will only state under solemn oath that the one conversation of a personal nature I ever had with him lasted exactly ten minutes. He wanted to find out about my romantic relationship with Pablo Escobar and—once I responded that our friendship was strictly political—Barón informed me that my contract was canceled, because his production company was not in a condition to continue paying me $1,000 a month. I know perfectly well that that director, so ugly and vulgar, had not sacrificed the North American audiences just to save a miserable amount of money: his new partners quite simply had demanded my head.

All the events of that terrible year of 1984 ended up making me a catalyst for a long and complex series of historical processes that would end up with the protagonists of this story in a tomb, in ruin, or in a jail; and all because of that karmic law of cause and effect for which I have always had so much respect and such reverential fear. Maybe it was with that same admiration, or the same dread, that a beloved Sufi poet of the thirteenth century summed up his cosmic vision of crime and punishment in two exquisite actions and only twelve words, to electrify us with a perfect synthesis of the most absolute compassion or, perhaps, to inspire its most sublime form:

"Pull a petal from a lily and you'll make a star tremble."

Me working as a radio and television journalist, 1981.

With Álvaro Gómez, eternal aspirant to
the presidency of the Conservative Party—
assassinated in 1995. The photo is from 1986.

Talking with President Belisario Betancur, 1984.

The laughter of those
happy years, 1984.

From left to right: Julio Mario Santo Domingo, me, Senator Miguel
Faciolince, and President Turbay listening to the candidate, Alfonso López
Michelsen, 1972.

In my gondola in Venice, announcing the stockings of Di Lido, one month before the assassination of Rodrigo Lara in 1984.

Virginia:
No pienses que si no te
llamo no te extraño mucho,
No pienses que si no te veo
No siento tu ausencia.

All that I had left of Pablo was this love poem.

LA CANCIÓN DESESPERADA

esperanzada —
De la vida.

Pablo — no tengo que
vivir horas estras, para
oerte presidente de
Colombia.
Tu amiga, que te
admiro y quiere.

Dora

The vain hopes of my friend, for Pablo.

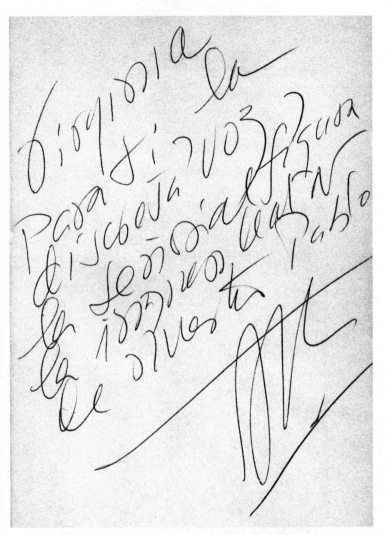

Dedication from Santofimio to Virginia.

A portrait of me by Hernán Díaz, 1987.

One of Pablo's favorites, 1972.

❧ *Under the Sky of Nápoles*

THE PLANE is as big as all eleven of Pablo Escobar's combined, and the man who descends from it, surrounded by his crew and by four young couples, looks like an emperor. He is sixty-five years old, walks as if he were the king of the world, and carries a months-old baby in his arms.

It is the beginning of 1985, and I find myself in the Bogotá airport chatting with dozens of people invited to Miami and Caracas for the book launch of *Love in the Time of Cholera*, the most recent work by Nobel Prize–laureate Gabriel García Márquez, and of the collection "Maestros de la Literatura Universal" ("Masters of World Literature"). Both will be distributed by Bloque De Armas of Venezuela. We—guests of the Colombian branch of the publishing house—are chatting with the editorial czar's local managers who will travel with us and several others who have come to the airport just to greet their boss. Armando de Armas distributes a large portion of all the books published in the Spanish language, and he owns dozens of magazines as well as newspapers and broadcasters in Venezuela. The baby he is holding isn't his grandson, but the youngest of his many children. And, it would seem, the baby's mother stayed behind in Caracas.

Once on the plane, De Armas finds out that I am the most well-known TV journalist in Colombia and that the recent edition of *Cosmopolitan* with me on the cover sold out in a day. Shortly before takeoff he receives a phone call; when he returns to his seat, he looks at me, and in seconds I understand just what one of his helpful managers on the ground has warned him of. It's clear that this man thirty years older than me is not afraid of anything and understands perfectly well that no woman who wears a $3,000 dress, crocodile accessories worth $5,000 more, and jewelry worth $30,000 or $40,000 could be "loaded up" with drugs. Much less if she is known by twenty million people and travels with three suitcases on the largest private airplane in Latin America to spend five days in Miami and Caracas. With the first glass of Cristal rosé champagne I ask Armando for the cover of *Bazaar*, "the only one missing in my collection." And to prove that he couldn't care less about what they say about a woman who looks like me, he responds, "Done!" In the first half hour after we meet, and in front of a dozen people who haven't noticed a thing, we have laid out the rules of the game for a strange and conflictive friendship that will last for years.

When we reach Miami, De Armas and a spectacular model who is traveling with us get into a wine-colored Rolls-Royce that is waiting for them by the plane's stairs. That night, at a very long table where he presides, I learn from his indiscreet managers that "Carolina Herrera," a Bloque de Armas brand that bears the name of his elegant compatriot, is generating considerable losses. The designer, whom I had met recently at a dinner given by the Crespi counts in New York that I attended with David, is married to Reinaldo Herrera, whose friendship with all the richest and most elegant people in the world is invaluable for someone as powerful and ambitious as Armando. While we are in Miami, De Armas asks the famous fashion photographer Iran Issa-Khan, cousin of the Shah of Iran, to take my photo for the cover of *Bazaar* and shoot an extreme close-up to show the world that I have no razor cuts or disfigurations. She spends hours and hours on the photo, but the results leave me terribly disappointed: though it's elegant, indeed, that serious face looks nothing like me. By the time we're in Caracas, and after a long conversation far from the rest of the group, De Armas tells me he is falling in love with me and wants to see me again as soon as possible.

Armando doesn't call me every day, no: he calls once in the morning, once in the afternoon, and again at night. He wakes me up at 6:00 a.m., and I don't complain. At 3:00 p.m. he wants to know who I was lunching with—because I have invitations almost every day—and between 7:00 and 8:00 p.m. he calls to say good night, because he is in the habit of getting up at 3:00 a.m., when we tireless young are just going to bed. The problem is, that is precisely the hour chosen by an extraditable psycho-rapist to call and beg my forgiveness—and, incidentally, to be sure that I am at home and in the arms of no one but the God of Sleep. I hang up the phone, thinking that this is what it's like to be caught between a devil with a fleet of airplanes and the deep blue sea. And that the generational time difference between these two men—one in Caracas and the other in Medellín—is going to end up driving me crazy.

I am working on the noon newscast now, the only one in Colombia that wanted to hire me as anchor. With a superhuman effort and a subhuman budget, we have managed to raise the rating from four points to fourteen, which still doesn't bring veteran journalist Arturo Abella, director and owner of the program, enough to pay fees to Inravisión, the official broadcasting entity. My romance with Pablo is an open secret in both of our professions, but it isn't commonly known, particularly among the type of Bogotá or European friends with whom I often have lunch at Pajares Salinas or La Fragata; in any case, both of us have always categorically denied it. For the past two years I have begged my closest colleagues not to refer to Escobar as a "drug trafficker" but rather as a "former congressman." Almost all of them have reluctantly agreed, perhaps with the secret hope that someday Pablo will grant them something more than an interview.

Every week, a mariachi band comes to serenade me, and following one of these visits, an "anonymous" call comes from a familiar strangler phoning to tell me the credit goes to "The Mexican," who is a world authority in *ranchera* music and who advised him, because he himself prefers hard rock and doesn't understand much about traditional Latin American music. I hang up. His next strategy is to appeal to my deep compassion for the poor and the suffering: "I only have eight planes left, they took the rest away!" he exclaims, and sends eighty orchids to accompany his words. I hang up without a word. Then, "Now I only have six planes left!" with sixty flowers of another color. I hurl the poor telephone in rage, wondering what those gadgets are made of so I can buy stock in the company. The next week it's "You see I'm a poor boy now, with only four planes?" and he sends forty phalaenopsis, as if I didn't know that the planes that aren't in the police hangar are in Panama, Costa Rica, and Nicaragua. Or as if I were ignorant of the fact that he has the resources to buy several replacements and, in passing, to give me a set of rubies or emeralds instead of so many patriotic *cattleya trianae*. And he keeps going, with "Cucurrucucú paloma" and "Tres meses sin verte, mujer," and "María Bonita" and the whole songbook of José Alfredo Jiménez, Lola Beltrán, Agustín Lara, and Jorge Negrete. Again and again, I tell myself, *What does a woman like me need a rapist with a personal airline for, when she has at her feet an honest man with only one airplane and a hundred magazines, who is always surrounded by pretty people, who finances Reinaldo and Carolina Herrera, and calls three times a day to tell her he's crazy for her?*

"Just imagine if you became Carolina's boss!" laughs David from London, in a complimentary tone.

Armando informs me that a Miami channel is looking for an anchor to launch their news program and they want me to try out. I fly there, give an impeccable presentation, and they tell me they'll let me know in a few months if I got the job. That night I have dinner with Cristina Saralegui, who works for Armando, and her husband, Marcos Ávila, who is happy because his band, with Gloria Estefan leading it, has become the sensation of the moment thanks to "La Conga." After several months of courting over the phone, I finally accept Armando's invitation to go to Mexico. This time we travel alone, and at the airport there's a red carpet from the plane's steps to the customs doorway, as if we were the president and first lady of the Andean Community. Since the superrich don't go through customs anywhere—unless they are rock stars suspected of some inspired hallucination—we head to his empire's Mexican facilities, surrounded by another cloud of managers. From an interior balcony I peer down at what looks like a supermarket with thousands of books and magazines grouped in tower after tower, several feet high. I ask what all that is, and Armando tells me they're the titles that will be distributed that week.

"*In a week?*" I exclaim. "And how much do you earn per book?"

"Fifty percent. The writer earns between ten and fifteen."

"Wow! So it's better to be you than García Márquez or Hemingway."

We reach the presidential suite of the María Isabel Sheraton, which has two bedrooms, and that's where the czar of distribution states the true purpose of all that love: he wants to fill me with children. He adores them, and he's chosen me as the lucky mother of the last, and surely the most spoiled, of his fertile existence, in which a dozen extramarital offspring coexist beside the children of his marriage.

"Ask me for whatever you want! You could live like a queen for the rest of your life!" he tells me happily, gazing at me as if I were the champion Holstein cow at the agriculture and cattle fair.

I reply that I love kids, too, but I wouldn't have bastards even with Carlos V, king of Spain and emperor of Germany, or with Louis XIV, the Sun King. He asks me if I would marry him and if once we were married we would have children. After examining his face I tell him no, not if we were married, either, but that I'm sure we would have a grand time.

He gets furious and starts to repeat what they've always said about me in the press:

"I'd heard that you hated children and that you didn't want to have them so you wouldn't ruin your figure! And to top it off you've brought me bad luck, because a strike has just broken out!"

"Well, if you don't have a ticket back to Colombia for me tomorrow, I'll join the picket lines and shout 'Down with foreign exploitation!' in front of all of Televisa's cameras. I don't want to hear another word about moguls with airlines or planes: they're all a bunch of tyrants! Good-bye, Armando."

A week later, he calls me from Caracas at six in the morning to tell me he passed through Colombia to see me after he settled the strike, but he'd had to flee because Pablo Escobar had tried to kidnap him.

"Pablo Escobar has three billion dollars, not three hundred million like you. He is thirty-five years old, like me, not sixty-five like you. He has a dozen planes and not one, like you. Don't confuse Escobar with Tirofijo, because by simple math it should be you thinking about kidnapping Pablo, not the other way around. And stop calling me at this hour! I get up at ten, like he does, not at three in the morning like you."

"So that's why you didn't want to be the mother of my children! You're still in love with the King of Coke. My managers told me you were that criminal's lover!"

I answer that if I were the lover of the seventh-richest man in the world, I would never have set foot on his plane—not in January with his group of guests, and much less go to Mexico with him—and I say good-bye.

I don't believe a word about the supposed kidnapping attempt. Two days later I find ten orchids, a newspaper clipping of my favorite photo, and a note from a man who tells me he now has only one little plane and can't spend the rest of his life without seeing that face on his pillow once more. He calls again and I hang up, and the next long weekend I decide it's time to stop suffering from so much maniacal stalking and return to the peace and calm of traditional values: in the Fountainbleu of Miami, David Metcalfe is waiting for me with a sun umbrella and a rum punch with its own umbrella. Julio Mario Santo Domingo arrives the next day, and when he sees me, he hugs me and spins me around twice, exclaiming, "Look at her, David! Now this is a woman! She came back; she came back! She's left the world of the richest men on the planet and come back to us, the poor ones!"

And, while David watches us with something that looks like the first twinge of jealousy in his entire life, Julio Mario sings laughingly:

"Helloooo, Dolly! It's so nice to have you back where you belong! You're looking sweeelll, Dolly, we can teeelll, Dolly . . ."

In the taxi to the airport where we're going to take the flight back on Avianca, Santo Domingo's airline, he and David are happy, laughing at Ivo Pitanguy's patients who are friends of both of theirs. Julio Mario says that since David saved him a fortune by paying the bill on his room, he is so happy that he'd "gladly stay in that marvelous taxi laughing with us for the rest of his life." When we reach Bogotá, I say good-bye to them, and I watch them as they're whisked away by an army of bodyguards in a dozen and a half vehicles that were waiting for them at the door to the plane. They don't go through customs, either, and someone who works for the Grupo Santo Domingo takes my passport and leads me quickly to another car. I think that it's people like Julio Mario and Armando—not like Pablo and Gilberto—who are the real masters of the world.

A couple of days later a journalist acquaintance of mine asks to see me. He wants to ask for a big favor, with the utmost discretion. I tell him I have a black-tie dinner to attend but that I'd be happy to see him. His name is Édgar Artunduaga, he had been director of *El Espacio*, the evening newspaper of bloody cadavers, and over time he will become a "Father of the Nation." He pleads with me to ask Pablo to help him financially. He says that after he helped Pablo go public with the video of Evaristo Porras's check to minister Rodrigo Lara, no one wants to hire him, and his situation is critical. I explain that dozens of journalists have asked me for similar favors, and that I've always referred them directly to Pablo. I'm not interested in learning of my colleagues' penury, and I don't like acting as intermediary with those kinds of donations. But in his case, I will make an exception, because what he tells me not only moves me deeply but also seems to require an urgent solution.

Pablo knows that I never call a man I'm interested in romantically, not even to return his calls. When I dial his private number and he himself answers, I immediately realize that he's delighted to hear my voice. But when I tell him I have Artunduaga in front of me and I explain what he's come for, he starts to howl like a raging lunatic, and for the first time ever he addresses me with the formal "*usted*."

"Get that sewer rat out of your house before he contaminates it! I'm calling back in fifteen minutes, and if he's still there, I'll borrow three boys from the Mexican, who lives ten blocks away from you, and send them there to kick him out!"

I don't know if Artunduaga can hear Pablo's shrieks and epithets on the other end of the line: he calls him everything from viper to blackmailer, swine, hyena, extortionist, small-time thug. I feel terribly uncomfortable, and when I hang up, I can only tell him that Escobar was annoyed because he doesn't usually touch on matters of third-party payments with me. I add that, if he likes, the next day I can talk with Arturo Abella to see if he'll appoint him as the political editor of the newscast. To bolster his spirits, I tell him I know the director will be happy to accept, because, it seems, he is negotiating the sale of a block of the company's shares to a group of very rich investors.

When Pablo calls back, I've already left for a dinner with David Metcalfe, where I see President López, who asks me who the tall Englishman with me is. I tell him he's the grandson of Lord Curzon, and godson of Edward VIII, and I introduce them. The next day, Arturo Abella tells me that the new prospective owner of the newscast, Fernando Carrillo, wants to invite us to dinner at Pajares Salinas, and that he wants to meet Artunduaga to decide about hiring him. He tells me that Carrillo, main owner of the Santa Fe soccer team of Bogotá, is a personal friend of such dissimilar people as César Villegas, right hand of Álvaro Uribe in Civil Aviation, and Triofijo. He adds that Carrillo has offered to lend us his helicopter so that a colleague and I can interview the legendary rebel leader in the FARC's encampment. Something tells me not to touch this subject in front of Artunduaga, and a couple of hours later I say good-bye to them because I figure David must have finished his business dinner and will be waiting for me so we can see each other before he returns to London.

Abella calls to ask me to stop by his office instead of going to the studio, because he has news. When I arrive he hands me a letter of dismissal, and he informs me that Artunduaga convinced Carrillo to cancel my contract and hire him as anchor. I can't believe my ears or my eyes! Arturo thanks me for the increase of almost ten rating points while I was in front of the camera and explains that the government's costs have ruined him. With tears in his eyes, he tells me he's had no other choice but to sell the entire news program to "those soccer gentlemen." When we say good-bye, I predict that the program will be off the air in six months, because no one turns on the TV, especially at lunchtime, to look at the face of Édgar Artunduaga, whom Pablo Escobar describes as a "sewer rat." (Before the year is over, the company will file for bankruptcy and Carrillo will lose all of his multimillion-dollar investment paying off the station's debts to the government.)

A solitary violinist plays outside my window: "Por una Cabeza," my favorite tango. He plays it three times in a row and then disappears. Two days later, Pablo calls again.

"I heard that someone saw you getting out of an Avianca plane with Santo Domingo and a foreigner. I'm not an airline owner like him, but I've had my own plane since I was thirty! You know I can't go to Bogotá for you; but we're going to stop this foolishness now, because life is very short and neither of us gives a damn about that jailbird. I am dying for the mind behind that face of yours, and I don't have the slightest intention of letting someone else have it, period! If you don't get on my last airplane now—so you can come and tell me why you're out of work—you will have to buy a ticket from Avianca, and that greedy old man Santo Domingo will become one hundred dollars richer with your money!"

Never have I heard a more convincing argument. Pablo may be the most wanted man in the world, but when it comes to the conditions of our relationship, I am the one who sets them. And I exclaim happily, "I'll come. But you'd better not be waiting for me in the airport! I'll come straight back to Bogotá in the first wheelbarrow I can find!"

This plane is a small one, and only the young pilot and I are flying. After a while a torrential rain starts to fall, and suddenly we're left without a radio. There is zero visibility, and with an inexplicable feeling of peace I prepare myself mentally and spiritually for the possibility of death. For a moment, I remember Jaime Bateman's plane in the Panama jungle. The boy asks me to come and sit in the copilot's seat, because four eyes see better than two. I ask him if we could land after 6:00 p.m., when the Medellín airport is closed and the possibility of crashing into another plane will be minimal, and he replies that that is, precisely, what he intends to do. When the weather clears up and we manage to visually locate the landing strip, we touch down with no problem.

I know that Pablo can't even get close to the airport, but two men are waiting for me in the same place as always. They bring me to the office first, to make sure that no one has followed me. If Armando de Armas's business looks like a supermarket, the offices of Pablo's cousin and partner look like a fast-food restaurant at lunchtime. Gustavo Gaviria alternates between pleasure at seeing me return to the excitement of nontraditional values and the telephonic handling of what seems to be a crisis of excess demand:

"It's so good to have you back, Virginia! Things are crazy around here today. . . . What happened with Negro's seven hundred kilos, huh? . . . I'm sending off half a dozen planes today, all rented, of course . . . Mona's four hundred, Holy Mother of God! If they don't fit, that woman will castrate me tomorrow! . . . Pablo isn't about to change for anyone, but you didn't hear that from me. . . . Yáider's six hundred, remember! . . . How do you always manage to look so well rested, huh? . . . The last one is full? . . . . You can't imagine the stress of this profession. . . . Now, that's tragedy, brother! . . . I mean, this work feeds a hundred thousand people, and indirectly a million. . . . Get me another plane, dammit! . . . You can't even imagine our responsibility with all those people. . . . Did this country run out of planes, or what? We're going to have to rent Santo Domingo's jumbo! . . . And the satisfaction of being able to serve the customers . . . oh, God! What are we going to do with the two hundred fifty for Smurfie? He's a new client and I forgot to include him! . . . Oh, they've come to get you, Virginia. . . . That asshole cousin of mine sure is a lucky man, not a poor slave like me!"

Finally I understand why Pablo sent that little plane. It wasn't the last one he had left: it was the last one in all of Colombia! On the way to see him I think about how the moguls' financial groups create one or two thousand jobs each, and feed around ten thousand people, and I wonder if figures like the ones Gustavo has just given me won't end up altering the scale of values. One million people . . . after some two hours on the road, three cars appear from nowhere and surround us. Horrified, I think I'm being kidnapped, or that the Dijín followed me. Someone takes my suitcase and demands I get into another car. After a few seconds of panic, I see that Pablo is driving! He kisses me happily, and we speed off toward Hacienda Nápoles while he tells me, "All I needed, after all these months, was for you to turn into Amelia Earhart on me! The pilot said you never complained for a second, and that you only made him feel calm and serene. Thank you, my love. I don't let rented planes on my landing strip because my security measures are becoming stricter by the hour. You can't imagine how careful I have to be now, and I have to be sure no one is following you! We're going to take advantage of you not having to work, and we'll spend many days together and get back the time we lost with all this stupidity, okay? Promise me you'll forget what happened last year, and that we'll never talk about any of that? Will you?"

I tell him I can't forget anything, but that I stopped thinking about all that a long time ago. Later, already in his arms, I ask him if we're not starting to be like Charlotte Rampling and Dirk Bogarde in *The Night Porter*, and I tell him the story: Years after World War II ends, a beautiful woman of around thirty is married to an orchestra director. One day, Bogarde, the guard who used to rape her in a concentration camp, attends a concert of the famous musician. Rampling and Bogarde recognize each other, and in that instant it begins, a relationship of the most obsessive and perverse sexual dependency between the elegant lady and the now respectable ex-Nazi. I don't tell Pablo that the roles of victim and victimizer are now reversed. It would be too sophisticated a concept for the criminal mind of a man who sleeps with paid teenagers because they remind him of the wife he fell in love with when she was thirteen and slender.

"But what horrible movies you've seen," he replies. "No, no, my love, you have never been unfaithful to your husbands, and I am not a Nazi rapist! Tomorrow I'm going to take you to the most beautiful place in the world so you'll see paradise on earth. I discovered it fairly recently, and I've never shown it to anyone. I know that you'll start to heal there, and to forget what I did to you that night. I know I'm a devil . . . and I couldn't control myself . . . but now I only want to make you happy, immensely happy. I promise."

He asks me to tell him in detail what happened with Jorge Barón and Arturo Abella. He listens to me in complete silence, and as I give him my version of recent events, his face darkens. I tell him, "I think it was Ernesto Samper's revenge for you going public with the checks you made out to him for Alfonso López's presidential campaign. Samper sent Artunduaga, who is his and López's lackey, to find out if it was true that I passed on bribes to journalists. That's the gossip of all those fat, ugly colleagues of mine who would give anything to fly in your jet and sleep in your bed. They all pretend to be my friends so they can get dirt about you and me, and I leave them hanging, because I never talk to anyone about you. Since you asked me to tell him that you wouldn't give him one penny, Artunduaga reported to Samper that you and I still saw each other—that is, you still tell me everything. Ernesto Samper called in a favor from his close friend César Villegas; Villegas asked a favor from his close friend Fernando Carrillo, and Carrillo bought one hundred percent of the newscast's stock. Samper and Artunduaga left me without work: one, because you gave him a ton of cash; and the other, because you didn't give him anything. I don't know how you know people so well, Pablo, but you're never wrong! You should stop counting so much on the people in your trade, because those guys are more jealous of you than my colleagues are of me—all those journalists who could never inspire the love of a millionaire."

Pablo tells me he can talk to Carrillo, who is just another client of the Mexican's, and have Artunduaga fired and rehire me for the spot.

I thank him, but I beg him to understand that I couldn't go back to TV because of a favor from him: I built my career alone, based on my talent, elegance, and independence, and I have never been part of a political deal or gone out with anyone from that world, even for a cup of coffee. I try to make him see how incredible it all is: now that his guild is taking mine over, the third-class *mafiosos* are allying with the politicians whom *Il Capo di Tutti Capi* had bought off and denounced, and they're calling for my head in the vocation that had put food on my table for thirteen years.

"They're taking revenge on you, Pablo, but it's no good for you to confront that wretched crook that 'Doptor Varito' left you in Civil Aviation, for my sake. Watch out, because if an insignificant associate of the Mexican's and a buddy of Alvarito's do this to me, what can you expect from the rest of that ungrateful guild you lead and defend with your life? In any case, I should tell you that I am almost certain that they're going to hire me as the anchorwoman of the newscast of a new Miami channel that's starting up soon. The people who saw the tape say I might be the best Spanish-language news anchor working today. And I think I need to leave Colombia before it's too late."

"But what are you saying? You can't leave me now, my love—you've just come back! You'll see—they'll start calling you for other programs soon. How are you going to live in Miami, when you can't drive a car and a Hispanic channel isn't going to give you a chauffeur? Anyway, they'll hire a Cuban, just watch. I'll die if you leave: I might have myself extradited just so you can come see me in Miami! And what are all the Florida newspapers going to say when they discover that a big TV star is visiting this poor prisoner every Sunday? It would be a scandal: they would fire you from the channel, deport you to Colombia, and separate us forever! We would both end up losing, don't you see, my love? Just wait; tomorrow you'll start to heal from all that suffering. . . . Starting now, you and I are going to be very happy, and you won't want for anything. I swear it on what I love most, which is my daughter, Manuela!"

The outdoor part of the next day—the only twenty-four hours of perfect happiness I ever knew when I lived in Colombia—begins at nearly noon, on a spectacular machine driven by one of the best motorcyclists in the world. At first I clutch his torso with both arms as if I were stuck to him with Krazy Glue, with my hair in the wind and my eyes squeezed shut in terror. But after an hour I feel calmer, and only occasionally grab hold of his shirt and his waist. With gradually opening eyes, I start to look out over all that he has never before wanted to share with anyone.

The most beautiful place that God created on earth is glimpsed from the top of a hill carpeted in perfect grass, neither very tall nor very short, where we are protected from the tropical sun, and also hidden, in the shade of a medium-sized tree. The temperature is also perfect and is unaltered by the occasional breeze that is the only reminder that time has not stopped just to please two lovers. There are nearly 360 degrees of plains for miles, green as jade velvet, with dots of water here and there reflecting the sun. There is not a trace of a human being, not a path, not a house or a sound or any domestic animals. There are no signs that 10,000 years of civilization have preceded us or ever existed at all. We go along discovering it together, pointing to things here and there, and we tell each other that we could be experiencing the first day of creation as Adam and Eve in earthly paradise. We talk about how cruel that couple's fate was, and I tell him that if God exists he must be a sadist. After all, He cursed Humanity to suffer unnecessarily, and he made it cruel to force it to evolve. I ask Pablo if all the land that extends to the horizon is part of Hacienda Nápoles, or if it's a new acquisition. He smiles and says that nothing is really his; then, looking out at the horizon, he adds that God merely gave him the task of caring for it, of keeping it intact and protecting its animals. He thinks for a while, and suddenly he asks me, "Do you really think we're cursed? Do you think that I was born evil, like Judas . . . or like Hitler? And how could you be cursed, when you're like an angel?"

I reply that I can be a devil myself, and I have my little horns. He smiles, and before he can come up with any reciprocal ideas, I add that as long as we're condemned to survive we will be cursed, and that no living being under the sky can escape that destiny. Contemplating all that beauty, an idea occurs to me:

"Do you know the lyrics of John Lennon's 'Imagine'? He must have written it at a moment like this . . . and in a place like this . . . but unlike in the song, everything that you and I are seeing really is worth killing or dying for! Right, Pablo?"

"That's right. For this whole sky, too . . . and I have to take care of it, because I think from now on I won't be able to leave much."

These last words cut to my soul. Since he doesn't realize it, I tell him that with all those passports he has, he should leave Colombia now and live like a king with a new identity.

"What for, my love? Here I can speak my own language, here I'm in charge, and here I can buy off almost anyone. I have the most profitable business on the planet, and I live in an earthly paradise. And here, on all this land of mine and beneath all my sky, you are with me. Where else am I going to get the most beautiful woman in the country to love me like you love me and say the things to me that you do? Where, tell me, where, if when I die the only thing from earth I'm going to be able to bring to hell is the vision of all this perfection, with you at the epicenter of three hundred sixty degrees multiplied by a trillion trillions?"

I am only human, and the truth is that such enormous tenderness cures the most bruised heart in an instant. On that day in May, everything is transparent, the air is diaphanous, and skin doesn't lie. Looking at that sky in raptures, something occurs to me:

"You know what I'm going to call the novel I'll write someday with your story, when you and I are old and have seen it all? *Heaven of the Damned*."

"Ohhh noo! What a horrible name, Virginia. It sounds like a Greek tragedy! Don't play tricks on me, we're working on my biography."

"But don't you realize that any journalist could write your biography if they put their mind to it? Your story, Pablo, is something different: it's the story of all the forms of power that people in this country have at their fingertips and manipulate like puppeteers. I think I could write it, because I know the stories of your profession and *la petite histoire* of the presidential families . . . and the rest."

"Why don't you tell me about all that while we're here these days?"

"What will you give me in return?"

He thinks for a while and then, with a sigh and a caress on my cheek, he says, "You will be the witness to things that no one else will know, because . . . if I die before you . . . maybe you could tell many truths. Look around. Since you have no sense of direction and you never know where you are, I think I can admit that all this is indeed mine. Beyond the horizon, too, so I have no weak flanks. Now look up: What do you see?"

"The sky . . . and the birds . . . and a cloud there, look! The enormous piece of sky that God lent you so you could protect everything below it, and so it would take care of you."

"No, my love. You are a poet, I am a realist: all this we're looking at above us is called airspace of the Colombian government! If I don't take down extradition, that's going to be my problem. That's why I believe I have to be thinking about getting a missile as soon as possible. . . ."

"A missile? But you sound like some kind of modern Genghis Khan, Pablo! Promise me you're not going to talk about these things with anyone else, because they'd think you've lost your mind! Anyway, even if you did get one—because with your money you can buy anything, and with your landing strip you can bring it all home—I don't think it would do you much good, my love. As far as I know, a missile can't be reloaded. So now: let's assume that with one missile—or ten!—you brought down all the air force's planes as they came to violate your airspace. What are you going to do with the gringos who invade us the next day, fire a hundred missiles, and don't leave an atom of paradise behind?"

He is silent for a moment. Then, almost as though thinking aloud, he says very seriously, "Yes . . . I'd have to go straight for a worthwhile target. . . ."

"Stop thinking about all that insanity. It would be easier and cheaper to pay the forty percent of Colombians in poverty to vote 'Pablo for President,' and take down extradition yourself! So tell me, what will I be witness to, and when?"

"Yes, you're right . . . forget it. And surprises aren't meant to be spoiled, my dear."

Now we've stopped being one and returned to two; like Adam and Eve, we feel cold and cover ourselves. He is absorbed, contemplating that airspace with his hands interlaced behind his neck; I am absorbed, contemplating that heaven of the damned with my head resting on his chest. He is dreaming of a missile, I of my book; he is working on his chess game, I'm putting my puzzle together again and again. Now our bodies form a T and I think to myself that we're immensely happy, that all this perfection will also be the vision of paradise that I take to heaven when I die. But . . . how could there be a heaven for me, if he won't be there with me?

IN THE MONTHS THAT FOLLOW, Pablo and I see each other once or twice a week. Every forty-eight hours I'm brought to a different location, and I learn to be even more obsessive about security than he is. I write nonstop, and since I don't watch TV or listen to the radio or read newspapers, I am ignorant of the fact that Escobar has assassinated Tulio Manuel Castro Gil, the judge who brought the case against him for Rodrigo Lara Bonilla's death. After he reads my manuscripts and makes observations and clarifications, we burn them. Little by little, I teach him everything I've learned about the three large powers that exist in Colombia, and the modus operandi of the country's richest families. I try to make him see that with the quantities of money and land he possesses, he should start thinking with more "dynastic" criteria.

"Once you get to know them, you realize some of them are so tight-fisted and so cruel that next to them, you're a decent human being, Pablo. Yes, just how you heard it, and please don't get offended. If it weren't for the bloody guerrillas and the magnates' own lack of greatness, the presidential families and financial groups would have crushed this poor country ages ago. As much as we detest those rebels, they are the only thing that scare and stop the powerful. All of the powers that be, absolutely all, carry the weight of crimes and murders: those they've committed, those of their parents during La Violencia, those of their landowning grandparents, those of slave-owning great-grandparents, or their Inquisitor or *encomendero* great-great-grandparents. Play your cards well, my love; although you've lived a lot, you are still a child, and you have time to correct almost all your mistakes, because you are richer, more astute, and braver than all of them put together. Remember that you have almost half a century of life left ahead of you to make this poor country into one of love instead of war. Don't make any more costly mistakes, Pablo, and use me to your benefit. You and I are much more than a pair of tits and a couple of balls!"

He soaks it in like a sponge, he listens to me and learns, analyzes and questions, compares and memorizes, digests and processes. Writing for myself, editing for him, I store away in my heart the memories and conversations of those days, the last happy ones that he and I will spend together before our 360-degree universe explodes into two 180-degree halves, and finally, into a million atoms that could never be put together again, or even be recognized. Life is cruel and unpredictable, and "God works in mysterious ways."

"Santofimio is coming tomorrow," Pablo announces to me one night. "Needless to say, he's going to ask me for tons of money for the presidential elections next year, and I'm begging you to come to the meeting and make a superhuman effort to hide all that hostility you have toward him. He's been telling everyone that he hasn't seen me since '83, and I want there to be witnesses that he's lying. Why? I don't know yet, Virginia, but I need you there. Please don't tell anyone; just listen, watch, and keep quiet."

"You know it's impossible for me to keep quiet, Pablo. You're going to have to give me an Oscar!"

The next day we meet in one of those huge houses that Pablo and Gustavo rent and constantly cycle through. It's night, and as always we are alone because the bodyguards withdraw when important people are coming. While Pablo talks on the phone, through the door to my left I see Santofimio arrive wearing the red shirt he almost always wears at political events. When he sees me, he makes a move to go back, but right away he realizes it's too late. He comes into the small office and greets me with a kiss on the cheek. Pablo asks us to wait in the living room because he is finishing up a business matter; someone brings us two whiskeys and disappears.

Santofimio asks when I arrived, and I tell him many days ago. He seems surprised, and he asks about the reasons for my absence from TV. I tell him that I, like him, have paid a very high price for my relationship with Pablo. Gustavo joins us, and I know that when the moment arrives, his mission will be to rescue me so Pablo and "the Doctor" can stay and talk about money. There are a scant ten months until the presidential elections of 1986, in which it's a virtual given that the Liberal Party's official candidate, Virgilio Barco, will win. Barco is an MIT engineer from a rich and traditional family, and he's married to an American. The other two candidates are Álvaro Gómez, of the Conservative Party—a brilliant man detested by the left, not so much for anything he did as for his father's crimes during La Violencia—and Luis Carlos Galán of the New Liberalism Party, dissidents from the majority party dominated by the ex-presidents López and Turbay. For a while, I listen patiently to predictions from Pablo and "Santo" about the voting in towns adjacent to Medellín. Before I withdraw to leave them holding forth on the subject they both like best, I decide to lead the conversation toward the one they hate the most.

"Arturo Abella mentioned recently that according to one of his 'trusted sources,' Luis Carlos Galán is considering conceding to Barco so he's not accused of dividing the party for a second time. Galán might even join the official party to help it reach an overwhelming victory over the conservatives, and in 1990, with the gratitude and backing of the liberal ex-presidents, he wouldn't have any rivals for the presidency."

"Abella's source is perfectly crazy! The Liberal Party will never forgive Galán!" Escobar and Santofimio exclaim almost in unison. "Haven't you seen he's coming in third in all the polls, light-years from Álvaro Gómez? Galán is finished, and Virgilio Barco doesn't need his four votes for anything!"

"Yes, yes, I know; but politics is the kingdom of Ripley's Believe It or Not. Galán is finished now, but only because he faced down the whole 'machinery' of the Liberal Party alone. In '89, with the machinery supporting him, you all are going to have to start thinking about what you'll do, because Ernesto Samper is still too green to be president in '90; he's only thirty-four years old. . . ."

"I'll finance Galán before that fucking son of a bitch!" exclaims Pablo.

"Well, Galán will extradite you the day after he takes over," comments Santofimio, annoyed. "If you eliminate him, on the other hand, you'll bring the country to its knees! And you have to make him see that, Virginia."

"No, Alberto. If you two take out Galán, you'll both be extradited the next day. Don't even think about it—we had enough with Rodrigo Lara! And what I'm trying to make you see is that for '90, you need to be thinking about another candidate."

"Galán is finished, and there are still five years until '90, my love," Pablo tells me with visible impatience. "The one we have to start maneuvering now is Barco, and that's why the Doctor is here."

"Come on, Virginia, I want to show you my latest diamond acquisitions," proposes his cousin. I say good-bye to Santofimio and arrange to see Pablo the next day. While Gustavo is taking out big cases from his safe, he tells me, "I'm fed up with all the politics, Virginia. Plus, I am a conservative! What I like is my business, race cars, motorcycles, and diamonds. Look at these beauties. . . . What do you think?"

I tell him that I hate all those politicians, too, but unfortunately, extradition depends on them. And with extradition in place, the only one of us who will be left is me.

"Please, God, let Barco be more reasonable than Betancur, because if he gives Galán the Ministry of Justice, I don't even want to think about the war that'll come next!"

And I start admiring those hundreds of rings that shine in an interminable succession of black velvet trays, twelve by sixteen inches. Gustavo clearly prefers diamonds to freezers full of cash and big cans buried underground. I have never coveted expensive jewels or valuable paintings, but as the saying goes, "diamonds are forever." And, as I look at them, I can't help but wonder with a certain sadness why it is that the man in the next room with three billion dollars to his name and who says he loves me, desires me, and needs me so much has never told me to choose one. Just one.

❧ *That Palace in Flames*

PABLO ESCOBAR has the most modern mind I have ever encountered. A true expert in Caribbean geopolitics, he has built the most profitable industry of all time in under a decade, and now he controls it with an iron fist as if it were a multinational corporation. He combines an exceptional talent for seeing the future with a kind of ancient wisdom that lets him resolve life's practical or urgent issues in a matter of seconds. Presented with a problem, somehow he always has an instantaneous solution ready, the kind that for another human being would be inconceivable and almost impossible to put into practice.

Pablo feels true passion for one thing: the exercise of power to the benefit of his interests. Everything in his life fulfills this purpose, and that obviously includes me. Since I love him and punish him in equal measure—and since I never give myself completely—I am a constant challenge for him. Because of that, he practices the same seduction with me on an individual level that he has started to employ on the collective level, with a country that he sees, treats, and tries to use as if it were merely an extension of Hacienda Nápoles. I am not just the only woman his age he will have in his entire existence, but also the only freethinking and educated one, and because of my profession, to him I will always be his lover behind a camera. When he needs to measure possible reactions to his political discourse, he coldly uses me as an interlocutor—a mixture of defense attorney, prosecutor, witness, judge, and audience—aware that while he is seducing the trophy woman, the camerawoman is analyzing, questioning, cataloging, and almost certainly comparing him with others of his stature.

Escobar is one of the most ruthless men produced in the entire history of a nation where men are often breastfed on hatred, envy, and revenge. But as time goes by and our love evolves, I've begun to see him as an overgrown child burdened with a cross that grows ever heavier. It is made of the responsibilities—some imagined and some bred in anger—typical of those whose ambition fuels an obsession to control and dominate absolutely everything: his circumstances, his environment, his destiny, and even the human beings who form part of his past, present, or future.

My lover is not only one of the country's best-informed men, he is also, like any good son of a teacher, ultimately a moralist, and when he is facing someone whose love or respect he wants to gain, he displays a rigorous ethical code. Every week, someone asks me for an appointment so he or she can offer him, through me, the most fabulous properties at the most laughable prices; with a smile and a caress, Pablo invariably replies, "No." A clear example of the reasons is his answer to the intermediary of Minister Carlos Arturo Marulanda:

"He's offering you his thirty thousand acres in the south of Cesar for only twelve million dollars. Bellacruz doesn't exactly border Nápoles, but with a few additional purchases that aren't worth much, here and here," I tell him, pointing at the maps they have left me, "you can join them farther on and build a gigantic corridor in the center of the country that will take you out toward the coast and into Venezuela. Soon it will be worth much more, because we all know that with the demand from your guild, the prices of land and real estate in Colombia are going to go sky-high."

"Marulanda is Enrique Sarasola's brother-in-law. Tell his emissary that I know Bellacruz is the largest hacienda in the country after some of the Mexican's in the Eastern Plains, where land is worthless, but that I won't give him even one million dollars for it because I am not a heartless bastard like the minister's father. And of course the value is going to double, my love! But first he'll have to find himself some other guy who's as unscrupulous as him and his brother, who's willing to kick out the descendants of all those poor people his father forced from their land in all the chaos during La Violencia."

He explains that there's a ticking time bomb in Bellacruz that sooner or later will end in a bloodbath. The minister's father, Alberto Marulanda Grillo, bought his first fifteen thousand acres in the forties and doubled the size of his huge estate with the help of "Chulavitas," the conservative police who set fire to ranches and raped, tortured, and murdered in the name of whoever contracted their services. Carlos Arturo Marulanda's sister is married to Enrique Sarasola, who is linked to the Spanish company Ateinsa. Sarasola, a close friend of President Felipe González, made 19.6 million dollars on commission and handled the awarding of the so-called engineering contract of the century, the Medellín Metro, to the Hispano-Alemán Metromed Consortium and its partners, among them Ateinsa. The manager of the Metro project, Diego Londoño White—a great friend of Pablo's and owner, with his brother Santiago, of the mansions that Pablo and Gustavo rent as their offices—was in charge of negotiating the contract and processing the juicy commissions. According to someone who had witnessed the rapacity and greed of the group headed by Sarasola, the awarding of the Metro "was more like a gangster movie than an auction for a civil engineering contract," with extravagant honoraria paid to everyone from Colombian lawyers Puyo and Vasco to the German spy Werner Mauss. It's an approach that another social democrat like Pablo Escobar seems fully to share.

The time bomb at Enrique Sarasola's brother-in-law's hacienda would explode in 1996, when Carlos Alberto Marulanda was ambassador to the European Union during the government of Ernesto Samper Pizano. Pursued by squads much like the Chulavitas his father had used half a century earlier, nearly four hundred peasant families would be forced to flee Bellacruz after their houses were burned down and their leaders killed in front of the army. Marulanda, accused of putting together paramilitary groups and violating human rights, would be arrested in Spain in 2001 and extradited to Colombia in 2002. Two weeks later he would be freed on the grounds that the crimes had been committed by paramilitary groups operating in the Cesar region, and not by the president's millionaire friend. According to Amnesty International, what happened on the Bellacruz hacienda constitutes one of the most abhorrent instances of impunity in Colombia's recent history. Diego Londoño White, like his brother Santiago, would later be murdered, and nearly all the beneficiaries of the Metro looting and the crimes of Bellacruz, or their descendants, today enjoy the most gilded exiles in Madrid and Paris.

"I think the time has come to introduce you to my friends who put me in touch with the Sandinistas," Pablo tells me as we're saying good-bye some days later, before I return to Bogotá. "We're preparing something very important, and I want you to tell me what you think of them. If things turn out according to plan, we're going to be able to live in peace. For security reasons, this time I can't even call you: in ten or fifteen days, a pilot will call and invite you to lunch in a certain restaurant. That's the password, and you can decide when during the following two days you want to travel."

In Bogotá I find a letter from Channel 51 in Miami. They want to do a second test and discuss a possible contract. The salary is $5,000 a month, and every day I have to be in the studio at 5:00 a.m. for makeup before taping several programs. A few days later, Armando de Armas calls to tell me that the offer is my best chance to restart my career in a big way, and he insists I not pass it up. I reply that in Colombia I was already making that much in 1980 on the *24 Horas* newscast, for only one daily program at 7:00 p.m. What I can't admit to him—or anyone else—is that I'm afraid that the moment someone sends photos of me with Escobar to a Miami newspaper, my contract with the American channel could be canceled amid a massive scandal. Back in Medellín I show the offer to Pablo, and I'm horrified to learn that he has continued to wiretap my phone calls:

"Five shows a day for $5,000 a month? What are those Cubans thinking?" And as he starts to burn the letter, he adds: "We're going to do something, my love: I'm going to give you

$80,000 while you find work with a broadcaster here that knows what you're worth, or with a channel in a country I can visit often. But I'm not going to send you all the money at once, because you'll run off to Miami with some Venezuelan millionaire, and I won't ever see you again. Even if you and I can't be together every week, now that you've come back I need you more than ever. I want you to be with me through a series of key events that will be happening in this country over the coming months."

What Armando de Armas said, then, is true: Escobar did run him out! But I still entirely dismiss the absurd idea that he tried to kidnap him. Since it's clear Pablo already found out who was behind the offer from the Cuban channel, I decide not to ask any more questions. Instead, I tell him about the Italian journalist's interest in his story for a possible film by the Cecchi Gori producers. At the possibility that his life could be brought to the big screen, he is bursting with pride. But even when he's radiant with happiness, Pablo Escobar is, before all else, a businessman.

"You see that there really are other work opportunities, and much more important and profitable ones for someone like you? Tell Valerio Riva that if he wants to meet with me through you, he'll have to pay you $100,000 for the synopsis and as an advance for the script. And that if he doesn't write the script in collaboration with you, there's no deal. If he refuses to pay, it's because those multimillionaire Italian producers aren't behind the project, and the guy just wants to use you to earn a fortune off the story that the whole world wants to know—and only more so after what's going to happen soon, because they won't be able to extradite me. You and I are going to be free to travel together almost anywhere, except the United States, of course.

And in any case, you can keep going there anytime you want a break from me . . . for a few days."

Exactly two weeks later, halfway through August 1985, I'm back in Medellín. Late in the afternoon, two boys pick me up at the airport in a discreet car, and the whole time we are on the highway, they never stop looking in the rearview mirror to be sure I haven't been followed by some persistent person wanting to learn Pablo's whereabouts. I don't ask where we're headed, and I nod off to sleep. I wake up when I hear the men talking on the radio, informing their boss we're almost there. As we are approaching the Nápoles gate, a small white car with three men shoots out like a bullet and disappears into the shadows and the silence of the night. The boys tell me the car belongs to Álvaro Fayad, top leader of the M-19. I am very surprised, because I was convinced that the rebel group and MAS hated each other unto death—and I turn around to try to see him. The man in the back seat of the car also turns around to see me, and for a few seconds our eyes meet. My car speeds onto the property and stops in front of the main house. At the end of the corridor under a yellow light, I can make out two or three men; they immediately withdraw with the men who've arrived with me. Since they hide when they see Pablo come out, I can't tell who they are. But I deduce that his guests are not only close confidants, they must also demand discretion in the subjects to be addressed, a prudent distance from subordinates, and exceptional security measures.

Pablo, an expert in communications, is always informed in seconds, by radio or walkie-talkie, of everything that happens around him. He comes right out to receive me, opens the car door, and leans in to embrace me. Then, he pulls me out with both arms and looks at me proudly as if I were some Renoir in his collection. His enthusiasm about something that he's clearly been planning for a while suggests that he can't wait to introduce me to his guest—who, I now know, is only one. He asks me to guess who it is, and I ask if it's that Saudi prince who transports huge amounts of money in his diplomatic plane, or some Central American revolutionary, or a Mexican three-star general, or one of the big Aztec or Carioca bosses, or maybe an emissary of Stroessner, the eternal Paraguayan dictator. When he tells me who it is, I almost can't believe my ears.

"I wanted you to meet two of the founders and top leaders of M-19. They've been great friends of mine for a while now, but I couldn't tell you until I was absolutely sure about you. After Martha Nieves Ochoa's abduction, we came to a nonaggression pact with them. Álvaro Farad has just left. He seemed worried about meeting you. But Iván Marino Ospina, the toughest of all the *comandantes*, is here. He didn't react when he heard your name, because he's spent years in the jungle and doesn't watch TV. Depending on how things go, we'll see if we explain who you are or if we leave you incognito." He puts his arm around my shoulders and takes on the bullfighter's accent he uses with me when he's happy.

"A little anonymity at this point in life won't do you any harm, will it, my love?"

"And how old is our nineteenth-century hero, Pablo?" I ask.

Laughing, he tells me around forty-three, and I tell him that the only Colombian men that age who don't know who I am are from those tribes in the depths of the jungle that still haven't heard about the invention of Spanish, or the brassiere.

"This one is a soldier from the Valle del Cauca who isn't even afraid of me, and he doesn't deal in intellectualism or bullshit! Promise me you're going to follow my lead, and that for once in your life, you're going to talk about national and local subjects. Swear to me, on what you most love, that you're not going to bad-mouth Pol Pot or the Cultural Revolution!"

"Are you insinuating, Pablo, that I can't ask the supreme commander of this country's star guerrilla group about the Montoneros' modus operandi, or about the Shining Path, the IRA and the ETA, the Red Brigades and Baader-Meinhof, the Black Panthers and the Tamil Tigers, Hamas and Fatah?" I tease him. "What did you bring me for? To talk about the ninth of April, the Sandinistas and Betancur? Surely I can ask about the Moncada Barracks attack, right? Havana is right there, between Cartagena and Miami . . ."

"Let him talk about Simón Bolívar and whatever he wants, because he won't say a word about Fidel Castro, I warn you. This man is the guy I've been needing to put an end to all my problems. . . . Let's not keep him waiting longer. And for the love of God, don't act like a movie star; it's enough you're wearing that dress! You just be simple and charming, as if you were just a nice, discreet girl, okay? One thing, I should warn you that my friend is very high . . . but you and I have seen it all when it comes to . . . other people's weaknesses. Right, my love?"

I imagine that the Amazonian commander will look like an army sergeant and wear camouflage, that he'll see me as an intruder in a meeting of very macho men, and that he'll do everything humanly possible to get rid of me so that Pablo will stay and talk about money. Iván Marino Ospina is a man of medium build, blunt features, wispy hair, and a mustache, and beside him Escobar looks like Adonis. I am sporting a short silk dress with high heels, and when he introduces me,

Pablo is overflowing with pride. I realize immediately that this legendary guerrilla chief really isn't afraid of Pablo or of anyone else, because from the moment he lays eyes on me he doesn't take them from my face, my body, my legs; he has an inflamed gaze that to this day I don't remember ever seeing in another man.

The M-19 leader is wearing civilian clothes, and he tells me he's coming back after spending several months in Libya. No one travels from South America "to do" Libya, as the middle-class tourists say: they go for business involving oil or arms, and the M-19 is not exactly Standard Oil. Since I know the fascination Pablo feels for dictators, I comment that Muammar Gaddafi made the decision to dethrone Idris I of Libya when he saw him lose five million dollars in a single night—figures at the end of the seventies—in the Monte Carlo casino. I ask Ospina if he knows him, and he says he's never laid eyes on him, because the M-19 only goes to Libya for combat training. When I try to find out if the "M" has good relations with the Arab League, the men exchange a glance and Pablo proposes we don't talk any more about the distant African desert, but rather of how hard life is in the Colombian jungle.

Iván Marino tells me he has spent many years in Colombia's Eastern Plains. The rivers, of colossal size in the rainy season, include the two hundred main tributaries of the Orinoco, whose basin covers 385,000 square miles of Venezuelan, Brazilian, and Colombian flatlands and jungle. Staring at me and measuring my reaction to every word he says, he starts telling me about *temblones*, a kind of worm. He explains that because of those creatures, the people fighting against the oligarchy in Bogotá and the imperialism in Washington have to be completely protected when they wade through those currents, especially from the waist down, and the boots and soaked clothing become additional cause for pain and suffering. Pablo and I listen in horror to stories of those animals like spiny corkscrews that tear their victims' flesh with a kind of forceps when they're pulled out, after a titanic struggle between the jungle doctor tending the "territory's" owner and the *temblón* in dispute of that ownership. And I fall into the trap of asking whether these blessed animals enter the body through the mouth or nose or ears.

"Much farther down. They get into all the orifices of the body, especially the ones waaaay down! And for our female comrades the problem is double," says Ospina, devouring me with his eyes as if he wanted to give a demonstration that would convince me.

Gloria Gaitán has always accused me of displaying abnormal doses of candor for a woman of my age and lucidity, and I show it off now as I ask the supreme commander of M-19, with widened eyes, "And you, Iván Marino, how many *temblones* have you had to pull out in all these years of revolutionary struggle?"

Staring at the wall with a certain sadness, as if he had suddenly remembered some dark and painful chapter he thought he had forgotten, he replies, "A few, a few." Pablo glares at me, and I get up to go to the ladies' room so as not to submit his friend to any more questions about the subject he chose in order to sell me his revolutionary ideology.

When I'm back, I stop behind the half-open door because I hear the guerrilla chief demanding something from Escobar in the most peremptory terms:

"No, brother, no and no. I want one like that. I don't want any other, period. Just like that one, who's not missing a thing.

Where did you get her, all perfect like that? Uuyyy, brother, the way she crosses and uncrosses her legs . . . and the way she smiles . . . and the way she moves! Is she like that in bed? What a heavenly little doll! Now, that's the kind of woman's woman I've always dreamed of. No . . . when I think about it, I want two like her! Yes, two in a Jacuzzi, and you can take it out of the million if you want."

"From the million . . . well, let me think about it, brother . . . because that's sounding good to me. But we have two problems: one is that, weeeelllll . . . Virginia is the most famous TV anchorwoman in Colombia. She says that's like being a movie star in a country without a film industry. Look at her here, in all these magazines, if you don't believe me. And two, since she knows about everything and talks about everything . . . she's my treasure. What I wouldn't give to have her in duplicate!"

"But why didn't you tell me, brother? Okay, okay, okay . . . sorry, man! Now that I think about it some more, then . . . two who look like Sophia Loren, you can find me that, right? Doesn't matter if they're mute . . . the more stupid, the better!" exclaims Ospina, rolling with laughter.

"Of coooooourse, man! I can get as many as you want of those: a brunette Sophia Loren, a blonde one, and even a redhead if she fits in the Jacuzzi!" exclaims Pablo with immense relief. "And don't worry, it won't cost you a thing, brother."

I am tempted to leave those two men alone and go to sleep, but I decide to go in. When I push the door open, I find the eyes of the most wanted criminal in the world looking in terror at the most wanted guerrilla in Colombia, as though imploring him to shut up; Pablo makes an affectionate gesture to have me sit next to him, but I ignore him and sit beside the table where both have left their machine guns. Since I see that

Ospina is still looking at my cover of *Al Día*—I'm kneeling and I look naked, but I'm really wearing a tiny flesh-colored bikini—I ask him if he wants me to autograph it so he can keep it as a souvenir.

"Don't even think about it!" exclaims Pablo, snatching the magazines to put them away in a drawer that he locks with a key. "Imagine if the army found them in a raid, and they interrogated you to find this *bandido*'s whereabouts? And mine, while they're at it!"

I ask Iván Marino why he entered the revolutionary fight. Looking off toward that point in space where we all keep our painful childhood memories, he starts to tell me how, after Jorge Eliécer Gaitán was assassinated in 1948, in his native Tulúa the conservative "birds" of the Valle del Cauca murdered three of his uncles, one of them with machetes in front of his eleven children. After a pause, and with profound sadness, I also start to tell him how it happened that my family lost all their land in Cartago—very close to Tulúa—because of those same "birds": during the first years of La Violencia, my grandfather—a liberal minister married to a conservative landowner—arrived every week at his haciendas and found the administrator dead, with his ears, tongue, and genitals cut off and in the belly of his young wife, impaled or sliced open. If she was pregnant—and the young peasant women always are—it wasn't unusual to find the fetus in the mouth of the dead husband or in the other torn cavities of the poor woman.

"You and I know that the only form of depravity that all those conservative 'birds' didn't practice with the peasant women was cannibalism. The men of my family never picked up arms, I don't know whether out of cowardice or Catholicism. Instead, they sold their land for pennies to the multimillionaire sugar family the Caicedos, who financed those monsters and were supposedly their friends and neighbors."

"But how can you compare your situation with ours?" exclaims Ospina. "In your family of oligarchs, 'the birds' killed the servants in the absence of their masters. In my family of peasants, they tore people apart in front of their children!"

I express my horror at all those atrocities, my compassion for all the suffering, and my deep respect for the origins of the Colombian armed conflict. I comment on how strange it is that three such dissimilar stories as ours are gathered here tonight on the country's most valuable estate: the head of a rebel organization, the number one drug trafficker, and a woman who owns not a square foot of land, but is related to half the country's oligarchy and is friends with the other half. I say that life takes many turns, and that Pablo is now a land-owner many times greater than my great-grandfather and his siblings combined, and that the size of one of his associates' properties far exceeds that of Pepe Sierra, the richest land-owner in the history of Colombia and friend of my ancestors. Since the two men stay silent, I ask Iván Marino why in June the M-19 broke the cease-fire they had agreed on with Betan-cur's government. He explains that once they had demobilized, their members and those of other insurgent groups included in the amnesty started turning up murdered by dark forces of the extreme right. I ask him if he's referring to MAS.

"No, no, no. Thanks to this man," he says, pointing to Pablo, "we don't mess with MAS, and they don't mess with us. He and I have a common enemy, which is the government . . . and as you know, 'the enemy of my enemy is my friend.' The minister of defense—General Miguel Vega Uribe—and the chairman of the joint chiefs of staff, Rafael Samudio Molina, have sworn to wipe out the left. If in Turbay's government they threw us in jail and tortured us, in Betancur's there won't be a single one of us left alive. Colombia is still in the hands of 'birds,' Laureano and his son Álvaro Gómez, only now they're military men who think these countries only get fixed with Pinochet's model: exterminating the unarmed left like cockroaches!"

"Yes, in my social circle almost no one hides their admiration for the Chilean model, but Álvaro Gómez is no Laureano, *comandante*. . . . And, though it may be hard for you to believe it, in 1981 I quit the highest-paid job on television for refusing, day after day, to refer to your group as a "band of criminals." In those days, I was the anchor of *24 Horas*, the newscast directed by Mauricio Gómez: Álvaro's son and Laureano's grandson."

Ospina seems surprised that someone like me could take such a costly political position, and I explain to him that since now I am one of those who have nothing, I also have nothing to lose. Pablo interrupts us to tell him, "Virginia had already been fired from another news program for supporting the creation of a technicians' union . . . and she's just turned down the offer from a channel in Miami because I convinced her to stay here in Colombia, even though all our enemies left her without work. Right there, brother, you're looking at a woman who's braver than the two of us put together. That's why she's so special, and that's why I wanted the two of you to meet."

He gets up and comes toward me. The guerrilla leader stands up to say good-bye, and it seems that now he is looking at me with new eyes. He is very high, and he reminds his host not to forget the favor he's promised. Escobar suggests that he go have dinner, and they agree to meet after midnight. Before saying good-bye, I wish him great success in his fight for the rights of the weakest:

"Take good care, and count on me when you need a microphone . . . if they ever give me one again."

"What did you think of my friend?" Pablo asks me when we're left alone.

I tell him that Iván Marino struck me as a brave, audacious man who is convinced of his cause, but that, in effect, he didn't seem to be afraid of anything.

"People who aren't afraid of absolutely anything have a suicidal personality . . . and I think he lacks greatness, Pablo. I can't imagine Lenin asking Armand Hammer for two prostitutes in front of a journalist; or Mao Zedong, or Fidel Castro, or Ho Chi Minh—who spoke a dozen languages—while they were high. And now tell me: What's that million for?"

"To recover my files and set them on fire. And without a record, there's no way they can extradite me," Pablo admits with a triumphant smile.

"But you won't get your innocence back, Pablo! The justice department and the gringos can rebuild your record! Did Iván Marino put that idea in your head?"

"You know very well no one puts anything in my head. That's the only way; there's no other. It will take them years to rebuild the case . . . and do you think anyone is going to volunteer to testify against us? Where are they going to find them—Suicide Anonymous?"

He explains that all the cases against him and his partners are already in the Palace of Justice, and the warnings he had sent to the Supreme Court haven't done him any good: in a matter of weeks, the Constitutional Court will begin to evaluate the cases in order to fulfill the U.S. requirements to extradite them all.

"And for grabbing a stack of papers from just one place you are going to pay him a million dollars?"

"It's no stack of papers, my love: we're talking about six thousand files. Let's say . . . a few boxes."

"I thought your record was a few phone books, not crates of phone books! My God!"

"Don't underestimate me, my love. You're in the arms of the world's biggest outlaw, and I wanted you to know that in a few months I'll be a man with no criminal history. I won't have a past, like you do. . . ." He laughs, and before I can answer him, he silences me with a kiss.

HE'S PUTTING ON HIS SNEAKERS, and he tells me he's going to go do his friend the favor he promised before he goes crazy.

"Pablo, it's true that the M-19 is used to pulling off spectacular hits, but the Palace of Justice is not the Dominican Embassy. . . . That strike was successful because the residence is on a quiet street, with wide access and exit roads. But the Palace of Justice looks out over Bolívar Square, which is huge and open. The only two exits are narrow and always congested, and the Presidential Guard Battalion is around the corner. What if they fire a shot and they kill some poor secretary with three kids, or one of those cops stationed at the entrance? That building is exposed to everything, my love. Getting into the palace must be easy. Stealing the papers, a little more complicated. But getting out of there is going to be impossible! I don't know how they're going to do it . . . and, well . . . the truth is, I don't really want to know."

He sits down on the edge of the bed and takes my face in his hands. For a space of time that seems like an eternity, he runs his fingers over it as though trying to memorize it. He stares at me, searching in my eyes to be sure that my evident disapproval of the plan doesn't hide the risk of some future indiscretion, and he warns me, "You can never, ever talk to anyone about what happened here tonight, understood? You never met Ospina or saw Fayad leaving. And if they ask you about me, you haven't seen me again. Don't forget for an instant that they interrogate people to death to get information about where these guys are . . . and things go the worst for someone who knows nothing, because anyone with information 'sings' in the first ten minutes! My friend is a skillful strategist, and everyone knows of his bravery in combat. Stop worrying, it's going to be a clean and fast hit. They're very professional in these things, and so far they haven't failed. I know how to choose my people, and that's also why I chose you . . . from among ten million women!" he says, kissing my forehead.

"So many . . . and why did you want me to meet Iván Marino, Pablo?" I ask him.

"Because he's a very important leader, and only someone like him can do me this favor. And you have to have another view of reality, different from that superficial and false high society you live in. And there are other things, too . . . but I can't talk about those. I can tell you about my business, so you understand why I can't call you or see you as often as I'd like, but I can't talk about my associates' matters. Now try to rest. In a couple of hours they'll come for you to get you back to the hotel before dawn. And you'll see, in a few weeks we'll be celebrating the operation's success with your rosé champagne."

He wraps me in a comforting hug and kisses my hair several

times, the gesture of a man comforting a woman he doesn't want to lose when he knows she's sad. He silently caresses both my cheeks, then stands up.

"I'll call you in a few days. And for the love of God, keep the Beretta in your pocket, not in the safe! I have a lot of enemies, my love."

We never know if we'll see each other again, but I've always been careful not to mention it, because it would be calling into question his absolute conviction that even when it comes to survival, he is above all other mortals. When he opens the door, he turns around for a second to blow me one last kiss, and I manage to say, "Pablo, the M-19 has always brought us bad luck, you and me both. I think what you're doing is crazy. . . ."

And once again I watch him go, carrying through the shadows the cross that only I know exists. I hear his whistle, and minutes later I see him move away from my window with a small group of men. I wonder if there is anyone else who knows the extent of the terror of extradition that weighs on this man's soul—this man, so rich and powerful, but so impotent in the face of legitimate power. I know that no one else could feel compassion for him, and I know, as well, that there's no one in the world to whom I could confess the fears that overwhelm me. I stay there alone, thinking of the causes of those two friends, one who fights for the poorest and one who fights for the richest, and the embedded pain or unmentionable terror that men and the brave carry in their hearts of flesh, lead, stone, and gold. I'm left sad and worried, wondering if it's Pablo who is manipulating Iván Marino with his money, or if it's the rebel leader plying the multimillionaire with his unique capacity to provide him the service on which, possibly, the rest of his life depends. And mine along with it. . . .

On August 29, 1985, some ten days after that night—the last I will ever spend at Hacienda Nápoles—I open the newspaper and read that Iván Marino Ospina has been killed in Cali in a confrontation with the army. On one hand, I feel sincere pain for the loss of that fighter; on the other, profound relief, because I imagine that without his fearless spirit, the absurd plan has been called off, or at least postponed. Like Pablo, I adore Simón Bolívar, who died in Colombia with his heart destroyed by the ingratitude of the people he liberated, and I offer up a prayer to El Libertador for the soul of the guerrilla commander whose path crossed mine during those brief hours. I wonder how long the army had been following Iván Marino, and with a shiver, I realize that it could have been Pablo who died. I think about what he must be feeling at the loss of his friend, and I know, starting at that moment, he will be reinforcing his security measures to the utmost and that we surely won't be able to see each other for weeks.

In the middle of September he surprises me with a serenade of my favorite tangos, among them "Ninguna" and "Rondando tu esquina." I think how that song, which I've always loved, now just reminds me of how surveilled I am. The next day Pablo calls to say that he misses me all the time, and to ask me to work seriously on the outline of the film, because if the Italians don't produce it, he is in a position to do it himself. At the beginning of October he announces that, given the possibility the Supreme Court will approve his extradition, he has to leave for a while. He implies that the plan of the Palace of Justice has been aborted, and he explains that he can't take me with him because it would mean putting me in danger. With the hope of seeing each other as soon as it's safe, he says good-bye with a mariachi serenade and the romantic promises of "Si Nos Dejan" and "Luna de Octubre."

In the following weeks I try to forget the events of that warm August night, but memories of Iván Marino's fearlessness and Pablo's triumphant tone throb from time to time in my memory like a black-winged butterfly. Again and again, we journalists hear rumors about threats from Los Extraditables and the M-19 against the Supreme Court magistrates, but no one pays attention because almost all of us who work in the media are used to hearing about threats and are convinced that, in Colombia, "a dog's bark is worse than its bite."

IT IS NOVEMBER 6, 1985, and I am with a colleague in the lobby of the Cartagena Hilton Hotel. We are covering the Miss Colombia Beauty Pageant for the radio; it's an event that, year after year, gathers most of Colombia's journalists in the city, along with hundreds of personalities and everyone who is anyone in the cosmetics and fashion industries. The queens make their arrivals with committees from their departments, which always include the governor's wife and the mayor of the capital. "Coronation Night" takes place at the Convention Center and is followed by a sumptuous black-tie ball at the Cartagena Club. The day before the event, the governor, his family members, and the dignitaries of each department make their entrance, along with media personalities from all over the country vying to interview many important politicians, and while they're at it, to admire so many pretty women. By this time, drug trafficking's penetration into the beauty pageants is common knowledge, and everyone is aware that without support from the department drug boss, the government couldn't dream of covering the expenses of the queen's committee (made up of one or two hundred relatives and close friends, two dozen high-society ladies, the ex-queens with their husbands, and the whole regional bureaucracy). Nor is it unusual for the Miss herself to be dating the boss—or the boss's son—and the relationships of the police commanders and the army brigade with the local king of coke or marijuana are much more intimate, stable, long-lasting, and profitable than the ones between the successful businessman and the reigning queen of the moment.

Anyone who has any doubt that the woman-as-object exists only has to attend a Miss Colombia pageant in Cartagena: the gowns and headdresses are similar to those of the *mulatas* in the samba schools at Carnaval in Rio de Janeiro, except those women dance and sing half-naked and happy, while the poor beauty queens drag feathered capes and flashy trains that weigh a hundred pounds, in temperatures of one hundred degrees Fahrenheit and on five-inch stilettos. The endless parades of carriages and themed boats over the course of an entire week leave everyone exhausted, down to the toughest marine officers, who are the ones tasked with escorting the girls.

It's eleven in the morning, there are five days left before the election and coronation of Miss Colombia, and the enormous lobby is buzzing with excitement at all the people who are here: radio journalists, photographers, singers, actors, fashion designers, the presidents of the firms that sponsor the pageant, former Miss Colombias who have only grown more beautiful and are now on the arms of their proud husbands. The judges are celebrities from other countries, and they're the only ones who hide from everyone so that later no one can say the committee manipulated them or the Miss's future father-in-law bought them off. The queens are in their rooms, getting ready for the first swimsuit parade. The hallways of the floors reserved for them are infested with ugly men in green uniforms and beautiful men in white uniforms, who all observe the whole gay population of makeup artists and hairstylists with utter contempt. These last, in turn, look at the navy officers with ferocious hatred and at the sailors with utter adoration.

At 11:40 a commotion breaks out and all the interviews and radio transmissions are interrupted. The M-19 has seized the Palace of Justice, and it seems they've taken the Supreme Court magistrates prisoners! My colleague and I dash to my suite and sit together in front of the TV. At first I dismiss the idea that what we are watching has something to do with Pablo, because I'm convinced that he is out of the country. The last thing that would occur to my friend is that I am Pablo Escobar's lover, or that one of the most visible leaders of MAS could have financed a guerrilla takeover. And the last thing that would occur to me is that my colleague is the girlfriend of one of the M-19 leaders.

Bolívar Square is an enormous expanse with a statue of Simón Bolívar in its center, looking toward the Primada Cathedral, on the eastern side of the plaza. Across from it is the mayor's office, flanked by the Senate, which looks north, and the Palace of Justice looking south. And behind the Senate is the presidential palace—the Casa de Nariño—guarded by the Presidential Guard Battalion.

Two days earlier, the security of the Palace of Justice, seat of the Supreme Court and the Council of State, had been turned over to a private company. That was precisely the day the Constitutional Court was to begin studying the extradition cases for Pablo Escobar Gaviria and Gonzalo Rodríguez Gacha, among others. The siege has been carried out by the "Iván Marino Ospina Commando Unit," in charge of the "Antonio Nariño Operation for the Rights of Man." Led by the commanders Luis Otero and Andrés Almarales, thirty-five insurgents have invaded the palace. Seven of them entered through the main door like ordinary citizens, and the rest forced their way in using two small trucks to barge through the basement door on a side of the building, coming in from one of the narrow and congested streets of downtown Bogotá. The guerrilla commando has already killed two guards and the palace administrator, and they've taken more than three hundred people hostage, including magistrates, employees, and visitors. Now they are demanding the radio transmission of a proclamation denouncing the abuses committed against those who accepted the amnesty agreement and condemning the ineffective Colombian justice that accepts Colombians being extradited and tried in other countries. They demand, as well, that the newspapers publish their program, that the government grant daily radio time to the opposition, and that the Supreme Court respect their right, enshrined in the Constitution, to force the president of the republic or his representative to appear in court. They want to subject him to judgment for betraying the peace agreements with the disarmed insurgent groups M-19, EPL, and Quintín Lame.

At noon, the building is completely surrounded by the army, whom the "Poet President" has ordered to recover the Palace of Justice whatever the cost. At two in the afternoon, tanks have already entered through the basement, the helicopters of GOES (Grupo Operativo Antiextorsión y Secuestro, or Operative Group Against Extortion and Kidnapping) have unloaded troops on the building's terrace, and a tank has knocked down the palace gates that open onto the plaza and gone inside, followed by another two loaded with men from the Presidential Guard Battalion and the artillery school. Belisario Betancur has convened with the former presidents, the presidential candidates, and the Senate and House presidents and is refusing to listen to the magistrates or the rebels. The offers from foreign nations to mediate between the government and the armed group don't even reach the ears of the president. He will not forgive the M-19 for breaking the peace process that was the foundation of his presidential campaign. And he won't forgive Iván Marino Ospina for supporting Los Extraditables in an earlier statement, even though the statement had been denounced by the other M-19 commanders:

"For every Colombian extradited, we must kill a U.S. citizen!"

The tanks open fire, and the radio stations start to transmit the voice of Magistrate Reyes Echandía, president of the Supreme Court of Justice—and also of the Criminal Court that had approved the extradition of Colombians to the United States some years before—begging the president to cease fire because they're going to end up killing everyone, but his calls are only answered by the police chief. The words spoken by the young colonel Alfonso Plazas from the artillery school to a journalist define the moment:

"Just here defending democracy, sir!"

And in Latin America, when a head of state gives the military carte blanche to defend democracy, they know exactly what they have to do. And what they *can* do: purge themselves of all that visceral hatred built up over years or decades of counterinsurgent fighting, leaving aside—finally!—all those restrictions imposed on them by laws designed by civilized men for the protection of unarmed citizens. Especially since the Colombian Palace of Justice houses—alongside all those files like books that contained the criminal records of Escobar and his associates—a few other boxes with 1,800 cases against the army and the security agencies for human rights violations. The voracious fire that inexplicably breaks out in the palace at six in the afternoon does away once and for all with the problems of a dozen extraditables, but, above all, with those of several thousand military men.

Hellish temperatures now oblige the guerrillas and their hostages to withdraw to the bathrooms and the fourth floor, and Andrés Almarales orders the women and the wounded to be evacuated. Late in the afternoon, the telephones on which Magistrate Reyes and Commander Otero had been communicating with the presidential palace go mute. When Betancur finally decides to talk to the court's president, it's impossible: technically, the military has carried out a coup. The events of the Miss Colombia beauty pageant are not canceled or postponed, with the argument that the happy, strong spirit of the Colombian people will not be broken by tragedy. Nor are the *cartageneros* about to let their parade be rained on for something that's happening "there in Bogotá."

The fighting goes on all night, and when the president's representative and the director of the Red Cross arrive in the early hours of the next day to negotiate with the guerrillas, the military won't let them enter the palace. Instead, they put them in the historic Casa del Florero alongside two hundred hostages who have been freed by Almarales or rescued by the uniformed officials, including the state councilor Jaime Betancur Cuartas, the president's brother. Each person is rigorously searched and interrogated by the director of the B-2 military intelligence unit, Colonel Edilberto Sánchez Rubiano, with help from the army's artillery and the F2 unit of the police. Several of these confuse innocent people with guerrillas, and dozens of judicial officials, including magistrates and counselors, are saved from detention only thanks to the pleading of their colleagues. Anyone who awakens the slightest suspicion is put into a military truck destined for the Usaquén Cavalry School in northern Bogotá. Of those, only two law students are later released, abandoned on a distant highway after being tortured.

At two in the morning the whole world outside Colombia watches on TV with incredulous eyes as a tank fires straight at the palace, blowing an enormous hole in the fourth-floor wall where the last groups of insurgents and hostages have taken refuge. Through the opening, police shooters stationed on the roofs of the surrounding buildings fire indiscriminately inside the palace, under orders from their commander, General Víctor Delgado Mallarino. Meanwhile, the army throws grenades while helicopters fly overhead. Though their ammunition is running out, the rebels refuse to surrender to a humanitarian commission for a later trial protected by guarantees, and as the rain of bullets is wiping out their resistance, the fire consumes what remains of the palace. The soldiers have been ordered not to leave anyone from the last group of sixty people alive, and they are all killed, including the magistrates who have witnessed the abuse and butchery. Among these last people standing are the president of the Supreme Court and the four justices who were to rule on the extraditions, including Manuel Gaona Cruz, a human rights defender. The defense minister orders all the bodies, without exception, to be stripped and washed, eliminating valuable evidence, and he forbids Forensic Medicine from going in to remove the cadavers.

While all of this is going on, and by order of the communications minister Noemí Sanín Posada—cousin of María Lía Posada, Jorge Ochoa's wife—the Colombian TV stations only show soccer games and news about the beauty pageant. Nearly twenty-seven hours after the siege began, a final explosion is heard, and inside the building everything is silent. At 2:30 p.m., General Arias Cabrales proclaims victory to the defense minister, and General Vega Uribe informs the president that the coup has been defeated and the Palace of Justice recovered.

"What palace? A pile of twisted iron with a hundred incinerated bodies inside?" we all ask, horrified.

At eight at night, Belisario Betancur addresses the country: "For better or for worse, the president of the republic takes responsibility."

Responsibility for what? The massacre of judicial power through army and police bombardment? I ask myself as I listen to that supreme commander of the Armed Forces, whom the Colombian people, eternally tempted by the illusion of a nonexistent peace, had believed in 1982 to be a leader.

From that whole massacre, three big winners have emerged: the military, Los Extraditables, and the two traditional parties—because, as a future political project, the M-19 and all the other insurgent groups have been left buried among the ashes of judicial power. Eleven magistrates are dead, along with forty-three civilians and thirty-three rebels, and eleven members of the Armed Forces and DAS. The news cameras had recorded the moment when a dozen cafeteria employees, their manager, and two rebel women were taken out of the Palace of Justice by the army. The next day, when their families ask for information about the whereabouts of the detainees, the response will be that they are being provisionally held in military barracks. No one will give a reason for this, or a location, and those people are never heard from again.

On November 12, I return home after that exhausting pageant, the last one I will cover in my professional life. The next day, November 13 of that annus horribilis, the greatest Colombian tragedy of all time occurs, and the world media forgets the hundred victims at the Palace of Justice and turns to the news of twenty-five thousand dead in Armero, in the rich rice and coffee region of Tolima. Thinking about the incredible luck of all those state-paid butchers, I tell myself that a curse has fallen on my poor nation and everyone in it. And I wonder if the man I had thought was the bravest of all has become merely the most cowardly of the monsters. I change my phone number, and with my soul shrunken by terror, I make the decision to never see Pablo Escobar again in my life. Overnight, I have stopped loving him.

ℭ Tarzan Versus Pancho Villa

THIRTEEN-YEAR-OLD OMAYRA SÁNCHEZ is in the throes of death in front of TV cameras from all over the world. Only her head and arms emerge from the hardened mud in which her legs are trapped under a concrete column. The panorama of desolation that surrounds the teenager—miles and miles of mud seem to stretch out infinitely—is broken only by the occasional treetop or bloated dead cow. Getting Omayra out and to a hospital where they could amputate her legs would take days. While the gas gangrene is invading her body, the girl transmits a message of hope to millions of fellow countrymen, and people from many countries watching her, feeling helpless, moved by her suffering and her bravery in the face of death. We Colombians know it is impossible to save her, and we can do nothing but watch over her final moments and pray that her pain ends soon. Seventy hours later that angel leaves us forever and flies to heaven, where the souls of the other twenty-five thousand victims are waiting for her, along with the hundred, innocent or guilty, who died ten days earlier at the Palace of Justice.

The child Omayra dies, but another twenty-one thousand have survived the drama in Tolima with injuries and property damage. In a matter of minutes, the Nevado del Ruiz volcano had erupted and swelled the peaceful Lagunilla River with lava and volcanic rock, and around midnight, it had descended over Armero now converted into a torrent several miles wide. The millions of tons of mud and rubble has literally wiped from the map a prosperous town that had existed for ninety years. There are warnings before all of Colombia's tragedies, and this one was no exception: for several months the volcanologists have been warning about the enormous fumaroles coming from the crater, but in its proverbial indifference the state decided to ignore them. Because how could the government evacuate fifty thousand people, and where could they put them up for days or weeks on end?

The two catastrophes in a row leave the country in deep mourning and with the most profound feeling of impotence. But the Armero disaster is a true blessing for the military men who've tired of raping and strangling the prisoners from the Palace of Justice, of yanking out fingernails, of pouring baths of sulfuric acid, of incinerating and throwing bodies into garbage dumps; now they want to recover at any cost their image as public servants in times of calamity. They put their men, resources, planes, and helicopters at the disposal of the thousands of people who have been left injured, wounded, or homeless. Overnight, they've stopped being villains and become saviors.

All that horror, the endless stories of unbearable suffering and irreparable loss, is shown morning, noon, and night on TV. And all those torrents of tears and collective pain combine with my own, and as I finally accept the selfishness, blindness, and irresponsibility of the man I had loved, I'm left feeling guilty for being alive and wishing only that I were in peace with the dead.

SOME TWO MONTHS LATER, my friend Alice de Rasmussen invites me to spend a few days at her house in the Rosario Islands, the small archipelago situated thirty-five miles from Cartagena de Indias. It is a national park, a collection of coral islands owned by the Colombian nation, but dozens of families from the traditional, well-off spheres of Cartagena, Bogotá, and Medellín have built all sorts of houses and mansions there. They are technically denominated as "improvements." In Colombia, the country where anything goes, common practices end up turning into legal ones. While the islands belong to the state, the surface land really belongs to whoever has appropriated it with the intention of "improving" it with sumptuous buildings. And who cares about the fact that the submerged part of an island in the Colombian zone of luxury tourism belongs to someone else? By 1986, there isn't a single vacant lot left, every lot is worth a small fortune, and the price of the most humble house doesn't go below a quarter of a million dollars.

Rafael Vieira Op Den Bosch is the son of one of the white colonists of the Rosario Islands national park and a Caribbean-Dutch mother. He is thirty-four years old, and though he doesn't have a zoo, he is an ecologist who is respected by the tourists, his neighbors, and the director of that reserve on whose domain he and his family have built the profitable business of the Oceanario Aquarium. Rafa, as everyone calls him, isn't rich, but he sells eight hundred lunches a day. He isn't short, ugly, and chubby, but rather tall, beautiful, and athletic. He doesn't have speedboats, just an old enormous fishing boat. He doesn't collect giraffes and elephants but rather barracudas and dolphins, and the only thing he has in common with Pablo Escobar is Pancho Villa: while Pablo kills people—and in photos where he's dressed in a traditional hat and charro costume he looks like the Mexican bandit reincarnated—Rafa has only kidnapped "Pancho Villa," a ferocious lemon shark, and in his minuscule bathing suit, he looks like a carbon copy of Kris Kristofferson.

I have been sad and terribly alone for months, and it's not hard for me to fall in love at first sight with someone as beautiful as Rafael Vieira, while he supposedly also falls in love with my smile and my breasts. He nicknames me "Pussycat," and I stay and live with him from the very first day. With him are his fish, his crustaceans, his dolphins, his sharks, and his cause: preserving marine life in a country and a national park where one of the oldest traditions is fishing with dynamite to save time and money, because what matters most is rum and today, not children or tomorrow.

In San Martín de Pajarales, the Vieiras' tiny island, there are no beaches or palm trees, and fresh water is a luxury. A dozen and a half Afro-Colombian workers who are descended from the island's original inhabitants live there, and so does Rafael's mother. His father and stepmother live in Miami, and his brothers in Bogotá. There are a dozen little houses, and the door of ours is always open. Rafa works all day on the expansion of the aquarium while I swim, dive, and learn the names of all the animal species of the Caribbean Sea in Latin, English, and Spanish. In the spirit of Cousteau, I become an authentic expert in the ethology of the crustaceans, and in the spirit of Darwin, I learn why sharks have evolved a perfect design over three hundred million years, while we humans evolved over only five million years and have all kinds of defects, like my myopia. I realize that it's because we descend from a bunch of simians who took millions of years to learn to walk on two legs and much longer to become hunters, and not from marine species, so much more inquisitive, adventurous, and free.

Rafa teaches me to fish and to dive with an oxygen tank. He teaches me to lose my fear of the manta rays that sometimes play with us and of the curious barracudas that swim around the humans to study that most predatory of species, the only one on the planet that tortures. He convinces me that the animals in the ocean don't attack unless they are stepped on or harpooned wrong, but I refuse to learn how to do it correctly because I don't like to kill or hurt any creature—I'd rather care for them all. With every day that passes I descend deeper without the help of a tank, and my lung capacity gradually expands. Since I swim six or seven hours a day, farther and farther, I become something of an athlete and I look several years younger. At the end of the day, Rafa and I always have a drink on a small pier he built with his own hands—like almost everything on the island—and watch the sunset over an incandescent horizon while we talk about environmental subjects, his trips to Africa, animals, and evolution. He doesn't like books, either, but he does like stories, and at night I read him Hemingway's. My life is now incredibly simple, and we are so happy we talk about the possibility of getting married down the road and even having children.

Every six weeks I spend a few days in Bogotá. The city now

seems like an inhospitable and strange place where you have to always keep up the usual defenses of *femina sapiens*—long, painted witch's nails, makeup, hairstyle, tailored suit with silk blouse, long stockings and stiletto heels. You have to be dependent on a bunch of cosmopolitan and malicious people who talk nonstop about infidelities and conspiracies, and who look at me with profound compassion and a bit of envy because I left behind my career, my trips, and my social life to go live "on a microscopic island, for the love of a beach boy known for being pretty and penniless." I stop by my apartment, pay the bills, and quickly return to my maritime life and Rafa's loving arms. One morning, on one of those visits toward the middle of 1986, as I'm going through my mail, I open a manila envelope that looks like it contains a magazine.

Nothing, nothing in the world could have prepared me for what it really holds: photographs of sixteen dismembered cadavers that return me to the reality of continental Colombia. And the anonymous text brings me back to the reality of a man I stopped seeing and loving months ago, whose memory is no longer the bittersweet taste of a forbidden fruit, but a series of memories, ever more faded, of uncertainties and agonies as costly as they are useless. It is clear that someone had learned about our meeting with the M-19, possibly a member of the security or military intelligence agencies involved in the most horrifying torture. The letter writer accuses Pablo and Gonzalo of crimes more atrocious than any I could have imagined and swears to make me pay with every drop of my blood and every inch of skin on my body. After crying for a couple of hours and praying to the victims' souls to ask for enlightenment as to what I should do, I decide to make two calls: the first is to an acquaintance in Medellín to say I have changed my mind about the seventy-two-carat diamond we had talked about. I tell her that now I do want to show it to the collector (the owner is asking a million dollars for it, and he's offering me $100,000 in commission for its sale). The other is to my friend Susanita, a real estate agent, to ask her to put my apartment up for sale. Then, instead of traveling to Cartagena, I take the first flight to Medellín.

Gustavo Gaviria receives me immediately with the same distant but sincere affection as always. While we talk about his business, my canceled contracts, and the situation in the country, I notice in the depths of his gaze what seems to be the start of a profound existential disillusionment. After a few minutes chatting, I show him the diamond that, according to what I've been told, once belonged to a European royal house. Taking a jeweler's glass that lets him detect the most insignificant carbon in the most apparently perfect stone, he starts to analyze that crystalline quail's egg that I've brought him.

"Really, it's one of the biggest rocks I've seen in my life. . . . It covers my finger from knuckle to joint. Yes, it must be from a crown. . . . From the price, it's obviously stolen. But it's not very clear . . . yellowish, not white or canary. It's not expensive . . . but I don't like the color and it has carbon flaws. . . ."

"For God's sake, Gustavo! You and I know that if it were D-flawless or canary, it would be worth four or five times more."

Someone knocks on the door, and without waiting for Gustavo's okay, he comes in and closes it behind him.

"Well, look who we have here! It's the Little Mermaid herself! Isn't she tan! And to what do we owe this honor?"

"She came to show me this, Pablo," Gustavo tells him, showing him the diamond. "They've canceled all of Virginia's advertising contracts, and she needs the money from the commission."

He takes that shining jewel between his thumb and index finger and studies it with his arm extended, at a distance, as he might hold a finger from the decomposing cadaver of his worst enemy. His face shows such disgust that for a second, I think he's going to throw the million dollars out the window. Then, as if he's had to overcome the desire to do just that, he looks at his partner and exclaims, "This is a drug business, not Harry Winston! And we don't make deals with her. If she needs money, let her come to me! And don't forget, brother, they're waiting for us in the meeting."

With a deep sigh, Gaviria tells me he doesn't buy diamonds of that size because in an emergency they're impossible to trade or sell for what he'd bought them for. I ask how someone with a billion dollars in cash could have liquidity problems of a million, and he, shrugging his shoulders with a resigned smile, replies that the rich cry, too. He says good-bye with a kiss on the cheek, and when I'm alone with his cousin, I hand him the envelope with the photographs and the anonymous letter.

"I think you should see this. It came in my mail and I had planned to leave it for you with Gustavo. It seems that because of something that you or the Mexican ordered done, someone wants to do the same to me. Who else knew about our meeting with Iván Marino, Pablo? And who was behind Álvaro Fayad's death in March?"

He opens the envelope and dumps its contents on the table. He is stunned, mute, and stupefied, and he sits down. He doesn't go pale, because nothing in the world can make him do that. Pablo Escobar has never trembled before things that would make a human being keel over. With Gustavo's jeweler's tweezers, he picks up each of the sixteen photos and studies them in silence. Then he reads aloud some parts of the text that accompanies them, and finally, he says to me, "I think you and I are going to have to talk. And for a long time.... Are you married?"

I reply that I'm not, but that Rafael is expecting me tonight in Cartagena. He asks me then to go return the diamond, lead my friend to believe that I'm going to travel, and then wait for him in his apartment until he can get free. What he needs to tell me, he says, is a matter of life or death.

"Call your boyfriend or whatever he is, and tell him you missed the plane and you'll be there tomorrow. And calm down, no one's going to hurt you, and I don't have the slightest intention of touching you. I'll keep these photos so I can have some friends of mine check them for prints. We'll find out just who this pervert is, not to mention the psycho who sent them to you, and the suicidal son of a bitch who's accusing me of paying for this bloodbath!"

"No, no, Pablo! Those photos already have hundreds of my prints, and you're going to make things worse. Don't show them to anyone or try to find out how they were taken, I beg you! I live on a little island with a man who's like an angel, and I'm not to blame for the crimes all of you commit," I tell him, bursting into tears and trying to get the photos back.

He stands up and puts an arm around my shoulders. When he manages to calm me down, he puts the photos into the envelope and promises me that he'll burn them once he's studied them carefully to see if the faces correspond to the disappeared people from the Palace of Justice; that is, what's left of their faces after the sulfuric acid did its work. He insists I spend that night in Medellín, and when I reluctantly agree, he says good-bye and hurries off. Following his instructions, I call Rafael to tell him I'll be there the next day, that my flight was canceled due to bad weather. I could never talk to him about the terror I feel, and much less about my reasons for sharing it with Pablo. When I reach the apartment and place my suitcase on the bed to unpack some things, I catch a glimpse of something shiny between the carpet's thick wool threads: it's a little gold bracelet, and I try it on. My wrist is almost as thin as a child's, but that worthless chain would have had to be an inch longer for me to clasp it.

When I see Pablo enter a few hours later, I realize that in this year he has aged five. He is barely thirty-six, but his walk seems slower and less sure. I notice he has gained weight and his temples are starting to turn gray; I think how mine are, too, but it's easier for women to hide it. He seems calmer than in the afternoon, but he looks tired and sad, as if he needed a good hug. His whole face is a question mark; mine, an enormous accusation. When he sees our separate reflections in the mirror that so many times reflected us together, he comments that I could be ten years younger than him and that I look like a golden statue. I thank him politely for a compliment that a year earlier I would have returned with a hundred kisses. He wants to know why I changed my phone number without telling him, and with a half-dozen short, curt phrases, I explain my reasons. After one of his downcast silences, he sighs, looks up, and tells me he understands. Then he looks at me with something like nostalgia for all the dreams that fled, smiles sadly, and adds that, really, he's very pleased to see me and talk to me again, even if it's only for a few hours. He asks if I mind if he lies down on the bed, and when I say no, he throws himself heavily onto it, puts his hands behind his neck, and starts to tell me stories about real life and of times as recent as November 6 of the previous year.

"Minister of Justice Carlos Medellín's secretary was taken to Simón Bolívar Hospital with third-degree burns. When the soldiers came for her, and the burn unit director tried to oppose them, they threatened to accuse him of collaborating with her, a *guerrillera*, and to take him to a barracks to interrogate him. They flayed that innocent woman for hours in the army cavalry school, and she died while those animals were literally pulling her flesh off in strips. One woman gave birth in an army truck, and they stole the baby; after the birth, they tortured her right there until they killed her. The dismembered cadaver of another pregnant woman was thrown into the Mondoñedo dump. Pilar Guarín, a young woman who was a substitute that day in the cafeteria, was raped for four days in the military garrison. They put her and several of the men into tubs of sulfuric acid, and they buried others in the "cemetery" of the cavalry school, where there are hundreds of bodies of people who disappeared during Turbay's government. And you know why they did all that? To try to get information about seven million dollars that I had supposedly given the M-19 to divide among the military and security organizations. The torture wasn't to find out who had financed the siege—they already knew that—but to find out where Álvaro Fayad and all that money was, including what I had already given Iván Marino Ospina."

"How much did you really give the M-19, Pablo?"

"I gave a million in cash to Iván Marino, and I promised them another million in arms and financial aid down the line. Thanks to the landing strip at Nápoles, we were able to bring in some explosives, but the weapons and munitions didn't make it on time, and that was the tragedy: the plan had to be moved up because that day the court was going to start to study our extraditions, and the evidence against us was overwhelming. The M-19 only wanted to make a proclamation and demand explanations from the president, but everything went wrong. The military set fire to the palace and assassinated the magistrates so there wouldn't be any witnesses to anything that happened inside. They told Gonzalo everything, and he told me. I can admit in front of you that that million and change was the best deal of my life; but close as he is to the B-2 and as much as he hates the left, neither the Mexican nor I paid the army to assassinate six M-19 commanders! That's the lowest blow I've heard in my life, because Fayad and Ospina weren't just my friends, they were also our connection to Noriega, the Sandinistas, and Cuba. I have no reason to lie to you, Virginia, because you know me very well and you know what I'm saying is true. And now I can admit that I wanted the highest M-19 commanders to meet you that night because I knew they were going to demand air time from the government, and I thought you could work with them."

I ask who else was in the know about his meetings with Ospina and Fayad, and he tells me only his most trusted men. I ask how many of them knew about my presence at the meeting in August 1985; he seems surprised, and he replies that, as always, only the two who had brought me and taken me back to the hotel. I tell him there's a traitor among his people: almost surely he told one of his passing little girlfriends about our meeting, and she called the security organizations to denounce me, so as to wipe me from the map or force me out of the country. Now someone with the most twisted mind on earth wants to sell me the idea that he and the Mexican paid the army to murder both the magistrates and the rebels so he wouldn't have to pay the M-19 what he'd agreed on if the siege was successful. He tells me that if he had really done that, he would have been at the beck and call of the army and the intelligence organizations for the rest of his days, and they would have been much more costly than the M-19.

"Pablo: I'm not interested in knowing who talked about our meeting with Ospina, but you have to start taking precautions with your own men and with those expensive whores you buy all the time. You have an army that protects you, but I'm at the mercy of your enemies. I am one of the most famous women in this country, and when they tear me apart or make me disappear, the details of our relationship will be public knowledge. You'll be accused of my death, and all your little beauty queens, models, and hookers will go running."

I fling the gold bracelet at him, saying it's too big to belong to his daughter Manuela.

"This is a little girl's! You're turning into a marijuana addict, and not only are you falling victim to your own invention, you're well on your way to becoming a pervert! What are you trying to find in all those virgins? Your only feminine ideal, the copy and duplicate of the woman who was once the girl of your dreams? The one who was thirteen when you fell in love with her?"

"I won't allow anyone to talk to me like that! Who the hell do you think you are?" he cries, standing up and leaping on me like a beast. And while he shakes me like a rag doll, I shout at him, unable to control myself.

"I think I'm your only real friend, Pablo! The only woman who never demanded anything from you, didn't ask you to keep her, didn't even think of you leaving your wife, didn't want to get kids out of you. The only iconic woman who has loved you and the only one who ever will! The only one who lost everything she'd worked for all her life for love of you, and the only one whom the seventh-richest man in the world left empty-handed and with no way to earn a living! Aren't you ashamed? And just when I thought that what we had was in the past and that I could live happily with a good man, I get a gift like this from a professional torturer. I brought you the photos so you would see what they did to all those innocent women because of your so-called cause, to talk to you about things that no one else would dare talk to you about, because I'm the only person who isn't afraid of you and the only one in your life who has a conscience! You know I'm terrified of torture, Pablo. Just kill me once and for all, before I fall into those degenerates' hands! Do it yourself, since you've 'offed' two hundred people and you're a world-famous expert in strangling techniques. But this time do it quickly, I beg you!"

"No, no, no! Don't ask me for something so horrible; you're an angel, and I only kill criminals. That was the last thing I needed to hear after all these months apart!" he says, now try-ing to soothe me, quiet me, take me in his arms, while I keep hitting him with my fists. Once I'm exhausted and, defeated, sobbing with my head on his shoulder, he kisses my hair and asks if I still care about him a little. I tell him I stopped loving him a while ago, but I'll care about him until the day I die, because he was the only man who was ever good to me . . . and to the poorest of the poor. In the long silence that follows, only my sobs are heard. Then, as if he were talking to himself while I'm recovering in his arms, he starts to talk to me with immense tenderness:

"Maybe it's better that you live on the island for a while, my love. I feel better with you there than alone in Bogotá. God does things for a reason . . . but you're going to get bored soon, because you need wings . . . and a real man. You're a lot of woman for a kid like that. You . . . as Jane with the Tarzan of the aquarium! Who would have thought?"

I tell him that after my Tarzan of the zoo, in my life anything is possible. We laugh with a certain resignation, and he starts to dry my tears. After thinking for a while, he says suddenly, "I'm going to propose a deal: Since now you have so much free time, why don't you include in the movie script the whole truth about what really happened in the Palace of Justice? If the Italians don't give you the $100,000, I will. And in advance."

I reply that the Italian journalist already said the producers wouldn't pay that much, and I add, "Plus, I would have to leave the country and say good-bye to my life with Rafael. In any case, you have to understand that at this point I couldn't write an apologetic version of what happened . . . nor of your existential reasons, Pablo."

He looks at me, offended, and with a deep sadness in his voice, he asks if now I see him as just a criminal, too, nothing but an outlaw with a ton of cash.

"If the man I loved most in my life were just a successful criminal, what would that make me? I know that what happened at the palace got away from you, and from the M-19 and Belisario. But I also know you're going to derail extradition with that massacre. Don't expect me to congratulate you, Pablo, because everything that's happening as a result of your business and your actions terrifies me. I can only tell you, now that you've brought the country to its knees, it doesn't make sense for you to keep killing people. Don't brag about that victory in front of anyone, and for the rest of your life, deny any involvement in that coup. See if you can finally rest from that hell you live in and let the rest of us live in peace. I'll keep the secret, if you can call it that, but you'll have to carry everything you've told me in your conscience. For their part, every one of those butchers will have to come clean with God sooner or later. And according to the Irish, it's historically proven that the curse of 'the crimes of the father' never fails: the debt for the father's unpunished sins will always pass on to his descendants."

Maybe to avoid thinking of his children, Pablo changes the subject and decides to talk to me about the pain he feels over the loss of Iván Marino Ospina. He tells me that the army killed him in Cali, in a house that belonged to Gilberto Rodrí-guez, and that the jailed head of the Cali Cartel mourned his death, too.

"Your friend, your partner in the siege, died in a house of Gilberto's? Imagine, the founder of MAS and the heads of both cartels, mourning a rebel commander! After that, the only thing left for me to see in this country is Julio Mario Santo Domingo and Carlos Ardila Lülle hugging and crying over Tirofijo after he dies ingesting a gallon of *refajo!*" (*Refajo* is a beverage made of half Bavaria beer and half Postobón soda.)

Next Pablo asks me why I also lost my advertising con-tracts, and I explain that according to the journalist Fabio Castillo of *El Espectador*, "Pablo Escobar gave me Medias Di Lido and a TV studio so I didn't have to leave the house to tape my programs." The Kaplan family felt insulted and can-celed my contracts. Arguing that a celebrity was very expensive, they replaced me with a model; women stopped buying their products, and the brand plummeted. I add that nearly all the country's journalists know that I couldn't fit a TV studio in my apartment, but not a single one of them has come out in defense of the truth, especially my female colleagues who have been scheming for years to get me off TV, especially Santofimio's cousin and her daughter, the daughter-in-law of ex-president Alfonso López. They're well aware that I have never been beaten and I have perfect skin, but they tell anyone who will listen that I suffered multiple facial disfigurations followed by an equal number of plastic surgeries, causing me to retire from the media to become only Pablo Escobar's kept woman.

"Those two women are like Cinderella's stepsisters . . . and *El Espectador* and Fabio Castillo orchestrated all those dirty tricks so you'd be left without work. I've heard that there's a consensus among the media honchos to do to you now what they wouldn't have dared do when you were with me. And the police colonel who brought the DEA to the Yarí labs was the same one who gave that miserable journalist a mountain of information for a book full of lies. But I'll take care of all of them, my love: 'sit in the doorway of your house and watch the dead body of your enemy go by,' because your enemies are, above all, mine."

I get up from the chair and sit on the bed near his feet. I tell him that my favorite Chinese proverbs are "A blow that doesn't break your back strengthens you," and "What happens is for the best." I tell him that if he topples extradition he has to promise me that he's only going to think about building the half century of life he has left and stop his blessed obsession with what the media says. I insist that neither he nor I are judges, or executioners, or gods. I give him a hundred arguments to show him that now far from all those wicked people, I am almost so perfectly happy that I don't even miss the fame or the social life or my career in front of the cameras.

He listens to me in silence, scrutinizing my eyes, my lips, every millimeter of my expression, with that look of a connoisseur that he reserves for others and rarely uses with me. Then, with that authority conferred on him by the certainty he knows me like no one else, he tells me I'm fooling myself, that I ran away to that island to avoid thinking about all the pain people had caused me, and I took refuge in Rafael's arms to forget him. Thoughtfully, he caresses my cheek and adds that it's strange that I have such a clean soul, and that in all those years at his side I was never contaminated by his, which is blacker than coal. Suddenly, he stands up as if spring-loaded, kisses me on the forehead, and thanks me for going to Medellín to bring him the proof of something so serious. Before he says good-bye, he makes me promise I'll give him my phone number every time I change it, that I'll always be there when he needs me—as he'll be there for me, on a private and very safe line—and that I won't leave his life completely.

"I promise, but only until the day I get married again. You have to understand that starting then, you and I won't be able to talk anymore."

I leave Medellín a little calmer than when I arrived and convinced that if extradition falls, Pablo will be able to start rebuilding his life on the legacy of that generous spirit and extraordinary vision I had fallen in love with nearly four years before. On the flight to Cartagena I pray to the souls of the tortured women and ask them to understand my silence. After all, I don't know where I can denounce all these crimes against humanity committed by state-hired assassins and thieves. I know that if I talked about the horrors Pablo has now confirmed, the media, so complicit with the powers that be, will demand I be thrown in jail for participating in God only knows what. And all for the entertainment of a country where cowards take their anger out on women because they aren't brave enough to face men like Escobar.

I want to wash my memory of those images of hair-raising torture and terrifying agony for which not even Pablo on the day of the Beretta could have prepared me, so I sink into the marine waters and start training to swim to the big island across from us. That one is still in its natural state because a foundation belonging to the Echavarría family bought it to keep it from being colonized. It's six nautical miles there and six back to San Martín de Pajarales, which means six hours' swimming if the sea is calm. I don't mention my plans to Rafa, because I'm not a good freestyle swimmer. I decide that in order to become one, on my next trip to Bogotá I'll have my eyes operated on so I can get rid of my contact lenses.

The first time I achieve my goal, with the help of flippers, mask, and snorkel—which let you swim without much effort and without taking your head from the water—I congratulate myself, radiant with pride and waving my hands in the air in victory. Because activity starts a little after dawn on our island, I'd left the house at 7:00 a.m. to reach my destination by ten. I didn't see sharks or large animals on my solitary swim, and I blame the dynamite fishing and the engines of the tourist boats, which destroy the coral reefs and are the only real danger in the small archipelago. I rest a few minutes on that deserted beach that fills up only with tourists on Sundays, and then I set off on my way back, now much more confident. I reach San Martín at 1:00 p.m., in time for lunch. When Rafa asks me why I'm so happy, I don't tell him the truth, because I know it would give him a heart attack. Instead, I tell him that I'm going to stop swimming and start writing in the abandoned shed on an island a few feet from us. I explain that in my double condition as vision impaired and banned from the media, I have always dreamed that my colleagues in the announcers' association could record audio books when they don't have work, so the sightless could listen to their marvelous voices. He tells me that people who are too lazy to read would also like that a lot, but that he would want to hear my stories narrated by me.

"And what are you going to write about, Pussycat?"

I tell him I'm going to write stories about the Mafia, like *The Godfather*, and about hunters and fishermen, like Hemingway's.

"Wow! The one about the shark and the ones about animals are fantastic. But don't even think about writing about those degenerate *mafiosos* who are ruining this country! I can recognize one of those traffickers the moment I see him, even if he's only wearing a bathing suit: that arrogant attitude ... the way they walk, or look at women ... or eat ... or talk ... everything. They're disgusting, filthy. They'd be capable of having you killed, and I'd be left without my pretty Pussycat!"

The next Sunday, I descend the rope stairs from the second floor where our bedroom and the terrace are, wanting to find out whose huge yacht is parked in front of the house. I come face-to-face with Fabito Ochoa—brother of Jorge, Pablo's partner—and his wife, who are admiring the little aquarium in the dining room while Rafa talks to their children about the pregnant sea horses, which are the males, and the

"Little Monster," my pet of an unidentified species. I assume that when it came to the royal family of narco-trafficking in Antioquia, Rafa decided to make an exception only because the Ochoas' true calling is in their love of animals: raising the most beautiful specimens of horses and bulls. Their other activity is only . . . a very profitable hobby.

Nearly everyone who passes through the islands visits the aquarium. The few who don't know Rafa Vieira know me, which means that our social life is much more active than one might think. One Sunday, while we are having lunch with Ornella Muti and Pasqualino De Santis—who are in Cartagena filming *Chronicle of a Death Foretold* based on García Márquez's novel—the cinematographer sits looking at me. He comments that I am *"veramente, una donna cinematografica"* and that he can't believe I've retired from the cameras. I know that many other people have asked about my absence from the screen and the microphones, and I'm also aware that only Pablo and I know the true reasons. In any case, the words of that legend of Italian cinema keep me happy for days, and even more so when I manage to repeat my twelve-nautical-mile feat the following week.

Rafa and I often attend parties on neighboring islands, especially those thrown by Germán Leongómez, whose sister is married to Admiral Juan Antonio Pizarro. Their son, Carlos Pizarro Leongómez, has become the new leader of the M-19 after the deaths of Iván Marino Ospina and Álvaro Fayad. Pizarro is popularly known as "Commander Papito," because he's the only guerrilla leader in history who looks the way Che Guevara does in photos, and not like an escaped inmate from Bogotá's Modelo prison. And, through the twists and turns of life, his rich uncle Germán, whom I had met as a suitor for the hand of the much richer Rasmussen widow, would soon become the boyfriend of the only Colombian congressperson who could aspire to a political career in France: Íngrid Betancourt.

A couple of weeks later I return to Bogotá, because in order to find out if I can operate on my eyes, I have to go without my contact lenses for two weeks. I decide to spend those days in my apartment in the capital, instead of on the island where I could have an accident, slip and fall, and end up in Pancho Villa's fins. In spite of the fact that only twenty people now know my telephone number, and all of them know I live in Cartagena, I find hundreds of calls on my answering machine. They range from the inevitable calls from David Metcalfe and Armando de Armas to the dozens who hang up without identifying themselves or leave messages threatening rape and torture. A few days after my arrival, Pablo calls.

"Finally, you're back! Did you get tired of living with Tarzan?"

"No, I'm not tired of Rafael. I came to see if I can have my eyes operated on before I go blind. And you, have you gotten tired of what you've always done?"

"No, no, my love: I enjoy making mischief more every day! But what do you do all day on that island, aside from swim and sunbathe? Have you worked on my script or on the book?"

"The novel won't come.... Every time I finish a chapter, I'm horrified at the thought that someone could read it, and I tear it up. I think you were the only person in the world I wasn't ashamed to show what I wrote."

"I love to hear that! Now that's truly an honor, my dear. I'm going to talk to you on a different phone every three minutes, okay? Change."

In half a dozen successive calls, Pablo tells me he wants to offer me the best business deal in the world: a unique opportunity that we can only discuss in person and in the most absolute privacy, and about which he can't tell me anything now. He says that for his own peace of mind he wants to secure my future definitively, because it made him terribly sad to hear me say my career had gone down the tubes because of him. I thank him for the offer and tell him I'm really not interested in getting rich. The next day he calls again to insist that he wants to make up for what I lost, once and for all; he asks me to imagine what will become of me if for some reason I separate from Rafael tomorrow and no one will give me work and— God forbid!—the doctors can't save my sight.

"Do you realize that if you had accepted that offer from the channel in Miami, you wouldn't have that whole happy life you're living? Imagine if you add what I'm going to offer you on top of all you have now. You could remove the thorn in your side from what they've done to you and secure your future! It's now or never, my love, because next week . . . I could be dead. Promise me that before you go back to Cartagena you'll stop by and see me. Don't make me suffer, it's for your own good . . . and your children's . . . because you told me you want to have kids, right?"

"I don't know. . . . You're going to set up a TV channel, and you want me to work there! That's it, right?"

"No, no, no! It's something much better than that. But I can't tell you anything now."

"All right. I'll go, but if it's not something worthwhile I'll never talk to you again as long as I live, and I'll renounce being your biographer. Let those beastly journalists write your story and say that you're nothing but a psycho with giraffes."

"That's the way to talk, my love! You should write how you know better than anyone that I'm a soulless psychopath so people will respect me and be even more afraid of me."

THE DOCTORS INFORM ME that they can't operate, but that my condition isn't serious. I think it's a shame to have to go on wearing contacts, and I can't wait to be back with Rafa, who calls me daily to tell me that he misses me. On the way back to Cartagena I stop for a few hours in Medellín to fulfill my promise to Pablo, who has sent a trusted aide to coordinate the details of our meeting. Once I'm at the apartment, he calls to tell me he's been delayed, and he begs me to wait a couple of hours; when two become four, I know he is forcing me to spend the night in Medellín. When he arrives, he excuses himself with the argument that every time he's going to see me, he has to wait until he's completely sure that "the coast is clear." He informs me that because of the material that was sent to me anonymously, he's had to bug my other phone again, the one that everyone has, but he couldn't tell me until we saw each other in person. He justifies himself by saying that if I were ever kidnapped, the identification of all those voices threatening me could lead to my location and rescue; but I wonder how long Pablo Escobar is going to keep exercising so many subtle forms of control over me. I decide that unless this business he wants to propose is really worthwhile and compatible with my new life, when the moment comes I'll tell him that I'm engaged to Rafa and that we can't see each other anymore.

He asks if I want some weed, because he's going to take a few hits. I'm surprised, because he's never smoked in front of me. I reply that I'd be happy to accept if marijuana produced any interesting effect on me, but it just makes me tired and I fall deeply asleep until the next day. He asks how I know, and I tell him that my Argentine husband smoked often, and I had tried it a couple of times without much success.

"That old *ché*? Now, that's a shocker!"

I tell him that "the Stivel Clan," maybe the most brilliant and important group of actors in Argentina, had undergone collective psychoanalysis with LSD in the seventies, under the supervision of a shrink who was crazier than all of them put together. I also tell him LSD is the only drug I'd like to try, to open the doors of perception, as Aldous Huxley says. I talk to him about my admiration for the British philosopher, disciple of Krishnamurti, and of his studies of peyote and mescaline, and I tell him how when Huxley was on his deathbed he asked his wife to inject him with LSD, because he wanted to cross the threshold to the other world with a total absence of pain and the absolute clarity he had glimpsed before, when time, space, and matter disappear. I ask him if he could get me some lysergic acid so I could try it once and save a little for the eve of my death.

"Are you suggesting, then, that I become an importer of hallucinogenic drugs? What a scandalous proposal, Cleansoul! I'm shocked!"

From that day on, Pablo will call me Cleansoul every time he wants to tease me, or mock what he describes as my "quadruple moral" when it comes to drugs: a visceral hatred for cocaine, crack, and heroine; a deep contempt for his adored cannabis; my interest in the peyote and *yagé* rituals of the Mesoamerican and Amazonian tribes; and my secret fascination with the idea of crossing the mythical river Styx en route to Hades: that something could help me replace pain and fear with absolute comprehension and a feeling of floating in a light and diaphanous ether, beyond all pleasures. A sublime delight, as described by Huxley, that would transcend all rational experience.

Pablo asks me if people do a lot of drugs on the islands, and I tell him that everyone except Rafa smokes and snorts by the ton. He insists on knowing whether I now love Vieira the way I used to love him, and to avoid giving him the answer he wants to hear, I explain that there are as many forms of love as there are of intelligence. I offer as proof the fact that things as exquisite as snail shells have been designed and built by primitive creatures based on the golden ratio, 1.618033. The same number is used in great Renaissance masterpieces, and is a recurrent pattern in the most successful works of architecture and the most impressive views in nature, including many human faces. I add that I have always been fascinated by the idea that minds as diverse as God's, geniuses', and mollusks' could, rationally or instinctively, apply the same proportion to rectangular compositions to make attractive geometric shapes.

From the bed where he is lying down, Pablo listens to me in silence, sunk into what seems to be a feeling of utter peace. From the same chair where he'd once blindfolded me and caressed me with a revolver, I coldly observe the king of drugs under the effect of a hallucinogenic he didn't produce. Suddenly he gets up and comes toward me as if in slow motion, and he takes my face in his hands, gently, as if he were going to kiss me and he didn't want to scare me. He studies me carefully and says that maybe it's the divine ratio's proportions that inspire the fascination he's always felt for my face. Uncomfortable, I tell him that had never occurred to me. Trying to wriggle free, I ask what he wanted to talk to me about. He caresses my cheeks and says he would like to know whether I talked to other very wealthy men about Irish curses and geometry. Surprised, I tell him no, that I had only learned things from those men. Staring at me hard, and without letting go of me, he asks if I feel any affection for those tycoons. Since we had talked before about the biggest financial groups, but not other men in general, I say I feel nothing for any of them, and I insist that he tell me once and for all why he made me come to Medellín. He asks if I would like to squeeze a lot of money out of those stingy old men, and when I laugh and say that the mere fantasy would bring a mental orgasm to anyone, he crows triumphantly that that is precisely what he wants to talk to me about:

"I am going to kidnap the richest men in the country, and I'm going to need your help. I'll offer you twenty percent . . . twenty percent of hundreds of millions of dollars, my dear."

So Armando de Armas wasn't lying!

Pablo had come into my arms still a child, and since at that age I was already a woman, I got used to taking care of him. He still doesn't know those men the way I do, and incredulous, I ask him, "Why do you need to kidnap those poor guys with two or three or five hundred million dollars, when you have three billion or more? You're richer than all of them put together, and if you become a kidnapper, your enemies are going to say that you are not only crazy but also poor, and they're going to eat you alive! Whatever you smoked isn't Samarian Gold, it's Hawaiian Platinum, Pablo. Holy Christ: How rich do you want to be?!"

"I've only taken three hits, and if you keep talking like that, I won't offer you any more good deals, Virginia. Look: I need liquidity, because the laws against money laundering have turned our lives into hell, and almost all the money from the business is held up outside the country. We can't bring money in appliances like we used to. Botero can't paint a picture a day, De Beers can't mine any more diamonds weekly, and no more Ferraris will fit in the garages. Extradition will fall, it's true, but the moment the gringos open cases against us in the United States, they are going to put a price on our heads, especially mine. And so, for the war that's coming, I need millions of dollars here in Colombia, not billions abroad. And there is nothing more expensive than a war. My friends in the M-19 taught me everything I needed to know about kidnapping, and with you I have an expert in the four richest men of the country and one of the few people I have total trust in. I have always thought you were a genius, and you could have phenomenal success in my world, if only you didn't impose so many scruples on yourself. Do you want to hear the plan, or are you going to be Cleansoul?"

Pablo seems not to have realized that he, now, is also one of the moguls of my past. With my best smile I ask what kind of partnership he proposes we form, and he, excited, falls into the trap.

"My first targets are the two bottlers: Santo Domingo is several times richer than Ardila, and I would kidnap him in New York, where he goes without bodyguards, or on one of his trips. You were seen getting out of a plane with him and your British friend . . . about a year ago, remember? Carlos Ardila has the advantage that he can't get away, because he's confined to a wheelchair. Luis Carlos Sarmiento answers your calls and gives you appointments . . . and I'm sorry for listening to your conversations, my dear. Then I'll look at Carlos Haime, the

Jewish owner of the oil and soap corporation, who is a close friend of Belisario Betancur. Since he's your neighbor, I'll need you to let me use your apartment while you're in Cartagena, so I can track him down."

As he goes on giving me details of how he plans to kidnap the four richest men in Colombia, I start to see that Pablo has a perfectly orchestrated plan for me. I explain to him that the Santo Domingo, Sarmiento Angulo, Ardila, and Gutt families have armies of at least a hundred men just as tough as his own, trained in the United States and Israel for one single thing: to keep the guerrillas from kidnapping any members of their families or taking a single cent from them.

"That terror is one of their favorite conversation topics, especially after Juan and Jorge Born were abducted in Argentina, and Camila Sarmiento, Gloria Lara, and Adriana Sarmiento were kidnapped here in Colombia. So far, the superrich haven't decided to hate you, because although they would never admit it in public, in secret they applaud the founding of MAS. If you kidnap a single one of them, they'll all forget any little quibbles they have among themselves and they'll unite against you. And you can't even imagine what Carlos Ardila's praetorian guard is like, or the kind of lifelong enemy that Julio Mario Santo Domingo can be! In front of a lot of people, he killed a caged viper just by spitting on it three times. To finish you off, it would only take four or five, Pablo!"

"Woooow . . . poor little snake! But don't you hate them? They never gave you a thing, and now they've had you banned from working and left you to die of hunger!"

"Yes, but it's one thing to detest them, and quite another to want to hurt them. When it comes to Luis Carlos Sarmiento, you should be thinking of meeting with him instead: he knows more about banking in Latin America than anyone else, and you could figure out a way to solve that little problem of your 'excess millions.' You put your army at his disposal when his daughter was kidnapped, and it's better business to have him on your side than as an enemy: Don't you realize that it's better to legalize one billion dollars than to squeeze him for fifty million? And since you listen to my conversations, you'll know that he had no problem giving an appointment to Gilberto Rodríguez."

His eyes flash.

"Well, unlike that jailbird, I don't like banks or credit cards—I prefer the smell of hard cash! And I hate taxes almost as much as Santo Domingo does; that's why he, the FARC, and I are the richest in the country. Let's forget about your ex-boyfriends, because it seems like you want to protect them. . . . Let's go to the next level: you know the Echavarrías, the sugar manufacturers of the Cauca del Valle, the flower exporters of the Bogotá savanna, and all those rich people who used to be your friends. Their wives turned their backs on you because of our relationship . . . and I only want to serve up on a silver tray the chance to pull out those thorns, my dear: one by one, all of them! And then there's another little gold mine: the Jewish community."

I tell him that at a moment when he has the U.S. government on top of him, plus the Colombian state and the press, he can't go after anyone with wealth or resources, at any level, above all the rebel groups that haven't messed with him since they abducted Martha Nieves Ochoa:

"You are Pablo Escobar, the richest magnate in Latin America, founder of Death to Kidnappers! You're not Tirofijo, and kidnapping is the FARC's business! How would you feel if Tirofijo got it into his head to become the new Czar of Coke?"

"I'd break him the next day! Don't you doubt that for an instant, my love. But you have to accept that kidnapping is so profitable that the FARC is richer than me. And I am not a magnate, understood? I'm the biggest outlaw in Latin America, and I think, speak, and act as such. Don't confuse me with those miserable bloodsuckers. I was born with different values!"

I try to make him see that no one, brave and fearsome and rich as he may be, can simultaneously face the gringos outside the country and everyone inside it, because it would be suicide. And when I run out of logical reasons, I tell him, simply, that his death would break my heart, that I loved him more than all my ex-boyfriends put together, and that I would shoot myself on the day when, between them all, they finish him off.

He looks at me in silence and caresses my face with the tenderness of old times. Suddenly, he hugs me and exclaims happily, "I was testing you, Cleansoul! Now I know that even if you stop loving me completely, and you even detest me, you would never conspire with anyone to turn me over to the gringos for all the money in the world the day they put a price on my head!"

He pulls me up with both arms, and with his hands on my shoulders, he adds, "In any case, I want to remind you that . . . there's only one way to test a person's loyalty: telling them something that no one, no one else in the world knows—whether it's true or not. And if the secret comes back to you, one month later, one year later, twenty years later, it was because that person betrayed you. Don't ever forget that lesson, because I care a lot about you, too."

I can only reply that if someday I told a single person about our conversation, not only would they lock me up in a mental asylum, but all my friends, family, and even my domestic help would go running, and I'd have to live the rest of my days not on Rafa's island but on a desert island. Before we say good-bye, I tell him, "You're very creative, Pablo, and I know you'll find a way to bring the money in without going after the rich and the guerrillas at the same time. For the love of God: 'Go in peace and sin no more.' We had enough with that incinerated criminal record!"

"I always know what's going to happen ... and you are not going to live the rest of your life with Tarzan, or have children with him. I can't offer you anything, Virginia, but before three months are up you'll be back here with me. And though you don't want to, you're going to have to see my face and hear my name every day of your life...."

On the plane to Cartagena I think to myself that it wasn't true that he was testing me: though he seems to have desisted from the idea of kidnapping the heads of the largest financial groups in the country, I know that sooner or later Escobar will become a kidnapper, and an incredibly efficient one. I was the one who once taught him that "he whom the gods love dies young," like Alexander of Macedonia. And although I couldn't swear it, I think Pablo is planning to risk his life, either at Russian roulette or in a very carefully planned way, for something that goes far beyond his fight against extradition, and much further than the control of an empire. But, above all, far beyond his time.

How Quickly You Forgot Paris!

I'VE BEEN SWIMMING through a school of jellyfish for two hours; there seem to be hundreds of thousands of them, maybe millions. If they were moon jellyfish, I would be dead, but thank God, they are only the inoffensive kind, the ones with little brown dots. Here and there I see one of the moon species, but I can dodge them. Today for the first time I have put on the wetsuit I brought from Miami to avoid the recurring problem of those stings, and I am also wearing my watch with a compass, indispensable to have in the ocean. I had left the house at 9:00 a.m., and though it's already noon, I still haven't reached the island that is my destination, which in the past I've reached in around three hours.

I must be feeling the effects of not sleeping a wink last night . . . and I shouldn't have left the house so late. So many relatives of Rafa's who came to spend Christmas on the island! And I'm tired of those tourists who come into the house to snoop around . . . they always want photos, and when I say no, they tell me I am conceited. As if I didn't know why all those men want to take photos with me in a bikini. . . . Not even my ex-boyfriends have photos of me in a bathing suit. But how many millions of jellyfish are there in the Caribbean Sea, my God? Well, I'm almost there . . . today is Sunday, and I can ask one of the tourist boats to take me back. . . . But I'm not tired, and that would be giving up. I must be careful the engines don't chop me into mincemeat. . . .

The beach that is deserted on other days is full of people today, the kind who arrive in boats by the dozen and end up having lunch at the aquarium. I take off my wetsuit and sunbathe while I decide what I'm going to do. The captain of one of the boats recognizes me and asks if I want him to take me to San Martín; I tell him no, because I'm going to swim back. He says he's never heard of anyone undertaking such a feat, and he advises me to start as soon as possible, because after 3:00 p.m. it will be much more difficult with the rising tide. After some twenty minutes, I feel rested enough to set off, and I decide that if I'm tired, I can ask one of the boats to pick me up once I'm close to San Martín.

But . . . it's a miracle, there's not a single jellyfish left! Where could they all have gone? It's like they were vacuumed up. What luck! Now there's nothing to stop me from making it back in under three hours. . . .

A while later I take my head from the water and see that San Martín looks farther away than usual. I turn to look back and I notice that the big island also seems to lie at a much greater distance. In any case, there's no point in going back because the tourist boats have already left. I don't understand what is happening, and I wonder if I'm seeing things because of the insomnia. I decide to swim as hard as I can, taking my head out of the water every five minutes, but the two islands move farther and farther away. Suddenly, I realize that I'm not in a straight line between two destinations but rather in the vertex of a *V*: a powerful current, the same one that carried millions of jellyfish away in twenty minutes, is dragging me out to open sea. There isn't a single tourist boat in sight because it's lunchtime, and not even a fishing boat because it's Sunday.

It is already three in the afternoon. There is a breeze and the waves are six feet high. I calculate that now I would need some five hours to reach San Martín. Since night in the tropics starts to fall around six thirty, in about three hours the first lights will come on and I'll be able to swim toward them. I know that no one drowns with snorkel and fins, because they let you float and swim without getting tired. But in the open water there are always sharks, and unless I find a yacht that has deviated from the usual route, on high seas I will have maybe seventy-two hours of life. I decide to prepare myself to die of thirst, but strangely, I don't feel afraid. I repeat that "he whom the gods love, dies young," and I wonder why Pablo ever bothered to save my life.

Pablo again . . . When will he stop killing everyone who wrongs him? Now he killed the colonel who led the DEA to Tranquilandia and the director of the newspaper who's been after him for four years! It's like a wound that won't scar over: every time I open a newspaper, there he is again . . . with that evil face of his. I wonder what the newest threats on my answering machine will be! Maybe God wants me to die in the sea and not at the hands of those butchers. . . . Yes, it will be a relief to end all the suffering. I love Rafa a lot, but in these countries you don't marry a person, you marry a family. Families are terrible . . . and his father is a horrible old man. I think I'm going to rest, because it's pointless to struggle against the current and I'll need all my strength to swim behind a boat, if one ever shows up. . . .

At 4:00 p.m., both islands are mere dots on the horizon. Far in the distance I glimpse—finally!—a beautiful yacht gliding slowly through the water. It seems to be coming toward me, and I tell myself I am incredibly fortunate. But a long time later it goes right past me, and I can see a pair of lovers hugging and kissing on the prow, and an island captain who is whistling on the stern. I start to swim fast behind the boat but no one sees me, and I realize it was a mistake to have bought a black wetsuit to make myself look thinner, instead of the orange or yellow one that Rafa recommended. For the following hours I yell until I have almost no voice, but the noise of the engines prevents anyone from hearing me. I know perfectly well that if I get any closer, the wake of the propellers could yank off my mask, and without the tube for breathing and my contact lenses, I would be even more lost. Around six thirty in the afternoon, when I'm about to lose consciousness from exhaustion after leaping hundreds of times in waves eight feet high, it looks like the captain's eyes meet mine. He turns off the motors, and I summon all the strength I have to leap again. He shouts to the couple that it looks like there is a dolphin following them, and they move to the stern to get a look. When I jump again and cry for help with the little voice I have left, they can't believe that they are seeing a woman out in the middle of the ocean. They pull me up onto the yacht, and I tell them I live in San Martín de Pajarales; that I don't know how to swim freestyle but I've spent nine hours in the water and more than five in the open sea; and that I was dragged out by a current. They look at me incredulously, and I collapse onto a bench lined in white plastic, wondering why the hell God has now saved my life fourteen times, and always at the last minute.

When I reach San Martín, Rafa pushes me into the shower and slaps my face over and over, supposedly to wake me up. Then he calls his father and his neighbor Germán Leongómez, uncle of Carlos Pizarro, the new M-19 commander. Those three men subject me to a war council and decide I have to leave on the first plane. Again and again I explain that I was dragged out by a current, and I implore Rafa to let me rest until the next day. But his father yells at him not to believe me and orders him to expel me from the island immediately—without even letting me pack my things—while Leongómez repeats over and over that I was trying to kill myself and I pose a risk for his friends.

At the wheel of his small, old boat and with his back to me, Rafael navigates toward Cartagena in complete silence. While I look out at that lead-gray sea, I tell myself that the man with whom I've lived for the past ten months has turned out to be nothing but a "daddy's boy" who lets other cowards tell him what to do with his woman. I think that Pablo was right, that Rafa isn't a man but a thirty-five-year-old child, and that at his age Escobar had already built an empire and donated hundreds of houses for thousands of people. When we reach the airport, Rafael tries to kiss me good-bye, but I turn my face away and walk quickly toward the plane. I reach Bogotá at ten at night, shivering with cold in my summer dress, because the Vieiras and their neighbor never even let me take a sip of water. I sleep for ten hours straight, and the next morning, when I get onto the bathroom scale, I see that I'd lost thirteen pounds—almost twelve percent of my body weight—in one single day.

Never again will I answer Rafael Vieira's calls. When I try to find out the names of the captain and the couple who rescued me from open waters so I can invite them to dinner and thank them, no one can tell me anything about them. Some months later, one person will tell me that "they were *mafiosos*, and they got killed," to which I'll reply that "you could also call people who build mansions and businesses on land stolen from the nation *mafiosos*."

A few days later I come down with a respiratory infection, and I visit the well-known ear, nose, and throat doctor Fernando García Espinosa.

"Did you fall into a sewer, Virginia? Because you have three types of streptococci that are only found in human feces! There's one that over time could seriously affect your heart, and I'm going to have to give you years of vaccinations."

Every time I'd gone swimming in the ocean, I had encountered "*gamalotes*," yellow islands twenty-five to forty feet in diameter made of decomposing plants and detritus. I had skirted them with disgust, and as it turned out, they were emitting millions of microbes into the water around them. But at the beginning of 1987, the infection was only the start of the odyssey that followed my miraculous rescue on the high seas. I had spent the night before crying, because I knew that in order to keep me from returning to TV at any cost, the media owned by the presidential families would make me pay for the newspaper director's murder. And now that Pablo wasn't my lover, and thus not my protector, state security organizations were free to do to me what they hadn't dared do when I was with him.

A few days after my return to Bogotá, Felipe López Caballero calls to invite me to dinner. The editor of the magazine *Semana* has three obsessions in life: Julio Mario Santo Domingo, Pablo Escobar, and Armando de Armas; though I am the only person who knows all three, I have always roundly refused to talk to him about them. Felipe is a tall and beautiful man with Sephardic features, like his brother Alfonso, who is always an ambassador to one of the world capitals. Although affable and seemingly shy, Felipe is a man of ice who has never been able to understand why he, so powerful, elegant, and "presidential," can't inspire in me the love I feel for that short, ugly peasant—and criminal summa cum laude—named Pablo Escobar.

His dinner invitation—the first he's made—surprises me, because while López has always had an "open" marriage, he would never risk being seen in a restaurant with someone who for years has been the target of the most visceral hatred from his wife and his mother-in-law, the unrecognized daughter of Santofimio's uncle. While we are dining in "The Library," the restaurant of the Charleston Hotel, he tells me about the recent scandalous events involving his wife, which all of Bogotá is talking about. The straw finally broke the camel's back, and he's decided to get a divorce. He is living temporarily in his brother Alfonso's apartment, and he invites me to see the place. In front of a long wooden table with two huge silver candelabra, Felipe asks me if I would like to marry him. It's a question I've heard dozens of times, and although I have always been gratified, it's been a while since I was impressed by it.

"*Semana* never tires of saying that I'm Pablo Escobar's lover. Since you've always had an 'open' marriage, do you want, then, to share me with him?"

López asks me not to pay attention to all that nonsense, because he can't control what every one of his journalists writes about me.

"Then I can only ask you this: If you looked like the King of Cuckolds when you were married to the ugliest woman in Colombia, what will it be like when you're married to the prettiest? I don't cheat on my husbands or boyfriends, Felipe, and especially not in public. Plus, I think I already know the only man who could get me to marry again."

He asks me who it is, and I reply that he's a European intellectual, eleven years older than me and from a noble family. I add that his greatest charm is that he still doesn't know that someday he will become the only intelligent choice I've made in my entire life.

THE DECISION to keep anyone from hiring me at any cost no longer knows any bounds imposed by journalistic ethics or logic: from Caracol Radio—directed by Yamid Amat, Alfonso López's attendant journalist—on down, all the broadcasters in Colombia crow that I threw myself into the ocean to kill myself because I have AIDS. Others swear that I'm dead and my humiliated family had to bury me in secret. An actress who has trained her voice to sound like mine calls the clinics of well-known doctors to say, in tears, that I'm suffering from the most embarrassing and contagious illnesses. The doctors, for their part, have no qualms about repeating left and right at all the cocktail parties that they're treating me for syphilis.

I'm calmly having lunch dressed in Chanel, in a Salinas restaurant, with Beatriz Ángel de Rugeles, the wife of an IBM executive. Suddenly the radio is shouting that if I'm alive, I should prove it once and for all by appearing before the microphones and cameras. Beatriz Ángel, who owns a chain of video stores, proposes that we should go to the Video Festival in Los Angeles together in order to forget about what happened on the island and escape everything they're saying about me. She is close friends with Felipe López and tells me he will be there, too, negotiating distribution for his film *The Child and the Pope*. López has taken advantage of Pope John Paul II's visit to Colombia to make a feature film with funds from Focine, directed by his close friend María Emma Mejía. And a loan of $800,000 in 1986, with no defined term—plus two hours of free acting from the Holy Father himself—have conspired to make what promises to be a smash box-office hit in Catholic Latin America, only exceeded by productions the size of *The Girl with the Blue Backpack*.

When I'm about to get on the plane—running, because I'm late—half a dozen photographers and journalists chase me though the airport corridors. They're from *Hoy por Hoy*, the magazine published by Diana Turbay, daughter of ex-president Turbay. The headline of the next issue, with me on the cover sporting a mink coat and dark glasses, will be: "Virginia Vallejo Flees the Country!"

The contents of the article will suggest that I'm not running from the paparazzi but from the law.

Beatriz and I stay at the Beverly Wilshire Hotel. Felipe López, who is staying at an economy hotel, calls to ask me if he can come to the main event as my husband so he won't have to pay for the fifty-dollar ticket. I have no choice but to accept, because how could I not help a movie producer save such a fortune in Hollywood? After we've been there for a while talking, López tells me, "Jon Voight hasn't taken his eyes off of you for half an hour, because you're the prettiest girl at the party. Now that I'm finally a free man, you really don't want to be my girlfriend?"

I look over at Jon Voight, laughing, and I tell Felipe López that according to the magazine *Semana*, the fearsome and sinister cartel boss Pablo Escobar Gaviria is not willing to share me with the son of the ex-president who turned him into a myth.

WHEN I AM BACK IN BOGOTÁ and unpacking my suitcases, the phone rings.

"But what is all this they're doing to you, my love? Why are they saying you have AIDS, that you're a fugitive, that you have syphilis? Is it true you tried to kill yourself? Are they tormenting you that badly? I'll tell you what: you're not going to answer any of these questions over the phone, and tomorrow I'll send a plane for you. You can tell me in person about everything those Vieiras did to you and what's behind what that pack of hounds are saying. I'm going to have all those butchers and quacks killed, and I'll castrate all those murderers with microphones! And Tarzan and his father, too!"

What woman in my situation wouldn't be dancing with happiness at that news? And even more so with the mariachi serenade that night, with "Amor del Alma" and "Paloma Querida" as incontrovertible proof that her Saint George will always protect her from the dragon? When he spins me around twice the following night and says the only thing that matters is that I've returned to his arms, I feel like the most protected woman in the universe. Now nothing and no one can hurt me, and for a few days I don't care about the threats and anonymous letters, the evil stepsisters and the butchers, the moguls and vipers, extradition and the dead, and whether all the rest of humanity loves or hates me. Nothing, nothing else matters to me except being next to that face, that heart, that torso, and in Pablo Escobar's arms. And when he swears that when he has me like that, all the other women disappear, that I'm the first and the only and the last, that his hours with me are the only true heaven that an outlaw like him will ever know, I float in the light ether Huxley talked about, because beside that masculine being, time and space disappear from my life, all the substance of which fear is made, and all matter that could contain the slightest bit of suffering. With Pablo I lose my reason, and with me he loses his head; and then all that's left are a man pursued by justice and a woman pursued by the media who know and take care of and need each other, despite the pain caused by all the absences, all his crimes and her sins.

"So the Vieiras forced you to get on a plane after struggling against a current in open waters and losing thirteen pounds in one afternoon?! They're a bunch of murderers . . . and you are a heroine! I'm going to blow that daddy's boy's boat to bits! There's a member of the ETA who's an expert in explosives and wants to come over from Spain to work with me. I'm told he's a genius, and I want to find out if it's true."

"But, Pablo . . . isn't the ETA . . . a little much to send to Tarzan? It's not as if San Martín de Pajarales is the Kremlin . . . or the Pentagon!"

"No, no, they're just common cowards . . . but I need the

guy to start practicing now, because there's a war coming. And I have other plans for the Pentagon: I'm going to get that missile whatever it takes, if I have to go to the ends of the earth."

I ask him what missile he's talking about, and he reminds me of the one he had initially planned to use to protect the airspace over Nápoles. Since a missile can only be used once, he's changed his mind: he plans to hit a worthwhile target, and it's not the Colombian air force or the presidential palace. The latter and the Presidential Guard Battalion can be neutralized with a few bazooka hits, without the need for a missile that's so expensive and complicated to get. But if he hits the Pentagon right in the middle of the building, the U.S. defense systems will be annulled, along with their communications with allies. That's why he's trying to contact Adnan Khashoggi, who is the richest arms dealer in the world and a man who balks at nothing.

"The Pentagon? Wow . . . woooow. But . . . haven't you seen the Pink Panther movies where there's a thousand-carat diamond protected by a bunch of crisscrossed rays that can only be seen with special glasses? How can you not remember? That's what you'll find at the Pentagon! Or don't you think the Russians would have hit the gringos with missiles a while ago, if it were that easy? There are thousands and thousands of miles of airspace protected by an impressive weave of invisible rays; yes, sir, I believe they're called lasers! And the White House and Fort Knox must be the same. Ay, my love! You're starting to seem like those bad guys in the James Bond movies. Like Goldfinger, willing to wipe out all of humanity in order to achieve their goal. Extradition isn't worth all that. . . ."

He looks at me wild with rage, and I think he's about to strangle me.

"That's what you think, Virginia! Extradition *is* worth all that and anything else I have to do. Everything, everything, everything, and don't say such an outrageous thing again or I'll throw you out the window! And the Pentagon isn't protected by any rays, visible or invisible. I've been thinking about how I'm going to send that missile. People are convinced the gringos are so invulnerable and smart, but it's not true. How do you think I get millions of tons of coke in there, which have already gone down from $50,000 a kilo to $14,000 since I've known you? Have you still not realized that we Colombians are much smarter than them?"

He tells me Reagan is obsessed with wiping him out, and Nancy with eliminating his business—which is why that little phrase "Just say no!" was invented—and that he won't let them or anyone else get to him. I swear to him that I saw a movie where a Russian missile directed at the Pentagon reached the limit of U.S. airspace and then, ipso facto, turned around and went straight back to the terrorist who had sent it. I try to make him see that if his missile bounces off American airspace and returns to Medellín, there will be half a million dead, like in Hiroshima or Nagasaki.

"Oh, God, what a fright! I think you're going to start World War Three, Pablo!"

He replies that Hollywood movies are made by a bunch of Republican Jews who see the world from Reagan's perspective, and that he's starting to think I'm turning into a chicken, like all the other women.

"I thought you were my other half and the only one who understood me, but turns out you're not just Cleansoul, you're also a moralist. Not to mention an imperialist! It's no good. But ... wait a second ... just a second, now ... Hiroshima, you said? Nagasaki? Oh, Cleansoul! . . . You really are a prodigy, a genius! What heaven did you come down from, love of my life?! And I was thinking I'd have to build a base in some banana republic . . . when it was really so simple!"

And as if he'd just solved the Taniyama-Shimura conjecture and Fermat's last theorem, he starts dancing and spinning me around, singing happily:

"*Por el día en que llegaste a mi vida, paloma querida, me puse a brindar!*" ("To the day you arrived in my life, dearest dove, I toast!")

I tell him one of these days they're going to put him in a straitjacket and lock him up. I beg him to stop thinking about such barbarities, because sometimes he scares me.

"You and I always used to talk about politics and history, but ever since I went to the islands you only talk about explosions and abductions and bombings. Neutralize the Pentagon! Do you think you're the USSR's minister of defense? There are beautiful things in life, Pablo: think of Manuela and Juan Pablo. Use that head and that heart of yours to build something, instead of dreaming of tearing everything down. I want to rest, too, after so many threats and dirty tricks. . . ."

He is thoughtful for a while, and then he tells me, "Yes . . . you should rest a while from all the threats. Travel all you like, as long as you always come back to me . . . but not to Europe, because it's full of temptations and you might stay there. To the United States, which is closer, okay? Even though you and I can't see each other every month, I go crazy every time you disappear on me. When you come back, I'll have the Tarzan job ready to go, and they'll know they can't keep messing with you, either. I'm sick of them tormenting you, poor thing!"

. . .

I HAPPILY GO TO MIAMI, and when I return, Pablo asks me to come to Medellín. He tells me he's done tracking down every member of the Vieira family, and he has everything ready to blow up Rafa's boat.

"I'm going to place the bomb in the marina where Tarzan keeps his boat when he goes to Cartagena! It's much easier there than in open waters, where the navy could grab my boys afterward."

Horrified, I exclaim that at the fishing club dozens of humble workers and tourists are going to be blown to bits, in addition to a hundred yachts. He replies that that is, precisely, the idea.

"I've told you that what I like most is making mischief, so don't you turn into Cleansoul on me. This will also set a precedent with all those psychos who've been tormenting you on the phone. We'll kill several birds with one stone, and no one, not the butchers, the vipers, the evil stepsisters will mess with you again. You have to demand respect in life. Period!"

For the next hour I beg him every way I can to not place that bomb, to think of all the innocent people and the Ochoas' yachts and that of the couple who saved my life, but he won't let his arm be twisted. He takes several hits of marijuana, and as he relaxes, I start to realize that the bomb fulfills a quadruple purpose: it punishes not only the Vieiras but also Rafa Vieira, and it sends a message not only to the butchers and the journalists but also, above all, to any man who could come between him and me. Since the days of the coke rocks for Aníbal and my express divorce, Pablo has sent two multimillionaire rivals running and asked me to help him kidnap my ex-boyfriends. He's used any pretext to take revenge on whomever he decides to blame for our separations after absences so long they seem like good-byes, and to hate anyone from my past. Now he asks me if he can lay his head on my lap, and I tell him of course; I caress his forehead and he, staring into space and talking as if to himself, continues:

"I've had enough of them humiliating you and persecuting you because of me. What they want to do is to take you out of my life for good . . . and you're my only true friend . . . the only woman who has never asked me for anything . . . the only one I can talk to about things you don't talk about with your mother or wife, only with other men. I can only trust three people now: Osito, Gonzalo, and Gustavo. And no one is happy with their brother, my love, and the Mexican lives in Bogotá, and my partner has changed a lot. Plus, all three of them are just like me, and I need someone who cares about me but challenges me . . . who has another scale of values, but who understands me and doesn't judge me. You've saved me from making a lot of mistakes, and I can't allow you to leave again . . . like after the palace, when I needed you and couldn't find you anywhere . . . you, who were always going off with someone richer than me . . . the owner of two dolphins and a shark! How about that?"

I tell him that, precisely, Pancho Villa III doesn't justify an attack from the ETA and Pancho Villa II. Finally, I manage to convince him to forget the bomb and replace it with a couple of the kind of phone calls he knows how to make. Reluctantly, he promises that's what he'll do, but only because the explosion at the marina could come back to haunt me. Remembering a recent event, I ask him, "Pablo, have you never thought about killing another man with your fists?"

Surprised, he asks me what I mean. I tell him how, at a recent dinner in the house of a well-known theater impresario, the boxer "Happy" Lora had asked for my phone number. I'd given him the number of the building's concierge, so that if he called, the doormen and my chauffeur would be very impressed. With absolute delight, I add, "Now, that's a fight the whole country would pay to see: Kid Pablo Escobar versus the challenger, Happy Lora! I think, in a twelve-round fight, the bets in favor of the world champion would be . . . around . . . a hundred to zero?"

"Noooo, my dear, you've got it all wrong! It would be a hundred to zero in favor of Kid Escobar! Because . . . why do you think *chumbimba corrida* was invented?"

We laugh, and we talk about other personalities of national public interest. He confesses that he plans to contact Fidel Castro through Gabriel García Márquez. The only expeditious way to get drugs into Florida is through Cuba, and he is willing to be more generous with Fidel than he ever was with Noriega or Ortega.

"Pablo, trying to get a Nobel laureate in literature to help you make drug deals with Castro is like asking the painter Fernando Botero to propose a brothel business to Gorbachev! Get your head out of that cloud, my love, neither García Márquez nor Castro is going to pay you any attention, and they're going to laugh at you. Ship your merchandise through the North Pole or Siberia, but forget about Cuba: Fidel has Guantánamo inside, and with what's happening now with the Contras after the Sandinistas started working with you, he's not going to risk an invasion or having the whole world accuse him of being 'a drug trafficker tyrant'!"

"The gringos financed the Contras with money that came from seized merchandise, did you know that? And I don't mean coke, but crack! Now that's an addictive drug that ends people's lives. . . . I've tried to block it, but I can't. If that's not a double standard, what is? Why doesn't Nancy Reagan tell Oliver North: 'Just say no, Ollie'? To kill communists, that guy made a deal with 'Piña,' convicted traffickers, and with the devil himself!"

I insist that the Castro idea is suicide, and I advise him to stop mixing so much politics in his business. Shrugging, he replies calmly, "And who said the president is the only option? I learned from the Mexican generals that the military doesn't have so many scruples. And if a president won't come to you, the generals under him will. In poor countries, every military man has his price, and that's what the reputation of being rich is for, my love. All of them, every one, are dying to work with me . . . and Cuba isn't Switzerland, is it? It's a simple matter of logistics: if it's not Fidel or Raúl Castro, it's whoever's below Fidel and Raúl. Period."

I try to make him see that if Castro finds out that someone in Cuba is working with Pablo Escobar, he's capable of putting him before a firing squad:

"And when that happens, the gringos aren't going to send Contras to Colombia, they'll come straight for you! Shoemaker to your shoes, Pablo—you're not a kidnapper or a communist, but a drug trafficker. Don't make political mistakes—you own an empire and that's what should matter to you. Otherwise you'll spend all your cash on wars and end up poorer than when you started. You're lining the pockets of those Caribbean generals and dictators while you do away with anyone who stands in your way in your own country. And if you want to go down in history as an idealist, you're doing everything backward, because 'charity begins at home.'"

"Whoever told you I wanted to go down in history as an idealist, my love? You still have no idea the kind of plans I have!"

GUSTAVO GAVIRIA has asked me to come by his office to talk about a very private matter. When I arrive, he closes the door and admits that I am the only person he can trust with a secret that's tormenting him. I imagine he's going to talk to me about his partner's crimes—or his *liaisons dangereuses*—because I know that they are seriously affecting the business's profits.

"I'm tired, Virginia . . . Pablo and the Mexican are practically living in hiding, Jorge Ochoa is in jail, and Carlos Lehder has just been extradited. All the responsibility for the organization falls on my shoulders, and sometimes I wonder if it's all worth it. Thank God, every time you come back Pablo gets reasonable for a while, but then you two separate again and he's left with no one to rein him in, just smoking weed in that world of hit men and little girls . . . surrounded by a family that looks at him like he was an omnipotent God. . . . And you know something? I've realized that there's only one thing that matters in life once you have secured the future of your children and of your grandchildren, but you can't leave the country to spend all your money. And it isn't accumulating diamonds, it's being happy with a beautiful woman who loves you, the way you love Pablo. That's the only thing that can put the brakes on a man. You know what I mean . . ."

I ask him who he is in love with, and he tells me it's a TV actress I must know. He swears he needs her, to adore her, to marry her if she accepts, to be faithful to her for the rest of his life. He repeats that she's the most beautiful creature in creation, that he's suffering horribly at the thought that she could reject him, and that for love of her he would retire from the business to become an honest man. And he offers me whatever I want if I just convince her to travel to Medellín and introduce them, because for security reasons, he can't leave his territory.

"Gustavo: I don't even want to know her name, because I wouldn't wish what I've suffered over these years to any other woman. Especially not one who works in the media. I have never been a matchmaker, and you are very married. Don't ask this of me, for the love of God—I've got enough on my plate with Pablo's latest ideas. Though it pains me to the core because I care about you, I can't do you this favor, nor do that to her."

He asks me what I most want in life, what my most unachievable dream is. I tell him that my life has turned into a hell of constant threats, and that I am going to confide a secret in him, too: I would like to leave the country and to go study simultaneous translation at the school in Geneva, Switzerland. If I had to stay, my goal would be to start my own cosmetics company. But Pablo is determined for me to become witness, and screenwriter or chronicler, of a long chain of events that scares me more each day.

"If you introduce me to Ana Bolena Meza, Virginia, I promise you will never regret it. And I swear I'll get you out of the country so you can start a new life, far away from all this. You don't deserve what they're doing to you because of us . . .

and what's coming is worse than anything you've seen yet . . . but I can't tell you any more. Promise me you'll try, so I can get rid of all this uncertainty that keeps me awake at night. You know I'm not promiscuous like Pablo: I am a one-woman man. I'm dying of love for that girl, and I just want to make her happy. Help me, you have such a big heart and you can't imagine how I'm suffering!"

He moves me so much, and I feel he's so sincere, that I promise to think about it.

And I go to San Francisco, to contemplate the ancient giant sequoias of Muir Woods and to see Sausalito again. I also visit that part of paradise on earth that once belonged to a certain General Vallejo, an ancestor of mine who didn't pass a single acre of Californian land to me. When I am returning from the Wild West and boarding the plane in Miami, two federal agents stop me. They ask if I'm carrying cash, and when they show their badges, I notice that the younger one's hand is trembling. I conclude that Pablo inspires terror even in the FBI. When I open my suitcases to unpack, I see that my entire luggage is in disarray and seems to have been meticulously searched for money. I never leave any country with more than $1,000, and I conclude that those are the things that happen when one travels a lot and tells customs agents that she's retired because she's sick of working.

Some time before, Joaquín Builes's girlfriend had called on the verge of tears to tell me that Hugo Valencia owed her more than two million dollars for jewelry, and he didn't want to pay. She begged me to talk to him for her, saying he no longer answered her calls, but he feels deep esteem and respect for me. I had called Hugo and explained that my friend was in serious trouble with her suppliers and was appealing to his generosity and his sense of honor to send her what he owed. I hadn't spoken with the Kid in two years, and his reaction had horrified me.

"I can't believe that you're calling me to collect other people's debts! Why don't you call your lovers instead, shameless old bitch? That schizo Pablo Escobar or that prisoner Gilberto Rodríguez? How dare you talk to me like that?"

"If you want people not to talk to you like this, Kid, pay your debts the way decent rich people do. And you know perfectly well I've never been Gilberto's lover."

"Ohhh, no? Well, his wife has a *marica* who goes from station to station paying the journalists to say you are! Hadn't you heard? Either you went deaf or you don't live in Colombia!"

After spending several minutes yelling things that not even our worst enemies would have dared to say about Pablo and me, Hugo had furiously hung up the phone. Two days later my jeweler friend had called, radiantly happy, to thank me—the Kid had just paid her one million dollars all at once. After I told her about the insults I'd had to bear in order to do her that favor, she'd replied that someone like me shouldn't pay attention to those things, because Huguito was just a boy going through a rough patch.

I go to Cali for the launch of a new product, and I decide to visit Clara while I'm there. Right away I see that she's changed a lot. After listening to my story about what happened on the islands, she goes to her room, comes back with a Cartier case, opens it, and shows me a necklace and earrings of emeralds and diamonds worthy of Elizabeth Taylor. Then, with a mixture of rage and pain, she tells me in an accusatory voice, "Did you know your little Pablito chopped Hugo Valencia into pieces? Yes, the Kid, who was our friend and who bought millions of dollars' worth of jewelry for his girlfriends! Now, Virgie, look closely at the size of these emeralds and guess who ordered them from Beatriz: it was Pablo! And guess who they're for? Some nobody beauty queen! That's right, with this $250,000 parure, Pablo bought a weekend with a little whore in a tin crown! And you, the most elegant and sought-after TV star in the country, a high-society beauty who only dated nobility and multimillionaires, not only did he give you nothing, he left you without work, with everybody gossiping about you, and persecuted by death threats! Look what that lover or ex-lover of yours with the face of a bus driver gives a forgettable hooker for spending a few nights with him! What has that miserable assassin given you in five years? You who were like a queen on a pedestal? What did that butcher give you? Look at it closely: a quarter of a million dollars for an ignorant little maid who will never wear it in front of a camera or at a ball in Monte Carlo, and who will sell it in an emergency for $5,000! Look at it, Virgie, so you never forget that what Pablo Escobar likes are expensive whores from his own social class!"

I have never asked anyone for jewels or expected them as gifts. The ones I wore on TV were costume Chanel, Valentino, or Saint Laurent; the ones I sported on magazine covers were only on loan from Beatriz. I had always thought that compared to the stingy magnates, Pablo was the most generous of men, the only lavish one, the only multimillionaire who had cared about making and seeing me happy. But the sight of those emeralds worthy of an empress and the description of their recipient, on top of what happened to the Kid and the harsh words from someone who for years had been my best friend, all wake me up from the dream I have been living in and return me to reality. I swallow my tears, tell myself that today I've truly reached my limit, and decide that the hour has come to follow Gloria Gaitán's advice and look for financing for my own cosmetics company. I ask for an appointment with the man who owns half the labs in the country, who has just returned to Colombia after a prolonged stay in Spain. And he sends word that he'll see me immediately.

I have never been inside a prison, but this one is the opposite of what I had imagined: it looks like a boarding school dorm, with happy people going up and down the stairs. There are almost no guards—just some smiling and well-dressed lawyers—and there's salsa music playing everywhere. In the Cali jail, Prisoner Number One is nearly as powerful as the pope in the Vatican, which means that no one asks my name, or stamps my hand, or opens my bag, or searches me. An officer leads me straight to the warden's office and withdraws.

"Our Lady of Mercedes has come to say hi to the ex-Extraditables!" I exclaim, like Scarlett O'Hara when she goes to visit Rhett Butler in jail, wearing that dress made out of the velvet curtains from the house at Tara.

"Ohhh, my queen, what is this vision come down from heaven?" cries Gilberto Rodríguez, giving me an affectionate hug.

"If it gets out that you're in jail here, half the country is going to line up to get in! This hotel is stupendous! Do you think they'd let me spend six months here once I manage to save an illegal fortune the size of yours?"

He laughs with a certain sadness and tells me I haven't changed a bit. We sit across from each other at a long table and start to talk. He tells me that though he's lucky to be back in his own country and on his own turf, the years in the European jail were terrible, hounded as he was by the thought that the Spaniards could turn him over to the gringos any day. After many negotiations between the governments of Belisario Betancur and Felipe González, he and Jorge Ochoa managed to get cases opened against them in Colombia for minor crimes so that national justice could claim them before the Americans did. That was what saved them from being sent to the United States.

"Here they bring me food from home or the restaurant of my choosing, but in Spain things were different. One gets used to being spoiled, my queen, and you can't imagine what it's like to have to eat unsalted spaghetti every day. . . . And the sound of those bars slamming morning, noon, and night, an infernal racket that won't let you sleep. But the worst part is thinking all the time that your woman is two-timing you."

"But who is the Beast going to cheat on you with? I'm sure she's a faithful beast!"

"No, no, my love, I'm not talking about her. I'm talking about how you and I had . . . Paris, remember? Did you forget already?" he asks, not hiding his sadness.

I could never tell him about what Pablo did to me when he found out about Paris. That terrible episode is one of our most intimate secrets, and in any case, I made him pay dearly. The debt is settled, and the pain almost completely forgotten. Plus, I've sworn to myself I won't ever talk about that with anyone. I decide to ignore the bit about "your woman." I look at Gilberto affectionately, comment that in those three years I only got one letter from him, and ask when he's going to get out. He tells me he'll be free in a couple of months, and that he would like to see me again. He admires my hair and suggests launching a shampoo with my name. I thank him for the compliment and tell him that what I'd like to launch, instead, is a line of makeup and skin care products, but I don't have capital. He promises that we'll talk about that when he gets out. To change the subject I ask him about the murder of Hugo Valencia, who owed a lot of money to a jeweler acquaintance of mine and to my friends at Raad for several cars.

"Huguito didn't pay his bills, and he made some very rough enemies in Medellín. Thank God, here in the Valle del Cauca such horrible things don't happen. . . . But let's not talk about that, I don't know anything about that business, because I'm retired. Really! You don't believe me?"

I tell him I believe that he's in forced retirement . . . and a provisional one. I realize that he no longer laughs easily, and he seems to have lost much of that malicious likability he used to have. But I think that compared to men who seem invulnerable, those with a temporary air of defeat hold a special charm for almost all women. I insist that he should consider himself the most fortunate man in the world, and he repeats that the years in jail marked him deeply and nothing will ever be the same: the stigma of a very well-known criminal passes on to his children. I tell him that's the price of inheriting a billion "stigmatized" dollars, and that his children should feel very grateful for the sacrifices he's made for them. With profound nostalgia, he explains that now he'll never be able to leave Colombia, because of the risk that another country will arrest him at the request of the American government and extradite him to the United States. Which means that not even with all his money will he be able see Paris again. We talk about his studies and readings in jail, about *Heart of Darkness* by Joseph Conrad and about Stefan Zweig, his favorite author, and how he would have liked to be an orchestra conductor. I know it's true, and when we say good-bye a couple of hours later, he promises that he'll come see me the day after he gets out. When I get back to Clara's house, I pass by the velvet case that contains some cold diamonds and emeralds—which could be worth cents or millions—and I tell myself that "God works in the most mysterious ways." And, like Dinah Washington, I sing happily:

"What a difference a day makes, twenty-four little hours . . ."

ARMANDO DE ARMAS proposes that I direct *Hombre de Mundo*, but I turn it down, because I know he doesn't treat the editors in chief of his other magazines well, and that with me he would be merciless. And since everyone around me seems to have an empire of some sort, I get to work designing my own: I study all the biographies of Helena Rubinstein, Elizabeth Arden, and Estée Lauder, and I decide it's time to create a Latin American brand with practical beauty products, colors that match the skin tones and features of Latin women, and economical prices, because the high prices of cosmetics only come from advertising and packaging. I ask Hernán Díaz to take some new photos of me and I find that, at thirty-seven years old, my face and figure look better than ever. I know that with a minimal investment from Gilberto, and with his enormous distribution chains, I could create a really successful business. After all, I can convince women to buy everything I advertise, so how about those creams that erase razor cuts and those vitamins that cure syphilis and AIDS? I buy all kinds of products to study them in detail and figure out which ones can be imitated or improved, and I think that, sooner or later, I will also launch products for men. I think I'm ready to start, and I count the days until my potential partner is free. But

I decide not to talk to him about my plans until I'm sure he shares my enthusiasm. Some weeks later, we talk again.

"I'm about to get out, but in this business the problems never end, *reinita*. Now your gentleman friend from Medellín is threatening us with war, because my partners and I don't want to do him a favor. I can't tell you what it is, because these are matters for men. And you should be careful, because he's going insane . . . and he's capable of having you killed."

I tell him that's a crazy idea, because even though Pablo and I aren't together anymore, he still considers me his best friend and he cares a lot about me. I propose he let me try to smooth things over, because now that Luis Carlos Galán has joined the official Liberal Party and is going to be the next president, he and Pablo need to think about creating a united and peaceful front against extradition.

"And I don't want to see you two kill each other or be extradited. We've all suffered enough as it is. . . . Stop this—the both of you are breaking my heart. Let me try for an armistice, okay?"

He tells me he's skeptical, because the mood is already pretty hot, but he doesn't mind if I communicate his willingness to reach an agreement to Pablo.

What I don't know at this point is the kind of favor Escobar is demanding from the Rodríguezes. Gilberto and Miguel have two main partners: "Chepe" Santacruz and "Pacho" Herrera, one of the few narcos who prefer young boys to beauty queens. Pablo is demanding that they turn over Pacho—his archenemy—in payment for a favor he did at the beginning of the year for Chepe: cut Hugo Valencia to bits. It's the kind of thing they don't do in Cali, but they do in Medellín.

Several days later I meet Ana Bolena Meza at the beauty

salon. The answer that sweet girl gives me is a lesson in dignity that I will never forget. We only exchange a few polite words, but her enormous blue eyes tell me more than she can express in words. In the depths of my heart I feel a profound relief at my failure, mixed with a strange and furtive feeling of joy: there are still people left in the world who can't be bought.

GILBERTO RODRÍGUEZ has told me he can't wait to see me; he got out of jail yesterday, and today he's already in Bogotá. It's five in the afternoon, and I'm in my living room making sure everything is perfect: the champagne, the music, the flowers, the view, the book by Zweig that he hasn't read yet. I hear the elevator door open and I'm surprised to hear laughter. When two men impeccably dressed in navy blue make their entrance looking radiantly happy, I can't believe my eyes: Gilberto Rodríguez has come to flaunt Alberto Santofimio in front of me, and Pablo Escobar's candidate has come to flaunt his rival. They inform me that they can only stay one hour because they're going to ex-president Alfonso López Michelsen's home; he's waiting for them there with Ernesto Samper Pizano to celebrate Gilberto's return to freedom.

I have spent my entire life in front of a camera and survived years of public insults, and I think I manage to hide how I feel about Santofimio. When the two of them say good-bye, I know that the Rodríguezes are going to finish Pablo. But I also know that first, Escobar will finish off half of humanity. If in the whole world only he and Gilberto were left, I think I would choose Pablo: he's pitiless, but with him you know what to expect. Like me, Escobar is carved from one piece. In five years I've called him maybe half a dozen times, and never to tell him I miss him or want to see him. But today I decide to follow my heart and do just that, for the first and last time: we have to meet urgently to talk about Cali, and I am going to travel in a commercial plane. I don't tell him or Gustavo that I'm going to say good-bye to both of them. And that this time, it will be forever.

In the past five years I have gradually become an impotent spectator of the designs wrought by all those men. Tomorrow I will do the impossible to try to dissuade Pablo from war, because the things gestating in his mind horrify me. I have just realized that I am witnessing the beginning of the end of two formidable newcomers to the world of power, and that once he and Gilberto have destroyed each other and the establishment has given them the coup de grace, nothing in the country will have changed. The same mean intellects as always will reign for another century with their pockets full of both men's money. Tomorrow I will see for the last time the only man who has made me completely happy, who has always treated me like an equal and never underestimated me, the only one in the world who has made me feel pampered and protected. I look at myself in the mirror and tell myself that in just a few hours I will say good-bye forever to all that he and I shared. I look at myself crying in the mirror, and behind the reflection, for an instant I'm reminded of Munch's *The Scream* once more.

∞ *A Diamond and a Farewell*

EXTRADITION FELL MONTHS AGO on procedural grounds, and Pablo has gone back to working in his office. When I arrive, I'm informed that he and Gustavo are in meetings, and they've asked me to wait a few minutes until they are free. I think about it being the first time that I've made use of Pablo's waiting room and, thank God, it will also be the last. While I wait, one of their bodyguards or *sicarios*—the name now given in Colombia to the Mafia's hit men—looks at my legs lasciviously and comments to his companion, in a voice loud enough for me to hear every word, that my successor definitely doesn't have my "class." Since I did the ad campaign for Di Lido pantyhose, many men stopped looking at my face and now don't take their eyes off my legs, because simple people always have more faith in what the media tells them than what their own eyes are seeing.

I look at those boys with their evil eyes and obscene tongues who don't hide their contempt for society and for women, and I think it's going to be a relief to say good-bye forever to that elite of an underworld that is ever more sinister, ever more powerful. Last night I decided that, for the first time since I met him, I am going to ask Pablo to give me money. Over these five years, and on my dozens of trips abroad, he has always sent me considerable sums for my expenses, which I accepted as tokens of his love and generosity. But, since he paid the debts of my television company in exchange for advertising time in January 1983, it hasn't occurred to me to ask him for anything, because I have always had enough from my work. I've never aspired to accumulate property or riches; for fifteen years, I've been one of the most sought-after professionals in Colombian television, and I never would have thought that at my age I could end up out of work. All this is to say, simply, that my savings are enough to live on for some twelve months.

Yesterday I'd been looking forward to talking calmly with Gilberto after his three years in jail, but the visit with Santofimio made alarm bells go off, and my instinct tells me I shouldn't expect any encouragement from him about the cosmetics business. That's why I have decided it will be better to ask Pablo for help, so I can go study languages in Europe and work in what I've always dreamed of since I was a child, until my marriage and later television got in the way. But first of all, I plan to do everything in my power to try to stop what seems to be an imminent war between the Medellín and Cali Cartels. That is, between their two top leaders: Pablo Escobar and Gilberto Rodríguez.

The door to Pablo's office opens and he comes out accompanied by a woman. She's around twenty-seven years old, and she's wearing a Colombian-made red wool sweater, a gold chain with a large medal of the Virgin Mary on her chest, and a black skirt. Although she is quite attractive and has a good figure and her hair is blown out, she could never be a model or a beauty queen. She has the look of a cosmetics salesgirl or an employee in a home-decor store. He introduces her as his girlfriend, and I congratulate him for having such a pretty girl at his side. She looks at me sweetly and without the slightest hint of envy of my expensive red Thierry Mugler dress, which gives me an hourglass shape and attracts everyone's eyes when I enter a Bogotá restaurant. I've chosen it from among more than 150 designer dresses from Milan, Paris, and Rome, because somewhere I read that the memory we conserve of a person is that of the last time we see them. And much as I still care about Pablo, I have decided that today I will say good-bye to him forever. Not just because we have stopped loving each other, but because our friendship has been turning into an inexhaustible source of problems, suffering, and danger for someone as visible but unprotected as me. I say good-bye to the girl with a smile and some polite words, and I say to him, "I'm going to ask your girlfriend to excuse us for a few moments, because I came from Bogotá just to bring you a message from Gilberto Rodríguez. And I think I should give it to you immediately."

And I head for his office without waiting for him to invite me. Pablo and the girl exchange some brief words, and he enters behind me, closes the door, and sits down at his desk. I can tell that he is seething with rage. The day before, I had said the word "Cali," and in punishment, he hadn't hesitated to expose and embarrass me in front of his "salesgirl." And, on seeing that woman, who can't be very important to him or me, the celebrity who sacrificed everything for love has not hesitated to respond with the name of his worst enemy. Pablo looks at me, and in a fraction of a second those eyes of a grizzly tell me everything: everything that awaits me for the rest of my life. The rest of my life without him. Without him, and nothing. Absolutely nothing.

"Let me warn you, I only have a few minutes, because my girlfriend is waiting for me. What did you want to tell me?"

"That Gilberto and Samper are going to massacre you, Pablo. But I can't explain how in just a few minutes, because finishing you off isn't so easy. And either you respect me or I'll go back on the next plane."

He looks at the floor, and after thinking for a few seconds, he looks up and tells me, "All right. I'll send someone to the hotel for you tomorrow at 9:30 a.m. and we'll meet at ten. And don't look at me like that. These days I get up very early. That's right, at nine! My day is full of meetings, and I have become a very punctual person. Gustavo is waiting for you. See you tomorrow, Virginia."

His curiosity tells me everything: a man who has paid $250,000 in emeralds for a weekend with one of so many beauty queens, but at the mere mention of Cali displays that "salesgirl" as his girlfriend, is losing his sense of proportion and is highly vulnerable. Together, the four big bosses of the Cali Cartel have more power and more resources than he does. And he's now alone, because his partners don't share his visceral hatred for Cali, and in particular for Gilberto Rodríguez. With a cool head, Escobar is a human calculator; with a hot one, he loses his sense and obeys only his wild passions. I have always known that he has the fiery soul of a warrior and that his rival has a soul of of ice, like all bankers. And I know

Pablo Escobar's strengths and weaknesses like no one else. I know that while he has the courage, pride, and tenacity of the exceptionally brave, he also suffers from the impatience, arrogance, and stubbornness of those likely suicidal men who one fine day decide to attack all their enemies not only at the same time but also prematurely. I feel a deep compassion—for him and for us—and the deepest and most painful nostalgia for what could have been and will never be. This fierce, unique being has not yet turned thirty-eight, and I once believed he was destined for great things.

A STRONG MAN is never more of a man than when he lets a tear fall. A furtive one for the irreparable loss of a child, a father, a dear friend. Or for an impossible woman. Between these other four walls, a man very much like Escobar, but diametrically opposed to all those subordinates outside, cannot hide his pain. He's just learned that the only being in the world for whom he would give his life, for whom he would leave everything behind, is a woman who someone like him can never have. Gustavo Gaviria begs me to tell him the whole truth, difficult as it may be for him to hear, and I am grateful for the trust placed in me by this man I had once thought was made of steel, ice, and lead. I confess that at the mere mention of his name and relationship to Pablo Escobar, Ana Bolena Meza went running. But first she'd told me, scandalized, "Virginia: you were this country's diva, and that drug trafficker ruined your career and your good name. I am just an actress who earns an honest living. Tell this Gaviria that not even for all the gold in the world would I subject myself to what those brutes let people do to you, or what the press is doing to you now. Tell him women like me only feel contempt for them. I'd rather die than let one of those narcos come near me!"

Gustavo asks me to repeat every word uttered by the impossible woman he was head over heels in love with. When he refuses to understand why that beautiful girl with enormous light eyes has such scorn for him, I remind him of what was written and said about me in the newspapers and on the radio: the stories of drug traffickers who beat me up horribly to take away my yachts and mansions, of women who had me cut with knives to take away my cars and jewelry, of authorities who raided my house to seize drugs and weapons, of doctors who treated me for syphilis and AIDS. I tell him that the media has disparaged me to keep me away from the screen and the microphone, in an attempt to deny me my right to work, my integrity, my honor, all the while demanding that any remnant of dignity, talent, or beauty be violently sliced, beaten, and kicked out of me.

Unable to contain or stop myself, and knowing that sooner or later he would share it with his best friend, I start to tell Gustavo all the things that I could never say to Pablo. Not just about the price I paid for having supported his ungrateful business associates and their nationalist position against extradition, but many other things. How can any poor devil sleep with a woman who really loves him when he knows, in the depths of his heart, that he is unworthy of love? Millionaires as they may be, for their whole lives, they will be doomed to pay the pretty ones for the mere illusion of love. I add that the Bible says, "Do not cast pearls to swine," and that men like Pablo don't deserve any love besides that of those pricey prostitutes he likes so much. And I end by saying that my mistake was to not have set my price from the beginning, when his partner had begged me to ask for whatever I wanted and I told him I wanted nothing, because iconic women educated like princesses don't love a special man because he's rich or poor—or so that he'll give them gifts—but rather because they want to make him happy and protect him from the outside world.

Gustavo has listened to me in silence, looking out the window. With a sad voice, he recognizes that I was clearly educated to be the wife of a prominent man and not a criminal's lover. But, he adds, that all of them are married to women who love and care for them, for richer and for poorer. I reply that those women only bear all the public humiliation because their men cover them in diamonds and furs, and if it weren't for those, almost all of them would leave. I describe the emerald jewelry worth a quarter of a million dollars—which couldn't have been ordered for that girl with the medal on her chest—and I ask him to help me convince his cousin to give me just $100,000 while I sell my apartment, so I can leave behind this country so hostile and lost to memory. I tell him I want to go to Europe and do the work I've always wanted: use my verbal and written mastery of half a dozen languages and basic knowledge of the Germanic and Nordic tongues.

Gaviria explains that they are going to need a lot of liquidity for the war that's coming, and he warns me I should be ready for his partner to say "No!" to an amount that, a few years back and it being for me, he surely would have given without thinking twice. He adds that neither is Pablo going to willingly accept my leaving for good, because he needs to know that his dear friend will always be there for all those things that he couldn't discuss with any other woman, or with his family.

Gustavo is a small and thin man who is always pushing a lock of limp hair from his forehead and who, like his cousin, doesn't look people in the eyes. After a brief silence and a deep sigh, he walks over to the safe, takes out his trays of diamonds, and places them on the coffee table in front of the sofa where we have been talking. He opens the cases full of hundreds of diamond rings whose sizes vary between one and two carats. He tells me he wants to give me one as a souvenir, because he *is* grateful for everything I've done for them.

Very moved, I tell him no and no, and thank him. But then, at the shining sight of all that thousandth millionth of his wealth, I change my mind: I take a Kleenex to dry my tears and I exclaim that I want the biggest of them all. Not only because I deserve it, but also because it's about time some blessed magnate gave me a jewel! He laughs delightedly, tells me he's honored to be the first, and urges me to take the purest, a diamond of less than one carat. I reply that I'll leave all that purity to Saint Maria Goretti, that no one can see the carbon except him with his magnifying glass, and that I want the fattest one with the fewest defects. I try on an oval one—uncommon, since the majority of diamonds are round (brilliant cut) or square (emerald cut)—and I have the ring on one hand and a Kleenex in the other when the door opens.

"But . . . what are you doing here? I thought you'd left a while ago! And what's this scene? Is the star getting engaged? Are you marrying . . . Don Gilberto?"

Gustavo looks at me with his mouth and eyes wide-open, and I can't do anything but burst out laughing and tell him his partner should be put in a straitjacket. Enraged, Pablo exclaims, "She doesn't get diamonds! She's different! She's not interested in diamonds!"

"What do you mean, different? Does she have a mustache, like you?" replies Gustavo. "I still haven't met a woman who hates diamonds! Do you really despise them that much, Virginia?"

"I adore them, and for five years I deceived your cousin here into believing I didn't so he wouldn't think I loved him for his dirty money! But he seems to think I've been deceiving him for years with a man behind bars, and I've had to come, like some Helen of Troy, to stop this war before they castrate each other and all feminine humanity is left in mourning!"

"You see she's with Cali, brother?" shouts Pablo furiously to Gustavo. Meanwhile, enraptured, I contemplate my first solitaire and prepare to defend it with my life. "Diamonds are for beauty queens who are on our side!"

"Don't talk nonsense, man; if Virginia were with Cali, she wouldn't be here!" Gustavo tells him in a reproachful tone. "Everyone wants to starve her to death, and I am going to give her something she can keep, something she can sell tomorrow if she needs to. I don't have to ask permission from you or anyone else, and plus, a diamond protects a person. And the only real queen you've had in your life is this woman here: before she met you, she had millions of men already pining for her!"

"Let her spend her time writing instead of posing for so many magazines and photographs!" replies Pablo, looking at my ring like he wants to cut off my finger and throw it into the toilet. "Yes, books, instead of so much talking! Stories to tell, that's what she has!"

"Oh, God forbid! Promise me, Virginia, that if you're going to write, you'll never, ever, say anything about us . . . or the business, for the love of God!" begs Gustavo, alarmed.

I swear, and he explains to his partner the reason for the gift.

"We're never going to see her again, Pablo. Virginia came to say good-bye to us for good."

"For good?" asks his cousin, disconcerted. Then, with the expression and tone of voice he surely uses to interrogate any poor guy accused of stealing one hundred kilos of coke from him: "What do you mean, for good? . . . Is this true, Virginia? Are you getting married, or what? Why didn't you tell me anything about this?"

I keep ignoring him, and I promise Gustavo that whenever I'm in danger of dying, like now, I'll rub the diamond as if it were Aladdin's lamp. I tell him I will never sell it, and I'll wear it to the grave.

Pablo says that he thought I was different from other women, and I raise my arms and exclaim that he was wrong—turns out I'm just like the rest, and I've discovered that I love diamonds, too! Gustavo laughs, and his cousin closes the door behind himself after saying, in a mixture of disgust and resignation:

"I'm disappointed in you, Cleansoul! Well . . . you and I will meet tomorrow."

The place of our final encounter is a little country house with white walls and geraniums in flowerpots, some thirty minutes from the Medellín Intercontinental, where two of his men had picked me up. He drives up in a little car minutes after we do, followed by another car with two bodyguards who immediately withdraw. A woman is sweeping the floor of the living-dining room, and she looks at me curiously. From personal experience, I know that when certain people are forced to get up at the crack of dawn, they are always in a bad mood. Pablo doesn't bother to ask the cleaning woman to leave, and right away he lets me know he's on the warpath.

"I can't give you more than twenty minutes, Virginia. I know you're here to intercede for your lover, and I've also already heard that you're going to ask me for money. Don't expect a single cent from me, or that I'll back off, because I'm going to destroy him!"

The woman cocks an ear while I tell her boss that the only life I've come to intercede for is his. And that someone who has spent three years in prisons in Cádiz and Cali couldn't be the lover of a person who lives in the Rosario Islands or in Bogotá. I add that, in effect, I didn't come to ask someone like him for guitar lessons; I came to ask him to get me out of the country before his enemies tear me to shreds. Looking at my nails while I contemplate my diamond, I add with utter calm: "I think that the Rodríguez family and Ernesto Samper are going to finish you. If you want to know how, I'll tell you all the details right here in front of this lady."

Pablo asks the cleaning woman to leave and come back later. The woman flashes me a furious look and vanishes. He sits across from me on a small two-seater bamboo sofa lined with brown flowered chintz, and I start to tell him everything about Gilberto's visit with Santofimio:

"They stayed less than an hour because they were going to Alfonso López's to celebrate Gilberto's freedom with the former president and Ernesto Samper. They were dressed very elegantly, and I couldn't believe my ears or my eyes! If you're going to go to war with Cali, Pablo, you can't keep trusting Santofimio: remember that his cousin is married to Gilberto's daughter, and that his partner in Chrysler, Germán Montoya, is now the man behind the throne in Virgilio Barco's government."

I ask him not to forget Machiavelli's advice, "divide and conquer," and I beg him not to get into a war that seems designed by the DEA to kill the two biggest bosses. It will leave hundreds dead, bring extradition back, and seriously sap both their fortunes.

"His, at least. It will be much harder for mine to run out!"

In my most persuasive tone of voice I remind him that if he were so rich, or so "liquid," he wouldn't have suggested I help him kidnap magnates; I add that, thank God, that secret stayed between us. He looks at me furiously, and impassive, I go on.

"The Rodríguezes don't have to support an army of one thousand men, Pablo, or all their families. I'm guessing that total is about six thousand people. . . ."

"My, how you've learned, Virginia! I'm impressed. And what about his army? Hundreds of congresspeople and journalists who are more expensive than all my boys put together! I think that in terms of costs, we're equal. And I invest in the people's affection, which is the best-spent money in the world! Or do you think any one of those senators would give his life for that guy?"

Again and again I repeat that the Rodríguez family has protection in their territory from the governor, the police, the army, and thousands of taxi driver informants. And that the M-19 doesn't mess with them, either, because Gilberto, aside from having been Iván Marino Ospina's friend, has been very close throughout his life to the family of commander Antonio Navarro who, according to him, "likes money a lot." I warn him that his enemy is a personal friend of several presidents and that given a choice between Rodríguez's silver and Escobar's lead, people's affections aren't going to waver. I try to make him see that he's dividing a guild that started out united around him and is now splitting into dozens of little, bloodthirsty cartels led by people without an ounce of greatness who will do anything to emulate him.

"A lot of clever people are fishing in those troubled waters, waiting to kill each other and leave the territory open. But if you and Gilberto join forces, your costs will be cut in half, your strength will double, and you both will win the final battle against extradition. Because if Galán is elected the next president, he'll enforce extradition the day after he takes possession. Gilberto has relationships with almost all the powerful people in this country, and you inspire a different kind of respect, the kind no one in his right mind would dare to question. Stop using those millions to kill each other, and let the rest of the Colombians live in peace—this country will forgive anything. You've always known what people are good for, Pablo: use me to stop this war. Go on, extend your hand and show him what greatness looks like. And the next day I'll leave Colombia so neither of you ever sees me again."

"He has to take the first step. He knows why, and there's no reason for you to know. They are men's concerns that have nothing to do with you."

I try to make him see that what matters isn't why the conflict started, but what an alliance with Cali could do for him.

"Well, if that guy seems so rich to you, and so important and powerful, why don't you ask *him* for money to leave?"

Never in all my life have I felt more insulted. I react like a panther and tell him that not only would I be incapable of asking anyone but him for money, but that I also never even spent one night with Gilberto Rodríguez. I add that my career ended because Pablo Escobar was my lover for a full five years, and not because of a five-minute affair that only three people know about, preceded and followed, it's true, by dozens of conversations that helped me learn how cheap presidents, governors, and half of Congress can be. Since I see we're not going to get anywhere, I remind him that he's a very busy man and we've been arguing for almost one hour.

He asks what time my plane leaves. I tell him it's at five, and that I should leave the hotel at three. He gets up from the sofa, and with his hands resting on the railing of the little balcony to my right, he looks off into the distance.

"And why do you want to leave . . . forever?"

I explain that I want to study simultaneous translation in Geneva. An excellent interpreter earns $1,000 a day, and I only need a loan of $100,000 because I would sell my apartment or rent it furnished to some diplomat. I add that, moreover, a translator with five or six languages will always be of great use to him, because he'll always be able to trust me with those kinds of recordings or legal documents he wouldn't want to leave in the hands of strangers.

"Well, you're not going with my money! There are millions of translators, and you are not going to end up married to some fat banker, giving dinner in Switzerland while I go through hell here. I don't care anymore if you love me or hate me, Virginia, but you're staying here and living through the things that are coming, so that later on you can write about them. Period."

I try to make him see that the day I do, corrupt people and all his enemies are going to cut me to bits, and that his selfishness is condemning me to starve to death in a country that can no longer offer me anything but daily terror. I ask him where he has buried his greatness. He looks at me, offended, and replies that it's the same place where my career is buried. Then, as if wanting to justify himself, he sighs deeply and says, "Do you really think you or I can choose our fate? No, my love! One only chooses half. The other half we're born with."

I get up from the chair and look out from the balcony at a bucolic landscape whose beauty, in other circumstances, I surely would have enjoyed. I tell him that someone who is going to turn thirty-eight years old with several billion dollars has no right to describe himself as a victim of fate, and that I should have known that someday his cruel streak could also turn against me.

"I've made this decision for reasons that I can't explain to you, but someday you'll understand. It's just that you . . . know me and understand me like no one else, and I also know you better than anyone. I know that even if you've stopped loving me, stopped respecting me, you will always judge me with noble parameters and you'll never betray my memory. Journalists won't be able to write my true story, nor will the politicians or my family, or my boys, because none of them has spent—or will spend—hundreds of nights with me talking about the kinds of things you and I shared. I chose you for your integrity and your generosity, and I think only you are prepared to communicate exactly what I think and what I feel . . . why I became what I am and what someday I will be. That's why I need to know—even if you're not with me but someone else, and even if you don't want to see me anymore, or hear from me, or talk to me—that you're out there somewhere, watching the madness that's coming with your unique clarity."

After a confession like that, I don't know what to say. I can only reply that we are both experts in feeding each other's ego when we're torn down. That everything he's said is nothing but an excuse not to give me a cent. That he has a wife and all the women he wants, and he doesn't need me for anything. That I still don't understand why, if I was really so important to him, he can't end my suffering with one stroke, the way he did with my company's debts five years before. When he replies that a war is going to start very soon, I laugh incredulously and admit that my good friend showed me a set of jewelry worth a quarter of a million dollars for a woman he's almost surely already forgotten. He comes toward me, takes my chin between his thumb and forefinger, and with all the irony he's capable of, in a tone of voice either reproachful or threatening, he says, "And the next day you went to see him in jail. Right, my dear?"

He lets go of me quickly and changes the subject. He asks what I think of his new girlfriend. I tell him I'm happy he has such a sweet and pretty girl to take care of him and love him. But I also warn him about a proven fact that he's already experienced with blood, sweat, and tears:

"Don't forget that in this country, there are certain women of lesser means who, when they know they're loved by a man like you, only seem to have one thing in mind: a baby, a baby, a baby, as if humanity would go extinct without them! Remember that by Colombian law, every child of yours, legitimate or not, is worth one billion dollars. I know that heirs horrify you almost as much as me, and I think that's why you and I lasted so long together: it never would have occurred to me to possess you, Pablo, or to get rich off of you."

He is lost in thought for a long while, and I know he's

thinking of Wendy. When I turn to look at him, I see that he seems deeply sad, as if suddenly he's been left alone in the world and has nowhere to go. He comes toward me, puts an arm around my shoulders, and pulls me to him. Looking off into the distance, he starts to talk to me with a longing I have never seen in him.

"It wasn't because of that. It was because you gave me the kind of love that really mattered to me. You were my intelligent love . . . with that head and heart the whole universe fit inside. With that voice, that skin . . . you made me so incredibly happy that I think you're going to be the last woman I love madly. I'm well aware that there will never be anyone else like you. I'll never be able to replace you, Virginia, while you will marry a better man. . . ."

His words move me to the last fiber of my soul and I tell him that coming from the man I've loved most, they are an homage that I'll keep as a treasure in the most hidden corner of my heart. But I've forgotten that Pablo Escobar always collects on his moments of gallantry with gallons of cold water: next thing I know, and with the utmost calm, he lets me know that all of that is precisely why he's decided to leave me with my hands completely empty.

"That way when you write about me, no one will be able to say you're writing an apology because I bought your heart or soul. Because we both know that they'll always say I bought your beauty with my money."

I can't believe what I'm hearing. I tell him that after his words of recognition, memorable and sublime, after all his generosity toward me—with his words, time, and money—this is nothing but crude revenge with roots in an absurd jealousy. Without looking at me, his voice now heavy with sadness, he replies that he has never been jealous. He says that someday I'll be grateful for his decision, because he always knows everything that is going to happen. I am distraught, and I just want to be alone so I can cry in peace. I tell him that we've been talking for two hours now, and there are a lot of people waiting for him.

With his body leaning out and his hands resting on the balcony railing, he stares silently at the horizon as if contemplating his destiny. Ignoring the passing of the hours, he starts to tell me that he is on a path of no return toward outright war against the state that could be the end of him. But before he dies, he plans to finish off the Cali Cartel and everyone else who gets in his way; starting now, things aren't going to happen with lead but with dynamite, even if the innocent pay for the guilty. Standing next to him and looking out in the distance as well, I listen to him in horror, my face bathed in tears, wondering why this man who is so incredibly rich has a heart burdened by such enormous hatred, such a need to punish us all, such ferocity and so much desperation. I ask myself why he can't ever rest, and whether all that rage built up and about to explode like a volcano is really just his impotence to change a society that's driven by others nearly as pitiless and unscrupulous as him. Suddenly, he turns toward me.

"Now stop blubbering. You won't be my widow!"

"Do you really think I could cry for someone like you? I'm crying for myself and for the fortune you're going to leave to your widow, who won't know what to do with it! Why do you want so much money if you have to live like this? And I'm crying for our country! Dynamite against this poor nation just for your selfish cause? How evil you are, Pablo. You could just strengthen your security and be done with it. Do you think that some platoon of brave soldiers is going to dare come looking for you?"

He replies that he does. That platoons and platoons are going to come for him sooner or later, and that it's for all of them that he needs dynamite and missiles. I comment that if someone were to hear him talking they would lock him up, not in a prison but in an insane asylum, and that we should thank God that until now he's had me to listen to all those crazy things he thinks of. Because every day he's seeming more like Juan Vicente Gómez, the multimillionaire Venezuelan tyrant from the beginning of the century.

"On her deathbed, his mother made him swear he would forgive all his enemies and stop torturing and murdering his opponents. When the old lady breathed her last, the president-for-life came out of the room and told his flunkies about that request: 'Of course I could swear it by God, because that poor old thing didn't know anything about politics: the last of my enemies has been buried for twenty years!' The difference between him and you, Pablo, is that Gómez lasted almost eighty years, while at the rate you're going, you won't even last five more."

"And you're sounding like one of those old wives who don't do anything but lecture!"

Calmly I reply that those old wives are always right about everything, because their old husbands are brutish and stubborn. And I remind him that Josefina was ten years older than Napoleon, while he and I are equally "old." Though I look ten years younger because I have a twenty-four-inch waist, he looks older because he's turning into a fat man like Santofimio from eating so many beans. And I end by saying that we've been talking for three hours now and that Gilberto Rodríguez warned me that one of these days he would have me killed. Yes, even me! Like any Juan Vicente Gómez, for supposedly being on the enemy's side and for giving lectures!

"You, my love? He's even more miserable than I thought! I only ask God that the day I end his life you're not with him, because if I have to see you in the morgue beside him, I will want to shoot myself." After a pause, he asks me, "Has he promised you anything? Tell me the truth, Virginia."

I tell him only the production and distribution of a shampoo with my name, and he exclaims, "A shampoo?! No wonder! Only a *marica* would notice your hair. With labs of my own, and that face and that head of yours, I would build an empire! The guy is a coward, my love. He's more afraid of that witch he's married to than of me, and you're going to find that out sooner than you think. . . ."

I beg him, then, not to force me to ask anything from his enemy, the only person who offers to finance me, though possibly with a miserable sum. I remind him that I am terrified of poverty and that I practically have no family left, or friends, or anyone else in the world. Again and again I implore him not to subject me, either, to the sight of all the terror he's been describing:

"Why don't you save me from so much suffering, Pablo, and just send one of those hit men who obey all your orders as if you were God? We both know you've wanted to. Why don't you just do it, my love, before someone else does it first?"

It seems that this last plea finally touches some fiber of that leaden heart, because when he hears it, he smiles tenderly and comes to the end of the balcony where I am. Standing behind me, he wraps me in his arms and whispers in my ear, "But no one kills their biographer, my love! And I couldn't bear the sight of such a beautiful cadaver, and with a twenty-four-inch waist! Do you think I'm made of stone? What if I wanted to revive it and I couldn't?" And, kissing my hair, he adds: "Now, that would be a worse tragedy than Romeo and Juliet! No, more like Othello and Desdemona. Yes, them and Iago, Iago Santofimio!"

On learning that he'd found out who Iago was, I can't help but laugh. Relieved, he comments with a sigh that over those years we really taught each other many things and grew a lot together. I tell him he and I had been like two little bamboo trees, but I don't tell him what I'm thinking: that this will be the last time I feel his arms around my body, the last time we would laugh together, the last time he will see me cry . . . I know that whatever happens and whatever he does, for the rest of my life I will miss all that happiness Pablo and I shared together. And since I feel that inexplicable pain on having to leave him, that terror of being unable to forget him, that fear I will start hating him, I insist that if he sent someone to kill me with one shot, I wouldn't feel a thing, and he could throw my remains in the whirlpool with some wildflowers. I add that I could watch over him better from heaven than I can from Bogotá, and even do some public relations for him with all those he sent there. He breathes in my perfume and is silent for a while, then tells me that he's never felt so insulted: he would never, ever leave me without a good headstone! A luxurious, stolen one that would say:

Here lie the delicious flesh and exquisite bones
That adorned Cleansoul, the Beauty
While she was the guardian angel
Of Blacksoul, the Beast.

I celebrate his singular talent for composing instantaneous verses and epitaphs, and his genetic predisposition for all things related to the mortuary business. And he explains that it is just habit: every day he composes dozens of death threats for all his enemies and sends them by mail with his fingerprints on them so no one can dispute his intellectual authorship. I remark that one of those people is going to end up cutting me with a razor, and it occurs to me to ask him if I can keep his Beretta . . . at least for a while.

"I've always said you shouldn't separate from it even in the shower, my love."

I feel an enormous relief, and I decide not to ask him for my key chain with the gold heart until the day he sends for his gun. He caresses both my cheeks, swears that as long as he's alive no one will touch a hair on my head, and gives me an argument more lapidary than all those marble headstones put together.

"Anyone who dares touch this little face, I'll cut both his little hands off with a chainsaw! And then I will do the same to his horrible daughters, his mother, wife, girlfriend, and sisters. And to his father and brothers, too, so you can rest easy."

"Now, that's going to be some consolation prize, Pablo! 'Blacksoul, the Beast' . . . that's going to be the perfect name for the protagonist of my novel, a bandit just like you but with Tirofijo's face . . ."

"Then I *would* toss you into the whirlpool, and alive, Virginia! But, if you give him the face of 'Commander Papito' of the M-19, you would sell more books. And those Italians would make a movie out of it and you can send me a copy dedicated 'to my Fairy-Godfather, who inspired this story. Alias Cinderella.'"

We laugh together and he looks at the clock. He says that since it's now 2:00 p.m., he's going to take me to the hotel so his boys can pick me up at three. But that first I'm going to put some makeup on my red nose, which looks like a strawberry after so much crying, because the employees at reception are going to whisper that he beat me up to try to take my diamond away.

Since we'll never see each other again, now I can ask him why I was the only woman he never gave furs or jewels to. He takes me in his arms, kisses me on the lips, and says into my ear that it was to maintain the illusion that he never had to buy the most beautiful woman of all. And the bravest and most loyal, although, it's true, somewhat unfaithful . . . I powder my nose with a little smile of satisfaction while he watches me with a proud expression. He comments that the makeup is really a marvel, and that it's a shame he only has coke labs and not cosmetics labs, like that *marica* from Cali. He adds that if I "pirated" his formula and gave it my name, I'd get richer than him. Laughing, I ask when he's ever going to come up with some legal business, and with a loud peal of laughter he replies, "Never, my love! Never ever! My whole life I will be the world's greatest outlaw!"

Before leaving the little house—and with a strange gleam in his eyes—he announces a surprise he has for me so I don't go away sad: he wants me to spend an entire month in Miami so I can take a break from all the death threats.

"Carlos Aguilar, 'El Mugre,' is there with another one of my trusted men, and they will take care of picking you up at the airport and taking you back, so I know you won't run off to Switzerland! Have a nice time, and when you come back, I'll call you to talk about something they're going to show you. I think you're going to love it, and I'd like to know your thoughts."

We set off with him at the wheel, followed by another car with only two of his men in it. I am surprised at what seem to be minimal security measures, and he explains that he now inspires so much respect in Medellín that no one would dare touch him. I note that in my language "respect" is sometimes called terror, and I ask who he's going to assassinate this time while I'm gone. Pinching my cheek, he replies that he doesn't like to be spoken to like that.

I tell him that according to what I've been told, those stories about narco-traffickers taking yachts from me seem to have come from his office after what happened with Vieira. Shrugging, Pablo replies that he can't control every word his boys say. And since the Cali gentleman's wife had originally designed that formula to make him look like an idiot and his wife look like a psycho, it's not his fault that now anyone can call a radio station and say that "Tarzan" is a narco, his old boat a yacht, and my emergency in the sea a suicide attempt.

"And you have to accept that now, thanks to that viper, the media will always label any man who gets close to you a drug trafficker."

"No, Pablo, don't be so sure! A few months ago, Felipe López asked me to marry him; and you must already know that, because you have my phones bugged. He's the son of the most powerful former president of Colombia, tall and beautiful, and a fledgling Citizen Kane. And *Semana* magazine has always treated you suspiciously well, considering that you're more than . . . a mere rival of the owner."

I don't even turn to look at him. After a few seconds, he

asks what "Cinderella's" reply was. And I tell him word for word what I said.

He laughs hard and comments that Felipe López would be capable of anything to get his hands on all his secrets . . . and those of the stingy moguls.

"Better, more like the secrets of the drug cartels' generous contributions to his father," I say. And I tell him that the Lópezes rigorously follow the advice Winston Churchill gave George VI: One day, the king asked his prime minister why he had stuffed his cabinet with "all those awful Labour Party members." Churchill, who used the same language as George VI because he was the grandson of the Duke of Marlborough—and, in any case, they were among men—replied, accompanying his words with an elegant gesture of two 180-degree arcs, there and back:

"Sire: because it's better to have them inside the tent pissing out, than outside pissing in!"

We went on laughing, and he remarks that what he's going to miss the most are all my stories. I reply that his are even better, and that's precisely why he wants to keep me in "the Cabinet." He says he will never forget that I was the only woman who opened elevator doors as if I were Superman and who didn't cry at tear gas but cried rivers at everything else, without worrying about her makeup. He adds that he's never met anyone who had twenty lives, and I tell him what he should never forget is that he only has one and that the day he loses it I'm going to want to shoot myself, too. We go on playing the same verbal ping-pong that we've played a thousand times before, but this will be the last time. We stop at a red light, having rarely if ever done that before, because at night he always drove like a fugitive from justice and not at this leisurely afternoon pace. I look out the window to my right, and I notice that the driver of the car next to us has recognized us and can't believe her eyes. We both wave at her, and Pablo blows her a big kiss. She smiles, enchanted, and I tell him that now that he's on his way to becoming a sex symbol, he has to swear to me that he will make more love and less war. He laughs, takes my hand, kisses it, and thanks me for having given him so much happiness. With the last of his mischievous looks, he promises that from now on he's going to try to eat fewer beans. And I tell him, "Tonight, when that happy woman tells her husband that you flirted with her, he'll just tell her to make an appointment with a shrink or the eye doctor. In a mocking voice, and without taking his eyes from the newspaper, he will tell her she's a liar who needs to go on a diet, or that you are an adulterer and I am a sinner. That's why husbands are so boring. . . ."

And since when it comes to him I have nothing to lose, I take advantage of all that happiness to go back to the original reason for my visit.

"Pablo: Luis Carlos Galán is going to be the next president, and the next day he's going to reinstate extradition. You need to make a peaceful alliance with Gilberto and design a formula for peace with him and the M-19, who are intelligent people and friends of both of yours."

"No, my dear: Galán will never be president!"

"Stop fooling yourself, he will be elected in '90. But all Colombians have a price, and if anyone knows that, it's you."

"Maybe he'll be elected, but he won't take his oath! And are you perhaps suggesting that I buy him?"

"No, you couldn't. I think Galán's price could be a peace

accord, if the Mexican would forget his blind hatred of communists and try to have a truce with the Patriotic Union and the FARC, and you would leave that stupid war with Cali and join with Gilberto and the M. If you kill Galán, on the other hand, history will turn him into another Jorge Eliécer Gaitán and you into another Roa Sierra. That's not what you are, my love, and I don't want to see you die like that, because you don't deserve that fate. You're a formidable leader, you have stature, a national presence, and you can handle the media. A lot of people need you, Pablo, thousands of poor people. You can't just leave them to their fates."

"Things are a lot more complicated than you think: I have the police on top of me, plus DAS, which is with Cali. The Mexican and I need the army, and beside military intelligence—the B-2, which is ours—the police and DAS are a bunch of nuns! Santo also has a lot of contacts in the security organizations and in the military's high ranks; I know perfectly well that he provides services to both cartels—because politicians aren't loyal to anyone—but I use him, just like the Rodríguezes do. Terrible things are going to happen here, Virginia, and there is nothing, nothing you can do to change the course of events."

I try to make him see it from the perspective of those powerful and perverse minds that run the country; they must be rubbing their hands in glee. With DAS—which is theirs—and the money of the Rodríguezes, who are a bunch of social climbers as politically naive as him, they will just sit back and let him and Gonzalo get rid of any candidate who threatens their nepotism, their embassies, and the advertising budgets for their media.

"You two will merely be useful idiots for the presidential families and the financial groups. When they kill you, Gilberto will take your business and Alfonso López and Ernesto Samper will be in power forever. I can see what's going to happen with you, too."

He repeats that he doesn't like to be talked to that way. I turn toward him and see that he looks tired and seems to have suddenly aged. We have been talking for four and a half hours, and I have spilled all the truths I never would have dared say to him before. I've mentioned his rival again and again, and I'm saying good-bye to him for good. I remark that the problem with all of them is precisely that they don't have anyone who will tell them the truth, because behind every filthy rich man there's only a great accomplice or a great slave. He turns to look at me, surprised, and asks me what that means. And since I know that my words will echo in his ears and be etched in his memory, I explain, "That your wife is a saint and your enemy Gilberto's is a viper, and something tells me that they will both be your perdition. Don't ask me why. I can only tell you that I will carry you in my heart for the rest of my life. Go with God, my love."

We stop a few feet from the hotel door, and we say good-bye forever.

We both know it's the last time I will see him alive.

He puts his hand behind my neck and kisses me on the forehead for the last time.

In complete silence, he and I caress each other's face for the last time.

With eyes full only of infinite absences, he and I look at each other for the last time.

He contemplates me for a few seconds with those eyes that seem to contain every danger and announce every tragedy, his sad black eyes that seem to carry every tiredness, every condemnation. And so that he will forever remember me as I always was, before I get out of the car I make a superhuman effort to swallow my tears, and I give him my last, fleeting kiss, the last of my most radiant smiles, my last couple of affectionate pats, and a look that can only offer him all those simple things that Billie Holiday's dreamy voice sang in "I'll Be Seeing You."

WHEN WE REACH THE AIRPORT, Pablo's two men point to a young man with the look of someone important. When he sees me, he smiles and comes right toward us, and he and his two companions effusively greet mine. It's been several years since I've seen that promising politician with the intelligent eyes and studious look, and I'm happy to be able to congratulate him on his recent election as senator. We talk for a few minutes, and when he says good-bye with an affectionate hug, he tells Pablo's boys: "You two say hi to El Patrón for me!"

The man who sits next to me on the plane turns out to be one of Aníbal Turbay's many acquaintances. These are the advantages of going back to traveling "collectively" and not in a private jet.

"I saw you with Pablo Escobar's boys and talking to Álvaro Uribe Vélez. Without him, Pablo wouldn't be a multimillionaire; and without Pablo, Alvarito wouldn't be a senator! Uribe is a cousin of the Ochoas and a distant relative of Escobar, didn't you know? But what world do you live in, Virginia? Here in Medellín this is all national history!"

And he starts to tell me the life and times of the whole guild: about Alberto Uribe Sierra, Alvarito's father; when the war is going to start and who will win and who will lose; how many kilos one ships from Cali and how many the other from Medellín; how many of this one's "fell" and how many of that one's were "crowned." And how it was that he'd escaped the Feds in a Manhattan court during a recess between two cases, before the gavel came down in the second, the judge shouted "Guilty!" and gave him life in prison. After a movie-like odyssey he reached Colombia one year later, kissed his native soil, and swore he would never leave again. Now he lives with his wife on a small farm—happy, even though he's the only ex-narco in history and doesn't have one cent to his name!

I think that this incredibly friendly man—who rolls with laughter and has teeth like Mack the Knife, and who used to sell "merchandise" to the Italian Mafia in New York—is, definitely, a much greater treasure than the ones Manolito de Arnaude used to look for. And over the next five and a half years, and almost until Escobar's death, I would adopt that loquacious conversationalist as my own local version of Deep Throat—the mysterious real-life character from *All the President's Men*.

The day I said good-bye forever to Pablo was also the second and last time I talked to the first two-term president of Colombia (2002–2006, 2006–2010). I would never see them again—neither Escobar nor "Doptor Varito"—and I would only talk with Pablo again over the phone. But, through the strange designs of divine providence and thanks to "Deep Throat," for the next five years I would know absolutely everything that was happening in Pablo Escobar's life and his world. That up-and-down world, terrifying and fascinating, of "the Band of Cousins."

PART THREE

Days of Absence and Silence

I have no mockings or arguments—I witness and wait.

—WALT WHITMAN, *Leaves of Grass*

❧ The Cuban Connection

I HAD ONCE TAUGHT PABLO that when making an important life decision, one should try to achieve at least three things to ensure that if one or two don't work out there is always the consolation that something else might still be gained.

The good-bye trip he's given me fulfills at least half a dozen purposes: the first is obviously to close our relationship with a grand finale that ensures I will be well disposed toward him, while still guaranteeing I'll stay in Colombia. The second is to distance his ex-girlfriend from the eternal rival who, the day after getting out of prison, is already arm in arm with his president and his candidate. I will soon learn the other reasons, as well as his monstrous mind's true capacity for machination.

Some weeks after his visit to my apartment with Santofimio, Gilberto Rodríguez calls me from Cali to ask me about the reply from my "gentleman friend" to his proposed armistice. Pablo had asked me the same question some fifteen days earlier, and I had replied that I still hadn't talked with "the man from the Valley." I added that if he did call, I certainly wasn't going to tell him Pablo was planning to destroy him, much less turn the two of us into the next version of Bonnie and Clyde, this time on the morgue floor. When he remembered what Gloria Gaitán had said about us, Pablo asked me to say hi to her, and we agreed to talk on my return.

I think that Escobar is still wiretapping my phone, so I watch every word I say. I tell Gilberto that he, who has always had the reputation of being a gentleman, should extend his hand to "the man from the mountain," who is very willing to fix the problem between them. I tell him that Pablo and I have said good-bye forever, and that he suggested I go for a long rest in Miami; I inform him I'm going to travel in a few days to put a definitive end to that chapter of my life.

There is silence at the other end of the line. Then Rodríguez exclaims incredulously, "If he was really willing to talk, we would be meeting in your house and he wouldn't be getting you out of the country! I don't know what you said to him, my queen, because now he's crazier than before! So crazy I've had to come to Cali, and I think I won't even be able to go back to Bogotá. When you're back, I want you to come here so we can talk about our project, and I'd like you to also invite your friend Gloria Gaitán, because I'm dying to meet her. Tell her I venerate her father: Jorge Eliécer Gaitán is what I most love in life after God and my mother!"

I tell him I'm almost sure she will accept, and that as soon as I'm back I'll go to Cali to talk about the business, and he can explain to me once and for all what is happening with that grumpy gentleman, because when we said good-bye he'd only commented that he held him in high esteem and wished us success in our project. He tells me that if that's the case, so I can really have a good time on my vacations, he wants to give me something for my expenses: when I get to the hotel one of his employees in Florida will bring me twenty grand.

I am surprised and pleased, and I think it is the best kind of omen. This time, I decide to leave the money Pablo has sent me in the safe with the Beretta, to deposit half of Gilberto's gift into my account in small amounts, and to spend only the other half. And I fly happily to Miami, to forget about Pablo Escobar and to buy myself some tailored business suits.

Never before had I met with people abroad who were tied to drug trafficking, and I had only occasionally exchanged a couple of polite words with Pablo's employees. Carlos Aguilar is a young, good-looking man who doesn't look like a criminal, even though he bears the nickname "The Dirt"; since I would never be able to call a human being by that name, I call him "Águila" (eagle). The other is a tall, thin, ungainly boy who never smiles and has a surly expression, a unibrow, and light eyes that scream *Danger! Mafia hit man!* I haven't been able to remember his name, but I saw his face years later in a newspaper among pictures of the hundreds killed in Pablo's dozen wars.

I ask him how they manage to enter and leave the United States without being arrested. With a condescending smile, they reply that that's what their passports (plural) are for. They tell me that this time the boss has sent them to move eight hundred kilos from one warehouse to another, because the place is "hot" and the DEA could be on it any minute, or the "*Federicos*" (the FBI).

"Eight hundred kilos? Wow!" I exclaim, amazed at the value

of the merchandise and the bravery of the men. "And how do you move it: a hundred at a time?"

"Don't be so naive, Virginia! What world have you been living in all this time?" says Aguilar, staring at me with deep pity. "For Pablo Escobar, eight hundred kilos are nothing! We move several tons a week, and I'm in charge of sending the money to Colombia: tens of millions of dollars in cash. Here and there a million gets lost, but it almost always makes it."

I know perfectly well that without authorization from El Patrón, the cartel's employees would never talk about the extent of the business with journalists or "civilians," but especially not with a woman. My ex-lover knows my heart like no one else, and he knows exactly what I'm going to feel when I hear what his subordinates are confiding.

I think it was that day when I finally stopped loving Pablo and began hating Escobar. For being the seventh-richest man on the planet and tasking his financial chief with making me feel like the poorest and most punished woman on earth. For forcing me to beg for charity from his enemy, whom he planned to run out of the country before he could give me anything. For using me as a punching bag to take out all his hatred of the Cali Cartel, and for trying to make me feel guilty for a war that would only leave hundreds of people dead.

Once, I had told Pablo about Quirky Daisy Gamble, a character in the Broadway show *On a Clear Day You Can See Forever*. Daisy knew things that no one else in the world knew, and she could do things that would be simply impossible for normal people. After I'd told him the story and we laughed for a while, we had concluded that—on days that weren't too cloudy—only I could correctly guess everything that only he was able to conceive of, plan, and execute.

Several days after I arrive in Miami, Carlos Aguilar announces, "The boss asked us to take you up in a plane so you could see the Florida Keys. He told us to say that from the air, on a clear day you can make out the Cuban coast, which will always be there. We'll go on a sunny day next week, and we'll let you know. . . ."

El Mugre and his companion—who has shown me that he keeps two revolvers on him, one in each sock—pick me up at the hotel and drive me to an aviation school about an hour away. There, they introduce me to three boys who are training to enter Escobar's service. They are very young—twenty-three to twenty-five years old—and short, thin, and dark-skinned. I notice they have exceptionally hard eyes for people their age and that they don't make the slightest effort to hide their surprise at my arrival and their discomfort with my presence. I've met a dozen pilots from the organization, and immediately I realize that these young men could never fit the profile of the cartel's aviators, who are civilians, rich men with the look of successful upper-middle-class professionals, absolutely sure of themselves and always smiling. These, on the other hand, look like little men of steel from humble origins, and I think that they can't be training to carry cocaine to Cuba, although maybe to bring it from there. But to fly in his tons of drugs from the Caribbean to Florida, Pablo has always had the most experienced American or Colombian pilots, which means that he doesn't need novices . . . nor is the merchandise moved to other markets by plane; in any case, as far as I know, distribution to all American territory is a matter for the Medellín Cartel's clients, not Escobar or his main partners. . . .

Suddenly, the true reason for my trip falls on me like an asteroid and flattens me like a steamroller: what Pablo wants to tell me is that he just laughs at all my advice and warnings. He's saying that any ex-boyfriend of mine is the king of something, and any Gilberto could be the King of Coke. He, on the other hand, plans to become a legend before he dies. Yes, he is preparing to go down in history not as just any old king, but as the King of Terror. He wants me to know it, and before I leave his life forever he's going to show me what his monstrous mind is capable of: he's going to display before his future biographer everything he hid from his lover, she who tried to rein him in, she who would have lectured him, she who processes information in a way that only he knows and who possesses a brain that he learned to manipulate to perfection.

El Mugre informs me that these boys are Nicaraguan, and they've just arrived in the United States. They entered through "the Hole," which means they crossed illegally over the Mexican border. I know what that means: they are Sandinistas, very possibly soldiers, and almost certainly fanatical communists willing to do anything for the Revolution. What Pablo wants to show me is that when money is pouring in and one plans things carefully, any, absolutely any mischief is possible. He wants me to see with my own eyes that these young aviation students with furrowed brow and humble aspect are preparing for something that an American or Colombian pilot wouldn't be willing to consider for all the gold in the world.

Pablo is also telling me that to do business with Cuba he doesn't need Castro's approval, and that when a dictator refuses his proposals out of fear of the Americans or the Contras, the generals below him have a price that someone all-powerful in terms of liquid resources, like him, is in a position to pay a million times over.

My instinct tells me not to accept the invitation to get into one of those planes, to view from the air something only the two of us could see forever on a clear day. And when we reach the mall where I want to buy some things and we sit down to lunch, I'm glad I made that decision: suddenly, two camera flashes blind us momentarily. We try to locate where they came from but can't. For the first time since I met Escobar, I see his men get scared about something. They both want to leave immediately, and I decide that I've had enough of Miami in these two weeks, and I'll return to Colombia the following day.

It's October 11, 1987. When I arrive at the airport, two FBI agents approach me and tell me they need to ask me some questions. I think that this time they're going to want to interrogate me about the boys or the pilots from yesterday, but again, they only want to know if I'm carrying cash. Relieved, I reply that that kind of money travels to Colombia in the same containers as the drugs and not in the purses of TV journalists with master's and doctorate degrees in narco-trafficking. I say it with the absolute calm of knowing for sure now that DAS is reporting me to foreign authorities every time I travel outside the country. Also with the absolute certainty that it was these special agents who took my photo the day before so they could find out from their Colombian counterparts who my companions were.

When I reach the airline counter, I find out that Bogotá International Airport is closed: the lawyer Jaime Pardo Leal, the former Patriotic Union candidate for the Colombian presidency, has been assassinated after being stopped at a military checkpoint as he was driving his modest car down a highway. In a country that supplies bulletproof vehicles and bodyguards to any third-rank civil servant, that little car and DAS's utter abandonment of the left's presidential candidate are a warning of what awaits anyone who is not with the ex-presidents of the two traditional parties, Liberal and Conservative, and the people anointed to replace them in power. Colombia's presidential families—who divide among themselves the embassies and high public positions, while they milk the state advertising budget through their media companies—are leaving the dirty work in the hands of General Miguel Maza Márquez, director of DAS and the man in charge of protecting the candidates. Maza, in turn, is leaving the dirty work in the hands of the army's military intelligence. And the B-2 is leaving the dirty work in the hands of "the Mexican" Gonzalo Rodríguez Gacha, the same man who has already exterminated hundreds of activists from the Patriotic Union. For the small group of lifelong, hereditary monarchies that control both public opinion and the nation's resources, the big bosses of the drug cartels are turning out to be the perfect instrument to eliminate their challengers without getting blood on their hands, and to eternalize the power that would give sustenance to several generations of their descendants.

I know that Escobar is not involved in Pardo Leal's death, because he is a liberal freethinker who doesn't kill for ideological reasons; he only kills those who steal from him or have spent years persecuting him. When we'd said good-bye, he told me there was nothing, nothing I could do to change the course of history. Since I know that he would never confess his impotence against anything, or any weakness or defeat, I understand what it was that he really wanted to say with those words: there will be nothing, nothing that *he* can do, with all his ferocity and his billions of dollars, against the sum total of established power, the security organizations that serve it, and his best friend and partner's obsession with exterminating anything that smells like communism.

The day after I return, I write to Pablo. I do it in code and sign off with one of his many nicknames for me. I recommend he not forget the enormous power Fidel has in the Non-Aligned Nations and with all the de facto governments in the world. I warn him that the day Castro discovers what his subordinates plan to do or are doing, he's going to line them up before a firing squad and use the event to polish his image. I remind him that sooner or later he is going to have to flee Colombia with his whole family, that no rich country is going to receive them, and that Castro will block their entrance into all those third-world dictatorships that have given him passports. If anyone does let them in, it will quite surely be with the intention of selling them to the gringos later for a reward. I tell him that if he thinks he can face down the Cali bosses, the Colombian state, Fidel Castro, and the Americans at the same time and all on his own, it's because he's already lost all sense of proportion and is in the process of losing his mind—the only thing one can never lose after being stripped of everything else—and he's on the home stretch toward suicide. And I end by saying that I'm tired of being persecuted simultaneously by his enemies and the intelligence organizations, that I'm not going to risk having my American visa revoked, that we are no longer friends, and that I don't plan to become an observer-accomplice of his existence. I tell him I'll do everything I can to forget all the reasons why one day long ago I fell in love with his lion's heart, and to become from now on only the hardest observer-judge of his actions.

"If you open your mouth, you're dead, love of my life," he

whispers one night at three in the morning, and I know he's been smoking marijuana.

"If I talked, no one would believe me and they'd lock me up with you, and I'd rather avoid that torture. You know that if you killed me, you'd be doing me the biggest favor of my life. And if you hurt me physically, I'll go to the media and no woman will come near you as long as you live. For those reasons—and because I cannot expect anything from you—I can give myself the luxury of being the only unarmed human being who isn't afraid of you. Pretend that you never met me. Forget me, and never call me again. Good-bye."

IN NOVEMBER I meet with Gilberto Rodríguez Orejuela in Cali. Every time I see him, he seems like a different man. In jail he seemed sad and defeated, but the day he and Santofimio were going to visit Alfonso López he looked like the happiest and most triumphant multimillionaire on earth. Now he looks terribly worried. If there is anyone else on earth who isn't afraid of Escobar, it's him, who is as rich as Pablo or more so; but Medellín has already declared war, and it's only a matter of days or weeks before one of the two cartels fires the first shot. Sitting across from me, Gilberto calls the general manager of his labs and orders him:

"I want you to know that I care a great deal about Virginia Vallejo, who is here with me listening. She's going to call you later, and I ask that from now on you collaborate with her on everything she could need."

That's all he says, only adding that as soon as he resolves some problems, we'll talk again. He knows that I don't have a cent, and I know perfectly well what that means: everything depends on whether there is war with Escobar, and for the moment, I am just one more reason for conflict between the two of them. And a particularly sensitive one at that, not because Pablo is still in love with me, but because he's not going to allow all his secrets and vulnerabilities—that whole treasure trove of information I carry in my memory and my heart—to fall into the hands of his worst enemy. I realize that Pablo is still tapping my phones and that, somehow, he's already let Rodríguez know that in this matter, he could turn out to be more territorial than all his hippopotamuses put together.

In December, Gilberto invites Gloria Gaitán and me to Cali. They both seem enchanted to have met, and the next day I see him alone. He confirms what Pablo had told me would occur sooner or later, and what I had already sensed.

"Every time the Beast sees you on the screen, she shouts at my eleven-year-old son: 'Come and look at your stepmother on TV!' You are any rich man's dream, and the fantasy of any cosmetics lab owner, but you've come into my life too late."

I remark that since he's obviously referring to my age and nothing else, I am at my best moment.

"No, absolutely not, it's nothing like what you're thinking! What I mean is that I've been married twice to women even more déclassé than me, while you are a princess, Virginia. But last night the Beast tried to kill herself, and when she recovered she told me that if I ever saw you again in my life, she would take away that little go-cart champion boy who is what I adore most in the world. He's the only reason I'm still with her and the only reason for my whole criminal career. I was faced with a choice between my favorite child and the business with you."

I reply that if he finances my cosmetics business with a decent amount, I swear I'll build an empire, no one else will know we are partners, and for the rest of his life he'll be able to turn to those legitimate funds in any emergency, because the new laws against illicit gain—the so-called forfeiture laws—are going to start to squeeze him mercilessly. With a paternalistic expression and a condescending air, he replies that he already has hundreds of legitimate companies that pay a true fortune in taxes.

After saying good-bye to him forever, I think how that cunning man was much more dangerous than Pablo Escobar and Gonzalo Rodríguez put together, and that God does things for a reason. Back in Bogotá and looking at myself in the mirror, I decide to encourage myself with Scarlett O'Hara's famous words in *Gone with the Wind*: "Well . . . tomorrow is another day!"

And we'll see what happens in 1988. Let them kill each other if they want, because there's nothing more I can do. Gilberto is human, and when Pablo crosses swords with someone, even the most macho and the richest go running. I still have $12,000 in the bank and $30,000 in the safe. I'm thin, I have an IQ as high as the number of designer dresses in my closet, and I'm going to Careyes, which is supposedly beautiful!

Careyes, on the Mexican Pacific, turns out to be one of the paradises of the richest and most elegant people on earth. Angelita, the beautiful model, has invited me to go with her so she won't be alone amid all those French and Italians while her boyfriend, a Parisian polo player, supervises the construction of the field. We don't say a word about Pablo, who five or six years before had yearned for her, or about my life over the intervening years. Our first night there I am introduced to

Jimmy Goldsmith, who presides over a mile-long table full of his children, their boyfriends and girlfriends, wives and lovers past and present, grandchildren, and friends, all of them beautiful, tanned, and happy. When the legendary French-English magnate shakes my hand and smiles, I think he is perhaps the most attractive man I've seen in my life, that he must be a friend of David Metcalfe's, and that there's a reason people say: "*El hombre que se casa con la amante, deja el puesto vacante!*" (The man who marries his lover leaves the position vacant!)

Sir James has just sold all the shares of his company before the stock market crashed, has ended up with a fortune of six billion dollars, and had been married to the daughter of Antenor Patiño. I look at those *palapas* owned by the Bolivian tin magnate's descendants as they celebrate his daughter Alix's birthday by listening to the most sublime mariachis on earth, and I wonder why our stingy tycoons can't live with a little style, as Metcalfe would say. And I think about Pablo and Gilberto, who have half or a third of this man's money and are only two-thirds his age and who could choose to be happy in a place like this, to enjoy the exquisite and perfect things in life, like this ocean, this climate, those infinity pools, the singular architecture with enormous vines climbing the columns that hold up the mansions' thatched roofs. And instead they think of nothing but killing each other.

Why won't the Mexican come listen to these mariachis, instead of assassinating presidential candidates? Why does Pablo prefer the Putumayo queen over these girls, who are so beautiful? Why doesn't Gilberto see the potential of this land they're practically giving away, and that will be worth a fortune in a few years? All these rich and noble Europeans realized, and came to colonize it before it's all bought up!

I conclude that it takes several generations to instill good taste and acquire a certain beauty so that people don't mock the excesses of fast money. And I think that, at the rate things are going in terms of longevity, the ugly billionares are going to take at least half a millennium to achieve it.

Back in Bogotá and after having dinner with some friends one night, I arrive home around eleven. Five minutes later my doorman rings and tells me that William Arango has brought me an urgent message from his boss. The visitor in question is Gilberto Rodríguez Orejuela's secretary, and although it seems strange for him to come so late, I let him up. I think that maybe his boss is back in Bogotá, or has changed his mind about the business or the war and doesn't want to say anything over the phone. And, as I do every time I press the button to let up the elevator that opens directly into my apartment's foyer, I put my favorite work of art into my jacket pocket.

The man is completely drunk, and when he comes into the living room, he collapses onto the sofa across from the banquette where I am sitting. Looking at my legs with glassy eyes, he asks me for a whiskey. I reply that in my house the whiskey is for my friends, not their drivers. He tells me that his boss makes fun of me in front of all his friends and employees, and so does the psychopath degenerate Pablo Escobar in front of his partners and hit men. He says that Gilberto Rodríguez has sent him to collect the two bosses' "leftovers," because it's about time the poor got a little something. With utter calm, I explain my problem: over the past seventeen years, the six richest men in Colombia and the four most beautiful have sat right there where he is sitting, and a destitute dwarf with the face of a pig isn't fit to replace them. He exclaims that it's true I'm a prostitute, just as doña Myriam says, and that's why he also has a little gift for me from her. Impassive, I reply that if he calls that low-class woman "doña," a chauffeur like him has to call me "doña Virginia" and not "Virginia." Not because I am an Infanta of Spain or married to a Mafia don, but because my family has belonged to the upper class for twenty generations.

He exclaims that he's going to give me what I deserve, and that now I'll find out what good really is. He tries to get up off the sofa, which is very low, and puts his hand in his pocket. He sways for an instant and leans on the coffee table to keep from losing his balance. When half a dozen candles in two silver candelabras fall noisily, he glances down. And when he looks up again, he has a 9 mm Beretta pointed at his forehead from five feet away. In my most controlled voice, I tell him, "Get both your hands up, you filthy chauffeur, before I shoot and you stain my sofa."

"As if someone as snooty as you, Virginia, could ever kill anyone, poor thing! And that little gun, I'm sure it hasn't a license from the army!" he exclaims, laughing with the cold blood of one who knows he has the support of the highest bosses.

"I bet it's a toy, and if it's real, I bet it's not even loaded. And we're going to find out right now so I can go to DAS and denounce you so they'll throw you in jail for carrying an illegal weapon and for being Pablo Escobar's ex-whore!"

When he stands up, I take the safety off the Beretta and tell him he's not going anywhere. I order him to sit down beside the phone. He obeys, because I explain that he's right: in effect, I don't have a license to carry the gun and it isn't mine—

its owner left it when he came to see me that afternoon, and two of his secretary-drivers are already on their way over to get it.

"Here on the handle it reads PEEG. It's pronounced 'Pig!'—the word that its owner yells every time he uses it. Since you surely don't know English, I'll translate: Have you heard of El Chopo, El Tomate, El Arete, La Quica, La Garra, and El Mugre?"

The man goes pale.

"See how easy it was to guess the owner's name? Turns out you're not as ignorant as I thought! And since you're so intelligent, and I have my hands so full, I'm going to ask you to act like a good secretary and help me out by dialing this number. We're going to tell that Vienna Boys' Choir to hurry it up, because I'm home now and they said they'd be here between eleven and twelve to get this gun. That's right, the degenerate psychopath Pablo Emilio Escobar Gaviria left it behind when he came this afternoon to make love to his whore—not his ex-whore. He left it right there where you're sitting, right where I'll be disinfecting tomorrow. Go on! What are you waiting for?"

And I give him a Bogotá number that I know will have been disconnected, given to me by the Mexican years before to use in case of an emergency.

"No, doña Virginia! You're not going to let all don Pablo's *sicarios* kill me! You've always been a good lady."

"But how could a genius like you expect that a 'prostitute,' one who a car thief and a drugstore messenger are starting a war over, will be some kind of angel, huh? Keep dialing that number, and if it's busy it's because that psychopath degenerate is talking with Piña Noriega. . . . Luckily, they never talk for long. And how could you think I'm going to let them tear you to shreds in front of me! Ugh, no, no, disgusting! Nor would I want to watch while that boys' choir does what you came here to do to me, to your daughters or sons, your wife, your mother and your sisters. Thank God they won't be long now . . . because tomorrow I have to get up early to take that furious madman to the airport—supposedly he wants to show me a new plane!"

"No, señora Virginia! You wouldn't let those thugs—sorry, those men—touch my family!"

"I'd like to help you, but this gun's owner has the keys to my apartment, and when his secretaries see me aiming it at Gilberto Rodríguez's secretary, they're not going to believe me if I say that the boss of the Cali Cartel sent a revolting drunk to smoke the peace pipe with the boss of the Medellín Cartel, are they? I have a little gift for you, too, so you can choose between two options. For you, personally, which do you prefer: some chainsaws that our sadistic carpenter has just gotten from Germany—and that he's dying to try out!—or half a dozen lionesses that have been dieting for a week, because they were getting fat off so many leftovers they sent to the Nápoles zoo? Okay, let's stop calling. They must have left a while ago, they'll be here soon. . . ."

When I get tired of describing all the things they're going to do to the poor woman who has to sleep with a repugnant pig like him and bear him piglets, I tell him to be grateful that I am a guardian angel of his family and I'm throwing him out of my house before those butchers come to cut her up before his eyes. With the Beretta aimed at his head, I order him to get into the elevator, and although at the last minute I want to kick him, I stop myself: I could lose my balance, and Pablo taught me that when you have a gun in your hand you have to keep your head not just cool, but freezing cold.

"God does things for a reason." When the door closes behind that depraved man sent by Gilberto Rodríguez to take revenge on Pablo Escobar—or by his wife to get revenge on me—I lock all the doors to my apartment and my room, I kiss the Beretta and bless the day when the man who took my heart of gold left me his pistol so I could train to defend myself the instant his enemies would come for me. I swear to God that no drug trafficker will ever again set foot in my house or have my phone number. I curse them all, that they not have one single day of happiness in their lives, that their low-class women cry tears of blood, that they lose their fortunes, that all their descendants be known as the Damned. And I promise the Virgin that in thanks for her protection, starting now I will cooperate with the foreign antidrug authorities any time I can be useful to them. I will sit in the doorway of my house to watch the dead bodies of my enemies and their children go by, and to see the survivors loaded onto DEA planes in handcuffs, even if I have to wait a century.

The next day, I call the only female friend who would never tell anyone what I'm going to confide in her. Solveig is Swedish, elegant as an ice princess, discreet and different from all those society women and journalists Pablo has always referred to as "the vipers." She and I rarely share confidences. I've always swallowed my pain alone, and in these last years I've gotten used to not trusting anyone. Today I tell her about what happened, not because I need to unburden myself, but because I know that now, especially, Escobar is tapping my phones and recording my conversations to find out whether I'm seeing his enemy. I also know that, though I hate him now and he doesn't love me, Pablo will always care about me. He'll hear me on the phone while my stunned and incredulous friend asks how someone like me could ever have gotten mixed up with people like that and why I let one of those guys into my house. He'll hear me telling her that I thought I could still stop a war that will leave hundreds of people dead. Since servants and secretaries never act without authorization from the boss, I don't tell Solveig the name of William Arango, because I know Pablo would shred him with a chainsaw the next day, and I don't want to carry the weight of that death. The only purpose of my confession to Solveig is to make Escobar loathe the man he always called a "social-climbing pig" even more. Not to mention his evil-sickened wife, who, with all those calls to the media accusing Victoria Escobar of slicing faces to steal gifts, was the one who really started that whole war between the two cartels.

SOMETIME LATER I receive in the mail a torn newspaper page: a hairdresser in Cali was killed, stabbed forty-five times—not ten, or twenty, or thirty—during a homosexual orgy. Since the minds who give the orders are a thousand times guiltier than the beasts who carry them out, I say a prayer asking compassion for the dead man's soul, and I offer up to God all my pain and the humiliation from the mouths of those lowlife elites— who differ neither genealogically nor morally from their hit men and servants. Then I ask Him to use me as a catalyst to eliminate them and their fortunes that were built on the shame of my country, the blood of their victims, and the tears of our women.

And on January 13, 1988, the war breaks out. While Pablo is

in Nápoles, a powerful bomb shakes the Monaco building—his wife and children's residence in one of the most elegant areas of Medellín—and the surrounding neighborhood to its foundation. Victoria, Juan Pablo, and little Manuela, who were sleeping in their penthouse bedrooms, are miraculously saved from death and emerge unscathed, but two guards lose their lives. Deep Throat tells me that the revenge was the work of Pacho Herrera, the fourth in the hierarchy of the Cali Cartel, and Pablo wanted to chop him to bits the same way he'd done to the Kid at the request of Chepe Santacruz, third in the hierarchy after Gilberto and his brother Miguel. Of the building, occupied entirely by Escobar's family and bodyguards, only the concrete structure remains; his valuable antique cars and Victoria's art collection suffer irreparable damage.

The war is leaving thirty people dead each day, and it's not unusual for the bodies of young models savagely tortured to appear in the morgues of Cali and Medellín, because the violence even reaches the beauty salons where the cartels hire informants. Pablo's enemies know I am not with him anymore, but they think I'm very close to his affections; I'm in a doubly vulnerable position because I no longer have his protection. The threats are worse than ever, and changing my phone number no longer does any good. Fewer and fewer people have my number, and I start to cut myself off from the world. The money in the bank runs out quickly, because my priority is to make the payments on my apartment while I wait for one of my paintings to sell, none of which are worth more than a few thousand dollars. And in Colombia, selling an artwork not by one of the half-dozen famous national painters takes months, if not years. When I offer my few gems to the jewelers I've frequented since I was twenty, they offer me 10 percent of their value, almost the same as a pawnshop. I decide not to sell my apartment, which has cost me nearly twenty years of work and sacrifice, because I would have to let dozens of curious people into my private life and subject myself to all kinds of indiscreet questions.

To keep busy, I start to organize my notes for the novel I'll publish one day if a miracle saves me, but it only serves to indelibly fix in my memory the nostalgia for all that has been lost since that curse named Pablo Escobar crossed my path, and to exacerbate all the shame that was the only thing he left me. After the bomb, in under a week, Pablo has already kidnapped Andrés Pastrana, candidate for mayor of Bogotá and son of the ex-president Misael Pastrana Borrero, and brutally murdered the prosecutor Carlos Mauro Hoyos. Since extradition has been reinstated, and he plans to bring the state to its knees, he's now paying between $2,000 and $5,000 for every dead policeman or officer. As the war comes into focus, eight hundred members of state institutions are murdered, and to prove that he has enough ammunition for the Cali Cartel and the state at the same time, the bodies of some of his victims carry more than one hundred bullets. It's clear that the days of low liquidity—unknown to the public—are in the past, and that the "Cuban Connection" is bringing him a true fortune.

With the parade of terror, threats, and murders, I've been sinking further into a deep sadness: almost nothing interests me now, I rarely leave the house, and I decide that as soon as the money in my safe runs out, I'll fire a bullet into my ear where Pablo taught me to, because I can't stand the fear of the poverty I see approaching with giant strides. My family only feels contempt for me, and their insults are added to the ones I hear every time I show my face in a supermarket. I know I couldn't even count on a loaf of bread from any of my three rich siblings, who blame me for the ridicule they have to bear at the Jockey Club, at restaurants, and at parties.

I've gone to say good-bye to Dennis, an astrologer friend from the United States who is leaving soon to go back to his native Texas because he was threatened by kidnappers. I want to ask him, while I'm there, when the terrible suffering I'm going through will end. He looks at my astral chart and some special tables that tell him where the planets will be on future dates, and he announces worriedly, "Your pain is only getting started . . . and it's going to last a long time, darling."

"Yes, but how many months? Tell me."

"Years . . . years. And you'll have to be very strong to bear what's coming. But if you live for a long time, you'll receive an enormous inheritance."

"Are you telling me I'll be very unhappy, and then I'll be the widow of a very rich man?"

"I only know you're going to love a man from a distant land, from whom you'll always be separated. And don't even think about committing any crimes, because you're going to have legal trouble with foreigners, and they're going to last years and years, but in the end justice will be on your side. Ohhhh! Not only are you doomed to solitude, but you'll also lose your eyesight in your final years. You will suffer until Jupiter comes out of the house of hidden enemies, prisons, and asylums, but if you are strong, in around thirty years you'll be able to say it was all worth it! Fate is written in the stars . . . and there's nothing we can do to change it, my dear."

"Is what you're describing a destiny, Dennis? It sounds more like a crucifixion!" I tell him, swallowing my tears. "And you're saying it's only getting started? Are you sure the tables aren't inverted, and the pain is going to end soon?"

"No, no, no. You have to pay karma because you were born with Chiron in Sagittarius. And like the mythological centaur, you'll want to die to escape the pain, but you won't be able to!"

That night I tell Gloria Gaitán over the phone that I'm thinking of committing suicide to escape the pain of dying of hunger. I tell her I plan to shoot myself so it will be fast and definitive. Since she is a friend of Fidel Castro's, I don't mention anything about escaping the pain of having to wait thirty years in a gringo prison until my innocence and that of the Cuban dictator are proven. Or in an insane asylum along with Pablo—a Sagittarius—until my sanity is proven, and on his deathbed that centaur leaves me his fortune for having lectured him for thirty years.

A couple of weeks later I accept the invitation of an acquaintance of mine to spend a long weekend at her country house. Since I'm convinced that I'll soon be leaving this world, I want to see nature and animals one last time. When I return to my apartment, where everything is always kept in perfect order, I realize that a thief visited me while I was gone. My desk is in disarray and the first seventy-eight pages of my novel are gone—patiently handwritten over and over, because I don't have a typewriter and the personal computer hasn't made it to these parts yet. Also gone are the cassettes from the interviews I did with Pablo in the early days, the cards from his orchids, and the only two letters he ever wrote me. With a terrifying premonition, I run to the safe in my bedroom and find it open. The $30,000 has disappeared—everything I had left in the world—and except for the two apartment keys, the safe is empty. While the velvet cases full of jewelry are open on the desk with nothing missing, the thief has taken my gold heart locket and has also taken my toy boat, the "yacht" *Virgie Linda I*. But worst of all, what I will never forgive that headstone thief for as long as I live, is that he has taken my Beretta. Yes, it was his, but he knew perfectly well that it had become mine and that it was the last hope I had left.

The theft of all my money, of months of work as an amanuensis, and of that gun that was my most precious company sinks me into the deepest depression. The cruel man I loved so much has lost his mind and is condemning me to a slow death over months. My mother has gone to Cali to take care of a sick sister and didn't leave a phone number, because mine is a nonexistent family. I wouldn't dare ask anyone else for money, or talk about my poverty to friends more remote every day, or relatives who were born distant. I don't even have the strength left to go out and sell anything, and I decide I won't wait thirty years until some karma is paid off. I'll let myself die of hunger, like Eratosthenes when he learned he would soon lose the last light in his eyes.

Since I know that from somewhere in the cosmos the noble spirits of the immortals can hear the supplicating voices of mere mortals, I beg that wise man of ancient Greece to give me strength to bear the three months that await me if a miracle doesn't occur. I had read that the worst days are the first ones, and after that you achieve a singular lucidity and almost don't suffer at all. At first you don't feel anything, but on the fifth and sixth day, the pain starts. It gets sharper with every hour that passes, with such a feeling of extreme abandonment and desperation, such agony in the heart—now ripped apart, as if all that remained of you were just some strips of flesh seared by flames. It's not life abandoning your body forever, but rather the little sanity you still have fleeing to hell in horror. And, so as not to lose my mind and to console myself, I turn to the only part of me that still seems full of something:

Right now, there are almost a billion people feeling the same agony I am. I saw how the richest people on earth live, and I saw how the poorest live in that garbage dump. Now I know how one of every five children who come into this world dies. If some miracle occurs in my life, in thirty years I'll be able to put all this pain in my heart into a book about God the Father and God the Son that I will call Evolution versus Compassion. *Or someday there will be true philanthropists, and I'll make a TV show about them that I'll call* On Giving.

From Olympus, where he lives now, the compassionate Eratosthenes seems to have heard me: eleven days later I get a call from my mother, who has returned to Bogotá. When I tell her I haven't been able to buy food, she lends me all the little money she has. A few weeks later, the miracle happens and a painting sells. Then I decide that to try to recover the millions of dendrites lost during my fast, I urgently have to study something that will challenge my brain.

Yes, I am going to study German so I can translate the Scholia *by the philosopher Nicolás Gómez Dávila, because they are a marvel of wisdom, meter, and synthesis: "The true aristocrat loves his people at all times, not only in times of election." Could it be that, according to the Colombian wise man of the right who hates modern apparatus, the Pablo Escobar whom I first met was more of an aristocrat than the Alfonso López of always?*

Three months later, my friend Iris, fiancée of the minister-counselor of the German Embassy in Bogotá, gives me some news.

VIRGINIA VALLEJO

"There's a scholarship available at the Institut für Journalismus in Berlin for a journalist who speaks English and has
basic German. It seems perfect for someone as passionate
about economics as you. Why don't you take it, Virgie?"

And in August 1988, I happily leave for Berlin—following
the designs of Divine Providence that, according to Dennis,
are written in the stars, and that half of fate that, according to
Pablo, you're born with. I don't go for one reason, no. I happily
go for one million reasons, as many reasons as there are stars
in the sky.

ℭ *The King of Terror*

"THE PEOPLE OF EAST BERLIN are eaten away by boredom and sadness. . . . They can't take any more, and they're going to tear that wall down any minute now! I think we'll see that magnificent avenue joined again in under a year," I remark to David, who stands beside me on an observation tower looking out at the Reichstag and the Brandenburg Gate.

"Are you crazy? It's going to be there longer than Hadrian's Wall and the Great Wall of China!"

The winds of fate have carried me to West Berlin in the last year of two Germanys, and the year before the fall of the Iron Curtain. Like one of those powerful tsunamis invisible from the water's surface, all kinds of hidden things are happening in the place that only fifteen months later will become the epicenter of the collapse of communism in Europe. But it's not exactly for political reasons that now, when I arrive at an international airport, all the alarm bells seem to go off.

The DAS in Colombia know that the world's biggest drug dealer practically exports his tons of drugs in containers, ships cash in industrial freezers, and so far hasn't needed to use his ex-girlfriend as a "mule," the lowest rank in the growing and now multinational industry designed by him and a dozen of his billionaire associates and rivals. And I've realized that the sudden interest I inspire in the FBI and the European police seems to be coinciding with the fact that lately whenever I travel from Bogotá to another country, members of the drug-trafficking elite occupy a large portion of the plane's first-class seating.

I've also noticed that every time I return to Berlin after a trip to another city with the German government grantees, when I enter my room at the student pension, the papers and bottles on the vanity are not in the precise order I had left them. The officials of the Institut für Journalismus have started to look at me suspiciously and ask me questions, like why my clothes are more fit for an executive than a student. I know what they're thinking and what the authorities have been asking about me. I know they have been following me and why. And I'm utterly happy.

One day I gather my courage and decide to call the American consulate in Berlin—in 1988, the embassy is in Bonn—from a public phone, to offer them my cooperation. I tell the person who answers that I think I have information about a possible conspiracy between Pablo Escobar and the Cubans and Sandinistas. At the other end of the line, the switchboard operator asks, "Pablo who?" She remarks that communist dissidents call all the time to say the Russians are going to blow up the White House with an atomic bomb, and she hangs up. When I turn around, my eyes meet those of a man I think

I saw some days earlier in the zoo near the Europa Center, where the institute is. I often go there to delight in thinking how, compared with the one in Berlin, the zoo at Hacienda Nápoles really looks like the little Berlin Wall beside the Great Wall of China.

A few days later, a man stops me as I am about to board a plane. He identifies himself as an antinarcotics officer from the Bundeskriminalamt (BKA), or Interpol Wiesbaden. When he tells me that they would like to ask me some questions, I ask him if they were the ones following me at the zoo and the day I called the American consulate, but he assures me it was not the BKA.

I meet with him and his superior, and from the start they inform me that I have every right to sue them for invasion of privacy: they have searched my room weekly, listened in on my phone calls, opened every last envelope of my mail, and have investigated every person I've been seen with. I explain to them that, far from suing them, what I want is to give them the names and ranks of all, absolutely all, of the drug dealers and money launderers I have met or heard named in my life, because I feel a visceral hatred for those criminals who ruined my good name and that of my country. But first, they need to tell me one thing: Who has been reporting me every time I travel? After days of byzantine discussions, they give me the name: it's Germán Cano, from DAS.

I start to talk. The first thing I tell them is that while I was traveling on my student ticket seated in the back rows of the plane, Guillo Ángel, one of the most visible members of the Medellín Cartel, sat in first class with his associate named Abadi, a money launderer and member of one of the richest Jewish families in Colombia. When we arrived at the Frankfurt airport, the two of them went on their way free and clear, while all the police came to examine my suitcases. Presumably, they needed to find out whether the girlfriend or ex-lover of the seventh-richest man in the world had herself a kilo or two, and was risking ten years in jail to earn $5,000 for one more Valentino or Chanel dress.

"If Germán Cano still doesn't know who the top drug king-pins are and who are the big money launderers, it's because DAS is protecting them. I think the DAS Department of Immigration has people at the airlines who tell them when I'm going to travel; they inform their narco friends, and when the day comes, they use me as a decoy to distract the foreign authorities. This is happening all the time, and I don't believe in coincidences."

I add that the antinarcotics police in my country have been on the DEA's payroll for years. I say I won't ask them if DAS receives anything from Interpol or not, but I imply that it's perfectly plausible they're taking money from their European colleagues with one hand and from the top narcos with the other.

"Tell me how I can help you. I only ask that you give me a passport or travel document so that DAS doesn't know when I leave Colombia and when I return. I'm doing this on principle, and I don't have the slightest intention of asking your govern-ment for asylum, or work, or for a single cent. My only prob-lem is that I swore to myself I would never again see anyone from that business, and my only source of new information is a former drug dealer. But he seems to be the best informed in the world."

And like that, because of what the leaders of the two biggest cartels did to me, and the denouncements from the Colombian security agency, my cooperation with the international antidrug agencies begins. I think that if the FBI hadn't been so concerned with searching my suitcases to see if I was carrying $10,000 or more for a non-liquid Pablo, and had instead been as efficient with their endless tracking of El Mugre and the Sandinista aviators, they would have been able to ruin, thwart, or smash the Medellín Cartel's impressive Cuban connection and its financial structure in a matter of weeks. And if instead of following me and my chic European friends, Interpol had tracked the big narcos and launderers who arrived on my plane, they would also have been able to cut off at its root the Cali Cartel's European connection that blew up the next year.

Police all over the world will always consider their colleagues to be more valuable than their informants. That's why I give those European friends of DAS all the names of the narco-traffickers and their accomplices, but I decide not to talk to them about Caribbean politics and to wait instead for a chance to contact the Americans directly. But as it turns out they don't need my cooperation: Pablo's connection with Cuba falls apart on June 13, 1989, and by July 13, Fidel Castro has already executed General Arnaldo Ochoa—hero of the Revolution and the war in Angola—and Colonel Tony de la Guardia. I receive the news of the general's death with deep sorrow, because Ochoa was always a man of extraordinary bravery who didn't deserve to die by firing squad, accused of high treason.

A war is the most costly thing in existence. Weapons and dynamite must be bought by the ton. Not only must soldiers have to be paid generously, so do all kinds of spies and informers, and in Pablo's particular case, also the authorities in

Medellín and Bogotá, plus politicians and friendly journalists. These hundreds—maybe thousands—of people are equal to the payroll of a corporation, and there are not enough tons of coke to withstand that daily bloodletting of resources. I know that right now Escobar has two problems in life. One of them, everyone knows, is extradition; but for the well-informed, like Deep Throat and me, his problem is money. After the Cuban connection's collapse, Escobar faces an urgent need for massive liquid resources for a war that is polarizing all his enemies: the Cali Cartel, DAS, and the police. It's already cost him hundreds of men, and since he never abandons the family of a person who gave his life for his boss, every dead *sicario* is multiplied into several mouths to feed. But most serious of all is that the war has provoked a stampede of his former associates toward the Valle del Cauca, because Pablo has started to charge taxes on his guild for the fight against extradition. Anyone who doesn't pay in cash, merchandise, vehicles, planes, or property pays with his life. Tired of his extortion and the cruelty of his methods, many bosses, like the one who was on the same plane as me, have switched to Cali's ranks.

I know that Escobar will turn more and more to kidnapping in order to obtain capital, and also that he will tear Bogotá apart and manipulate the press ever more coldly in his quest to cripple the state. He feels such contempt toward a media that criticized him pitilessly when he was with me— and *because* he was with me—that he has named one of his houses "Marionetas" (Puppets) in their honor. From my solitude, I watch silently as those same colleagues who had once pelted me with the ugliest epithets for loving the *paisa* Robin Hood now kneel before the King of Terror. They all woo him eagerly, but he's the one who needs them, and desperately.

And the megalomaniac obsessed with fame, the extortionist who knows the presidents' prices better than anyone, learns to manipulate them to sell an image that grows more terrifying and all-powerful every day, precisely because every hour he becomes more vulnerable and less rich. The foreign press has created the impression that Pablo is the leader of a nationalist organization, like the PLO, the ETA, or the IRA. "El Chopo," "el Arete", "el Tomate," and "la Garra" are his military wing, and the Dirt heads the financial wing of the Medellín Cartel. But while those groups fight, respectively, for the right to a Palestinian homeland or for Basque separatism or for a part of Ireland, the cartel and its wings fight only for one man's cause: to keep El Patrón from being extradited.

And while nearly a thousand police are killed, the Colombian justice that takes twenty years in coming—that eternal tool of victimizers—also falls victim to its own indifference: in 1989, the narco-traffickers assassinate more than two hundred functionaries of justice, and now no judge will dare rule against them.

In 1989, I return to Europe with all the information I have been able to gather for Interpol. It seems to me that in matters of narco-trafficking, the Germans prefer to deal with the FBI and DAS and to leave the Colombian police to the DEA for whom they don't seem to feel any great admiration. But the truth is that in August of that year I'm not thinking much about public events or the news in Colombia, because my father is dying and I'm worried about my mother's suffering. Only sometime later do I learn that on the sixteenth of that month, my ex-lover ordered the murder of the judge who had opened the case against him for the newspaper editor's death. Also that on the morning of the eighteenth, he did the same to the Antioquia police commander Colonel Valdemar Franklin Quintero, for having purged officials on Pablo Escobar's payroll and detained "The Nanny" and Manuela for several hours to interrogate them about his whereabouts. On the nineteenth, my father dies, and that night I tell my mother I won't be traveling to Colombia to attend the funeral, because he never loved me and hadn't talked to me since 1980.

But there is another reason for not being with her, a terror I can't share with anyone. The night before my father died, Pablo committed a crime that was only one among thousands but it was the most significant of all: on August 18, 1989, eighteen *sicarios* with IDs of the army's B-2 unit assassinated the man who would have been president of Colombia from 1990 to 1994, having secured 60 percent of the vote. He was the only Colombian statesman of the second part of the twentieth century who was truly irreproachable. A month earlier, General Maza Márquez had replaced the candidate's trusted bodyguards with a group of men led by a certain Jacobo Torregrosa. I knew that if I traveled for my father's funeral, DAS would surely have men waiting for me in the airport to question me about Escobar and the reasons for my frequent trips to Germany, and I would end up in the hands of a dozen animals in one of their dungeons or in the army cavalry school. I also knew that the media, thirsty for revenge, would believe anything that General Maza chose to tell them, and they would furiously applaud any brutality that the DAS or the B-2 wanted to use against me, as they had applauded the mythical beatings and mutilations for years. Because that presidential candidate was named Luis Carlos Galán, and for Pablo Escobar he was the first and the last, the worst and the greatest of an ever-growing list of enemies built up over a life marked by hatred and destined only for the most ruthless forms of revenge.

Three months after Luis Carlos Galán's assassination, Pablo Escobar blows up an Avianca airplane with 107 people aboard, one of whom was supposed to be the *galanista* César Gaviria—now the Liberal Party's official presidential candidate—who at the last minute had decided not to board. For this crime, a New York court would later give the *sicario* La Quica ten life sentences. Investigators would conclude that the explosive used was Semtex, the same one used by Middle Eastern terrorists, and that the detonator was very similar to the one used in December 1988 by a terrorist sent by Muammar Gaddafi to blow up a Pan Am jet carrying 270 passengers over the Scottish village of Lockerbie. Libya had recently paid compensation in the millions to the victims' families. Manolo from the ETA had taught Pablo and his men how to build the most powerful bombs, and that's how I confirmed once more that international terrorism was interconnected, the same way narco-trafficking was interdependent with the establishment powers that be in my country and nearly all of the surrounding ones.

In November 1989, the Berlin Wall falls. It's the official beginning of the end of the Iron Curtain and the communist governments in Eastern Europe. That December, George H. W. Bush invades Panama, and General Noriega is overthrown and brought to the United States to be tried for drug trafficking, organized crime, and money laundering. Carlos Lehder becomes the most valuable narco witness against the ex-dictator, and his sentence is reduced from almost three life sentences to fifty-five years.

In December of that same year, a bus with 8,000 kilos of dynamite rocks the DAS building and tears it to its foundation. Only General Maza survives, and only because his office was surrounded by concrete reinforced with steel. There are almost one hundred dead and eight hundred wounded, and in front of that Dantesque scene, I no longer weep for the dead but for the living. Two weeks later, in an army ambush on the Caribbean coast, Gonzalo Rodríguez Gacha falls. While the country explodes in jubilation at the Medellín Cartel's vulnerability, in Pacho, the heart of the Mexican's territory, thousands of people cry over their benefactor's death. I know that from now on, General Maza and the Cali Cartel will be a solid block of concrete and steel against Pablo, who has been left without his only friend and unconditional ally of his own stature. And now with Gonzalo's enemies on the extreme left added to Pablo's on the extreme right, paramilitary squads would over time become the most ferocious catalyst of all the hatred Escobar inspired.

The series of wars resulting from the first becomes more polarized as the days pass. Including Bernardo Jaramillo—the next presidential candidate of the Patriotic Union—and Carlos Pizarro Leongómez, from the now-demobilized M-19, four candidates for the presidency have been assassinated. No one dares ask for explanations from the person whose job it is to ensure their safety: the immovable director of DAS.

In addition to my scholarship and my cooperation with Interpol, there was another reason I was in Germany for a good portion of the four years that passed between my good-bye to Pablo in 1987 and my next contact with him.

In July 1981, I had been the only Colombian journalist sent to London to cover the wedding of Charles and Diana, the

Prince and Princess of Wales. After carrying out a marathon broadcast of six hours by myself, I was returning happy and proud because both the BBC and the Crown's information service had offered me jobs. I had declined, because the prospect of starting my own company with Margot overshadowed any Hollywood movie opportunities or prestigious international positions. On the flight from London to Paris, where I had a long layover before taking the flight back to Bogotá, a charming girl had sat next to me, and we spent the trip happily chatting about the royal wedding. When we reached Paris, she had introduced me to her brother, who was waiting for her at Charles de Gaulle to continue together to the South of France. While she took her little nephew to buy an ice cream, he and I had stayed talking. He was the son of a German nobleman and a Lombard beauty, and it seemed that, like me, he was not happily married. When we said good-bye, we both knew that one not-too-distant day we would see each other again. When I returned to Bogotá and David Stivel had told me he was leaving me to go off with his actress, I had said calmly, "Do it today, because yesterday in Paris I met the only man who could convince me to marry again. He's beautiful, ten years younger than you, and one hundred times more brilliant. You only have to sign the document my lawyer will send you in a couple of days, and I hope you'll be as happy as I plan to be."

One of the three reasons I had fallen in love with Pablo was the gift of my freedom: one Monday in January 1983, he had told me that on Friday, as soon as I was free of my ex-husband, I had to have dinner with him before some other ogre got to me first. Starting that night, I had loved that man from my own country so much I hardly ever thought about the one from a distant land. The superior man Pablo predicted I would marry someday—and the one whom, according to Dennis, I would love—would return to my existence and, for a short time, bring me all the forms of happiness I had believed were reserved for the just in paradise; and he would also return to play the strangest role in Pablo's death, and an even stranger one in my life.

He has now been divorced for a couple of years, and when his sister tells him I'm in Germany, he comes to see me the very next day. Bavaria is one of my earthly paradises, and Munich one of my urban paradises—the perfect neoclassical city of the Mad King and his composer of *The Ring of the Nibelungs*. For several weeks we walk around the Old Pinakothek, with its timeless treasures and Rubens's titanic *The Rape of the Sabine Women*, and the New Pinakothek, with so many other jewels of his and my time. We stroll through the Bavarian countryside, one of the most bucolic God has created, and we are incredibly happy. Sometime later he asks me to marry him, and after thinking about it for a few days, I accept. He puts on my finger an engagement ring with an eight-carat diamond—the number of infinity—and we set the date for May of the following year. His mother tells me that soon we'll travel to Paris to order, six months in advance, the haute couture Balmain wedding dress that she wants to give me. For the first time in my life, everything is approaching the divine perfection dreamed of by the most sybaritic of the epicureans, or by my adored Sufi poet of the thirteenth century.

A few weeks later, my future mother-in-law sends her chauffeur for me because she wants me to sign some documents before the marriage. When I get to her house, she puts a prenuptial agreement in front of me: in the case of divorce or the death of her son—one of the heirs of her second (and multimillionaire) husband—I would receive a portion of my spouse's fortune that is so ridiculous I can only interpret it as the insult it clearly is. In an icy voice she tells me that if we don't sign, she will disinherit her son. When I ask her for an explanation for her sudden change in attitude toward me, she takes from her desk an envelope full of photos of me with Pablo Escobar, accompanied by an anonymous letter. I ask her if my fiancé knows about what is happening, and with great irony she replies that she could never stand in the way of her son's happiness, but that in the next hour he will be informed of all the reasons for her and her husband's decision. I tell her that my fiancé already knows about that relationship, and that she is destroying all our dreams, because I could never marry someone who is not going to be my partner and companion on completely equal terms in all circumstances of life, good or bad, and because without me at his side, her son will never be happy again.

My fiancé begs me to give him a few days to try to change his mother's mind, but his pleas fall on deaf ears: I return his ring, and that same night I go back to Colombia with my heart destroyed.

WHEN I ARRIVE, I learn of the violent deaths of two people I know, total opposites of each other: Gustavo Gaviria Rivero and Diana Turbay Quintero.

The first leaves me sad for many days, not just for him, but because without the solid rock that his cousin was for him, Pablo will go even crazier, and the country will end up paying for it. He no longer has the strength and support of the

417

industry's founding bosses, and he only has his brother Roberto left. Although he's a man of utter confidence in accounting matters, Osito doesn't have Gustavo's impressive command of the business or his obsession with absolute control. He is missing that ruthless character so essential to managing an empire of organized crime, especially with a partner who is almost always absent and demands more and more resources for a war against an entire state with armed forces and organized agencies. I know that in spite of his brother's unconditional loyalty and talent, without his cousin Gustavo, Pablo's business will collapse and his enemies' will rise. And I know something else that by now he must also know: the next death will be his, and the greater his cruelty before he dies, the greater the myth he leaves behind will be.

Pablo has always known that women suffer more and that female victims inspire more compassion than male ones. That's why this time he has chosen Nidia Quintero, the ex-wife of President Julio César Turbay, as the forced spokeswoman for his cause. While Turbay Ayala's brutal government was responsible for thousands of disappearances, the size of the social foundation Nidia directs has made her into one of Colombia's most beloved people. When her daughter Diana Turbay is on her way to interview the priest Manuel Pérez, leader of the ELN (National Liberation Army), for the newscast she directs, Escobar's men intercept her. Now the most admired woman in Colombia in recent times is clamoring for the new president, César Gaviria, to stop the war, listen to Los Extraditables, and save her daughter. But Gaviria does not sacrifice the rule of law to the man who assassinated his *galanista* predecessors and who blew up a plane he should have been on; the government lashes out against all. In an attempt to free

Diana, a police officer blind with hatred toward Escobar's men and desperate to take revenge for the deaths of hundreds of colleagues confuses the victim—who is wearing a hat—with one of her kidnappers. Diana dies in the shootout, and the entire country accuses the police of shooting first and asking questions later. They cry that the president lacks compassion before the pleas of the victim's mother, the press, the Church, and an entire country sick of watching funerals on TV, day and night: burials of the hundreds of humble dead and multitudinous processions for the illustrious dead. Escobar has already announced:

"The only thing that has been democratized in this country is death. Before, only the poor died violently. Starting now, the powerful will, too!"

But if there is a pain that I will never forget, it's that felt by my journalist friend—girlfriend of an M-19 commander and whose name I will keep quiet forever—sobbing in my arms as she tells me how she was raped by DAS agents who entered her house at night. They warned her that if she reported them, they would torture her to death. Before they left, while she was crying in the bathroom, they put unlicensed guns in another part of her apartment. Minutes later, the police came with a search warrant, and she was thrown in jail, accused of illegal arms possession and of collaborating with the rebels.

"The thing that has saved you, Virginia, is the absolute terror that Pablo Escobar inspires," she warns me. "Never, never talk badly about him, because what protects you is that everyone is convinced that you went off with the German but he made you come back. It's better that they believe that than for you to end up in the hands of a bunch of animals who will tear you apart and then plant guns or drugs on you. If they do the same things they did to me to a beauty like you, the media will applaud for days, because around here the press is sicker than anyone else. They know you know the price they sell out for, and they can't wait to see you carved up or kill yourself so you'll carry their secrets to the grave. I don't understand why you came back. . . . The few people who care about you say behind your back that you could only have returned to this hell out of love for Pablo Escobar. Don't even think about setting them straight! When they ask you about him, just tell them that you don't allow people to bring the subject up."

Along with Diana, Pablo abducts two journalists I've known my whole life: Azucena Liévano and Juan Vitta, plus two cameramen and a German journalist, who are all later freed. Diana's death becomes Pablo's most effective and convincing argument against the new government. But things don't stop there: to force the highest spheres of *galanismo* to come out in favor of dialogue with him and acceptance of his conditions, Escobar now kidnaps Luis Carlos Galán's sister-in-law and her assistant, and later Marina Montoya, sister of President Barco's secretary and Gilberto Rodríguez's partner in Chrysler. Later, Escobar murders Marina Montoya in cold blood in retaliation for an attempt to free the rest of the women. And in September, he kidnaps Francisco Santos, son of one of the owners of *El Tiempo*, to force the country's main newspaper to come out in favor of a Constitutional Assembly that would amend the Constitution and prohibit extradition.

This is the climate when I leave the man from a distant land and return to my own country. Nidia's daughter and Aníbal's cousin dead at the hand of the man he introduced me to. My friend raped by enemies of Pablo and the M-19. My colleagues Raúl Echavarría and Jorge Enrique Pulido murdered by the man I'd loved so much. People dear to me, like Juan and Azucena, kidnapped by my *paisa* Robin Hood, along with schoolmates like Francisco Santos and my relative Andrés Pastrana. All of them, as media personalities, guaranteed Pablo a public outcry in a country that is emotionally overwhelmed and still convinced he is the seventh-richest man in the world. Only those who were once part of his intimate circle know that this whole wave of kidnapping responds precisely to his desperation at the depletion of his forces and the bleeding out of his liquid resources. Given the problems presented by the armies of the four wealthiest multimillionaires, Escobar descends now to the next level of great Colombian fortunes and kidnaps Rudy Kling, son-in-law of Fernando Mazuera, one of the richest men in the country and a great friend of my aunt and uncle. Almost all of Pablo's latest victims have some relationship to me: a friend or child of friends of my family, a colleague or relative, a schoolmate or a lifelong acquaintance. When the editor of *El Tiempo* calls on behalf of Francisco Santos's father to beg me to intercede for his son, I reply that I wouldn't even know how or where to locate Pablo, but he implies he doesn't believe me. Every time I enter a restaurant I read the contempt on the patrons' faces. And since I have no other defense mechanism, I become more and more distant and take refuge in that elegance I had polished so much in recent months in order to be up to the demanding model set by my future mother-in-law, but it only exacerbates people's hatred, because they attribute it to my wealth.

My ex-fiancé calls constantly to tell me he's worried about that climate of hostility and lawlessness I live in, and I reply that, sadly, this is the only country I have. He promises that in a few weeks he will come to visit me, because he can't stand to be away from me. I beg him not to come, because I'm not going to sign that prenuptial contract, allow him to be disowned, or live with him without being married, and I insist that for both of our good, he has to try to forget me.

I have sold my Wiedemann painting and my little car, and with that money I've managed to pay my expenses and save my apartment, but my resources are about to run out again.

I had worked with Caracol Radio years before, but now Yamid Amat, its director and one of Pablo Escobar's most loyal journalists since the days of his public declaration of love for Margaret Thatcher, is scandalized when I ask him for work. The same thing happens with the managers of RCN Radio and Television, owned by Carlos Ardila, the soda tycoon. Finally, Caracol Television, owned by Julio Mario Santo Domingo, calls to tell me they have the perfect job for me. I imagine they want to offer me a job as an anchor, because the truth is there are a lot of requests from the public for me to return to television, and news of my return to the country has led to all kinds of rumors and speculations. My favorite is that Ivo Pitanguy had to use Pablo's millions to put me back together head to toe, because my figure was terribly damaged after I'd given birth to a set of twins, whom I'd abandoned in a London orphanage! And since my ex-partner, Margot Ricci, has always said that people in Colombia don't turn on the TV to see me or hear me, but to see what I'm wearing, I go happily off to the interview with the channel's president wearing Valentino. Knowing that a professional TV personality with a wardrobe like mine is a benefit for any channel in a developing country, she asks me, "And who makes your clothes?"

I don't hesitate to answer with my most radiant and confident smile: "Valentino in Rome and Chanel in Paris!"

In my infinite lack of knowledge about recent local events, I have forgotten that Canal Caracol is not Televisa of Mexico or O Globo of Brazil. Because for that woman, the person there asking her for work is none other than the ex-girlfriend or still-girlfriend of the biggest criminal of all time. Yes, sir, none other than the pyromaniac who burned down the country house of the man to whom she owed her job: Augusto López, president of the Santo Domingo Group!

She offers me a leading role in a telenovela, and surprised, I tell her I'm not an actress. With a shrug, she replies that with my twenty years of experience in front of a camera, who the hell cares? Didn't I turn down offers to act in Hollywood?

"Telenovelas reach all socioeconomic strata. Even children watch them. They are an export product that goes to dozens of countries. Now you really will be famous all over the continent!"

I sign the contract, and a few days later the phone calls start from the entertainment media asking for interviews. In total, I give thirty-two for radio and TV. *Aló*, the main magazine of the newspaper *El Tiempo*, insists I give them a print media exclusive, and when I decline over and over because my statements to the written press have always been distorted, with words I never said put in my mouth, the director promises she'll respect my right to approve every word of my answers before publication. When I accept, the first thing she asks is whether I'm going to see Pablo again, and then she asks for the name and address of my ex-fiancé. I'm not going to allow the man I love to be mixed up with a criminal who has caused me so much harm, and I keep his information to myself. About Escobar, I say: "It's been years since I've seen him. But . . . why don't you ask him about me instead, when you interview him?

If he gives you one, because as I understand it, he hasn't exactly been giving interviews."

Two days after the interview is published, my phone rings. Now all the media have my number, and I answer the phone myself.

"Why are you saying such ugly things about me?"

"I'm not going to ask how you got my number, but I'll tell you: because I've had it up to here with people asking me about you."

Pablo tells me he's using a brand-new phone—especially for me—and so we can talk without interruption. He already had mine checked for bugs before calling, and he found both are clean!

"I wanted to welcome you back. It seems you've been missed by a few million people . . . not just by me. How do you find the country after being gone all this time?"

"I think it was on page twenty-eight of *El Tiempo* that I read, in a single five-line column, that there were forty-two thousand homicides in Colombia last year. I am coming from a country where three dead bodies are reported on the front page as a massacre, and to answer you, well, I would have to first ask: How many of those thousands do we owe you, honorable father of the nation?"

With a deep sigh, he replies that now that the Constitutional Assembly will be held, the country will return to normal, because everyone is tired of so much war. I comment that many journalists seem to agree that "those gentlemen from the Valley" have already bought off 60 percent of Congress, and I ask him whether he has the same proportion of the Constitutional Assembly.

"Weeeeell, my love . . . you and I both know that those

guys just spread a little dough around here and there. I, on the other hand, use real silver. I have my guys, the tough ones from Magdalena Medio, and their *plomo,* the ones of 'lead,' that guarantee me absolute victory. I can't tell you about it on the phone. We are going to change the Constitution so no Colombian can be extradited!"

I congratulate him on his friend Santofimio's proverbial efficiency. Terribly annoyed, Escobar exclaims that he's not his friend but his errand boy, and that as soon as the assembly is over he won't need him for anything again. He says that he would rather forgive Luis Carlos Galán—wherever he may be—than Santofimio. Surprised, I ask if he means he regrets doing "that," and he replies, "I regret nothing! You're very smart and know perfectly well what that means. I'm changing phones."

After a few minutes, the other one rings. Now in a very different tone, he asks, "Let's talk about you. I know all about your German boyfriend. Why didn't you marry him?"

I tell him it's none of his business. He swears that he cares for me a lot, says he can imagine how sad I must be, and insists that I've always been able to tell him everything. Just so he'll know the price I'm still paying for my old relationship with him, I decide to tell him about the letter to my fiancé's mother with the photos of him and me, and about the prenup I refused to sign. Again and again he begs me to tell him how much the percentage was, and worn down, I tell him.

"They offered you that vice president's salary for managing several houses?! You're right when you say behind every multimillionaire there is always a great accomplice or a great slave: the old lady is her husband's accomplice, and she wanted you to be her son's slave. What a witch! Anyway, how do you manage to get these filthy rich men to get stuck on you all the time, huh? Why don't you give me the secret, my love?"

"You know it very well. And it must be that the older I get, the more elegant I become. I think eighty magazine covers help, too. You have just as many . . . but for different reasons, of course."

"Yes, yes . . . but on that cover of *Aló* you look horrible! I didn't want to tell you, but you look . . . old. Changing phones."

I sit thinking about what I'm going to say when he calls back, which he does a few minutes later. After talking in general about my return to work after years of being black-listed, I comment that on-screen I look better than ever—and definitively better than him—because at forty-one I weigh 117 pounds and I look thirty. And I explain why they published that photo taken at the wrong moment, the only ugly and really vulgar one of my life.

"How were they not going to publish it, when you had the magazine's owner kidnapped? I had to ask for work from the people whose houses you burned, and they've only offered to use me as the star of a trashy soap with third-rate leading men before throwing me into the street to die of hunger, suppos-edly on the orders of Santo Domingo, whose planes you blow up with the sons-in-law of my friends inside."

"But why are you talking to me like that, my love, when you mean so much to me? A dream of a woman like you wasn't born to work like a slave for those bottler tyrants. You deserve to be very happy . . . and you'll see that that man you left will come back for you very soon! You can be veeeerrrry addic-tive . . . I should know!"

I reply that, in fact, he's going to come in a few days, but I have decided I am not going to subject myself to his mother's magnifying glass for the rest of my life. After a silence, Pablo tells me that, at my age, I should be thinking about becoming a businesswoman instead. He says good-bye and tells me that after the Constitutional Assembly, we'll surely talk again.

My boyfriend comes to Bogotá four days later. Again, he places the engagement ring on my finger and repeats that if we get married and I make him very happy, his mother will surely soon change her mind and annul that contract. I explain that I can't break my commitment with Caracol, under threat of paying triple what I'm going to receive in payment. I add that once I have a video reel with recent material, I will leave Colombia forever, and I'll almost certainly get excellent offers in the United States. He begs me not to do that, and I tell him he's putting me in a terrible bind. Since in a few hours I have to go to Honda, where the first episodes of the soap opera will be filmed, we say good-bye and agree to meet the next month somewhere in the Caribbean.

Around three hundred people have been invited to the cocktail party for the premiere in Bogotá. Amparo Pérez, the head of public relations for Caracol, picks me up in her car, and on the way she asks me, "Nothing more was heard of your German boyfriend! Right?"

"Yes, more was heard. He was here two weeks ago and left me this." And I show her my diamond, four times bigger than Gustavo's and D-flawless.

"Oh, take that ostentatious thing off, before Mábel thinks Pablo gave it to you and fires you for going back to keeping bad company!"

"Pablo could never give me an engagement ring, Amparo, because he's already married. And I'll turn the ring around, because clearly, people in this country think Pablo Escobar is the only man in the world who has enough money to buy a diamond."

The next morning my fiancé calls to ask how things went in Honda and about the premiere. I describe the evening filming amid clouds of mosquitoes that devour us and the infernal heat that, under all the lights, is around 110 degrees Fahrenheit. After a brief silence, and with sadness in his voice that he doesn't try to hide, he tells me in German: "I don't understand why you signed a contract like that. And there's something I need to tell you: I was followed from your house to the airport. . . . I know it was him. I think he's still in love with you, kiddo."

And the whole world falls in on me. How could I have been so stupid? Why, at this point in life, do I still not know Pablo Escobar? I should have known that after the robbery in 1988 and three and a half years apart, he wouldn't be calling to reiterate his affections. He wanted to find out whether what he'd heard was true, whether I resented the man I had just left or his family, and whether I could be useful to him!

Before hanging up, terrified, I only manage to tell him, in German: "No, no, no. He hasn't been in love with me for a long time. It's something much worse than that. Don't ever call me again. I'll call you tomorrow from another phone and you'll understand everything."

A couple of days later, at midnight, Pablo calls.

"We both know that you stop loving your husbands or boyfriends the day after you leave them, right, my dear? I don't know how you do it, but you always manage to replace us in a matter of days! What Caracol is doing to you is public knowledge, and all I want is to ensure your future. I'm worried about you . . . because you're not getting any younger, are you?

That's why I'm going to send you a written proposal that is very serious. Don't ever forget that I can make the media say whatever I want about you: I just bombard them with calls for a week ... and you'll never work again. *Adiós*, my love."

The note says that he already has all the basic information but he needs my cooperation. The proposal consists of 25 percent of the "profits," and it is accompanied by a simple list: some residential addresses, a few private phone numbers, some financial information, bank accounts, names of children—if there are any—and the date of my ex-boyfriend's next visit to Colombia, or my next trip to Europe. On another page with names and newspaper clippings glued to a piece of yellow paper, is this addendum:

Ultima Hora Caracol, Yamid Amat!

Mr. X has been killed in an attempted kidnapping. Son of Mrs. X, wife of Mr. X, CEO of the company Such-and-such, established in the City of X. The former TV anchor Virginia Vallejo, accused of possible participation in the crime, is currently being detained in the DAS jail, where she is undergoing interrogation.

For hours and hours I rack my brain thinking about how he could have gotten those names. I remember his voice eight years earlier: "If you plan carefully, any, absolutely any mischief can be accomplished," and I conclude that maybe someone in his organization traveled on the same plane as my boyfriend, and after days of tracking him down, once they were in Germany, he found out who he was. Another possibility is that he had me followed on one of my trips. . . . I wonder if he knows about Interpol, if he could have sent the man in the zoo, if the photographs and letter to my future mother-in-law could just be another form of revenge. . . . Every possibility passes through my mind, and then I realize that at the place where my fiancé works it would be relatively easy to find out who he is. All I know is that when it comes to getting fast money in large amounts, for Pablo "Paris is well worth a mass." When he calls again, this time at dawn, he says that sooner or later, with or without my help, he will achieve his goal.

"You're seeing that with some extra calls to DAS, you could spend a few years in jail while they investigate whether or not what my witnesses say is true. And who do you think they will believe? Maza and your enemies in the press . . . or you, poor thing? What wouldn't that old Nazi lady give to get her son back? . . . Right, my love?"

I am chilled as he explains—with those short sentences followed by silences that I'm more than used to—that he needs me to speed up things that would otherwise take months, because he doesn't have trusted translators in several languages. It's a matter of choosing, not between silver or lead—because he knows death doesn't scare me—but between money and jail! In a few days he'll call me, and in the following days he'll give me a demonstration that he's serious. And he hangs up.

I get a call from Stella Tocancipá, the journalist writing a profile on me for the magazine *Semana*. She informs me that she chose to quit her job rather than say all the nasty things about me that her superiors would have expected her to write. Someone else who doesn't have Stella's bravery or conscience writes everything they dictate, and after I am fired from Caracol, he's rewarded with the Miami consulate.

What *El Tiempo* publishes is even worse: now I'm the lover of another drug dealer—no one knows his name—and I've become nothing but a vile thief of all kinds of sumptuous things, and for that I've again been hit, kicked, and mutilated without mercy. What Pablo Escobar is telling me is that—as had happened with Rafael Vieira—for the rest of my life, any man with whom I have a serious relationship will be described by journalists who take dictation from his *sicarios* as "another narco-trafficker, only anonymous." Also, that instead of spending the rest of my life condemned to solitude and unemployment, I should start to think like a "businesswoman" and abandon my scruples. Since the authorities who are not on the payroll of the drug cartels are on my enemies', I cannot denounce Escobar's blackmail. The stories are so sordid—and the phone stalking and the mockery every time I go to the supermarket so terrible—that I develop anorexia, and for several days I seriously consider the possibility of killing myself.

Then I think of Enrique Parejo González, the *galanista* minister of justice who signed the first extraditions after the assassination of his predecessor, Rodrigo Lara. As Colombia's ambassador to Hungary in 1987, he has become the only person to survive a personal attack from Pablo Escobar: five point-blank shots in the garage of his house in Budapest, three of them to the head. This brave man—today miraculously and completely recovered—embodies like no one else the narcos' power to reach the most places very far from Colombia when it comes to taking their revenge. In my country without a memory, Escobar does not forgive.

I know that Pablo already has a lot of information about my fiancé's family, but my instinct tells me that as long as he doesn't come to Colombia and I don't go to Germany, he won't be in danger. After thinking about it all night, my conscience dictates my only option: I will remain alone, and since I don't have recent material to show an international artists' agency, I will accept my fate and live in my country. From a public phone, I ask my boyfriend to meet me in New York on an urgent matter. On the saddest day of my life, I return his ring and tell him that as long as that monster is alive, I won't be able to see him and he can't call me again, because Escobar will kidnap or kill him and accuse me of involvement in his crimes. More than six years would pass before we were both free of our circumstances, but by the end of 1997 he would already be very ill, and the last of the torments Pablo Escobar left me would begin.

When I return to Bogotá, I change my phone numbers, and I only give the new ones to four people. I am so terrified by the possibility of my own kidnapping that when my two girlfriends close to the extreme leftist groups ask me about my ex-fiancé, I reply that he was only one of the media's many inventions.

THE CONSTITUTIONAL ASSEMBLY OF 1991 has the country immersed in a climate of hope and dialogue, in which the traditional parties participate alongside the rebel groups, ethnic and religious minorities, and students. Antonio Navarro of the M-19 and Álvaro Gómez of the Conservative Party shake hands, and after a few months, the Constitution is amended, extradition is eliminated, and the good and bad people of Colombia prepare to start the new era in a framework of understanding and harmony.

But things are not so simple in a country where the rule of law is always being sacrificed on the altar of some peace agreement—which, for the narco-terrorist group of the moment, will always consist of some kind of amnesty. That way, they can make fun of the judicial system and not be extradited. The beginning of the nineties sees the birth of "Los Pepes," short for "Los Perseguidos por Pablo Escobar": people persecuted by Pablo Escobar. Again, everyone down to the last village idiot knows that the group's members are also in the paramilitary groups commanded by the brothers Fidel and Carlos Castaño, the Cali Cartel, dissidents of the Medellín Cartel, police and intelligence organizations that were Escobar's victims, and one or another foreign adviser in the finest style of the Contras. After the new—and seemingly definitive—fall of extradition, and to protect himself from the Pepes who are stalking him ever more mercilessly, Escobar agrees to turn himself in if a prison is built especially for him in Envigado, on a seven-acre plot of elevated land of his choosing, where he'll be attended by his own surviving boys of his choosing, with guard personnel approved by him, a 360-degree view, protected airspace and electrified fences, and, of course, all the basic comforts and entertainments that modern life can offer. The wealthy classes in Colombia will always enjoy the legal concept "La Casa for Cárcel," or house arrest. And Gaviria's government, in order to get a break from Escobar, tells him, "Okay then! Go right ahead and build your soccer field, your bar, your nightclub, and invite anyone you want to come dance in it, but just give us a break."

Pablo's surrender becomes the event of the year. Obsessed with his only weak flank—which we both know well—he demands that no airplane fly over Medellín during the day he has chosen to proceed, amid a caravan of official vehicles and the national and international press, to his new retreat paid for by the Colombian government.

The problem with desperate presidents and the good people of Colombia is that they still don't know the owner of "Puppets." Everyone believes he is worn out and his intentions are good; but from the prison, baptized "the Cathedral," he goes on managing his criminal empire with an iron fist. In his free time he invites big soccer stars like René Higuita to play with him and his boys, and at night, before their well-deserved rest, he invites dozens of good-time girls to play with them all. Like a king, he receives his subjects: his family, his politicians, his journalists, and the bosses of other regions of the country who still aren't affiliated with the Pepes. Everyone comments that "in Colombia, crime *does* pay," but any protest is furiously hushed in the name of peace, because—finally!— Pablo is contained.

Now only Todelar, the third-largest radio chain, offers me work, and only on the condition that I obtain my own advertising budget. I ask for a meeting with Luis Carlos Sarmiento Angulo, now the richest man in the country, and beg him to save my life, because among the big media there seems to be a consensus to kill me with hunger. That noble man gives Todelar advertising for some $10,000 a month, and the station pays me the 40 percent agreed on, allowing me to live without anxiety for the first time in several years. Since I don't have an office, once again everyone has my phone number. (After Pablo's death, my contract will be canceled without explanation and Todelar will keep 100 percent of the advertising money.)

One day, Deep Throat tells me that some friends of his were visiting Pablo in the Cathedral. One of them commented that an acquaintance of his had seen me recently at a restaurant in Bogotá and said that I looked beautiful and that he would die to go out with me. When he heard that, Pablo cried, "Hasn't your friend heard that Virginia tried to keep the yacht of some colleagues of ours, and they had to take it back by force? And I'm sorry for that poor friend of yours: he's blind, and he should get some glasses! Who wants an old woman like that, when there are so many young ones? She's just a lonely and broke fortysomething, forced to work at a shoddy radio station so she doesn't die of hunger, because no one will hire her for TV anymore."

"My friends couldn't believe what they were hearing," Deep Throat tells me, visibly bothered. "They said it was the last low blow that asshole hadn't taken!" And he goes on talking: "Get this: one of them is very tight with 'Rambo'"—Fidel Castaño, head of the United Self-Defense Forces of Colombia (AUC)—"and a few days ago we were on his ranch in Córdoba, and suddenly the guy comes up on a bicycle. He chatted with us for a while and then he left, same way he'd come: alone and pedaling, nice and calm! In this country everyone knows each other. . . . There's a reason why they all kill each other. This Rambo seems made of steel: even though he goes around unarmed on a bike, no one in their right mind would dare mess with him. That's the guy who, sooner or later, is going to finish your Pablito, the Ungrateful—"

"Well, God bless Pablito the Possessive! Could you tell your friend to tell Rambo, in detail, how much Escobar hates me, to see if the Pepes will stop tormenting me? Ask your friend to tell Castaño about a couple of men who call me at midnight, put a chainsaw on the phone, and whisper that they're sharpening it for 'the whore of the Envigado psycho.' You can't imagine the terror I live in: every night, when I leave work at eight and I'm waiting for a taxi, if I see one of those SUVs with tinted windows go past, I think it's the Pepes coming for me! Tell him I'm begging them to stop those threats, because I'm just one more person persecuted by Pablo Escobar. And ask him when he'll let me interview him for that shoddy radio station, to see if he'll tell me how he's going to finish off the Monster in the Cathedral."

After a few days the calls lessen considerably. It seems that this time, my poverty or old age has saved me, and now that I am seemingly under the Pepes' protection, I can finally sleep in peace until the next of Pablo's enemies appears. Because when it comes to threats, the only ones missing are the Pentagon missile and the Kremlin's atomic bomb!

Chainsaws have become the weapon of choice for all the groups. Somewhere I read that in a village in the Antioquia or Córdoba Departments—the AUC's center of operations—the shrieks of the victims could be heard from one end of town to the other, while drugged-up paramilitary men raped the women in front of their young children. When Escobar finds out that the Moncadas and Galeanos, associates of his, have hidden five and twenty million dollars, respectively, he invites them to the prison and starts to cut them, using that weapon that doesn't need a license because it's in the prison workshop. After forcing the treasure's location out of them, not only does he get his hands on it using the men he still has on the outside, but he also goes after all the associates and accountants of both organizations, torturing them until they hand over their remaining capital, including haciendas, livestock, planes, and helicopters.

And when the story that Escobar has also built his own dungeon and a cemetery right under the noses of his guardians reaches the presidential palace, César Gaviria decides he's had enough. He sends the vice minister of justice Eduardo

Mendoza—the son of old friends of mine—to see if something so spine-chilling can be true or if it's just the invention of the Cali Cartel and the Moncada and Galeano families. When he's told that an army contingent is coming to transfer him to another prison, Escobar thinks the government plans to turn him over to the DEA; and when the young official enters the jail, Escobar takes him hostage. After a series of confused events of which many different versions exist, Pablo comes walking out past the guards—who don't move a finger to stop him—and flees with his men through some tunnels they've been working on for months. A marathon live broadcast begins at all the stations in the country; while the new director of the Todelar newscast station—in the service of the Cali Cartel—won't let me take the microphone all afternoon, Pablo makes Yamid Amat of Caracol believe that he's been hiding for three hours in a big tunnel near the Cathedral. In reality, he is already miles away and protected by the dense jungle.

I am happy, because I know that with his escape, Pablo has signed his death sentence. The authorities immediately form a police "Search Bloc," trained in the United States with the single mission of finishing him off once and for all. From the start, the Pepes offer their full cooperation. After intensive training, the Navy SEALs and Delta Force also enthusiastically join the Search Bloc, and the DEA, the FBI, and the CIA send Vietnam vets. German, French, and British mercenaries follow them—hoping for the twenty-five-million-dollar reward—and a total of eight thousand men are allocated in various countries to a multinational war against a single individual, whom the Americans want alive and the Colombians want dead. Because only death guarantees his silence.

In retaliation for the interrogations and deaths of a few underworld martyrs in the name of the rule of law, Escobar places one bomb after another, practically one per week, and his hit men, now converted into media stars, begin to appear on magazine covers and on the front pages of every newspaper. As if Pablo were some Resistance leader, the media publish everything they say and everything he dictates to them:

"Terrorism is the atomic bomb of the poor! Although it's against my principles, I have to use it!"

Pablo Escobar has always known how to act the poor man when it's convenient. In 1993, I am miraculously saved from the worst of all the recent attacks, a bombing at the elegant Centro 93 mall, but I'm left weeping at the spectacle of a little girl's severed head atop a lamppost, and of hundreds dead and wounded.

By now I have sold my apartment, because I can't stand my phones being tapped and all the insults, and I have rented a new one on the first floor of the chic El Nogal condominium. My neighbors include a former first lady who is a relative of my father, three children of former presidents, and Santo Domingo's niece. All of their bodyguards guarantee me relative protection, half a dozen residents share my DNA, and I can finally rest from the telephonic buzz of chainsaws. After the sale, Deep Throat asks me for a loan of $2,500. Though I never see him again after that, I resignedly tell myself that the information he'd given me over these six years was worth all the gold in the world.

The last thing that my source had told me was that Pablo is hiding in houses he's buying up in middle-class neighborhoods around Medellín. It surprised me, because in the most clandestine phase of our relationship, the men who drove me to his hideouts told me that he had five hundred country houses scattered throughout the Department of Antioquia. Deep Throat's friends had told me that, seconded by the Search Bloc, the Pepes were determined to kidnap Pablo's closest family members to exchange them for members of both groups who have fallen into his hands. Since he is desperate to get his family out of Colombia, I am convinced that he will put off the good-bye until there is nothing more for him to do, because—since he surely will never see them again—that day will break his heart into a thousand pieces. If he still has one.

In any Latin American country, the Escobars would be an easy target for Pablo's enemies, who could kidnap or extort them for the rest of their lives. The United States would never receive them, and flights to the East or to Australia from Colombia are nonexistent. In 1993—before the 2001 Schengen Agreement—Germany is the only country in Europe with direct flights from Bogotá, by which Colombians could enter without a visa or many customs checks. I know that several members of Pablo's family are already in that country, and I know that sooner or later his wife and children, his mother and siblings, will also head for Europe.

The only thing I feel for them now is a deep compassion. But the compassion I feel for Pablo's dead and for myself is greater, because after ten years of insults and threats, I've been forced to bear the sorrow for Escobar's victims and the rage of his enemies. And the straw that finally breaks the camel's back is Wendy's death. During a luncheon at the home of Carlos Ordóñez, the guru of Colombian cuisine, a famous comedian tells me she had been married to an uncle of Wendy's, and that Wendy was murdered under Pablo's orders during a trip she took from Miami, where she lived, to Medellín. He had

adored Wendy; and he had left her with a fortune of two million dollars in 1982, the equivalent of around five million today.
The two of us were opposites in everything, and though I'd
never met her, the story of the abortion at the veterinarian's
had chilled me, and I had always felt a great compassion for
her. I think it was this death—not slandering me in the media,
or mocking me in front of his colleagues for the poverty and
solitude he had condemned me to—that was the last offense
that cowardly monster could commit. Gilberto had told me
six years earlier that someday Pablo would order me killed,
too. . . . Because of all those things, from some very distant,
immaterial point, an inexplicable strength—maybe the spirit
of that other poor woman who had loved him almost as much
as I did—tells me that the time has come to add my humble
grain of sand to the scales, to help bring an end to all that
infamy once and for all.

I HAVE BEEN WAITING six years for my moment, and after thinking about it for several days, I make a decision: one day toward
the end of November 1993, I go to a public phone and make
a call to a European institution in Strasbourg. I have always
had the phone number of the brother of the man with whom
I could have been happy, and he has always felt a great affection for me. For the next half hour I explain to him why I
think that at any moment, those people will fly to Europe and
try to enter through Frankfurt. Using all the arguments I can
think of, I beg him to explain to the upper levels of the German government why, the day after they are in a secure country, Pablo Escobar will be free to destroy mine as he pleases.
Although hundreds of people of different nationalities haven't

been able to catch him, everything seems to indicate that the Search Bloc and the Americans have him cornered, thanks to the most advanced phone tracking system in the world. And though Escobar is an expert in communications, it's only a matter of weeks or months until they locate and kill him. After a few minutes, my friend asks why I'm so passionate on the subject, and why I know the modus operandi of a terrorist like that.

I can't tell him that, nine or ten years before, that criminal had spent more than two million dollars on airplane fuel so he could have me at his side or in his arms for more than two thousand hours. Nor can I explain that—with a woman who loves and understands him with the intelligent perspective of a free heart—a man lets vulnerabilities show that no one else knows. To the human being listening to me, I can only confess that I know every fold in that monster's mind better than anyone in the world, just as I know his Achilles' heels. At the other end of the line I can feel his surprise and then shock. I continue:

"He's going to go crazy looking for a country that will take his family in, because his enemies, the Pepes, have sworn to exterminate them all like cockroaches. Some people in his organization already fled to Germany, and if you allow entry to the only people in the world who really matter to him, sooner or later, he'll come after them, and the Pepes will come after him. Escobar is now the best kidnapper in the world, and if he goes there, the days of Baader-Meinhof will seem like child's play! If you don't want to believe me, ask your brother to show you the letter Pablo Escobar sent three years ago."

With something of reproach in his voice, he tells me, "He lives in the United States now, kid. He got tired of waiting for you, and . . . he got remarried in March. I'm going to talk to him first, and then with a friend of mine in Washington who specializes in counterterrorism and who can tell me what's going on. . . . He's someone who knows a lot about these things. I still don't understand why you're so sure those people are coming to Germany. But I'm going to look into it, and as soon as I know anything, I'll call you."

It's not only on a clear day that you can see forever. Also on a dark one, and a black one, and one of the saddest of my life. Why did I need to make that call, my God? To receive news like that, punishment like that, such a bucket of cold water over my head?

On the way to the radio station in the rain, I think how I am the most solitary woman on earth and how terrible it is not to have anyone with whom to vent so much suffering. That night I cry myself to sleep, but the next morning I am awakened by a call from my ex-fiancé. He tells me he knows how I'm feeling with the news of his wedding, and I can only reply that I know how he's feeling with the news of the police net closing around the man who separated us. In French, he tells me that his brother has started to make inquiries in Washington: everything seems to indicate that the *krimi* is really nearing its end, and he's going to try to convince the German minister to keep a close watch on the Frankfurt airport I'd always flown into. I congratulate him on his marriage, and when I hang up, I know the only feeling I have for Pablo is the most fervent wish that someone kill him very soon.

At lunchtime I get a call from Strasbourg, and my friend asks me to talk from a public phone. He says that he finally understands what happened between his mother and me, and he asks if I think Escobar would retaliate against European citizens or companies. I reply that now that his brother is in the United States I feel deep relief, because he would have been Escobar's first abduction target in Germany. I explain that in other times he would have surely blown up the embassy in Bogotá, and the Bayer, Siemens, and Mercedes buildings there. But he has always been utterly ignorant in German matters, and in his present circumstances, to plan large attacks in Bogotá he would need to tend to many communications fronts and prepare very complicated logistics. His desperation to get his family out of the country, on the other hand, is going to lead him to focus on that one thing, which will be a real blessing for the people who are tracing his calls.

"Oh! Warn Berlin that they will definitely travel on a Sunday, so as not to give the governmental agencies time to decide to block their entry. Flying on a commercial airline would be suicide, because everyone would find out. That's why I'm sure they will try to travel in a private plane, although in Colombia—aside from a few tycoons who would never lend them—no one I know of has planes with that kind of flight autonomy. But the cartel has been renting planes for fifteen years, and there must be dozens available in Panama . . . I can only tell you that I'll eat my hat if they don't go to Europe. And if you let them into Frankfurt, in less than one month the Pepes will be bombing the Escobar family, and Escobar will be blowing up the Cologne Cathedral! This is a guy who's spent years dreaming of blowing up the Pentagon—you heard me right. Tell them that his only Achilles' heel is the family, the family, the family. He would give his life for his family!"

On Sunday, November 28, a phone call wakes me up. From New York, I receive some stunning news.

"You were right, kid. They flew to my country, but you were

wrong about one thing: they made the mistake of flying on Lufthansa! My brother already talked to the highest level of government, and he wanted me to tell you that an entire army is waiting for them and won't let them set foot there or in any other European country. They are going to send that family of his back to Colombia so they can meet the same fate as the families of all of Escobar's victims. It's confirmed, and only a dozen people know. For your own safety and for ours, you can't open your mouth. The Washington experts say he's going to go crazy looking for someone to take them in, that he's surrounded and they don't give him one month. Now cross your fingers for Bayer, Schwarzkopf, and Mercedes!"

Thursday night, when I come home from work, the phone rings.

"Bravo, kid! The wicked witch is dead!"

Then, for the first time in eleven years, everything in my life goes quiet.

Pablo has lain dead since three in the afternoon.

❧ *There's a Party in Hell Today*

THROUGH THE WINDOW of the U.S. government's small plane, I look out for the last time in my life at the ground of my homeland and the sky of my country. A nine-hour flight may seem an eternity to someone else, but I'm used to spending entire days without talking to anyone. During that time, all the reasons why I am going to the United States and will never return to Colombia, except to be buried there, go parading through my memory. . . . All the events of recent days have conspired to turn me into a key witness of the attorneys general in both countries, and in past and future criminal cases of exceptional significance: the assassination of a presidential candidate in Colombia, a trial in the United States over more than 2.1 billion dollars, the holocaust of judicial power in my country, a multimillion-dollar money-laundering operation in thirty-eight countries. . . . Now, I'm headed toward the nation that has saved my life because, had Pablo Escobar not been my lover, I wouldn't have just two quarters in my wallet and all the names of his biggest accomplices in my memory.

How could I forget what happened after his family was returned from Germany? Pablo's voice on all the radio stations the next day, threatening to turn German citizens, tourists, and companies into "military targets"? If you knew all his subtleties, you knew it was the voice of a man exhausted, cornered, overwhelmed by suffering, now unable to terrorize anyone. A man whose family had been run out of the elegant Santa Ana neighborhood and was now hiding in the Tequendama Hotel, property of a compassionate police department that fulfilled its duty to protect the wife and children of their victimizer while the entire country protested, enraged.

At my microphone during the day, silent in front of my TV at night, I waited patiently for the denouement.

THE FOLLOWING THURSDAY, four days after the family's return and desperate because no country will accept the only human beings in the world he cares about, Pablo talks to his sixteen-year-old son for twenty minutes, something that in other circumstances he would never have done. Since his flight from the Cathedral, he has maintained obsessive discipline in his communications, and he rarely uses phones. But now he starts desperately making calls in search of a way to relocate his family, whom the Pepes have sworn to exterminate. In his eternal obsession with manipulating the media, Pablo explains to his son in detail how to answer questions sent to him by *Semana*, the magazine that over the years has honored him time and again with its cover. An efficient police officer who has been tirelessly tracing his communications for fifteen months finally locates him through radio triangulation and immediately passes the information to the Search Bloc. Minutes later, the police locate the house in a middle-class neighborhood of Medellín, and they can see Escobar through a window while he's talking on the phone. He and his bodyguards also see them, and a wild shootout begins; like Bonnie and Clyde's, it lasts one hour. Gun in hand, Escobar goes running out barefoot and half-dressed and tries to jump from the roof to a neighboring house, but it's no use: seconds later he collapses on the roof with two bullets in his head and several more in his body. Now the most wanted man in the world, the number one public enemy of the nation's entire history, the man who for more than ten years subjected the rule of law to all the deliriums of his megalomania, is only a two-hundred-fifty-pound monster who bleeds out in front of two dozen enemies who celebrate their victory with rifles in the air, delirious with pride and crazed by unprecedented joy.

The paroxysm spreads to thirty million Colombians, and the verses of the national anthem with "*Cesó la horrible noche*" ("The horrible night has ended") resound from all the radio stations in the country. I can only remember two previous events that were similar to the collective phenomenon that followed Pablo's death: the fall of the dictatorship of General Rojas Pinilla when I was seven years old and the riots after a soccer game against Argentina that Colombia won 5–0 that left eighty people dead. Watching and listening to all that, from the silence imposed on me by the jubilant director of the Todelar newscast on the payroll of Gilberto Rodríguez, can only be compared to the dimensions of that explosion of joy described by Pablo eight years ago, on a noonday and under the sky of Nápoles, when he had sworn to me to take to Hell in the instant of his death only the vision of our two bodies merged in the epicenter of 360 degrees multiplied by one trillion trillions.

But that was a long time ago, because when you've suffered so much, eight years can seem like an eternity. . . . And that man who had come into my arms still a child, and had left them a man determined to become a monster to go down in history as a legend, had done it in the end: now the president of the United States, Bill Clinton, congratulates the Search Bloc, and "all of humanity"—as the national anthem would put it—congratulates Colombia. The celebrations throughout the country last for days and days, and while in Cali the Rodríguez Orejuela family cry tears of joy for the victory, in Medellín, dozens of mourners, hundreds of drunkards, and thousands of poor people throw themselves at Pablo's coffin as if wanting to keep something of him for themselves, the same way they had in that garbage dump where, eleven years ago, I had fallen in love with him. Back when he was a human being and looked like one, when he didn't flaunt his riches before me, but rather displayed all the bravery and heart he possessed at that time. Now I see that body with its face disfigured by selfishness, fat, and evil, and with a mustache like Adolf Hitler's; the Search Bloc had kept one end as a souvenir and the DEA the other. His own mother had exclaimed, "That man is not my son!"

And beholding that repugnant and loathsome sight, I also said to myself, crying, "That monster was not my lover, either."

Now my phone has stopped ringing. I have no friends left, and Pablo's enemies have finally let me rest. None of my colleagues call me, because they know I would hang up without a word. *Sit in the doorway of your house and watch the dead body of your enemy pass by*, I say to myself as I watch that human tide on TV, the twenty-five thousand people who attend his burial: *There goes my torturer and that of my whole country, wrapped in visceral hatred, covered in infamy, surrounded by the scum of society. Yes, those people are the families of his hit men and all those young men who thought he was God because he brought a weak and corrupt state to its knees . . . because he was rich and audacious like no one else . . . because he kept the gringos in check. Yes, one mourner for each of his victims, that's all.*

A while later, trying to find a plausible explanation, I say to myself incredulously: *But . . . twenty-five thousand . . . isn't it a lot of people for someone who did so much evil? What if he had done good? Are those crowds a mix of* sicarios *and also . . . thousands of grateful poor? Could it be that eleven years ago, when everything started, I wasn't so wrong after all?*

And I start to remember how Pablo had been when he was still so young and I was still so innocent . . . how he had planned to make me fall in love with him in that dump, and not in the Seychelles or in Paris . . . how he'd sent his Pegasus for me every week so he could have me for hours and hours in his arms . . . how—because love makes us good—each of us had inspired the best in the other and he told me I would be his Manuelita . . . how he loved me and while I loved him he had dreamed of being a great man . . . how it was that our dreams were shattered and those who destroyed them ended up dead . . .

Because, once the initial jubilation has passed, my heart has been turned into a giant red onion, just a poor onion of raw and bloody flesh, and every sixty minutes someone rips off another nerve layer without anesthesia, and then wraps it pitilessly with yards of barbed wire until the next hour. Then

I go to my library and look for Neruda's *Twenty Love Poems*, the only thing of his that Pablo couldn't take away the day he took my money, my manuscript, the letters, the cassettes, the *Virgie Linda I*, and the Beretta, because it was mixed in with my hundreds of books. And reading Neruda again, and Silva, my beloved and suicidal poet, I let myself be wrapped in their verses. And I remember Pablo as he was during that last autumn when, six years before, we had seen each other for the last time, and my voice still tried to find the wind to touch his ear.

And I remember the night of one of those days when my thirty-three-year-old lover received nearly a hundred million dollars a month, was loved by the most famous, elegant beauty of his country, and, proud as could be, left her house with all his best friends on the way to the home of Colombia's most powerful president, with the secret dream of also being president someday . . . that night as ominous as Silva's "Nocturne," with the videocassette of the future Minister Lara, when Pablo had first presaged, perhaps seen with true horror, the possibility of losing everything that had fallen into his hands and arms, almost as suddenly as it had arrived . . . that night, impossible to forget, when all the happy attendees ignored Neruda's "Song of Despair," the poem so heavy with tenderness that it inspired *Il Postino*. . . . Now that all his premonitions have come true, all his terrors have materialized, I sink into the heartrending sorrow and the oceanic depths that describe like nothing else the ignominy of his destiny, condemned and cursed as Judas, and all the tragedy of that destiny of ours . . . his impotence to change anything and my impotence to change him.

Now he is asleep for all eternity, and in that rigid earth he lies alone. And I start to remember how, when he thought

I was asleep, he would kiss me gently so as not to wake me up . . . and then again and again, to see if I was awake. How he told me that the whole universe fit inside my heart, and I replied that I only wanted all of his to fit . . . that man's enormous heart of gold that, before my terrified eyes and with me unable to stop it, turned into the enormous lead heart of a monster . . . that lion's heart that couldn't change anything, but did teach me to feel everything and to cry for what couldn't be changed so that, one clear and not-too-distant day, all that rage and those longings of his could travel alongside my sufferings, in my books and in my story.

That little old poetry book I was on the verge of burning a hundred times, with its two signatures and a sad quatrain, its cover damaged by the tears I still shed ten years and ten months after that night, would be the mute continent of two star-crossed lovers' broken dreams. Perhaps one day it will end up under thick glass in the museum where the remains of failed loves and doomed passions rest. With time, it will be all I have left of Pablo, because five years later, in Buenos Aires, two muggers would snatch off the watch that had accompanied me for almost fifteen years. I haven't missed it for one single second of one single day, because I will never miss the lost possessions, only "the lost birds that return from beyond to meld with a sky I will never get back again."

IN NOVEMBER 2004, as I watch on television an extradited man in handcuffs boarding a DEA plane headed for the United States, accused of trafficking two hundred thousand kilos of cocaine, I say to myself: *There's a party in Hell today, Gilberto!*

Like him and his brother, I also came to this sky and this

land in a DEA plane, but for different reasons: in September 2006, without going to court and before I can testify against them, the Rodríguez Orejuela brothers plead guilty to all charges. They receive a sentence of thirty years, and their fortune of $2.1 billion is split equally between the Colombian and U.S. governments.

Today I can only say that God works in the most mysterious ways, and that sometimes he condemns us to the deepest and most prolonged forms of suffering because he has chosen us as catalysts for strange, perhaps even historic, events.

THEY PULL A SKULL from the dirt, all that's left of Pablo, his horrible skull coated in infamy. Thirteen years after his death, against the wishes of his mother, they have exhumed his remains for a paternity test. I wonder who the mother of that child of his could be, and I feel only deep compassion for the women who once loved him and now argue over his fortune, because none of them want his name. I think about the three who directly or indirectly had something to do with his death, and the pain of those of us who really made him dream and suffer, laugh and rage: his wife, Wendy, and me. Pablo sacrificed his life for the wife who, now jailed for a time in Argentina, repudiated the name Escobar and the names he chose for their children—but not his fortune—and in doing so left him without succeeding generations. Wendy, murdered by Popeye, a cowardly *sicario* who envied Pablo's lovers and dressed like a woman. And me, condemned to die of hunger and solitude, and thrown to the wolves to let them tear me apart.

"What would you tell Pablo if you could see him for five

minutes?" I'm asked by a sweet girl who came into the world on Christmas Eve 1993, three weeks after Pablo's death.

Feeling again the pain of the two women whom he first adored and then destroyed—murdered or ruined by Pablo, exposed to the threats of his worst enemies, vilified by the most profane journalists, targets of mockery from his low-born family, slandered by gutless thugs—I reply without hesitating:

"I would ask him who he's been reincarnated as: one of those terrified little girls in Darfur, torn apart by twenty animals like him? . . . Or as an angel of compassion like my friend Sister Bernadette of the Missionaries of Charity? . . . Or as the next, or definitive, version of the Antichrist? I think, from that unfathomable eternity made of the freezing nights and endless solitude of those who have no possible redemption, his voice would almost certainly say to me: 'Well, my love . . . you, better than anyone, know that we demons were once angels!' And then, before disappearing forever in some firmament of deepest midnight, now with no moon and no stars, that black soul would very possibly add: 'You know, I finally understand the law of cause and effect. You were right, Virginia! Maybe . . . if down there on earth you pulled a petal from one million lilies, from here I could make one million stars tremble . . .'

"My firmament, *liebchen*, is always lit," I tell her, smiling at that wise creature who understands all.

EIGHTY-SIX DAYS HAVE PASSED since my arrival, and I'm settling into a small apartment with spectacular views that I have always dreamed of. Thirty-five floors below lies the financial district of Brickell, and around it, several dozen luxury condominiums on avenues lined by palms that look cloned. Finally, any time of day I can look out at the sea that I've always needed like a second skin, the sailboats and yachts that pass on their way to crossing under the bridge, and the seagulls that dance outside my balcony against the background of a perfect, cobalt-blue sky. I am deeply and immensely happy, and I can't believe that, after bearing twenty years of insults and threats and living eight years in fear of poverty, I can finally enjoy so much beauty, so much freedom, and such peace, before the light leaves my eyes forever.

When night falls, I go out on the balcony to contemplate the moon and stars. With the eyes of a fascinated child, I watch planes go by overhead, arriving from all over the world loaded with tourists, business, and hopes, and the helicopters that come and go between South Beach and the airport. Farther on, in Key Biscayne, someone is celebrating their birthday with a profusion of fireworks that from this side of the water I receive like an unexpected gift from God. The ships' foghorns sound in the distance, and above and below me the murmur of motors vanishing in the distance is a lively music that joins the smell of salt and the warm breeze to wrap me in a rhapsody whose notes I thought I had forgotten. A thousand lights from banks and condominiums have turned on above the city that glimmers below, and with my heart flooded with gratitude, I observe the enormous Nativity scene of this tropical future Manhattan. It seems that now my remaining visible nights will shine like Christmas Day.

The scene is a celebration of the senses, and I wonder if someday I will also passionately love or sing to this privileged land where I have been so happy and where nearly all dreams are possible: the nation of the Statue of Liberty and the Grand Canyon, of Cahokia and California and New York, of the universities where a hundred Nobel Prize laureates teach future winners to think; the nation of inventors and architects and visionary engineers, of giants of cinema and music and sports, of trips to the moon and the Hubble and the Galileo, of titanic philanthropists and a thousand ethnicities and sounds with the flavors of every corner of the earth; the nation of the persecuted members of the human race, and of the enterprising people who once arrived here with empty pockets and built a country through ambition and sacrifice, with an obstinate idea in their heads, a dream of freedom in their hands, a song of faith in their hearts.

I am just one of the many refugees who on a day like any other—though historic in their own lives—set foot on its beaches, fleeing from enemies or hunger. And from the place where I arrived on an unforgettable day in 2006, I could finally tell the story of a man and a woman from two opposing worlds who once loved each other in a country at war. It would have been impossible for me to start to tell it, to finish writing it, or to even dream of publishing it in the country where I was born and that I had to abandon forever that July day.

A month after I arrive, Diego Pampín and Cristóbal Pera of Random House Mondadori, one of the world's most prestigious publishers, enthusiastically welcome my idea of relating my intimate view of the most terrifying and complex criminal mind of recent history.

Pablo will not be written into my books again, but Blacksoul the Beast will always live in them—in my new stories of love and war in that country of one million dead and five million displaced, inhabited by the cruelest and the sweetest people on earth, at the eternal mercy of armed bands and dynasties that, with their pack of accomplices, courtiers, and henchmen, passed down power and treasure from generation to generation. Stories of a political class that one fine day discovered the business of building golden bridges between criminal bands and presidential ones, and of a media that would soon discover another, even juicier business: the frenzy of hiding imperfect pasts and howling accusations at anyone who dares uncover them. As Oscar Wilde said of the aggressors of his time:

What seem to us bitter trials are often blessings in disguise.